5/2014

LOST PLANTATIONS OF THE SOUTH

# *Lost Plantations of the South*

Marc R. Matrana

UNIVERSITY PRESS OF MISSISSIPPI   JACKSON

www.upress.state.ms.us

The University Press of Mississippi is a member of the Association of American University Presses.

Unless otherwise noted, illustrations courtesy of the Library of Congress, Prints and Photographs Division, Historic American Buildings Survey.

First printing 2009

∞

Library of Congress Cataloging-in-Publication Data

Matrana, Marc R.

    Lost plantations of the South / Marc R. Matrana.

            p. cm.

    Includes bibliographical references and index.

    ISBN 978-1-57806-942-2 (cloth)

    1.  Plantations—Southern States—History. 2.  Plantations—Southern States—History—Pictorial works. 3.  Plantation life—Southern States—History. 4.  Southern States—History, Local. 5.  Southern States—History, Local—Pictorial works. 6.  Plantation owners—Southern States—Biography. 7.  Slaves—Southern States—Biography. 8. Southern States—Biography. 9.  Historic sites—Conservation and restoration—Southern States. 10.  Historic preservation—Southern States. I. Title.

    F210.M36 2009

    306.3'49—dc22                              2009008538

British Library Cataloging-in-Publication Data available

DEDICATED TO MY GRANDPARENTS


*Frank John Matrana (1900–1979)*

*Augustine Molaison Matrana (1904–1996)*

AND

*John D. Jordan (1925–1992)*

*Wanda Taylor Jordan (1929–2009)*

You too proceed! Make falling arts your care,
Erect new wonders and the old repair . . .

—Alexander Pope

When by the Ruins oft I past
My sorrowing eyes aside did cast
And here and there the places spy
Where oft I sate and long did lie.
Here stood that Trunk, and there that chest,
There lay that store I counted best,
My pleasant things in ashes lie
And them behold no more shall I.
Under the roof no guest shall sit,
Nor at thy Table eat a bit.
No pleasant talk shall 'ere be told
Nor things recounted done of old.
No Candle 'ere shall shine in Thee,
Nor bridegroom's voice ere heard shall bee.
In silence ever shalt thou lie.

—Anne Bradstreet, "Verses upon the Burning
of our House," June 18, 1666

# Contents

Acknowledgments   ix
Introduction   xi

CHAPTER 1. *The Upper South, East:*
*Virginia, West Virginia, and*
*Maryland*   1

Rosewell   5
Oak Hill   7
Ossian Hall   9
Ravensworth   14
Marshall Hall   17
George Washington's Rock Hall
(Bullskin) Plantation   21
Bush Hill   22
Chatsworth   26
Malvern Hill   27

CHAPTER 2. *The Upper South, West:*
*Arkansas, Kentucky, and Tennessee*   31

Sylvan Home   35
Rosedale   39
Sunnyside   40
Mount Brilliant   43
Reverie   46

CHAPTER 3. *The Carolinas*   49

Pooshee   53
Millwood   57
Prospect Hill   59
Eutaw   62

Springfield   68
Stoney-Baynard   70
White Hall   71
The Rocks   74
Devereux   79

CHAPTER 4. *Georgia*   81

Casulon   83
Mulberry Grove   87
Hamilton   90
Hampton   91
The Hermitage   93
Retreat   100
Horton House   104

CHAPTER 5. *Alabama and Florida*   109

Rocky Hill Castle   112
Forks of Cypress   117
Umbria   120
New Smyrna   126
Bulowville   129
Yulee Plantations:
Cottonwood and Margarita   131
Mount Oswald   134
Verdura   136

CHAPTER 6. *Mississippi*   139

Goat Castle   143
Brierfield   146
Hurricane   150

Windsor  151
Prairie Mont  155
Malmaison  159
Homewood  167
Windy Hill Manor  174

CHAPTER 7. *Louisiana*  177

Le Petit Versailles  180
Belle Grove  184
Woodlawn  192
Orange Grove  199
Seven Oaks  202
Uncle Sam  211
Elmwood  220

CHAPTER 8. *Texas*  227

Lake Jackson  229
Clay Castle  231
Eagle Island  233
Ellersly  234
Wyalucing  237
Orozimbo  242
Glen Eden  243
Peach Point  246

*Conclusions*  251

Notes  261
Bibliography  279
Note to the Reader  299
Index  301

# Acknowledgments

First, I must thank my many friends at the Westwego Historical Society for their backing and assistance. Mayor and Mrs. Daniel P. Alario, Sr., of Westwego—the founders of the society and my dear friends—provide a steady stream of encouragement and support, as does Westwego Historical Society president Kenneth Cantrelle.

My dear friend Mrs. Charmaine Currualt Rini, of the Jefferson Historical Society of Louisiana, provided much useful advice. President Frank Borne of the Jefferson Historical Society and Dr. Mary Grace Curry have both been a great encouragement.

Glenn Falgoust, a great Louisiana historian, has provided much aid and research assistance. Our mutual friend, famed chef John Folse, Louisiana's official Culinary Ambassador to the World, has done much to promote my work, as has his director of communications, Michaela York.

I certainly must thank all of the individuals at the many libraries, archives, and collections I visited and corresponded with. Lee Freeman at the Florence-Lauderdale Public Library in Florence, Alabama, was most helpful, as were Bill Warren of the Florence City Schools in Alabama, John A. Leynes of Jacksonville, Florida, Eleanor Ruth Briggs of the Harrison County Historical Museum in Marshall, Texas, and Jamie Murray of the Brazoria County Historical Museum in Angleton, Texas, among many others. And, of course, Dr. Florent Hardy, Jr., administrator and director of the Louisiana State Archives, has been a major supporter of my research projects.

Much appreciation is extended to my friends at the University Press of Mississippi, particularly editor-in-chief Craig Gill and marketing director Steven B. Yates, who are both a joy to work with.

Many thanks also go to my many friends who have kept me sane while I tried to juggle my medical career and the writing of a book, especially Heather Green, Dr. Sarath Krishnan, Dr. Shawn Ragbir, Shane Mabry, Sherie Dry Gerdes, Angelle Bencaz, and Jacques Levet, Jr. Also, I thank my extended family, who is always there for me. Finally, I owe a great debt of gratitude to my parents, Daniel and Jonnie Matrana, for their constant and unwavering love, encouragement, and support.

Enjoy the book.

# Introduction

During the height of antebellum agricultural production, it is estimated that there were nearly fifty thousand plantations in the slaveholding states of the South.[1] Today, only a small fraction of these remain, and most are significantly altered from their antebellum state. These plantations represented estates ranging in magnitude from moderately sized farms with as few as twenty or so slaves to massive properties that sprawled across tens of thousands of acres and individually exploited thousands of enslaved human beings. Collectively, these estates spread from the old tobacco fields of Virginia and Maryland down to the flooded coastal rice fields of South Carolina and Georgia, through the massive cotton belt of Mississippi, Alabama, and other states, and onto the sugar lands of Louisiana and east Texas. Together these family-owned farms, powered by their massive slave labor force of several million persons, created a thriving agricultural economy for the unique region that has never been duplicated. These estates and their inhabitants also nurtured a deep, rich culture of color, class, and conflict that pervaded the entire South, but took on intriguing nuances in various regions and social niches. The estates and their inhabitants carved from the barren landscapes built environments that left unique, memorable, and important footprints. But, even as we imagine the quintessential plantation and its larger associated economy and culture, the unique essence that exactly defines a "plantation" and distinguishes it from other agricultural estates still eludes historians today.

Originally, during the earliest days of English colonization, the word "plantation" referred simply to a settlement. Before long, as the agricultural potential of the vast open lands of North America was quickly realized and large farms were organized, the term took on another meaning more closely resembling what we describe as a plantation today. While the technical definition of a southern plantation has been a topic of hot debate, this volume will define this particular entity as a large farm or agricultural estate of the colonial or antebellum South that exploited the labor of at least twenty enslaved individuals, although most of the estates profiled here had many more slaves. Furthermore, a plantation's inhabitants, both free and slave, usually conformed to certain cultural mores and social conventions of the day. Plantations were most always owned by families and routinely passed down through generations, even in the situation of absentee proprietorships.

The estates themselves nearly all had easily recognizable patterns of settlement and improvements within their built environments. Although the columned mansion was the exception rather than the norm, a master house or cabin of varying size and style usually existed even on estates where the owning family did not reside regularly. There was in most cases a clear delineation between the dwellings of white masters and those of their slaves. On larger plantations the virtually ubiquitous slave quarters with their closely arranged cabins were easily distinguished. There were neatly arranged fields that grew a variety of crops for consumption on the estate, but usually only produced one major cash crop that was largely defined by the plantation's geographical location. Also, there were distinct areas set aside for production. Buildings with highly specialized functions were characteristic. Ice houses, tobacco barns, sugarhouses, dovecotes, blacksmith shops, sawmills, and horse stables are just a few examples of the many structures created for specifically defined purposes within the plantation complex.

Plantations were landed estates, much like English manors. Their value came directly from the land and from the work that was done on the land by enslaved individuals. Profits that funded the estates largely came from the sale of cash crops and their derivatives (i.e., granulated sugar, processed cotton, blue dye from indigo, etc.). These crops were the direct products of land and labor. Likewise, the built environments of these plantations, from the grand mansions of the white masters to the lowly cabins of slaves, were usually direct products of the land improved by labor, rising from the earth much like the crops in the fields. Bricks that were used in construction were routinely made from sand or clay from the plantation lands, molded by hands of slaves and fired in kilns or allowed to dry in the sun, soaking up the solar rays much like the leaves of the crops. Nowhere was this more true than at the Hermitage in Georgia. Every building on the entire estate was produced from fine bricks made on the plantation. Likewise, wood for the construction of buildings, fences, bridges, and other planta-

tion structures often came from wooded areas of the estate. Slaves chopped trees from the land and made them into something much different—their forced labor transformed the chaos of nature into the order and symmetry of the southern plantation landscape. And no icon was more associated with this landscape than the plantation mansion.

Traditionally, most scholarship has focused on the plantation mansion itself for several reasons. First, the great houses were more likely to survive than the rest of the plantation complex. Secondly, plantation mansions were usually the most elaborate and arguably the more architecturally interesting structures on the plantation. And finally, until recently, most scholarship and local history focused on the lives of the white masters rather than their slaves. Likewise, much of this volume focuses on the master houses for some similar reasons—there is simply more information available about lost mansions as compared to lost slave cabins and barns.

But, as much as plantations were built places, they were also essentially people and production. And it is for this reason that the stories of the families and individuals who called these estates "home" are included in this volume. In order to grasp the importance of any one of these estates, it is vital to have some understanding of the people whose lives were intricately intertwined with them. Mostly, the personal and family histories that have survived over time are those of the white owners, many of whom left diaries, plantation journals, letters, and other ephemera that give glimpses into their worlds. Often, little is known of enslaved people whose labor fueled production. However, regarding lost estates, where information is known about enslaved individuals and the built environments they called home, the stories of slaves and their architectural legacies on the plantations are discussed.[2]

Additionally, information is also included in this volume regarding the lost architectural imprints of the productive aspects of the plantation environment. Besides the grand mansions and humble cabins of the typical plantation, there were generally many buildings for the processing and storage of crops, preparation and storage of food, shelter of animals and implements, and other various productive purposes. Some of these buildings were quite simple—plain storage sheds or small smokehouses, for example—while others were elaborate, such as large multiroom barns or grand brick sugarhouses, which, exteriorly, were sometimes as architecturally ornamented as the mansions themselves.

It has been said that plantations of the Old South and their inhabitants bequeathed to the future the most striking architectural relics ever created by an agrarian people. Certainly in North America few could argue against this case. Sadly, those great relics have been slipping into oblivion at an alarming rate over the last 150 years.

Today, little physical evidence of the South's plantation past is left. Throughout the region only a small percentage of plantation mansions are still standing, and far fewer slave dwellings remain. Furthermore, intact antebellum agricultural and productive structures are quite rare.

Of those plantations that do exist in some form, many have been greatly altered, and certainly few retain their original outbuildings such as slave cabins, barns, etc. And those which do boast a slave cabin or two usually have only a small portion of the entire original ensemble of ancillary structures.

Many existing plantations are endangered by progress, neglect, and other threats. Germania Plantation, for example, near Donaldsonville, Louisiana, is literally falling apart, reverting to its natural state. And Le Beau Plantation in St. Bernard Parish, Louisiana, doesn't fare much better. It was in a sorrowful state of decay before Hurricane Katrina struck, and the storm only caused more damage to the once magnificent palace.

Of those plantation homes that remain in good condition, only a few hundred are open to the public, and the great majority of these exist as romanticized depictions of southern antebellum life. The fact is, the great majority of the Old South's archi-

tectural and agricultural legacy has vanished, and much more is disappearing every year.

Most of these lost estates exist now only in antiquated court documents, census records, old family papers, and other ephemera. Some are remembered in history books or articles, while a few leave extensive written accounts. But many leave no evidence of their existence at all, and have since faded out of the grasp of history altogether, sinking deep into the unknown.

But before we can delve into the fascinating histories of these often mysterious and forlorn estates, it is important to define what is meant by "lost" plantations. The framework this volume will use to delineate that which is a "plantation" from that which is not has already been outlined. Working within this definition, this study will address estates whose man-made physical structures and associated agricultural operations have been completely destroyed or left only in the most basic rudimentary, often ruinous, form. The definition has wider implications because deep within the physical demolition of plantation structures one finds the ideological, economic, and cultural obliteration that often spearheaded and more often than not preceded these physically destructive events.

This volume is in no way meant to be a complete survey of each and every plantation that at one time existed in the South. Nor is it a comprehensive analysis of the downfall of the plantation system or of the cause of every architectural loss. Such undertakings would fill many libraries. It is instead simply a study of a number of plantations of various sizes, styles, eras, and functions that at one time thrived, but have since been lost to time. As noted above, these range from huge estates in which hundreds or even thousands of individuals were enslaved to modest farms with only a few slaves.

Readers will note the volume makes no attempt to present an equal number of estates from each southern state, but instead focuses mostly on the Deep South and East Coast, although every southern state is represented with at least one lost plantation. This is for several reasons. First, the Deep

South and original southern colonies represent the older, more settled areas of the young country, where a more established plantation system and slave society was in place. The great majority of the built environments of plantations were found in these areas, as were most of the large, iconic plantation mansions. Secondly, for the most part these areas have done a good job of preserving plantation records and documenting lost estates. Information on more plantations from these areas is available. Finally, and least importantly, this trend represents in some ways the author's own preferences and personal academic interests.

The histories of thousands of lost plantations have been examined by the author, and sixty essays have been chosen for final inclusion in the book and categorized by state. Many were selected because their rise and fall proved to be representative of what was happening to other plantations regionally, and, therefore, their histories provide a wider context to the limited scope of a single volume. Often estates were included because they had unique significance in their own right. Some plantations were chosen for inclusion because of the architectural importance of their master house. This was the case with Belle Grove in Iberville Parish, Louisiana, once the single largest, most elaborate, and arguably one of the most beautiful plantation mansions in the South. Others were selected because of the value and interest of their overall physical structures and layout. Louisiana's Uncle Sam Plantation is said to have been the most complete plantation complex to ever exist, and it was certainly one of the most meticulously aligned. It was included for this reason. Still others found a place in this volume because of the significance of their owners. George Washington's West Virginia estate and David Levy Yulee's Florida plantations were added because of their famous proprietors. Yet others joined the collection because of momentous or historically significant events that took place on the site. Mulberry Grove Plantation in Georgia was the place where young Eli Whitney invented the cotton gin, certainly an event that changed both the fate of the South's plantation system and the history of the American economy in ways no one could have predicted. And, finally, many estates were chosen because the stories of their demises illustrate wider principles and deep concepts of how and why the plantation landscape of the South has been and is being lost. Plantations such as Georgia's Casulon and Kentucky's Mount Brilliant certainly fit into this category. Some of the plantations included embody many of these important aspects. Seven Oaks and Orange Grove, both in Louisiana, for example, were significant on many levels. Regardless of why a certain plantation was included, the author strived to create a collection of estates that complement one another historically and aesthetically while communicating a broader idea about the changing face of the South's landscape and life.

The stories of these lost plantations and their fatal endings are not formal academic histories based purely on primary sources. Such sources have been scrupulously consulted and cited where appropriate, but reliable secondary sources have also been widely utilized. Sometimes more definite histories of these estates exist and are widely available (as is the case with Seven Oaks, Belle Grove, and others), and this volume is certainly not meant to supersede such documents. In other cases the brief summaries provided here represent the largest collection of information gathered on the estates. Either way, this volume does not seek to be an encyclopedia of lost plantations nor an academic tome, but rather strives to showcase the variety and richness of these unique properties along with the stories of the people who lived and worked there, while noting their diverse demises—all in an effort to collectively compare and contrast their rise and fall for the general reader and historian alike. Furthermore, although the book focuses on the fading architectural legacy of the South amid the massive social, cultural, and economic shifts that proceeded after the Civil War, again, it is in no way meant to be a treatise on the demise of the plantation system; many monographs and dissertations attempt this goal.

☙

If one is to accept that history is written in architecture, then it is paramount that one consider lost architecture along with extant structures in order to fully grasp a comprehensive and accurate picture of the past. The stories of these plantations—their emergences and their ultimate devastations—seek to augment those sagas of remaining southern estates, which often receive a relative lion's share of attention.

Some of these plantations were destroyed even before the Civil War, but most survived this uniquely American conflict. Universally though, for those that survived, the years after the war were dramatically different from those before it. Some of the plantations continued to operate as they had in antebellum days, using former slaves or others as laborers.

Others later took on other nonagricultural functions. The famed Seven Oaks Plantation of Jefferson Parish, Louisiana, was transformed into Columbia Gardens, one of the nation's earliest and most successful resort attractions; Marshall Hall in Maryland served a similar function. Seven Oaks was then later used as a military barracks. Wyalucing Plantation in Marshall, Texas, was purchased by former slaves and was used by them as a college. And Lake Jackson Plantation in Brazoria County, Texas, like many other Texas plantations, was transformed into a prison farm. The conditions on these former plantations varied widely depending on their function, but those listed herein had one thing in common: they each met an eventual end.

Some of these estates were victims of progress. For example, Northampton and other South Carolina plantations drowned when the Santee Cooper power company flooded the plantation lands, creating a number of lakes during a major environmental and navigation project. Others were torn down so that subdivisions or other environments could be built. Many plantations were destroyed by fire, weather, or other natural disasters. Yet others sadly succumbed to neglect, reverting to the elements, as no one was there to halt the process. Some historic mansions were simply destroyed without reason by their owners, often after heated battles with local preservationists. Such was the tragic fate of Louisiana's Seven Oaks and Kentucky's Mount Brilliant.

These stories and others provide interesting and essential examples of preservation battles in action and also the consequences of a lack of community preservation effort. The analysis of such tragedies should provide some insight into the workings of preservation battles and will, it is hoped, be of some small use to future preservation conflicts. These histories exemplify why the protection of historical sites—specifically plantation structures—is so crucial to the South and to the nation.

The histories of these "lost plantations" and of the many people whose lives were intertwined with them provide an important glimpse into colonial and antebellum life. The stories of their decline and ruin are each unique, but they hold a common thread in that all of these estates have been lost physically, economically, socially, and culturally. The era they represent is equally lost, a time when human beings were forcefully held as property and when these vast agricultural enterprises and many more like them comprised the backbone of the nation's economy and the South's landscape. To fully understand this era we must not only look to the few estates which remain, but also consider the thousands that have been lost. They collectively represent the South—the good and the bad—and ultimately they reflect upon us and how we as a society deal with our own intricate, complicated past.

# CHAPTER ONE

# The Upper South, East: Virginia, West Virginia, and Maryland

We shape our buildings; thereafter, our buildings shape us.

—*Winston Churchill*

Now, just as one more or less consciously reads the face of every person one meets, to discover whether it is friendly or withdrawn, happy or sad, at home in the world or baffled by it, so buildings are the faces on which one can read, long after the events themselves have passed out of memory or written record, the life of our ancestors.

—*Lewis Mumford*, The South in Architecture

Queen Elizabeth I granted Sir Walter Raleigh a charter to establish a colony north of Florida in 1583. A year later, he explored the Atlantic coast, calling it Virginia, in honor of the "Virgin Queen," Elizabeth, who never married. After the tragic and mysterious loss of the Roanoke Colony in present-day North Carolina, the first permanent English settlement in the New World, Jamestown—named for King James I—was founded in 1607, by Captain Christopher Newport and Captain John Smith. During the winter of 1609–1610, nearly 90 percent of the population died during a period known as "the starving time," when the third supply ship to the colony was lost.

Despite hardships and tragedy, the population grew as settlers and servants continued arriving. In 1619, the House of Burgesses was established as the colony's governing body. The same year, the first Africans were introduced to augment the indentured laborers, although slavery was not fully codified until 1661. Even during these first few decades, plantations flourished in the colony and huge fortunes were being made in tobacco.

Meanwhile, in 1629, George Calvert, 1st Lord Baltimore in the Irish House of Lords, applied for a new royal charter for what was to become Maryland. He had recently suffered financial failure in Newfoundland's Avalon colony, and sought to recoup his losses through tobacco after hearing of the successes in Virginia. Calvert simultaneously sought to create a New World haven for Catholics. George Calvert died in April 1632, but the charter was granted to his son, Cecilius Calvert, 2nd Lord Baltimore.

Both Virginia and Maryland grew through the eighteenth century, as agriculture enterprises fueled local and regional economies. Plantations flourished and their built environments blossomed. In both colonial Virginia and Maryland, the Georgian style that so dominated the North American English colonies could be seen abundantly in many structures, including plantation houses and associated buildings. Later, the so-called Federal style, which blended Georgian and neo-Palladian elements, was also popular. Rosewell, built in Gloucester County, provided the highest, most lavish example of high architectural style in the region. But while the founding fathers focused on the architecture of the plantation estates, they also began thinking about the design of government and the inequalities colonists faced under the governance of England.

By the fifth decade of the century, dissent and outright disgust with British leaders besieged many colonists. Speeches by Patrick Henry and Richard Henry Lee concerning taxation without representation led the royal governor to temporarily dissolve the House of Burgesses. Eventually, both Virginia and Maryland joined other colonies in the revolt against England, later becoming the tenth and seventh states to join the Union, respectively.

While Virginia's plantation economy and slave society became more engrained in the colony's culture in the post-Revolutionary, antebellum period, Maryland's history took a divergent path as compared to other slaveholding states. Cereals such as wheat began to eclipse tobacco in Maryland, requiring only seasonal laborers and negating the necessity of slaves on many estates. The free black population grew, and Maryland's slave culture dwindled.

Before the young nation's first centennial, sectionalist sentiment and divisive debate about slavery led to outright civil war. Virginia seceded from the Union in 1861, and joined other southern states in forming the Confederate States of America. In 1863, forty-eight counties in the northwest portion of the state—whose economy and culture was for the most part quite detached from the plantation and slave society of the east—separated from Virginia and returned to the United States, thereby forming the state of West Virginia. Despite strong support for the Confederate states from Maryland's wealthy and influential slaveholding minority, the state did not secede and remained loyal to the Union. It has been widely suggested that Governor Thomas Holliday Hicks's temporary suspen-

A pencil drawing of Virginia's elegant Mannsfield Plantation House. The flanking dependency was connected by a curved walkway. A second symmetrical structure was connected by a similar curved walkway. The house was destroyed in the Civil War.

The ruins and foundations of Mannsfield Plantation were excavated in 1934, revealing thousands of artifacts and much information about the history of the estate and region.

sion of the legislature and President Abraham Lincoln's subsequent arrest of many of its proslavery, prosecession members were largely responsible for Maryland's allegiance to the United States.

Despite differences of opinion and differences in uniforms on the field of battle, war brought with it much heartache for families on both sides. The plantation system was all but annihilated by the emancipation of slaves, and many Virginia plantations were destroyed. In spite of tragedy and economic collapse, most plantations in the region physically survived. Most, however, later succumbed to disaster, development, and demolition over the years.

This chapter details seven lost plantations once located in present-day Virginia and one each from Maryland and present-day West Virginia. Of course, there were thousands more. For example, Mannsfield, built by Mann Page III, who had grown up at Rosewell and married Mary Tayloe of Mount Airy, was an exquisite example of high Palladian style built in Spotsylvania County, Virginia. It carried many of the stylistic and formative features of Mount Airy, a house that still stands today, including flanking dependencies connected by curved walkways, much like those of Washington's Mount Vernon. The Mannsfield house also had a large central hall and was reported to have marble floors. The plantation house was destroyed by artillery fire during the Civil War. Its ruins and foundations were excavated in 1934, revealing thousands of artifacts and much information about the history of the estate and the wider region. Likewise, the famed domed mansion of the illustrious Randolphs on Virginia's Turkey Island was also destroyed during the Civil War. It had been completely renovated and possibly totally rebuilt c. 1770, at which time it was described as a two-story brick house with a large central dome and one-story flanking wings.

In Forest Glen, Maryland, Edgewood Plantation, originally the home and tobacco estate of the Brent family and later the Keys family, was small, but showcased an unusually grand Greek Revival master house, an oddity in the state. The plantation site later served as the home of the Forest Inn hotel, and later National Park Seminary and National Park College. The estate became part of the Walter Reed Army Medical Center Annex in 1942, and the celebrated mansion was razed by the military in the 1960s.

There are several dozen notable plantation houses that still stand in the Virginias and Maryland. Among them is Wilton House, the estate of William Randolph III, now in Richmond, which is open as a house museum. Due to encroaching industrialization, it was moved to its present location in 1933, by the National Society of the Colonial Dames of America. Chatham Manor, a quintessential Georgian-style mansion built between 1768 and 1771 by William Fitzhugh, sits along the Rappahannock River in Stafford County, Virginia, opposite Fredericksburg. It was the center of a large, successful plantation. Its last private owner, John Lee Pratt, gave the estate to the National Park Service, which uses the plantation as the headquarters of the Fredericksburg-Spotsylvania National Military Park. Portions of the house are open to the public as a museum. Westover, in Charles City, Virginia, was built c. 1730 by William Byrd II, the founder of Richmond. It is a massive three-story brick Georgian house with two wings that were originally separated from the main house. The east wing once

contained more than four thousand volumes of the famous Byrd family library. The east wing and library burned during the Civil War. The present east wing was built around 1900, and both wings were connected to the main home at that time. The grounds at Westover are opened daily to the public, and tours of the house can be arranged by appointment. Of course, the most successful plantation museums in both Virginia and the United States are Washington's Mount Vernon and Jefferson's Monticello. These not only provide visitors a glimpse into the lives of the founding fathers and into life and labor on these large southern estates, but provide prime examples of preservation successes on a grand scale.

In Maryland, extant examples of antebellum plantations include Sotterley Plantation, the sole surviving tidewater plantation in the state, which was home to the Bowles, Plater, Briscoe and Saterlee families. In the eighteenth and nineteenth centuries, Sotterley served as a thriving port and landing. The La Grange Plantation in Cambridge is now home to the Dorchester County Historical Society, which purchased the estate in 1959. The society uses the house as a museum open to the public and for special functions.

Estates such as the Jenkins Plantation survive in present-day West Virginia. Originally, the area was part of Green Bottom in what was then western Virginia, and the Jenkins family owned four thousand prosperous acres. They built a handsome brick home in 1835 that has survived multiple trials and tribulations to serve as a public interpretative site of the West Virginia Department of Culture and Tourism.

Scholarship is varied concerning these states of the Upper South. Many of Virginia's most important lost plantations and other demolished structures are featured in *Lost Virginia: Vanished Architecture of the Old Dominion*, an exceptional book that accompanied a 2001 Virginia Historical Society exhibit of the same name.

Maryland's architecture is analyzed in several volumes by Henry Chandlee Forman, including *Early Manor and Plantation Houses of Maryland*

and a sequel volume, *Tidewater Maryland Architecture and Gardens,* as well as *Maryland Architecture: A Short History from 1634 through the Civil War.* These works provide excellent information on many extant and some vanished plantation homes, while the state's architectural legacy is further explored in several county-specific volumes. West Virginia's architecture is highlighted in S. Allen Chambers's *Buildings of West Virginia,* among other works.

The present-day states of Virginia, West Virginia, and Maryland each had a unique plantation history, and they dealt with the issue of secession in dissimilar ways, but they are similar in the fact that, like the rest of the South, the great majority of the architectural and built evidence of their colonial and antebellum past is now gone. Through closer examination of such lost estates and recognition of these plantations in wider history, we can hope to gain a better understanding of our unique and fascinating past.

# Rosewell

Rosewell Plantation of Gloucester County once featured the largest and most extravagant mansion built in colonial Virginia, but today the remarkable home exists only as a ruin. Located near Carter's Creek and the York River, the plantation originally had a smaller wood-frame master house, but this structure was destroyed by fire in 1721. At this time, Rosewell owner Mann Page I set out to build a home that would not only rival the newly completed Governor's Palace near Williamsburg, but would surpass it in size and style. At the time of Page's death in 1730, the house was still not complete, and its ownership passed to his wife, Judith. Construction was halted for years, but began again in 1737, after Judith inherited money from her father, Robert Carter. The same year, Mann Page II took over the administration of this gargantuan construction project, finally finishing it.[1]

Once completed, the mansion included three stories atop a raised basement. Not one, but two cupolas rested above the roof, and four large brick chimneys symmetrically framed the structure. Inside, the six-foot-wide staircase—often touted as one of the most elaborate staircases ever built in the Americas—dripped with embellishment and decoration. Corinthian capitals throughout the stairs were accented by an array of carved vines, flowers, rosettes, leaves, and other wooden foliage.

Outside the house, a number of buildings of various forms and functions dotted the plantation landscape, among them a large circular icehouse and a massive stable. The original plan called for two connecting units to link the house with two large dependencies, but these were apparently never constructed.

Mann Page II left Rosewell in 1765, and his son John Page took over as plantation master. By 1771, John Page and his wife, Frances Burwell Page, had undertaken redecoration and renovation of the mansion. John later had a difficult time financially with the plantation, and was not able to keep up all the routine repairs and maintenance needed on the home. Despite his troubles in business, he still managed to play an important role in community and social affairs. He served as a member of the House of Burgesses.

John Page died in 1808, and his second wife, Margaret, inherited the plantation along with a large number of slaves. The house was virtually abandoned for much of Margaret Page's tenure as mistress, during which time she resided at Williamsburg.

In 1837, after Margaret's death, Rosewell was sold to Thomas B. Booth, whose many "improvements" to the mansion, which included removing marble from the floor of the great hall, taking out exquisite paneling and mantels, and demolishing the double cupolas, actually did more harm than good. After completing his renovations, Booth sold the estate to his cousin John T. Catlett, some ten years after his purchase. Catlett resided in the house and actually enhanced the structure. After Catlett's death in 1881, the plantation passed through various hands.

Rosewell met its death in 1916 in a tremendous

Rosewell Plantation House
was the largest and most
extravagant house built in
colonial Virginia. Today the
mansion exists only as a ruinous shell, which has been
expertly preserved by the
Rosewell Foundation.

The Rosewell Plantation
cemetery.

fire. All that remained thereafter were remnants of the building's outer structure—a great shell reminder of a proud colonial past. In 1935, Congress passed a bill to develop a Colonial National Historical Park that would include Rosewell. The property and ruins, however, were never purchased for this purpose. In 1979, the owners of the ruins donated them to the Gloucester Historical Society. The Rosewell Foundation was then established to manage the site.

Since that time, the Rosewell Foundation has played an exemplary role in its care of the ruins. It has promoted research into the history of colonial Virginia, most notably through archeological exploration of the site. The foundation has stabilized the ruins, preserving them for future generations. The group has also been instrumental in sharing the ruins with the community and communicating their significance by opening the area to the public and establishing a visitors center and museum onsite. Certainly Rosewell is an example of how all plantation ruins and other culturally significant sites should be preserved and shared. In the remains of Rosewell, southerners can find their past, a physical testament to the duality of proud heritages as well as shameful indignities, but an accurate, authentic example of what used to be.

## Oak Hill

Samuel Hairston's Oak Hill Plantation of Pittsylvania County, Virginia, survived the Civil War and well into the twentieth century, only to burn to the ground in 1988. The estate was located near the North Carolina border on the Dan River, and it was the site of an important hospital established by General Nathaniel Greene for his troops during the Revolution.[2]

The Hairston family's progenitor, Peter, had come to North America in 1729, from Scotland, and his descendents successfully amassed a plantation empire unrivaled in the South. The Hairstons owned dozens of estates across the South, but most were clustered in lower Virginia and in North Carolina. Oak Hill was among several Hairston estates in Pittsylvania County, but its importance was paramount to the family as it served as a headquarters for operations, especially for Samuel Hairston's branch of the family.[3]

Oak Hill, like many other Hairston estates, principally grew tobacco, a cash crop whose cultivation formed the central economic bastion of the region. Raising tobacco was no easy task, and after the plants' leaves had been harvested, they still had to cure. A large log barn on the property served this purpose. Here, tobacco leaves were hung on racks, and a fire in a trench on the floor provided the smoke and heat needed in the drying and curing process. One unfortunate slave would have had the scorching job of tending to the fire —constantly making sure it was large enough to serve its purpose, while not getting out of hand. It was this tobacco, cured in such a way, that spurred the Hairston fortune and provided the funds for the construction of the mansion at Oak Hill.[4]

The celebrated master house was built by Hairston between 1823 and 1825. It was an impressive two-story, five-bay symmetrical brick structure with a one-story front porch boasting four white columns supporting a plain pediment. The back porch, which was added later, was longer and larger. Two sets of tall chimneys—four in all—framed the house at both sides. A little brick annex was later added to one side of the house.

The interior of the house was originally filled with mahogany furniture, most of which was produced in Milton, North Carolina. The walls were furnished with oil paintings of the family that had been commissioned in 1861. One of the wooden mantels was stained red with a mixture of polk berries.[5]

Outside, the master house was surrounded by an abundant garden divided by boxwoods. A seventy-five-foot pine tree acted as a landmark for the plantation, as it could be seen for up to four miles away. The gardens sloped downward from the house on a series of large, magnificent earthen terraces that were carved into the landscape by slaves.[6]

There was a little brick schoolhouse in the garden that served the Hairston children. Such schoolhouses were fairly common on large plantations, where well educated private tutors were usually brought in to teach the young white children. One such tutor at Oak Hill was William Marshall Treadway, Jr., of Chatham, Virginia. Hairston also allowed neighbor children to attend school in his gardens. Columbia Stuart attended the school, where she met Samuel's son Peter Hairston. Columbia and Peter later married. Columbia's brothers, James Ewell Brown ("Jeb") and Willie Stuart, also attended lessons in the little garden schoolhouse and lived on the property at one time. Jeb later became a famed Confederate general.[7]

Beyond the gardens were the slave quarters. In his book, *The Hairstons: An American Family in Black and White,* Henry Wiencek interviewed modern-day descendents of both Hairston slaves and masters. Descendents of former Oak Hill slaves recall stories that were passed down about life on the Hairston plantation. Daniel Hairston recalled that his grandfather Gus, who was a slave at Oak Hill, often recounted a story about butter. Apparently, the slaves were not allowed to have butter, but one day, Gus took some and hid it under his hat. While he was being whipped for another infraction, Gus's hat fell off, along with the butter. When the overseer realized what Gus had done, he gave him a second whipping. Both Gus and his own descendents found this story humorous, but it, along with other tales, weaves a picture of active slave resistance.[8]

Other stories of slave opposition at Oak Hill recounted by Wiencek include a yarn about how the slaves would sneak out late at night while the master and his family slept. They would steal a fence rail and a hog that they would roast over a hidden fire in the woods, using the fence rail as fuel for the flames. It was imperative that this was done quickly and that the hog's uneaten remains, from skin to bones, were burned completely to hide any evidence of the insurrection from the master or overseer.

Another anecdote related how Oak Hill slaves, who were prevented from prayers or worship, would go again to forested areas to hold religious meetings. They brought along a large metal pot that was used in the slave quarters for washing clothes. This pot was placed upside down, as it was believed that this would prevent whites from hearing the preaching and singing. Wiencek notes that this tradition was rooted in African beliefs that an upturned pot in the middle of the house would invoke the protection of a god.[9]

The number of slaves at Oak Hill grew as Samuel Hairston continued to prosper and his plantation expanded. By the middle of the nineteenth century he was considered the richest man in Virginia. In 1850, it is said, he marched about seven hundred slaves from Oak Hill to Martinsville, roughly twenty miles away, so that he could present them all as a wedding gift to his daughter, Alcey.[10]

These enslaved people and all others at Oak Hill and elsewhere were freed by the Emancipation Proclamation of 1863. One of the first things the freedmen of Oak Hill did was to establish their own church, after having been forbidden to worship openly for so many years. The Piney Grove Primitive Baptist Church is still in operation today, and many current members count themselves among descendents of Oak Hill slaves.

Samuel Hairston lived until 1875, when his son George took over the plantation.[11] George, like his brother Peter, attended the University of North Carolina, but he dropped out after poor performance. He married Anne Elizabeth Lash in 1855.[12] The couple had two sons, William and Samuel. The family lived principally at Berry Hill, a nearby Hairston plantation. After George's death in 1925, his son Samuel inherited the plantation.[13]

Samuel married May Jopling of nearby Danville, Virginia. They had seven children. Samuel was an active dairy farmer, real estate broker, and railroad director, in addition to his agricultural work at Oak Hill. The plantation mansion itself remained in a pristine state of repair until 1988, when it was destroyed by a "mysterious" fire.

Today a ruinous brick wall and remains of the chimneys are all that are left of the master house, and some vestiges of outbuildings can still be seen, although the property has largely reverted to a natural state, overgrown with vegetation. Wiencek notes in *The Hairstons* that descendants of Oak Hill slaves often visit the ruins even today, as many feel immensely connected to the estate where their ancestors spent their lives and their bones now rest.[14]

# Ossian Hall

Once located near Annandale, a small community just inside the Capital Beltway in Fairfax County, Virginia, Ossian Hall had been one of several plantations owned by the noted Fitzhugh family. The plantation's master house was occupied until the early 1950s, when it was abandoned. Less than a decade after it was deserted, the historic mansion was set aflame by the local fire department in a sadistic public spectacle that drew onlookers from far and wide.

The land that was to become Ossian Hall Plantation was originally part of the large Ravensworth Plantation tract, a land grant that was acquired by the Fitzhughs in the late 1600s. The family carved out the estate that became the domain of Henry Fitzhugh, a cousin of Ravensworth's William Fitzhugh, via inheritance.[15]

The family called the estate Ossian Hall in honor of Ossian or Oisín, a legendary poet/warrior of the Fenian Cycle of ancient Irish mythology. The name Ossian was also that of the narrator of *The Works of Ossian*, an influential cycle of poems by James Macpherson, which he supposedly translated from ancient Scots Gaelic sources.[16]

By 1694, the property was occupied by tenant farmers. Henry Ftizhugh's son Nicholas reportedly built the mansion at Ossian Hall for his large family that included twelve children. Traditionally, 1730 has been the date of construction noted, but sources note that it could have been built as late as 1780.

Regardless of the construction date, the house was an impressive sight. It was a wood-frame two-story structure with a five-bay façade. On the earlier side of the house, there was a gabled roof with a large central pediment extending the length of three bays. At the center of the pediment a large fanlight illuminated the commodious attic floor and principally the large stairwell leading to the attic. Framing the pediment were two tall dormers, and beyond this the entire structure was framed by thick brick chimneys. Below, a one-story gabled portico supported by four little columns gave welcome to guests and friends. Benches, thought to be a later addition, were built between the columns of the portico.

The opposite side of the house was probably originally quite plain. However, later, in the mid-to-late 1800s, an impressive colonnade was added, paying homage, no doubt, to that at Washington's Mount Vernon. Six square columns supported a heavy entablature and intricate balustrade above. On this side of the house, there was no pediment, but instead three dormer windows peeked out from the gabled roof.

On one side of the house a thin one-story corridor attached an adjacent larger wing to the rest of the house. The interior of the house was of a standard central hall plan. On the first floor, the central stair hall was flanked by a single large room on one side and two smaller rooms on the other. The smaller rooms had adjacent corner fireplaces that shared a central chimney. The second story was more divided, with two rooms flanking each side of the stair hall, each having a corner fireplace, similar in plan to those below. One end of the broad stair hall was also divided on this level, creating another small chamber. Above, the large attic was further divided, creating several small chambers.

In 1804, Dr. David Stuart, a statesman and planter, purchased Ossian Hall. Stuart, a close friend of George Washington's, married Eleanor Calvert Custis, Martha Washington's former daughter-in-law.[17] The Stuarts had seventeen children of their own, as well as four from Eleanor's former marriage to John Parke Custis. The family grew, filling the plantation house as David Stuart's reputation and career rose. He was chosen as one of the three

The mansion at Ossian Hall Plantation featured a front façade that was dominated by a large central pediment at the roofline (which was flanked by attic dormers) and a pediment-topped portico below.

In the mid-to-late 1800s, the rear of Ossian Hall was adorned with a Mount Vernon–inspired colonnade with a heavy balustrade.

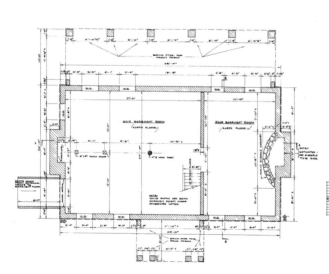

Ossian Hall. Basement plan.

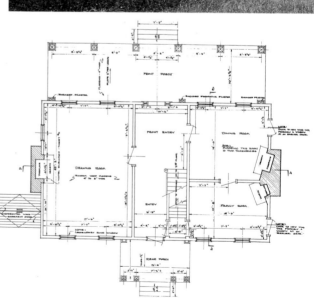

Ossian Hall. First-floor plan.

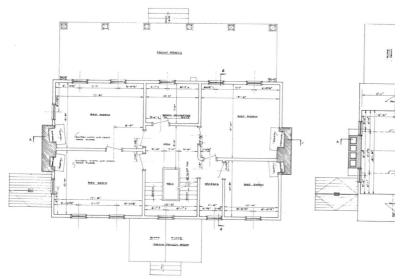

Ossian Hall. Second-floor plan.

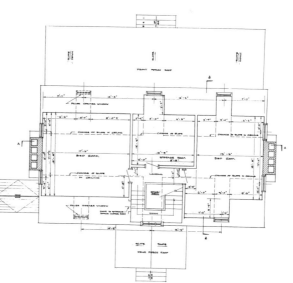

Ossian Hall. Attic-floor plan.

The Annandale Volunteer Fire Department's logo featuring Ossian Hall Plantation House, the historic structure that the fire department deliberately destroyed.

commissioners to oversee the plan of the Federal City (now Washington, D.C.). Later, he served in Virginia's House of Burgesses.

Eleanor Stuart died in 1811, and her husband died three years later. The plantation was passed down to the younger generation, who continued agricultural enterprises at the estate. During the Civil War, Ossian Hall was home to even more friends and family—many with close ties to Robert E. Lee and his wife, Mary Randolph Custis Lee—who sought refuge from Union-controlled territory.

The plantation passed through various hands until it was purchased by Kansas senator Joseph L. Bristow in 1918. In retirement from his public career, Bristow relished agrarian life. He resided at Ossian Hall until his death in 1944.[18]

Members of the Bristow family continued to reside at Ossian Hall until 1951, at which time they vacated the historic mansion. This created an open holiday for vandals and treasure hunters, who ripped intricately carved woodwork from the walls and stripped the mansion of its fine metal furnishings. It is said that in 1957, a truck pulled up in the middle of the night and stole all of the brass door locks and mantels from the house. Later, some of these wooden embellishments fortunately made their way into Twiford, a historic estate in Westmoreland County.

Stripped, the shell of the once magnificent plantation mansion was burned in 1959. Unlike the mysterious arsons at nearby Ravensworth or at Georgia's Casulon Plantation or even the lightning-caused fire at Alabama's beloved Forks of Cypress Plantation, the fire at Ossian Hall was a publicly planned and well-plotted undertaking. The fire, which took place on September 9, 1959, was billed as a "training exercise" for the Annandale Volunteer Fire Department. The group further marketed the deliberate destruction of one of their community's most historic and significant structures as a public service, to make way for the new Bristow Subdivision, itself named after one of the plantation's last famous residents. Six other fire departments assisted in the cruel demolition, first setting fire to each room individually and sequentially squelching the flames. Finally, they cast a giant blazing bonfire upon the whole house as over five hundred spectators looked on in awe, astonishment, and abhorrence. Adding insult to irreparable and appalling injury, these courageous men crowned their behavior by pulling down the house's still-standing brick chimneys.

Later, the fire department had the insolence to emblaze upon the center of their logo the image and name of Ossian Hall! It sits there like a stuffed animal head on a hunter's mantel, giving only a glimpse of what it was like in life. The ironic images of the lost plantation still proudly appear on the official uniform patch, Web site, and even the fire trucks of the department!

Today, a suburban development sprawls over the majority of the former plantation lands. A small elevated and undeveloped plot is thought to have been the plantation cemetery. Here members of the Stuart-Custis family lie in unmarked graves, and no evidence of their former lively presence or that of their historic Ossian Hall Plantation can be found.

## Ravensworth

Like Ossian Hall, Ravensworth, which shared the same original land grant, was also a seat of the famed Fitzhughs, and it was also later associated with the Lee-Custis clan. Ravensworth's history can be traced back to the late 1600s, when the original land grant—the largest such grant in northern Vir-

The large symmetrical mansion at Ravensworth Plantation featured a low central portico and Palladian window above. The main portion of the house was connected to two identical side wings.

Ravensworth Plantation House. A small dining area.

ginia—was deeded to John Matthews. In 1685, family progenitor William Fitzhugh of Bedford, England, purchased 21,966 acres from Matthews.[19] The sprawling property was an irregular axe-shaped plot that provided for easy access to local waterways. Fitzhugh called this property Ravensworth in honor of an ancestral seat in England.[20]

Fitzhugh never resided on this tract, but instead made his home at Eagles Nest in King George County. It is clear that by 1686, Fitzhugh was cultivating his lands at Ravensworth, which he referred to as a "plantation." Of the estate, he also wrote that it was "convenient and good Land enough to seat 140 to 200 fam'lys upon one Divided wch [sic] contains 21,966 acres, which I will either sell them in fee at 17 [pounds] sterling for every hundred acres, or else lease it to them for three lives paying 20 shillings p. annum for every hundred acres . . ."[21]

Fitzhugh leased large portions of the property to, among others, French Huguenots, who had fled Europe to avoid religious persecution. These settlers, however, found the Ravensworth tracts to be primitive and difficult. Their only shelters were scanty wooden huts, and the settlements were regularly besieged by Native Americans. There was also the threat of attacks by wolves and other wild animals.

While his tenants battled the problems of agrarian life and tobacco cultivation in the still largely unclaimed wildness, Fitzhugh found much success in his legal practice at Stafford County. Aside from his membership in the court, he also prided himself in his role as commander of the Stafford County Militia. He died in 1701, and at the time of his death he had amassed over fifty-four thousand acres of land in the region.

The Ravensworth estate passed to Fitzhugh's two eldest sons, William, Jr., and Henry. William, Jr., inherited the southern portion that would later be home to Ravensworth Plantation House, while Henry retained the northern portion. Henry's portion later became Ossian Hall Plantation. Over the years various plots of land were sold or acquired, accounting for the ever-changing boundaries and acreage of the plantation.

William Fitzhugh of Chatham, great-grandson of the original William Fitzhugh the immigrant, was the first family member to build a plantation house on the estate.[22] His house was an expansive Palladian mansion. Its central wing was a two-story, five-bay structure that was dominated by a central pavilion with a low pediment. A one-story portico with four small columns framed the central front door with its surrounding fan transom and sidelights. A large central Palladian window stood above the portico balustrade, and, above this, the pediment center was occupied by a bull's-eye window. Framing the central portion of the house were the two symmetrical side wings that rested lower than the main house. Two-story connecting halls linked the one-bay wings to the central part of the house. Each wing boasted a crowning pediment echoing that found atop the central pavilion. The rear of the house was dominated by a wide two-level piazza that ran the length of the central portion of the house. It was likely inspired by the famed piazza at nearby Mount Vernon.[23]

Outside the main house, the usual dependencies including kitchens, barns, shops, and slave cabins could be found. But of particular interest at Ravensworth was the unusual stables building, designed in the classic Jeffersonian style. The brick structure, thought to have been constructed in the first years of the nineteenth century, featured an arcade on one side enclosing a porch. One end of the structure had a large recess supported by flanking Tuscan half-columns. This recess was topped by a frieze and had a central opening—later a set of windows, but probably once a large doorway. The interior of the building was outfitted with several large stables and a second story was divided into several separate storage areas.

Given the physical structure of their plantation and their busy public and social lives, it seems that the Fitzhughs had established themselves as one of the great planter families of the South. By 1786, William Fitzhugh was regularly dining at Mount Vernon with the Washingtons, according to George Washington's own writings. Fitzhugh's daughter Mary Lee later married George Washington Parke Custis, who was Martha Washington's grandson. She therefore became mistress of Arlington House, and her own daughter, Mary Anna Randolph Custis, later married Robert E. Lee.

Ravensworth was eventually held in trust for Mary Anna Randolph Custis, and it was to Ravensworth that Robert E. Lee's mother, Anne Hill Carter Lee, had been brought when she became ill. Then a young cadet at West Point, Robert E. Lee had been summoned to Ravensworth upon the news of his mother's convalescence. The matron died and was buried at Ravensworth, although her body was later moved.

During the Civil War, Mary Lee fled Arlington House and used Ravensworth as a refuge, but she stayed there only briefly, opting to go further south, where she felt she and her family would be safer. Ravensworth eventually was inherited by the Lee children, and two of Robert E. Lee's sons, George Washington Custis Lee and William Henry Fitzhugh "Rooney" Lee, lived there. Rooney Lee died in 1891, and the house passed to two of his sons, Robert E. Lee III and Dr. George Bolling Lee. Dr. Lee eventually obtained total ownership after his brother's death in 1922.

On August 1, 1926, the plantation house was mysteriously burned. The fire, which destroyed the mansion, was thought to have been set by arsonists. Many of the priceless Lee-Custis family portraits displayed in the plantation mansion had been moved over the years, but seventeen remaining portraits were destroyed in the blaze.

Dr. George Bolling Lee died in 1948, and his widow sold the Ravensworth tract to developers in 1957. The noted stables were demolished in 1960 to make way for new subdivisions, including one called Ravensworth Farm, which still stands on the site today. A lone historical marker erected by the Department of Historic Resources in 1992 reminds residents of the property's historic past.

## Marshall Hall

Said to have been the largest home in southern Maryland documented to date before the 1740s, and obviously one of the most architecturally significant, the master house at Marshall Hall Plantation—right across the Potomac from Washington's Mount Vernon—housed numerous generations of the Marshall family, served as an amusement park for several decades, and was finally gutted by a great fire and later further damaged by a motor vehicle accident.

William Marshall I was born in England in 1607. He traveled to Maryland in 1640, just six years after the colony's first settlement had been established.

Marshall Hall. Front elevation. Colonial proportions
and styling are evident.

Marshall Hall. Plan of the
first floor.

Marshall Hall. Plan of the second floor. The later extension
did not communicate with
the older parts of the house
on the second story.

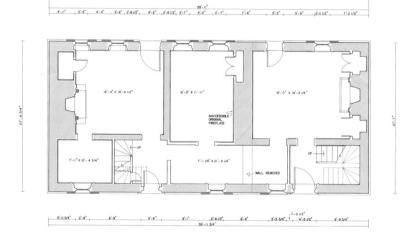

FIRST FLOOR PLAN

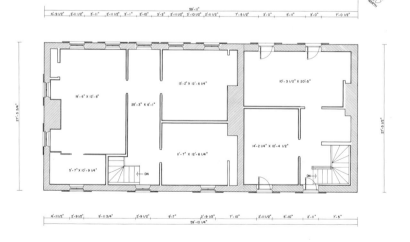

SECOND FLOOR PLAN

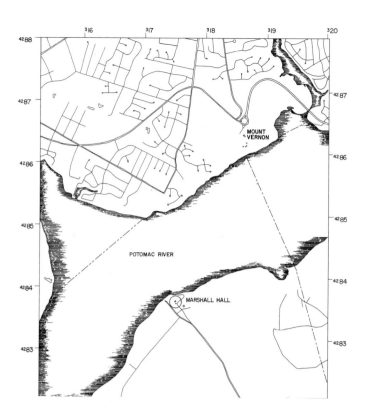

Map showing the proximity of Marshall Hall Plantation to the Potomac and to Washington's Mount Vernon on the opposite bank of the river.

It is thought that Marshall arrived as an indentured servant; however, in less than ten years he not only earned his freedom, but also actively began purchasing and selling land of his own. He even requested land grants from the colonial authorities in exchange for his work in bringing more English colonists to Maryland.[24]

In 1650, Governor Leonard Calvert issued a warrant providing five hundred acres of land for William Marshall.[25] Marshall named the tract after himself and developed a farm on the property. He soon married Katherine Hebden, the widow of Thomas Hebden. The couple had three children.

By the time of William Marshall's death in 1673, he owned over a thousand acres that were divided among his young children. A variety of livestock was also equally divided among the children.

William Marshall II married Elizabeth Hanson, the daughter of Randolph and Barbara Hatton Johnson Hanson. Randolph had settled much of the area that comprises the current-day Piscataway Park. Among William II and Elizabeth's four chil-

dren was Thomas Marshall I, who built the master house at Marshall Hall. Thomas obtained the land upon which he constructed the house from a portion of property that had been overlooked on previous surveys. He called his patent "Mistake." In 1726, at the age of thirty-one, he married Elizabeth Bishop Stoddert, the widow of surveyor James Stoddert. Together they had five children. After Elizabeth's death circa 1749, Thomas later married Sabrina Truman Greenfield, although this union produced no offspring.

Thomas erected the plantation house between 1725 and 1730. The house itself was a one-and-one-half-story brick structure with steeply pitched gables and flared eaves. The first story originally contained four rooms and a small stair hall near the rear of the house. The second story originally contained a hallway that transversed the center of the house with chambers on either side. A narrow ladder to the attic could be found in one of the bedrooms.

The interior of the house was finely finished

with heavy baseboards, chair-rails, and ceiling cornices. A major addition to the house was built around 1760. It was constructed in such a way that no seam could be noted in the exterior brickwork. This extension of the house contained a large first-floor room and fireplace, a stair hall, and a passage on the first floor to the original part of the house. Interestingly, the new stairway led to the second story, but there was no communication on the second floor between the original rooms of the house and the two new bedchambers of the extension.

Around the same time that the extension was constructed, a kitchen was built nearby, about thirty feet from the house. The grounds also contained a noted stable and carriage house renowned for its large size, Flemish bond brickwork, and graceful arched openings.

Also found on the plantation were a major warehouse and wharf where Thomas I ran a very successful mercantile business, importing goods for local consumers. Of course, his primary business was agriculturue. He developed a very successful tobacco plantation on his lands at Marshall Hall. For example, in 1759, thirty-one enslaved laborers on the estate produced eleven thousand pounds of tobacco. Smaller crops of wheat and corn were also cultivated on the plantation. In addition to slave labor, Thomas I also employed several tenant farm families; in exchange for a portion of their crops, they were allowed to live on and farm a specific portion of property.

By 1760, Thomas Hanson Marshall II had inherited his late father's estate. He built upon his father's success to become one of the wealthiest planters in Charles County. He was well known in the area, serving in several state conventions, and was awarded a captaincy in the American Revolution.

Thomas II was an acquaintance of General George Washington, whose Mount Vernon estate rested nearly directly across the Potomac from Marshall Hall. The two planters traded lands, crops, seeds, and other supplies, although there is no indication that the neighbors were close friends.

Thomas II married Rebecca Dent in 1756, and they had six children, including Thomas Marshall III, who inherited the plantation. Thomas III became a physician and served in the Continental Army during the Revolution. By 1780, he was a senior surgeon in the military's hospital department.

In 1795, Dr. Marshall married Anna Calgett. Together the couple had four children. Anna died within ten years of the marriage. Dr. Marshall then married his cousin, Margaret Marshall.

Dr. Marshall, like his father, was also an acquaintance of Washington. The first president's own diary mentions that Dr. Marshall visited Mount Vernon for tea in 1758, and later that year he spent the night at Washington's estate.

Dr. Marshall died in 1829, and his eldest son, Thomas Hanson Marshall IV, inherited Marshall Hall. He married Eleanor Ann Hardesty in 1821, and they had seven children. Thomas Hanson Marshall V inherited the plantation in 1843. He was the father of sixteen children, six by his first wife, Sallie Magruder Lyles, and ten by his second wife, Henrietta Eleanor Lyles (who was a cousin of Sallie). Eight of these children survived into adulthood.

After the Civil War, Thomas V was forced to sell Marshall Hall Plantation due to debts he incurred as a result of the war. The estate passed through various hands until it was purchased by the Mount Vernon and Marshall Hall Steamboat Company in 1895. Marshall Hall was used as a pleasure resort known as Marshall Hall Amusement Park.

The amusement park was a grand success, with many visitors coming regularly by steamboat from the nearby Washington area. The company installed a variety of Victorian park structures, gardens, croquet and jousting greens, gazebos, and concessions on the grounds of the mansion amid the early farm buildings.

In the mid-twentieth century these nineteenth-century park structures, along with the interspersed eighteenth-century farm buildings, were demolished to construct a modern amusement park. The Marshall Hall master house and nearby kitchen building were spared. Surrounding these older structures a new building was constructed called Happyland; it contained 185 slot machines.

Also built was an ice rink, roller coaster, Ferris wheel, shooting gallery, "frontier railroad," and several other rides and attractions.

Around this time, there was talk of restoring Marshall Hall as a historic tourist attraction for the park, as it was currently being used as a home for the park manager. This idea, however, was abandoned. Park manager Lorenzo Addison said that "they decided that a dead president pulls too many people to Mt. Vernon and dropped the idea."[26]

The new park operated through the 1970s, when a concerted effort to preserve the rural setting of the Mount Vernon overlook was undertaken by private citizens and government officials. The amusement park had been sold to Joseph Goldstein and Star Enterprises in 1969. He envisioned a large, Disney-like park called Spirit of America on the site. But when he began clearing trees along the shore and exposing a view of the amusement park to Mount Vernon, both preservationists and elected leaders cried foul.

The National Park Service took over the site in 1974. Subsequently, various laws were passed over the years preserving the Potomac shorelines in and around Washington's historic estate. Piscataway Park was created and eventually encompassed the Marshall Hall property.

On October 16, 1981, the historic master house at Marshall Hall Plantation was destroyed by an arsonist's fire. Officials found that the barbed-wire fence surrounding the property had been broken into. Besides the house, a Victorian carousel house—the only remnant of the nineteenth-century park structures—was also destroyed in a similar blaze set the same night. No obvious motive was identified.[27]

Only the charred outer walls of the house remained. Mount Vernon resident director John Castellani said, "It's very upsetting to those of us in historic preservation, because it was a fine building with great prospects." Before the blaze, the National Park Service had considered moving their National Colonial Farm, a living history museum, to Marshall Hall.[28]

The next year, the remains of the amusement park were removed from the grounds and the ruins of the house were all but abandoned. In 2003, adding insult to injury, an eighteen-wheeler accidentally barreled through the decaying structure, leaving a massive gaping hole in the crumbling ruins.

Today, the Marshall Hall Foundation, an organization of concerned citizens, has incorporated itself with the central mission of safeguarding the memory of Marshall Hall Plantation. They have established a Web site (http://marshallhall.org/) to communicate the importance of this estate, and are actively involved in local preservation efforts.

## George Washington's Rock Hall (Bullskin) Plantation

Rock Hall Plantation, part of a larger estate known as Bullskin, was owned by George Washington. His brothers held the other plantations that made up the Bullskin lands and included Harewood, Claymont Court, Blakeley, and Happy Retreat. In Washington's day the plantation was located in Virginia, but today the lands form part of Jefferson County, West Virginia. The master house that Washington built was totally destroyed by fire in 1906, although some scant evidence of the original estate still exists.[29]

George Washington first encountered the lands that would later make up his Rock Hall Plantation when he was sixteen and he and young George William Fairfax[30] were invited on a surveying expedition under James Glenn. The party measured the boundary of Lord Fairfax's lands, which totaled over 5.2 million acres. It was at this time that he first dreamed of owning a plantation at Bullskin.

Soon, Washington began saving the money he earned from surveying and started lending it to his brothers with interest. Washington made a second trip to Bullskin in 1750, when he traveled with his ailing brother Lawrence to the healing Indian springs there. Lawrence was equally impressed with the good lands there and purchased over

2,000 acres. At age eighteen, George Washington purchased over 450 acres of Bullskin lands from Robert Rutherford, calling his estate "My Bullskin Plantation." He expanded his holdings with 550 acres purchased from Lord Fairfax and later two additional tracts of more than 1,000 acres, purchased from James McCracken and George Johnson.

Lawrence Washington died in 1752. At this time the Washingtons owned over 4,000 acres at Bullskin. A portion of this property was given to younger brother Charles, who developed Charles Town, today the county seat of Jefferson County, West Virginia. Lawrence's widow and young daughter (who died soon after) inherited his Bullskin lands as well as Mount Vernon. George purchased Mount Vernon from her in an effort to keep the property in the Washington family.

It is clear that Washington had developed a plantation at Bullskin called Rock Hall as early as 1755. The original house is thought to have been a two-story stone building with a wide front porch and stone chimneys. By 1760, Washington wrote of a smallpox epidemic that was ravaging the slave quarters at Rock Hall. He instructed his overseer to have slaves in the "upper quarter" who contracted the disease removed to his own house and to call for the nurse. The original house was later enlarged by Washington.

In addition to producing his own crops, Washington also began dividing the plantation into two-hundred-acre tracts that he leased to tenant farmers. These farmers were to each build a twenty-foot-long dwelling house and forty-foot-long barn on their tracts. Washington also gave very specific instructions to the farmers about what crops they were to plant and what animals they were to keep. He further instructed each of them to plant an orchard and vineyard, preserve woodlots, and maintain fences.

Washington retained possession of Rock Hall Plantation throughout his life. He died in 1799, and the Bullskin lands and Rock Hall were thrown into a family quagmire over who should inherit the properties. The battle raged on for twenty years un-til it was finally settled in court. The property was purchased by Lawrence Lewis, who later sold it to Matthew Ranson. Ranson later sold the plantation to Thomas Hite Willis and his wife, Elizabeth.

Interestingly, the Rock Hall Plantation would soon return to the Washington family. John Augustine Washington III, George Washington's great-grandnephew, could no longer maintain Mount Vernon. He sold it to the Mount Vernon Ladies Association in 1860. His daughter Jane Charlotte Washington married Nathaniel Hite Willis, who was the son of Rock Hall owner Thomas Hite Willis. The couple eventually inherited Rock Hall and raised their large family there, until the master house burned in a kitchen fire in 1906. The family then moved to Charles Town, the city George Washington's brother had earlier established.

The plantation property was sold to John Burns in 1912. He leased the lands to the Victor Products Company. The plantation was then called Romance, and became a part of R. J. Funkhouser's Victor Farms. Funkhouser later purchased and restored several of the other Washington brothers' houses at Bullskin, some of which are now on the National Register of Historic Places. Today, a few overgrown stone structures and foundations are all that is left of our first president's beloved plantation.

## Bush Hill

Bush Hill, near the independent city of Alexandria, Virginia, had a long, complex history stretching back over 270 years. The estate served as a large farm, the principal residence of the prominent Scott family, a headquarters for Union forces during the Civil War, a detention site for Hitler's foreign affairs counselor during World War II, and later a private nursery school. Its senseless destruction by arson in 1977 left local citizens angered and perplexed.

The site of the former Bush Hill Plantation is located near Back Lick Run in Fairfax County. It was the location, according to archeological evi-

The master house at Bush Hill Plantation.

dence, of two prehistoric Native American settlements dating back thirty-five hundred and fifteen hundred years. The history of European settlement on the site can be traced back to 1706, when, on December 23, Lord Fairfax and Lady Culpeper granted over forty-six hundred acres to William and Thomas Harrison, Thomas Pearson, and Major John West.[31] Roger West, the major's son, later inherited his father's share of this Virginia acreage, and in turn sold it to Charles Lee in 1787. The property eventually ended up in the possession of Josiah Watson, who is said to have constructed the original plantation house sometime in the second half of the eighteenth century.[32]

The house, a two-and-one-half-story structure, was laid in Flemish bond with sixteen spacious rooms occupying the main house and an additional wing.[33] Surrounding the house there was, according to an antebellum advertisement in the *Alexandria Gazette*, "a frame granary, log corn house, cow and sheep shelters, Overseers' houses, negro

quarters, dairy, blacksmith shop, ice house, smoke house, &c. . ."[34]

The first notation of the plantation being referred to as Bush Hill is from a 1797 real estate transaction. It was also during this year that the estate was expanded to include some additional acreage from a neighboring tract. Furthermore, it was during 1797 that Bush Hill was sold by Watson to Richard Marshall Scott, collector of revenue at Dumfries.[35]

Scott, a prominent businessman, was the son of John Scott, a merchant who came from Glasgow to Virginia in 1753. He married Mary Love, the daughter of Samuel Love of Salisbury, in 1788. Richard and Mary moved to Bush Hill between 1796 and 1797. The couple lived very happily and prosperously there for nearly a decade and a half, until Mary met an untimely end.

She died tragically in January 1812, after suffering injuries in a horrific theater fire that broke out on the evening of December 26, 1811. The fire claimed the lives of dozens of people, including Virginia governor George W. Smith and Senator and Bank of Virginia president Abraham B. Venable.

After the death of his beloved wife, Scott was left alone. He remained a widower for some sixteen years. The first years following his wife's death were among the saddest of his life. In January 13, 1813, he wrote, "This day and hour, ten o'clock, terminates twelve months of the most unhappy year of my life." The next year he wrote only, "The second anniversary of my wretched widowed state."

During these years Scott devoted himself to developing Bush Hill and keeping a continuous journal of the day-to-day activity of the plantation. Diary entries recount Scott's passion for gardening and planting during these lonely days. The plantation in modern times was noted for claiming two of the tallest American holly trees in the eastern portion of the county, but in antebellum times the estate was ripe with a variety of fruit trees, including apricot, apple, cherry, peach, and lemon. Scott also cultivated strawberries, asparagus, grapes, melons, currants, raspberries, gooseberries, hyacinths, and tulips, among other fruit-producing and flowering plants. In fact, it was Scott who provided a large number of the fruit trees to the Washingtons for their Mount Vernon estate.

Scott was an acquaintance of George Washington, and his diary recounted dining at Mount Vernon plantation numerous times. He also regularly dined at Marshall Hall, directly across the Potomac from Washington's estate. Scott further records a visit to the White House to call upon President Madison and his wife, Dolly, on July 4, 1811.

In addition to his active life in agricultural and social affairs, Scott often busied himself with managing his many slaves. The 1820 federal census records Richard M. Scott as the master of thirty-three slaves at Bush Hill—seventeen males and sixteen females. In addition to his slaves at Bush Hill, Scott also owned slaves at his city residence, 312 Queen Street, Alexandria, four miles from the plantation. He later purchased Farmington Plantation, upon which he settled his parents and other relatives whom he supported. Scott acquired half a dozen or so plantations during this time, including, among others, Dipple at St. Marysville, Cherry Hill in Piccawaxen, Waterloo, and Mount Air. He also acquired Marboro Iron Works and other commercial properties. In total, Scott is said to have owned nearly 150 slaves, some that he hired out for both town and plantation work.[36]

Childless, Scott became the principal caregiver and foster father to numerous children in need. He devoted much of his time to taking in and rearing youngsters, from needy relatives to unfortunate orphans. Many of these he supported into adulthood, all the while managing his agricultural operations at Bush Hill.

The plantation experienced a great fire in 1823. On April 8 of that year, Scott wrote:

> On my return from Alexandria I found my servant hall, my barn, stables, carriage house, covered way, barnyard, hay, straw, plough, cartwheels . . . 13 cords of wood consumed by fire, which broke out in the servants hall on Sunday the 6th, and was carried by a high south wind to the barn. The fire was occasioned in the absence of a mother by her little children setting fire to a straw bed. All my people were in town except Tom and Moses who retuned in time to save the horses, mules and oxen which were in the stable, and also the corn house attached to the barnyard—the barn a large wooden building 60 x 30' two storeys [sic] high—the carriage house 134' x 16' two storeys high and two covered ways 12' x 14'.[37]

Tired of managing plantation affairs alone after a long period as a widower, Richard Scott remarried in 1828. At the time of their marriage, Eleanor Douglass Marshall, the youngest daughter of James Marshall and niece of famed U.S. Supreme Court Chief Justice John Marshall, was in her early twenties. Scott was nearly sixty. Soon, she gave birth to Richard M. Scott, Jr. Upon the child's birth, Scott wrote, "I have prayed to the Lord, day and night, for upwards of thirty years, to bless me with a child of my body."[38] Sadly, the child's mother took ill with a "bilious fever" on the third day following delivery and died a few months later.

After three years, at the age of sixty-three, Scott married his third wife, Lucinda Fitzhugh, a member of Virginia's celebrated Fitzhugh clan.[39] In 1833, a single son was born to the couple, whom they named John Mordecai Scott. Seven months later, Richard Marshall Scott, Sr., died at Berkley Springs, Virginia. Shortly before his death, he wrote: "My body when it shall be deprived of my soul I commend to the care of my surviving relation and friends, with an humble but earnest request that it be interred between the bodies of my affectionate and departed wives Mary and Eleanor Douglass and near those of my honored Father and Mother, brother and sister in the family burying ground on my farm called Farmington."[40]

Richard Marshall Scott, Jr., was taken in by a guardian and attended various boarding schools, including the School for Moral Discipline in South Boston. His stepmother, Lucinda, married Dr. Edward H. Henry in 1846, at which time Richard took full ownership of Bush Hill. His brother, John Mordecai, eventually took over Farmington Plantation.

Upon Richard's arrival at Bush Hill, he began recording day-to-day plantation life in a journal much as his father had. On his first day at the plantation, February 18, 1846, he wrote: "This day I moved from Alexandria where I had been reading law with Francis L. Smith since Oct. 1, 1845, to Bush Hill the residence of my honored and departed father. O Lord! I have this day commenced a new era of my life and Grant Oh most merciful God that I may be faithful to my duty and able to bear the responsibility of a master . . . that I may prove a kind master to my servants and that they be dutiful and obedient to me."[41]

A month later he wrote: "The past four weeks since I came to my farm to live have been the happiest of my life . . . I can now say I am at home, a house I can call my own and I am truly proud of it for never in my life could I really say I had a home."[42]

Content at his new residence, young Richard Scott allowed his mind to turn to love. On March 15, 1846, he wrote, "I learned that Miss Gunnell from Washington is expected to spend some time in the neighborhood soon. Anticipate much pleasure with her society—a lady for whose most estimable and charming character I have much regard."[43] On May 11 of the same year, he wrote, ". . . glad to learn today . . . Miss Virginia Gunnell—is coming to visit the neighborhood very soon. Oh heavenly Father how thankful my cold heart would be if I were only blessed with a companion such as this . . ."[44] The next year, Scott, Jr., at the age of seventeen, married his sweetheart, Virginia Gunnell, the daughter of James S. and Helen Mackall Gunnell. Together the couple had four children: Eleanor Scott, born in 1847, Frank Scott, born in 1849, Anna Constance Scott, born in 1853, and Richard M. Scott III, born in 1851.[45]

Richard Scott, Jr., and his wife, Virginia, lived prosperously at Bush Hill with their family until Scott's death, after which, in 1853, she divided and sold the property.[46] One hundred acres was sold to W. Willoughby and the remaining 436 acres to Dr. Francis Gunnell, the brother of Virginia Gunnell Scott, who later served as surgeon general of the United States Navy from 1884 to 1888. During the Civil War, Union officers used the plantation's master house as a headquarters, and after the war, in 1870, Dr. Gunnell acquired Willoughby's interest in Bush Hill.[47]

On May 23, 1881, Dr. Francis Gunnell sold the great majority of Bush Hill to his brother Dr. James M. Gunnell for thirteen thousand dollars. In 1907, the plantation came into the possession of Leonard G. Gunnell, who lived there with his wife, Emily Nelson, until World War II, when the Bush Hill Plantation house was leased by the federal government for what was then a secret purpose. President Franklin D. Roosevelt used the home to house Ernst Franz Sedgwick "Putzi" Hanfstaengl, Adolf Hitler's close confidant and aide, who was well known for his skills in playing the piano.[48] He was valuable to the U.S. government because of his intimate knowledge of the German führer and his political associates, and, most especially, because of his keen ability to distinguish Hitler's voice from that of an imposter on broadcasts.

Leonard G. Gunnell died in 1946, and the plantation was divided into parcels and split among family members, including Donald B. and Mary Gunnell Phillips, Bruce Covington Gunnell and his wife, Virginia Burt, and Mark Mayo, Jr., and his wife, Amenie Gunnell Boatner. Bruce C. Gunnell constructed a modern home on the plantation lands, near the public road. By the 1950s, portions of the plantation lands were being sold to the Wellington Construction Company for the creation of a suburban neighborhood, and by the 1960s, the Bush Hill Woods subdivision and other similar developments were operating.[49]

It was around this time, in 1948, that the Bush Hill Plantation house was rented for a nursery school called Holly Hills Preschool. Sadly, the school ceased classes in 1977, after vandals broke into the plantation mansion, destroying furnishings and wreaking great havoc to the interior. The windows and doors were boarded shut to prevent intrusion, but this was of no use. On the evening of March 13, 1977, despite precautions taken by the plantation's owners, vandals again visited Bush Hill and set it afire. The plantation house was completely destroyed and no suspects were ever identified. The fire was one in a string of blazes of old and historic properties in the area, which ultimately destroyed numerous important structures. These losses greatly angered and perplexed local citizens and preservationists.[50]

Today, a large, colorful historical marker has been placed near the site of the once-fabled Bush Hill Plantation. The marker contains a summary of the plantation's rich history and of the personalities who once occupied it. It also contains reproductions of important primary documents, such as the *Washington Post* article that describes the mansion's destruction by fire. In addition, it contains the annotated version of a longer poem by an anonymous author published originally in 1825. The shortened version on the marker reads:

Retired and apart from the world's busy hum,
This rural and lovely retreat,
By the genius of talent and taste, has become
To the stranger and curious, a treat.

'Tis a model, deserving of copy from all
Who wish' to improve their estates;
'Tis a spot, where the spring & the summer and fall,
Man's bosom delighted elates.

Should I search far & wide, there is not a place
My soul would prefer to 'BUSH-HILL'
For Natural charms, and for many a grace
Conferr'd by industry and skill.

—*Phenix Gazette*, Alexandria, November 26, 1825

## Chatsworth

Chatsworth Plantation, near Richmond on the north side of the James River, was among the holdings of the famed Randolph family, arguably the most prominent, wealthiest, and most emulated family in colonial and antebellum Virginia. The Marquis de Chastellux, a French aristocrat who traveled to Virginia in the 1780s, noted that one "must be prepared to hear the name Randolph frequently," when visiting the state.[51] The progenitor of the clan was William Randolph I, whose own Turkey Island Plantation—with its great domed master house—was destroyed during the Civil War. The builder of Chatsworth, Peter Randolph, was the grandson of William and the brother of William Randolph III.[52]

Peter Randolph was born in 1717, and grew up in an environment of great privilege and opportunity. He seized much of this opportunity and, with his family's support and backing, became one of the wealthiest planters in the land. He amassed in total some 20,000 acres and over 250 slaves.

Peter married Lucy Bolling in 1738, and together the couple had four children: William, Beverly, Anne, and Robert. Beverly later became the eighth governor of Virginia from 1788 to 1791. Peter served in the House of Burgesses and was appointed surveyor-general of the customs for the Southern District of America in 1749. He also served on the governor's council.

By 1751, Peter had built his home at Chatsworth in Henrico County, near the famed Turkey Island estate of his grandfather and the original site of his brother William's Wilton Plantation.[53] Chatsworth was a fine five-bay home with a steep gabled roof and symmetrical chimneys on the ends of the house. Two one-story wings that may have been added later flanked the main structure of the house. An unusual porch and portico was likely also added at a later date. It included a one-story covered porch that ran the length of the main portion of the house and was supported by eight slender columns. Above this, extending from only the central bay was a short, disproportionate portico with four columns and a low pediment above. This portico served as a balcony from the second floor.

During his tour of America, J. F. D. Smyth noted that the structure was "a very good house with an agreeable perspective."[54] Peter Randolph filled his mansion with costly furnishings. He was described as a man with expensive taste in all things. Of particular note was the commissioning of portraits of himself and his wife to hang inside the house. The standard-size canvases that were traditionally used for this purpose were not adequate for Peter. He instead insisted that artist John Wollaston paint three-quarter-length portraits on larger canvases.

Peter Randolph died on July 8, 1767, at his plantation. Chatsworth passed to his eldest son, William, who married Mary Skipwith. They had two sons, Peter Skipwith and William Beverly. William died in 1774, at the age of thirty-four, and Chatsworth was passed to William Beverly, who remained on the estate for many years. William Beverly died childless and the estate was largely abandoned. It burned around 1915, and a new modern house was eventually built on the property, but not in the same location as the plantation house. Today, the plantation has largely been forgotten, and most of its history has long been lost, except for some original records and papers stored at the Library of Congress in Washington, D.C.

## Malvern Hill

Malvern Hill, once located near Varina in Henrico County, was one of Virginia's oldest plantation homes until it was destroyed at the beginning of the twentieth century.

The estate was first held by Richard Cocke, who emigrated from England and settled on the James River at Point Bremo, the present-day site of Curles Neck Farm. He was a prosperous planter who acquired large tracts in Henrico County, including the property he called Malvern Hills. The lands, it is said, reminded Cocke of the Malvern Hills in England that divide Hereford and Worcestershire.[55]

Richard Cocke and his wife, Temperance Bailey, gave the Malvern Hill tract to their son, Col. Thomas Cocke, who was born in 1639, and served in the House of Burgesses. It is highly probable that the Cockes were actively planting tobacco at Malvern Hill at this time, as this represented the region's major cash crop from 1612, when John Rolfe introduced a popular, milder strain of the plant.

Thomas married Margaret Powell, who was born in 1647. It was Thomas and Margaret who built the first house at Malvern Hill, a frame structure with a brick chimney. Little architectural information has survived about this precursor to the later modified master house. Thomas and Margaret raised six children in this home, including Capt. Thomas Cocke, who later owned the estate.

The younger Thomas, born in 1664, married Mary Brashers, the daughter of John Brashers and Mary Pitt, French Hugenots who settled in Nansemond County, Virginia. Like his father and namesake before him, Thomas raised his six children in the frame plantation house at Malvern Hill, including son James Powell Cocke, born in 1690, who later inherited the estate.

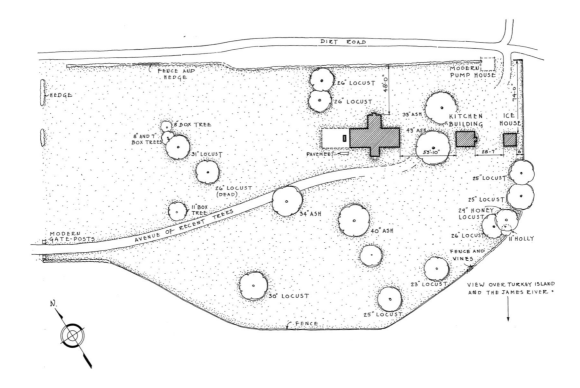

Malvern Hill Plantation. Plot plan.

Malvern Hill Plantation House. The Flemish bond brickwork and early lozenges can be seen in this image.

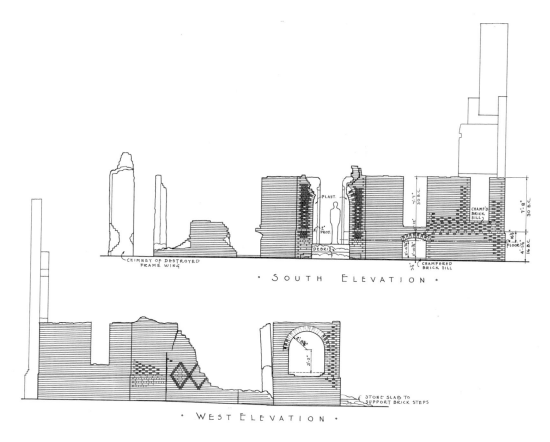

The ruins of Malvern Hill Plantation's master house as they stand today.

James Powell married Martha Herbert, the daughter of John Herbert and Frances Anderson, around 1718. It was likely James Powell who rebuilt the plantation house in the early eighteenth century, dismantling much of the frame structure of the earlier house and constructing a new brick home around the original brick chimney.

The new house was a one-and-one-half-story structure with a large gabled roof. The main portion of the house measured approximately twenty and a half feet deep by nearly fifty-one feet wide. A ten-foot-by-ten-foot square front porch covered with a steep roof and gracefully arched openings welcomed visitors. It may have been added at a later date. The façade was originally symmetrical, with five bays and dormers above. On the back of the house a nearly square room of approximately thirteen and a half by fourteen and a half feet contained a fireplace and may have served any number of purposes. The main floor of the house was subdivided simply into a dining room and a large, open parlor. A later frame addition to the northeast side of the house extended it out an additional twenty-eight feet, providing more living space. The precise floor plan of the half-story above the main wing eludes historians, but it is clear that this living space was subdivided and probably served as various sleeping chambers. Architectural historians have praised the original chimney that was incorporated from the earlier house for its attention to detail. Integrated into the Flemish bond brickwork of the chimney were intricate designs with glazed brick set by builders. On the lower portion of the exterior chimney, two diamond-shaped lozenges—one within the other—can clearly be seen, with a small ornament in the middle. Above, a similar motif of a single diamond was expertly laid. This fancy type of brickwork is quite unusual for the time period and represents dedication to style and design as well as true skill on the part of the brick-layers.

The plantation remained in the Cocke family until the late eighteenth century. It served during this time period as a campsite for Revolutionary War soldiers, including the Marquis de Lafayette. Malvern Hill was purchased by Robert Nelson, brother of Thomas Nelson of York Town, prior to the turn of the century. A few years later the plantation again served as a campground for soldiers during the War of 1812. Nearly sixty years later, in July 1862, Maj. Gen. George B. McClellan's Army of the Potomac claimed victory over Robert E. Lee and his Confederate troops from their vantage point at Malvern Hill. Not even an inch of land was gained by the southerners. The battle—in which 5,355 rebels were killed—became known as the Battle of Malvern Hill.

The mansion at Malvern Hill burned in 1905, and was subsequently pilfered. Today, the site is owned by the National Park Service, and the structural foundation, along with some brick remnants, still remain. The plantation/battlefield site was placed on the National Register of Historic Places on November 12, 1969. The famed site and horrific battle are immortalized in an 1862 poem by the celebrated author of *Moby Dick*, Herman Melville, entitled "Malvern Hill."

MALVERN HILL
by Herman Melville

Ye elms that wave on Malvern Hill
   In prime of morn and May,
Recall ye how McClellan's men
   Here stood at bay?
While deep within yon forest dim
   Our rigid comrades lay—
Some with the cartridge in their mouth,
Others with fixed arms lifted South—
   Invoking so
The cypress glades? Ah wilds of woe!
The spires of Richmond, late beheld

Through rifts in musket-haze,
Were closed from view in clouds of dust
   On leaf-walled ways,
Where streamed our wagons in caravan;
   And the Seven Nights and Days
Of march and fast, retreat and fight,
Pinched our grimed faces to ghastly plight—
   Does the elm wood
Recall the haggard beards of blood?

The battle-smoked flag, with stars eclipsed,
   We followed (it never fell!)—
In silence husbanded our strength—
   Received their yell;
Till on this slope we patient turned
   With cannon ordered well;
Reverse we proved was not defeat;
But ah, the sod what thousands meet!—
   Does Malvern Wood
Bethink itself, and muse and brood?

*We elms of Malvern Hill*
   *Remember every thing;*
*But sap the twig will fill:*
   *Wag the world how it will,*
*Leaves must be green in Spring.*

# CHAPTER TWO

# The Upper South, West: Arkansas, Kentucky, and Tennessee

History, insofar as it accustoms human beings to comprehend the whole of the past and to hasten forward with its conclusions into the far future, conceals the boundaries of birth and death, which enclose the life of the human being so narrowly and oppressively, and with a kind of optical illusion, expands his short existence into endless space, leading the individual imperceptibly over into humanity.

—*Friedrich von Schiller*

All I can say is that there's a sweetness here, a Southern sweetness, that makes sweet music . . . If I had to tell somebody who had never been to the South, who had never heard of soul music, what it was, I'd just have to tell him that it's music from the heart, from the pulse, from the innermost feeling. That's my soul; that's how I sing. And that's the South.

—*Al Green*

Landlocked Arkansas, Kentucky, and Tennessee each developed plantation economies and slave societies much later than their peripheral neighbors along the coast. The original colonies, however, supplied settlers to these undeveloped regions. And, as pioneers moved westward in search of fortune and most of all land, native inhabitants were moved further away, with many succumbing to unfamiliar European diseases to which they had no immunity.

By the mid-eighteenth century, a few brave settlers made their way in to the future areas of Tennessee and Kentucky. Much of what is now Kentucky was purchased from Native Americans in 1768 and 1775, in the treaties of Fort Stanwix and Sycamore Shoals, respectively. After this, the area grew rapidly and the settlements west of the Appalachian Mountains were founded.

Much of eastern Tennessee was considered a portion of North Carolina in the mid-eighteenth century. But, as the population of the region increased and settlers felt that their voices were not being heard on important issues such as navigation of the Mississippi River and protection from native raids, eight counties broke away from North Carolina in 1784 to form the independent state of Franklin, with John Sevier as governor. When North Carolina ratified the United States Constitution in 1789, it ceded these western lands, the Tennessee country, to the federal government. As Tennessee's population grew, it became the sixteenth state in June 1796.

Tennessee's new settlers brought with them slaves, and, by 1790, there were 3,417 slaves in the territory. With statehood, the population continued to grow as smaller farms and yeomen farmers populated the mountainous eastern part of the state, larger estates and commercial industries filled middle Tennessee, and large, formal plantations prospered in the cotton region of west Tennessee. By 1840, plantation culture and the institution of slavery were firmly established, especially in the west, and Tennessee had a population of 183,057.

Kentucky and Tennessee share similar histories. Permanent residents began settling the Kentucky region by the 1770s, bringing slaves with them. Tobacco plantations were established in the bluegrass region and in the western part of the state, although small family farms were by far the dominant agricultural unit.

Prior to the Louisiana Purchase, Arkansas was largely a vast wilderness, with only a small number of European inhabitants. After 1803, a trickle of settlers began to migrate from Tennessee and Kentucky, but it wasn't until after the War of 1812 that a larger number of Americans came. By 1819, the year the Arkansas Territory was organized, the region boasted a population of over fourteen thousand. The first settlers to populate the area were largely trappers and hunters, followed by sustenance farmers and yeomen agriculturalists. It wasn't until several decades later that a large number of aspiring planters and young professionals traveled to Arkansas to find their fortunes.

Because Arkansas's plantocracy developed later than most of the others in the plantation South, there was less rigid hierarchy and more opportunity for social mobility for ambitious white families during the antebellum years. By the 1830s and 1840s, sons of planters from established areas were joined by young doctors and lawyers and even yeoman farmers (who sought to improve their station) in migrating to the wilds of Arkansas to establish cotton plantations.

Whether migrating to unsettled Tennessee, Kentucky, or, later, Arkansas, an aspiring planter would typically travel to the territory a year or two ahead of his family or perhaps send a son or two in his place. Often they brought with them a few male slaves, and together these men would usually work side by side clearing land, building log cabins, and producing at least one season of crops before the rest of the household would arrive.

The journey for the planter's family and slaves was a difficult one, especially to remote Arkansas. Water transportation was expensive and trains were limited, so most plantation families opted to travel by land, risking their lives crossing rivers and canals, navigating the dense wilderness with horses, wagons, and carriages, and battling diseases that seemed to flourish during these long journeys. After months, fortunate families reunited amid the fertile fields of cotton.

After their long journeys, settlers first developed the areas along the Red and Arkansas rivers into cotton plantations. Later, the entire Mississippi River coast became a hotbed of cotton cultivation in Arkansas. These riverfront regions were favored principally due to their navigable water access to New Orleans, a crucial factor for Arkansas's large agriculturalists. It was in the New Orleans markets that Arkansas planters sold their cotton, and it was there that they purchased needed supplies for the year. It is said that New Orleans bustled with Arkansas planters in February and March, many staying a month or more.

By 1850, there were over six thousand slaveholders in Arkansas, and more than five hundred owned twenty or more slaves. A decade later, in 1860, the number of total slaveholders in Arkansas had nearly doubled, and the number of "planters" with more than twenty slaves had almost tripled. As more and more entrepreneurial planters developed their agricultural enterprises, they actively sought to reestablish the old systems and societies they had left behind in Tennessee, Kentucky, Virginia, and elsewhere. Most notably, the institution of slavery was quickly and strongly established, as families brought slaves with them during their migrations and purchased more slaves once they arrived.

In addition to swiftly instituting slavery, the planters of Tennessee, Kentucky, and Arkansas attempted to duplicate the built environment of the Old South plantations of their homelands, building slave cabins, barns, kitchens, accessory structures, and, of course, master houses. Because Arkansas's development was arrested in its adolescence by the onset of the Civil War, the grand columned palaces seen in Louisiana, Mississippi, Alabama, and other well-established southern states were simply never constructed in the region. Instead, most master houses on Arkansas plantations consisted of log houses or moderately sized frame houses produced from timber cleared from the plantation property.

Because Tennessee and Kentucky were developed earlier, more larger and refined mansions could be found, but few rivaled those of the Deep South, and certainly the number of such grand homes was considerably less in the Upper South.

The Greek Revival style was seen to some degree in all three states, but on a much smaller scale than elsewhere in the country. For example, Lakeport Plantation in Chicot County, Arkansas, provides one of the most striking extant examples of the Greek Revival applied to the wood-frame Arkansas plantation mansion, with its broad portico and pleasant proportions. In middle Tennessee one finds homes like Rattle and Snap in Maury County still standing, with its ten tall Corinthian columns and intricate lace ironwork details. And in Kentucky, Ward Hall in Georgetown provides a comparable façade with red brick walls and four white Corinthian columns quite similar in style to those at Rattle and Snap.

As elsewhere in the South, the onset of the Civil War devastated the relatively young plantation systems of Tennessee, Kentucky, and Arkansas. The states withdrew from the Union, and became the sites of numerous, mostly smaller battles during the Civil War. With the disintegration of the cotton economy and the emancipation of the slave labor force, the plantocracies of this portion of the Upper South largely collapsed, leaving planters collecting the pieces of their ruined lives and society.

Over the years, a combination of progress and neglect sent a death blow through much of the plantation architecture of these three states, while natural disaster and fire destroyed much more. Today, there are a few remaining examples of antebellum plantation structures, but most have long faded into the past.

There are no studies that specifically analyze lost architecture in Tennessee, Arkansas, or Kentucky, but there are excellent resources about the history and in some cases the architecture of these states. Several volumes are of particular usefulness. Clay Lancaster, who has devoted much of his life to Kentucky's architecture, has written an excellent summary of the state's early structures in *Antebel-*

Tennessee's famed Rattle and Snap Plantation mansion has survived to the present day.

*lum Architecture of Kentucky*. Donald P. McNeilly provides a fascinating synopsis of Arkansas plantation life in *The Old South Frontier: Cotton Plantations and the Formation of Arkansas Society, 1819–1861*. And James Patrick provides a great glimpse into the built environments of the Volunteer State in *Architecture in Tennessee, 1768–1897*. Also of particular interest is Mills Lane's *Architecture of the Old South: Kentucky & Tennessee*, part of a series of volumes on southern architecture.

Today, little physical evidence of the cotton plantations that once dotted the rivers of southeastern Arkansas and the western edge of Tennessee can be seen. And the bluegrass tobacco estates are all but vanished. But, even as much of the built environment of these estates has been lost to time, some of their histories remain. Hereafter are the stories of three of Arkansas's famed lost plantations and one each from Tennessee and Kentucky.

## Sylvan Home

The history of Arkansas's Sylvan Home and the family that owned the estate—the Bullocks—may well have faded into the past like the log structures that made up the plantation, had it not been for an old woman and her daughter. In 1929, at the urging of her daughter, eighty-year-old Harriet Bailey Bullock Daniel began penning her memories and recollections of life on the plantation near Arkadelphia that she and her family called home in antebellum days. She had been telling stories of her former life as a "southern belle" to her children and grandchildren for decades, and her daughter thought the project would be a good way to preserve this heritage, while giving the old woman something to do. What resulted is a remarkable and delightfully readable tale that was published some six and a half decades later under the editorship of Margaret Jones Bolsterli.[1]

Daniel's manuscript began with the birth of her father, Charles Bullock, in Warren County (now Vance County), North Carolina, on February 26,

1811. He was the ninth of eleven children born to James and Nancy Bullock. Charles Bullock grew up on his parents' large plantation. He was expected to marry his cousin Agnes Bullock, but when she unexpectedly married William Hare, Charles was forced to find marriage elsewhere. He met Sarah Jane Shepherd at a party; she was his partner for a candy-pulling contest. They were married soon after on January 29, 1833, at the home of Sarah's father, Thomas Shepherd. The couple resided with Charles's mother until after the birth of their first daughter, Fanny Lyne, in 1834.[2]

Thomas Shapherd moved to Fayette County, Tennessee, shortly after his daughter's marriage. Charles and Sarah sought to join Shapherd after the birth of Fanny Lyne. They prepared a great convoy of wagons and with Sarah's sister Arianna Shepherd Webb and hosts of slaves, the young family made their way west. They stayed a few days with Thomas's brother Robert Shepherd, for a much-needed sojourn from "rugged mountain passes" and "rough roads of the hill country."[3] They finally settled close to Dancyville, near Thomas Shepherd's place. Here the family lived for several years.

Over time Charles and Sarah's family grew. Within a period of some years, they had six daughters and two sons: Fanny, Nannie, Kate, Mary Helen, Anna Booker, Sue, Tom, and Kim. In time, some close neighbors, including Kimbrough Jones and Jesse Harris and their families, sought to join the thousands moving further west, pulled by a booming cotton economy along the Mississippi River. The Bullock family decided to join their friends, and soon Charles Bullock was on the move with his family and slaves once again.

Just prior to leaving Tennessee, Charles sold some of his slaves, including Lucy, a young mother. In an episode that provides great insight into the heart of slavery on the Bullock estate, Lucy's young son Shadrack was placed in a wagon with other black children and her infant Damon was handed to another female slave named Rose. When Lucy realized what was happening she began to wail and beg for her children. The caravan began moving,

and she chased the wagons until finally she tripped and fell, forever separated from her young sons.

Ironically, in a household where black mothers were ripped from their suckling babes never to be seen again, the white children were "required to be courteous and respectful to [the slaves] . . . and to treat them with due and proper consideration."[4] The paradoxical fact foreshadows the complex and seldom straightforward social and hierarchical relations between the Bullocks and their servants that would often define life in their household.

Although the family and their slaves briefly lived at another location, the Bullocks permanently settled on two thousand acres in Dallas County, Arkansas. The Bullocks initially lived in a quickly constructed kitchen building, until the mansion house was complete. Harriet Bullock Daniel provides a detailed description of the house in her writings: "Our dwelling house was a frame building of six large rooms, two wide halls, dressing rooms and closets . . . he built the front room of hewn logs, six by eight inches, which are dovetailed together, and then stripes were put on with large wooden pegs, before the house was ceiled and weatherboarded . . . It has wide glass windows with small panes. The top of the house was of shingles, and the floors were of dressed plank. The outside of the house was painted white; some of the rooms were light blue or dove colored."[5]

The house conformed to standard plantation architecture, with a broad central hallway flanked by two rooms on either side. Front and back porches added to the façade. Upstairs, the second story was made up of two bedrooms and a central hall. An unusual feature of the home gives much insight into the distinctions of gender with the family. The boys' room upstairs was accessible from the main staircase in the central hall; however, the girls' bedroom upstairs did not communicate with the rest of the second story—there were no doors leading to the hall and there was no balcony. This bedroom was only accessible via a stairway which emanated from the first-floor master bedroom. In order to get to their bedroom at night or leave their room, each girl had to first enter her father's bedroom, which acted as a gateway of sorts. The young ladies' boudoir was truly the "inner sanctum" of the Sylvan Home. In addition to providing "protection" for the young virgins, it also severely limited their movements. In comparison, the young brothers had easy access to and from their chamber without having to pass through any other family members' dwellings.

Outside the great house, double slave cabins were arranged in rows. The 1850 U.S. census notes that the Bullocks owned twenty-five slaves and later accumulated nearly forty. Harriet provides a description of these structures in her writings: "The Negro cabins were built of smaller logs, chinked and daubed, and had puncheon floors, stick chimney, wooden shutters for windows, and they were covered with split boards. The shutters of the windows had to be kept open, even on the coldest days to admit light."[6]

Before the Bullock estate was completely constructed, the family experienced a grave tragedy. Sarah Shapherd Bullock died in October 1852, leaving her husband a widower and her young children motherless. Before her death, she arranged for one of her older daughters to look after the younger children, a position that "Sister Nannie," as she was known to her young siblings, devoted her early life to.[7]

The death of his wife was a massive blow to Charles Bullock. His daughter recalled: "Aunt 'Riah said that after the funeral was over and all the folks gone, Pa went off alone and lay on a log near the branch in front of the house. He stayed there a long time, until they all got worried about him. Uncle Billy [a trusted slave] finally went out and sat down by him, but didn't say anything. Just after sundown Pa came to the house, leaning on Uncle Billy's shoulder."[8]

Again, the interactions between the Bullocks and their slaves provide insight into the intricate bonds between blacks and whites on this fascinating Arkansas estate. It is clear from her recollections that young Harriet Bailey Bullock spent more time with her black "family" than she did with her white relatives, especially after the death of her mother. She writes: "The doctors said I must not stay in the school room all day and I was sent to Aunt Rose's [a trusted slave] house to spin a brooch of thread as soon as I could turn a wheel. I liked to steal off right after breakfast and be at her house when the children were brought in for her to take care of while their mothers worked in the fields."[9]

Harriet further recalls the joys of often joining her young "colored" friends as they ate peas out of a skillet in the yard. She notes that if her father was coming, she would run back to her spinning. She continues:

> Once I ate too many huckleberries and thinking I was going to die, slipped off down to Aunt Rose's house for help. Her big bed was, to me, always spotless and no child dared touch it. On this occasion I was honored by being laid between her sheets . . .
>
> I used to have big meetings with the colored children. These were conducted in a corner of the fence around Aunt Rose's house. A plank stuck through cracks about three feet from the ground served as a pulpit and a long plank across the wide part of the corner was for the congregation to sit on. What singing and shouting we had with the preaching, particularly after a prorated meeting in our church.[10]

The dynamics of Harriet's relationship with the individuals her family enslaved and their relationships with her illustrate ironies and complexities of the bonds and social connections of whites and blacks in the plantation South. Young Harriet felt honored to rest in a slave's bed and relished eating with them in their yard, but on some level she understood her societally imposed superiority as she play-preached and pontificated from her makeshift pulpit.

Life for Harriet and her siblings changed greatly in the mid-1850s, when their father decided to find a new wife. He initially started secretly courting Mary Jones, a friend of his eldest daughter. When Kimbrough Jones, the young lady's father and a close friend of Charles Bullock, learned of his acquaintance's intentions with his daughter, he grew quite angry and sent her away to a boarding school out of state. Bullock's older daughters were away at school, and soon he undertook a trip to visit them. There he met another woman. Prior to his arrival home, he sent word that he would be bringing along a new bride, Mary Carter.

The young girls of the plantation did not take well to this news. "Sister Fanny," who had assumed the duties of plantation mistress on the estate, was especially distraught, even telling her siblings that she wanted "to go to Mother in heaven." Most of the Bullock daughters learned to love their stepmother; however, Fanny soon moved out of state to marry.[11]

Only a few years after his marriage, Charles Bullock found himself in hot debates with his neighbors about such issues as states' rights and secession. His daughter notes: "Although Pa thought holding to the Union was the only way to keep the slaves, he was ever a staunch Southerner. Yet some of the people in our part of the state thought he should be sent North or be killed, fearing that he would act as a traitor to the Southern cause. One man in the neighborhood, who held views like Pa's, was found by his wife one morning hanging dead from a tree in front of his house."[12]

As Bullock's two sons left for war, a mass of soldiers came to replace them. Soon the Bullock family found that their home was surrounded by a Confederate encampment. In her memoirs Harriet notes that several generals camped in the "front grove" and that General Joseph Shelby made his headquarters in the plantation office about 250 yards from the main house.

On April 18, 1864, the Bullocks were alarmed by cannon shots from nearby Poison Springs as General Samuel B. Maxey's cavalry unit captured a Union wagon train. Soon, wounded soldiers began making their way to Sylvan Home, and the plantation house became a makeshift hospital. An old tablecloth served some as dressings for wounds.

With war raging in front of him, Charles Bullock became keenly aware that the southern cause might not prevail. He began instructing his daughters to wait on themselves, in preparation for the time when there would be no servants. Harriet

notes that prior to the war, "Each of us had a Negro girl at our beck and call. Emily was the name of mine. She tied my shoes, brushed my hair, hung up my clothes, saw that I always had my sunbonnet on when I went out of doors and seldom, without permission, ventured out of the sound of my voice."[13] Such all-encompassing service was to be short lived, as Harriet notes in her writings:

> [N]ow I had to share the house work with my other sisters and I still felt keenly the change at home after the slaves were gone . . . Cooking, washing, housecleaning and attending to the milk were not easy for us girls. Sister Nanny bought a washing machine, but after her first attempt at laundry she stayed in bed a week. Being unaccustomed to hard work, we did not know how to go about it. This made us all fussy . . .
>
> Neither did things on the plantation go on so smoothly. Mr. Scott [overseer] who was still with us, could not get hands to plant and work the crops and the way had not been opened for Pa to take his cotton, accumulated during the war, down to New Orleans to sell. And the new system of labor was a problem. Once a hand spoke impertinently to Pa, who picked up a hoe and gave him a blow on the head. The Negro, though not seriously hurt, was infuriated and took the matter to court. The case was decided in favor of the Negro and Pa had another lesson in the treatment of freedmen . . .
>
> Everything seemed so changed by this time. Many of the old servants had gone and what work went on was under the reign of confusion. Pa had tried to prepare us for it, but such a change as was produced by freeing of the slaves had to be worked out by actual necessity.[14]

Charles Bullock was forced to sell much of his plantation lands after the war in order to provide financial stability for his family. His remaining younger children began marrying and finding lives of their own, much as their older siblings had done. Bullock remained in possession of his plantation house through the rest of his life. He died in 1886.[15]

The plantation house came into possession of Charles Bullock's daughter Mattie and her husband, Neill McCaskill. The couple remained at the plantation house until their deaths, in 1904 (Neill) and 1911 (Mattie). Their son William Fletcher McCaskill and his wife, Elizabeth Tatum, lived at the house, and Elizabeth gave birth to her daughter Martha there. William sold the house around 1917, and he moved his family to Arkadelphia along with a few prized pieces of antebellum furniture from Sylvan Home.[16]

The house was purchased by a Mr. Thomas, but later was returned to the Bullock-McCaskill clan when William's brother Charles Neill McCaskill purchased it in the 1920s or 1930s. The plantation was later owned by Charles's son Neill, who, in 1940, undertook an extensive renovation of the house. In addition to providing structural improvements, Neill updated the façade of the house, demolishing the old one-story porch and replacing it with an impressive and heavy two-story Greek Revival–style portico with four imposing square pillars. This was topped with an intricate balustrade. A small balcony was also added under the portico.[17]

On December 27, 1966, the master house at Sylvan Home Plantation caught fire and burned to the ground. In 1972, Neill McCaskill built a modern home on the site. He used old bricks from the original plantation house to construct a large fireplace in his new home. Physically, little is left of the old plantation—a barn, a few cedars, and remains of the old cemetery—but thanks to the stories of an old woman, the rich legacy and multifaceted lore of Sylvan Home linger on.

## Rosedale

The master house at Rosedale Plantation that was once located near the Manchester Township of Dallas County, Arkansas, has the unique distinction of being one of the few plantation houses to have been destroyed not once, but twice! Today, all that remains of this estate is an old barn.

The land that would later become Rosedale was originally owned by Reuben Rambo of Hot Springs County, Arkansas. Rambo did not pay taxes on this property, and therefore, it was eventually sold by the county officials. The land, which was near a Ouachita River landing called Montroy, was purchased by Colonel Joseph Allen Whitaker in 1857.[18]

Whitaker, who was born in September 1812, near Raleigh, North Carolina, had attended the University of North Carolina, where he studied medicine. He later served in the Mexican-American War and practiced his medical skills treating wounded soldiers. After the war, he abandoned medicine and decided to become a planter.

Whitaker married Rebecca Perry Yarborough, and together, the couple established Rose Hill Plantation in North Carolina. A house was believed to have been built there by Madison Griffin.

After losing two children in infancy, Rebecca fell into a deep depression, and Colonel Whitaker sent her to an "asylum" in Philadelphia. She was accompanied by two of the plantation's slaves, Jane and Louisa. Rebecca remained at this institution for two years.

Upon her release, Whitaker decided to relocate to Arkansas. He felt that a change in environment might remove his wife from the previous sorrows she had known at Rose Hill. The couple moved to Arkansas, and after acquiring the Rambo tract, Whitaker began purchasing multiple parcels of land. By 1859, he owned several thousand acres and twenty-six slaves.

Whitaker commissioned Madison Griffin, the architect who is thought to have designed his North Carolina home, to come to Arkansas and build a home similar to the Rose Hill house. Whitaker called his Arkansas plantation Rosedale, and although the location provided a change of scenery for his wife, the colonel also strived for some sense of familiarity in re-creating to some degree his North Carolina estate, using the same architect and opting for an analogous floor plan.[19]

The house was a two-story, five-bay structure with a wide central hall and crowning cupola. Outside, a large brick kitchen stood separate from the main house. The kitchen fireplace was much later integrated into a new home built on the site. Surrounding the house and kitchen complex, a garden of oaks, magnolias, cedars, and a variety of roses framed the stately home. Whitaker even imported peacocks to adorn the mansion's balconies, but this was short lived because the birds became quite a nuisance.

Soon after the builders finished constructing the house, Arkansas withdrew from the Union, and the Civil War began. Whitaker was too old at the time to serve in the Confederate military, but instead joined the Dallas County Home Guard Unit for Manchester Township. He also financially supported the southern cause.

Although Whitaker lost his labor force when the slaves were freed, he managed to remain in possession of over three thousand acres of land, and financially, he fared better than most. Unfortunately, although he retained his real estate, one of his greatest loves was taken from him. Rebecca became quite ill with tuberculosis after the war. She longed to go back home to North Carolina, and six weeks after arriving there, she died. Whitaker placed his wife's body in an above-ground vault, as one of her greatest fears in life was being buried.

Whitaker returned to Clark County, Arkansas, and later, at age sixty-one, sought a new wife. Family legend has it that a party was given in nearby Tulip, and Whitaker made it clear that he would attend in order to find a bride. Given that he was one of the wealthiest planters in the area, he was seen as a very eligible bachelor. It is said that there was great competition among the young socialites of Tulip and their counterparts in Arkadelphia to outdress and impress at this gathering. One story even recounts that some of the women from Tulip sent word to those in Arkadelphia instructing them to stay home since surely the Tulipians would outshine the less striking Arkadelphians. Regardless of who had the more beautiful gowns or the more charming conversations, it was a young woman from Tulip, Mary Elizabeth Amy Smith, the daughter of wealthy planter Samuel Webb Smith, who caught the eye—and soon the heart—of Colonel Whitaker.

The couple was married on February 20, 1873, in Tulip, and a large reception was held the next day at Rosedale. Soon, Mary gave birth to a daughter named Helen. In 1876, the family took a trip to the Centennial Exposition in Philadelphia. The Whitakers also visited the old home in North Carolina. Shortly after their return to Rosedale, Colonel Whitaker was involved in a riding accident and subsequently died. Several months after his death, Mary gave birth to the colonel's final child, a daughter named after him: Joseph Allen Whitaker. She was called Jodie.

The widow married James Strong in 1881, and shortly after the family was devastated by two tragedies. First, while away at school in Gurdon, Helen was badly injured while playing "pop-the-whip." She died. Then, in 1886, shortly after architect Madison Griffin had refurbished it, the mansion at Rosedale Plantation caught fire and burned to the ground. The family moved into the brick kitchen.

They hired Madison Griffin's son to design a new Victorian home on the site, but, tragically, this home was also destroyed by fire in 1919. Today, there are but few relics of Rosedale. The kitchen was destroyed, but its fireplace and chimney were incorporated into another house on the site. The large plantation barn was moved and restored by Ron McDowell, and it is now listed on the National Register of Historic Places. All other relics of Rosedale—the two mansions, the slave cabins, and other structures—have slipped into the past much like the old way of life Colonel Whitaker held so dear.

## Sunnyside

Once located near present-day Lake Village, Arkansas, Sunnyside was an enormous antebellum plantation that later became notorious for its use of Italian immigrants as field laborers and for claims of peonage. Today, only a roadside marker suggests the barren site's previous history.

The story of Sunnyside can be traced back to

one man, Abner Johnson, a native of Kentucky who migrated to the dense wilderness of southeast Arkansas in the 1820s. He, along with other speculators, saw much potential in the cheap, undeveloped lands of the region. Johnson became a leader among the group, and he was elected sheriff in 1832.[20]

By 1840, when Johnson and his wife decided to move back to Kentucky, he had acquired thousands of acres of property. His principal tract was called Sunnyside. It was made up of over twenty-two hundred acres with a variety of buildings. Johnson had forty-two slaves at Sunnyside, all of whom were included in the sale of the estate. Johnson sold Sunnyside to Elisha Worthington for sixty thousand dollars. Worthington also agreed to provide Johnson with 250 bales of cotton annually for a full decade.

Under Worthington's ownership, Sunnyside expanded and prospered. He added, among other improvements, a landing on the Mississippi River. His personal life, however, was not as smoothly undertaken as his agricultural enterprises. Worthington married a young lady on November 10, 1840, in Kentucky, and he soon brought her to Sunnyside, but less than six months later she returned home to Kentucky, claiming her husband was an adulterer. An 1843 act of the Kentucky legislature annulled this union.

Worthington was in fact in love with a female slave who bore him two children. He never married the woman, but evidence indicates their relationship persisted for years. The children, James W. Mason and Martha W. Mason, were raised at Sunnyside, and later both attended Oberlin College in Ohio. James later studied in France, but returned to Sunnyside before the Civil War.

Despite the fact that many of his neighbors vehemently disapproved of his lifestyle, Worthington became one of the most influential planters in Arkansas, largely because of the sheer volume of wealth he had amassed. During the 1850s, Worthington acquired several thousand acres of additional lands, all located in the Lake Chicot region. By the 1860s, he owned a total of over twelve thou-

sand acres in Chicot County and nearly 550 slaves. A portion of this land was incorporated into Sunnyside Plantation, which served as the chief Worthington residence and flagship of their plantation empire.

In the last months of 1862, Worthington left Arkansas, taking most of his slaves and livestock to Texas. His two children—James Mason and Martha Mason—remained at Sunnyside to oversee their father's property and manage plantation operations. The Mason siblings witnessed much battlefield action on their family estate. For example, on June 5, 1864, a large force of Union soldiers was sent to the Sunnyside landing to intercept Confederate troops who sought to interrupt boat traffic on the Mississippi. The next day the Battle of Ditch Bayou, which occurred nearby, cost many lives on both sides.

After the war, Worthington returned to his plantation. He was pardoned by President Andrew Johnson for his involvement in the Confederate cause, but like all planters he faced massive challenges. He was confronted with a new shortage of labor after his slaves were freed. Also, worldwide ebb in the demand for cotton and other economic factors caused a financial collapse of the cotton industry. In addition to his monetary tribulations, Worthington battled health problems. He finally decided to dispose of his property.

Sunnyside Plantation was transferred to the Pepper family, and in 1868, it was purchased by the William Starling Company. In 1881, John C. Calhoun, grandson of the famous politician, along with his wife, Lennie Adams, and brother, Patrick Calhoun, began acquiring several Chicot County plantations. Among those the three relatives purchased was Sunnyside.

The Calhouns organized the Calhoun Land Company, with the goal of bringing former slaves and their offspring back to the plantations as tenant farmers. Calhoun explained:

> We wish to make small farmers of our laborers, and bring them up as nearly as possible to the standard of the small white farmers . . . the first year we

contract to work with [the laborer] on the half-share system, and require him to plant a portion of the land he cultivates in corn, hay, potatoes, & c. For this portion we charge him a reasonable rent, to be paid out of his part of the cotton raised on the remainder. In this way all of the supplies raised belong to him, and at the end of the first year he will, if industrious, find himself possessed of enough supplies to support and feed a mule.[21]

Calhoun further noted that these sharecroppers would be more and more gradually acclimated to independence, and would ultimately reach "tenant" status, in which they would then own all of the implements of their labor, their homes and livestock, and other properties. They would then rent the lands of the plantation as independent farmers.

This plan revolved around these individuals obtaining their independence only through the Calhouns. For example, all sharecroppers-turned-tenants were pressured to purchase their supplies and comforts at the only nearby stores, which happened to be owned by the Calhouns. In the end, a variety of postbellum farming schemes could be found on Sunnyside. Some of the laborers became traditional sharecroppers, others worked as independent tenants, and some were in between. Still others worked directly for the company as wage laborers.

But the Calhouns' labor "experiments" were short lived. Investors in the scheme were shaken by a great flood in 1882 and a lack of railroad transportation to the area. By the mid-1880s, the Calhouns had abandoned Arkansas for New York, where they found much success on Wall Street. Sunnyside was eventually purchased by Austin Corbin, who had been one of the Calhouns' financial backers.

Corbin, the president of the Corbin Bank in New York and a noted railroad developer, founded the Sunnyside Company, which ran several Chicot County plantations. He was known as a rather iniquitous and infamous anti-Semite, who led a campaign to bar Jews from his Manhattan Beach resort, and later, served as secretary of the American Society for the Suppression of Jews.

The notorious Corbin aggressively improved Sunnyside during his tenure as owner. He built a small railroad to transport cotton from the fields to the gin, installed a telephone line to Greenville, Mississippi, and docked his steamboat, the *Austin Corbin*, in nearby Lake Chicot.

Despite his improvements, Corbin's plantation venture faced failure soon after its initiation due to the fact that most of the black laborers who had previously worked the lands were unwilling to farm under a "foreign" company. In 1894, Corbin signed a contract with the state of Arkansas creating a sharecropping arrangement with the state penal system. Corbin agreed to supply all of the lands, seeds, tools, and supplies necessary to grow cotton, while the state would agree to provide convict laborers. Each party would split the profits equally. That same year roughly 250 prisoners produced over a million pounds of cotton.

Corbin vigilantly sought more workers for his lands, and, in the mid-1890s, he devised a complex scheme to settle Italian immigrants at Sunnyside. Legend has it that Corbin's daughter married an Italian count who assisted him in the undertaking, but in fact she married René C. Champollian, a French artist who committed suicide about a decade prior to Corbin's ventures at Sunnyside. In truth, Corbin negotiated with an Italian immigrant agency in New York, Italian diplomats, and, most notably, Don Emanuele Ruspoli, the mayor of Rome.

Corbin divided out 250 twelve-and-a-half-acre lots. Upon each one he built a simple but sturdy house. Each lot with house was priced at two thousand dollars, which immigrants were required to pay in installments over twenty-one years at a rate of 5 percent. The Sunnyside Company would agree to purchase all of the cotton produced on these plots at market price, less freight and expenses. An arbitration board was created to handle any contract disputes that might arise.

By the end of 1895, the first Italian settlers arrived. They were greeted by the community not with southern hospitality, but with outright hostility. Irate newspaper editors spewed racial epithets and bigotry stereotypes in their columns, and many other leaders spoke out against "Corbin's dagoes," as the settlers had come to be known in certain circles. But, despite the hatred shown to them, the Italians proceeded to quietly and peacefully farm their little plots, while trying to improve their own lives, and their numbers grew as more boats arrived.

Austin Corbin died in a carriage accident less than six months after the first Italian immigrants arrived at Sunnyside. He was eulogized by Arkansans as a progressive hero and benefactor. After Corbin was gone, the Italians continued to reside at Sunnyside, and soon received an encouraging visit from Ruspoli. Shortly thereafter, a convention of planters and local businessmen made a visit to Sunnyside, where they cruised on the steamboat *Austin Corbin* and dined in the plantation mansion, then called Corbin House.

By 1898, the Sunnyside Corporation leased Sunnyside, along with other smaller Chicot plantations, to three distinguished gentlemen from Greenville, Mississippi: Hamilton R. Hawkins, Orlando B. Crittenden, and LeRoy Percy. Percy, a politician and planter, provided much publicity for the Italian "experiment" at Sunnyside, touting Italians as the saviors and future of the South's cash crop economy.

In reality, the plight of Sunnyside and its Italian settlers was something completely different. The immigrant workers grew unhappy with their contracts, the high prices at the plantation store, and most of all with unsanitary conditions. The laborers' water supply was filthy, and soon illness swept through Sunnyside.

By the dawn of the twentieth century, many of the Italian families had moved away to find better lives and greater opportunity elsewhere. They were slowly and incompletely replaced by a small number of black sharecroppers. In addition to the loss of labor, the operators of the plantation also faced accusations of peonage with regards to the use of Italian laborers. The United States Department of State took action, and Assistant U.S. Attorney Mary Grace Quackenbos waged a long inves-

tigation of Percy and the situation of Italian labor at Sunnyside. Also, devastating floods, boll weevil infestations, and other difficulties contributed to Sunnyside's decline.

After the First World War, the Sunnyside Company sold the plantation to W. H. Baird and J. C. Baird for nearly one million dollars, but the new owners defaulted on their debts. The plantation was sold at auction to the Kansas City Life Insurance Company for seventy-five thousand dollars. The insurance company subdivided the plantation and sold off pieces.

By the late 1930s, when workers of the WPA's Federal Writers' Project visited the site of the plantation, little remained. The railroad had been removed, the steamboat had been scrapped, and much of the built environment had been dismantled and/or destroyed by fire. Only two of the Italian families still resided on the plantation property.

Today, the Sunnyside plantation is but a memory. The lands are barren. A lone historical marker at present-day Lake Village notes the nearby property's history and its connection with Italian immigration. A cemetery where the Italians buried many of the loved ones who were victims of malaria and other diseases brought on by conditions at the plantation is today little more than a desolate field. It is marked with a solitary cross, as its individual grave markers have long since faded into the past. Many descendents of the Sunnyside Italian immigrants still reside in Arkansas today.

## Mount Brilliant

The over two-hundred-year-old mansion at Mount Brilliant Plantation near Lexington, Kentucky, was demolished by its owner in 2002, after a heated debate over the historic house's destiny. The vast estate, originally a two-thousand-acre land grant, was deeded in 1744 to Henry Russell, a nephew of Thomas Jefferson. Russell later died in the French and Indian War. The property was then passed on

Mount Brilliant Plantation house, front façade. Drawing by Martin Townley, Andrew Kesler, and Travis Roberts. Courtesy of the Center for Historic Architecture and Preservation, Department of Historic Preservation, College of Design, University of Kentucky.

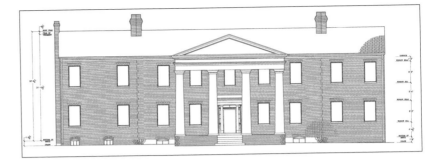

Site plan of Mount Brilliant Plantation house and surrounding area prior to the demolition of the house. Drawing by Martin Townley, Andrew Kesler, and Travis Roberts. Courtesy of the Center for Historic Architecture and Preservation, Department of Historic Preservation, College of Design, University of Kentucky.

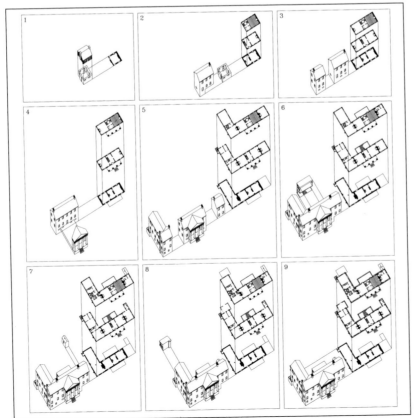

The evolution and transformation of Mount Brilliant Plantation house. Drawing by Martin Townley, Andrew Kesler, and Travis Roberts. Courtesy of the Center for Historic Architecture and Preservation, Department of Historic Preservation, College of Design, University of Kentucky.

to Gen. William Russell, the first owner's brother. William was married to Patrick Henry's sister Elizabeth. And it is from Patrick Henry's Virginia estate—Mount Brilliant—that the Kentucky farm borrowed its name. William Russell transferred ownership of the plantation to his two eldest sons, William and Robert Spotswood Russell.[22]

William was well known for his military and public service. At the young age of fifteen he joined Daniel Boone's Indian campaign and was soon after appointed an officer during the American Revolution. He led a company at King's Mountain, served twelve terms in the Kentucky legislature, and was elected sheriff of Fayette County. He ran for governor of Kentucky, but was defeated by James Garrard.

In 1786, William built Mount Brilliant's first house, a log cabin, near a spring and a large cave. Interestingly, the structure still exists and was renovated in the 1990s. Robert Spotswood Russell constructed a stone house at one end of the plantation, an area that later became known as Poplar Farm. This historic structure also still stands.[23]

The great house at Mount Brilliant was constructed in 1792, the year Kentucky gained statehood. The house went through up to six renovations, its final character being that of a large nine-thousand-square-foot, nine-bay farmhouse with twelve rooms. Later, four large Doric columns were added to the front of the house, providing an impressive visual statement.[24]

Hamilton Atchison, Jr., acquired the estate in 1832. He was a cousin of David Rice Atchison, a U.S. senator known as being "president for a day," between James Polk and Zachary Taylor. The senator is said to have visited the plantation regularly.[25]

Thomas Hughes purchased the property in 1861. He later owned two other historic Kentucky estates, Elk Hill and Clifton. In 1891, Arthur Delong acquired the plantation and sold it to James B. Haggin in 1905. His descendents remained at the plantation until the 1980s. In a 2002 article in the *Lexington Herald-Leader,* Nell Blair Vaughn notes that the Haggin descendents were extremely active in the campaign against polio, devoting much time and money to efforts to eradicate the disease.[26]

The estate eventually ended up in the hands of Kenneth T. Jones, Jr., a Guam businessman. In 1996, he sold Mount Brilliant to Greg Goodman, a Texas multimillionaire who grew up down the street from the Bush family and is a friend of former president George W. Bush. Goodman is president of HGG Investments in Houston and is also a horse farmer. His family owns Goodman Manufacturing, one of the nation's largest producers of whole-house air conditioning units.[27]

Goodman set out to transform Mount Brilliant into a dream resort for himself and his family, including his wife, Becky, and their four children. He began by replacing roads and fences, radically changing the face of the estate. He added numerous stables for horses, two outdoor show rings, and a farm manager's house. Next, utility lines were buried, a small pond was expanded into a six-acre lake complete with a sailboat and dock, a formal garden was planted, a pool and fish pond were constructed, and a maze was built.[28]

John Blackburn, an architect from Washington, D.C., and James Gehrmann, an interior designer from Houston, were contracted to transform a century-old carriage barn on the estate into the Goodmans' contemporary-styled private residence. The completed structure contained 10,400 square feet of living space, including a large sunken living room and huge fireplace, a wine cellar, five bedrooms and a master suite, a second-floor study area with a desk for each child, and a large "eat-in" kitchen. Next, an even older playhouse was similarly transformed to allow the Goodman children an ideal place for sleepovers. Two other historic buildings were renovated as modern guesthouses.[29]

But, for all his improvements upon the estate, Goodman failed miserably at one. The grand mansion at Mount Brilliant—the white-columned 1792 manor house—was not to be restored, but instead demolished! Sometime after 2000, Goodman decided to destroy the structure, wanting it off his property.

Goodman's ultimate motivation behind this act was never clear, but it seemed as if he felt the old house detracted from his estate. He said, "We've spent a lot of money fixing the farm up . . . and the house is not a pretty sight . . ." Goodman said that a restoration of the mansion would cost between two and three million dollars. "I'm sorry I don't have $2 million to spend on a house so people can drive by and look at it. . . ," he said.[30]

Local residents were appalled when they learned of the property owner's plans after he applied for a demolition permit. James Millard, who owns a farm near Mount Brilliant said, "My reaction is just absolute, entire disappointment that the property owner would not recognize that the county as a whole owns the cultural history of that building."[31]

Soon, the Blue Grass Trust for Historic Preservation got involved, scheduling several meetings with Goodman, which were described as "cordial, but candid." More than a hundred people attended an emergency meeting held by the Trust on August 9, 2002. A letter-writing campaign and a petition were discussed, among other things. Many felt like the Texas native did not appreciate Kentucky history, a theme that is often repeated in such preservation efforts, especially when nonlocals are involved. Goodman admitted that he did not think the house was particularly historic, except for its age.[32]

The Blue Grass Trust explored several options for preserving the home, including moving it from the property, which would have cost $360,000. Goodman offered to donate his demolition costs ($42,000) to such an effort, but still the sum was more than the Trust could pay. Goodman even agreed to give the Trust time to look into what could be done to save the house, but he was adamant in his desire to demolish it.

Finally, after many avenues had been explored, the Trust made a joint statement with Goodman, stating that the two parties could not find a way to save the mansion. Goodman agreed to give $25,000 to fund documentation and historic research on the house before its demise. The University of Kentucky's Graduate Program in Historic Preservation undertook this work.[33]

On November 22, 2002, after measured drawings had been made and other documentation completed, the great mansion at Mount Brilliant was demolished, not to make way for another structure, but simply because its owner didn't want it. Many local residents were dismayed. James Millard said, "Destroying that structure is needless. Had they wanted to they could have saved it." Greg Goodman said that he was "glad to be done with it."[34]

Sadly, this case illustrates the failing of organized preservation on a large scale. Mount Brilliant wasn't lost to nature or the elements. It wasn't destroyed in the name of progress. It was deliberately destroyed because its owner wanted it gone for good. One wonders why, if Goodman couldn't afford restoration, he couldn't have left the historic mansion as it was for future restoration by the next generation. Even in a ruinous state the mansion would have been better off than being destroyed. And such a fabled ruin would have been a novel attraction to his farm much like ancient ruins across the European countryside.

But ruins were not to be the fate of Mount Brilliant. Fortunately, some of the estate's old structures have been preserved, albeit in a greatly modified form. The Blue Grass Trust has made a point of stressing the importance of this tragedy as an example of what can happen to a community's historic treasures if they are not properly preserved. As such the Trust is spearheading efforts to protect other rural landmarks to prevent future preservation battles and losses in the region.

## Reverie

Once the oldest home in LaGrange, Tennessee, the mansion at historic Reverie Plantation survived the Civil War and other perils and was gloriously restored in the 1960s, only to be destroyed by fire in 1987.

The plantation property was the early site of a Chickasaw settlement and an important Native American trading post. Later, as planters immigrated from Virginia and the Carolinas seeking to establish plantations in the region, the property was held by Major Edmund Winston, who constructed the master house there around 1825. Major Winston owned a boys' military school called Chestnut Hill Academy in nearby LaGrange. His daughter Mary Eliza married Dr. Whitson Alexander Harris around 1848, and Major Winston presented them with the Reverie Plantation as a wedding present.[35]

At this time the plantation covered over eight thousand acres and produced a variety of crops for consumption, but it was cotton that served as the estate's principal staple and that fueled the economic engine of the region. Spurred by the financial success of his crops, Dr. Harris enlarged his master house into a true plantation mansion in 1854. He had his slaves produce bricks from clay and cut timbers from the estate's own forests for use in the major expansion. Workers from Ohio crafted a summer porch and added four additional rooms. They also moved the kitchen and dining room from the daylight basement to the main floor. But perhaps the most noticeable and dramatic change was the incorporation of a new Greek Revival portico with four tall columns and an impressive pediment that lent the house the iconic presence for which it was so celebrated.

Dr. Harris and Mary Eliza had five children; however, they all died tragically—supposedly of diphtheria—within a brief time span. In addition to this great misfortune, the Harrises faced much turmoil during the War Between the States. Their plantation was occupied during the Civil War and it is probable that the Harrises left the area. Some seventy large plantation mansions in the area were destroyed during the war—their timber was used for fuel and their bricks were used to construct fireplaces and chimneys within soldiers' tents. But a few of the great plantation homes were spared, as they served as officers' quarters. The mansion at Reverie was occupied by the Union more or less continuously during the war, and the grounds served as a camp for the cavalry. General John Aaron Rawlins, who later served as U.S. secretary of war and acted as a close aide to General Grant, stayed at Reverie while Grant was stationed at nearby Hancock Hall Plantation. General William Smith also lodged at Harris's plantation. And it was from Reverie's grounds and the adjoining Michie

The master house at Reverie Plantation was dominated by large square pillars and a crowing pediment. Photo by Allen Cogbill. Courtesy of John and Betty Walley, Bolivar, Tennessee.

Road that seventeen hundred men from nearby LaGrange assembled in April 1862, to begin their six-hundred-mile journey to Baton Rouge in a military maneuver known as Grierson's Raid—a tactical ploy to distract the Confederates from Grant's concurrent attack on Vicksburg.

After the war, the Harrises sold the plantation to the Myrick family, who in turn sold the estate to Thomas Bess Beasley in 1878. Beasley willed the estate to his son, Peter R. Beasley, a son-in-law of the Hancocks of Hancock Hill Plantation. The Beasleys' first child was born at Reverie around 1909, but the family moved out in 1916. Peter's father-in-law had grown elderly and infirm, and he agreed to give his son-in-law and daughter Hancock Hill Plantation in exchange for their staying and caring for him until his death.

Peter Beasley sold the plantation to Joseph Hamer, who retained the estate for sixteen years until he lost it in 1932. Robert Eldridge Hunter, a banker and store owner, then acquired the house and lived there with his wife until 1963, when the mansion along with three hundred acres were purchased by John and Betty Walley of Memphis.

John Walley had previously driven through the area of LaGrange while commuting on business trips to Jackson, Tennessee. He would often slow down to admire the beauty of the spot. "I was in another century," he said. "Everything was so quiet and lovely."[36]

His wife, Betty, agreed. "There's a history and atmosphere in LaGrange that you find no place else . . . It's up to us to see that the town is preserved."[37]

After buying Reverie, John and Betty spent fifteen long months restoring the house to its original grandeur. During the restoration, the Walleys made several interesting discoveries. First, they found the original contract for the expansion of the house between Dr. Harris and the Ohioan contractor "Laffrotti" written on wood on the inside of a door facing. It listed the name and county of origin of each of the craftsmen who worked on the house. They also found a hidden door in the northern wall of the west bedroom that opened to a chute where valuables could be stored. And, finally, they uncovered a small door in the east wall of the east bedroom that led to a secret room.

The Walleys spent a great deal of time and money remodeling. By the time they were finished they had hung 440 rolls of wallpaper on the interior walls and used 160 gallons of paint on the exterior of the house alone. The original random-width heart-of-pine floors remained, as did many other original elements. At this time the Walleys' three young children, Page, Scott, and Janis, were old enough (between six and nine years old) to enjoy the house as well and spent many long hours playing in the side yard. They relished finding artifacts scattered about the grounds and just below the earth, including multiple arrowheads, no doubt from the area's days as a Native American trading post. Betty Walley noted, "Living here is just like having your cake and being able to eat it too."[38] The Walleys lived on the plantation for nearly a quarter century, before tragedy struck.

A fire of unknown cause broke out in the early morning of November 11, 1987, at Reverie and quickly engulfed the mansion. John Walley immediately called the fire department. His plantation manager, Paul Camper, described what he saw to the Memphis *Commercial Appeal* in an article that appeared in the newspaper the next day. When he realized the house was on fire he immediately went to the back door to rescue the Walleys. "I saw the sky all lit up over here . . . They knew the house was on fire but they had no idea it was fixing to collapse on them. Once we all got out we knew there was no chance to think about going in."[39]

John Walley agreed: "The flames were just leaping down the way right at us . . . It was a runaway fire. I would say in all candor, another matter of seconds and we could not have gotten out the door. If it hadn't been for Paul rushing us we would not have had those seconds."

There were twenty-five firemen from LaGrange and neighboring Grand Junction who responded to the call, but as fireman John Parham noted, "By the time we got there it was too far gone to put it out."

During the blaze, many important antiques were lost, including an 1835 lounge chair which was original to the mansion, hundred-year-old Persian rugs, a twelve-foot-high bed made in 1820 in New Orleans, and a 1795 English sideboard. Also lost was the two-thousand-volume library, which included many first editions of history, language, and poetry, a complete set of the Oxford English Dictionary, and more than a hundred Civil War books, including *The Rise and Fall of the Confederacy* by Jefferson Davis. Also lost with the library was a rare 1823 copy of the *Tennessee Gazetteer*.

Even amid the smoldering ruins of their once-great plantation home, the Walleys showed great resilience. Standing in front of his home, now largely reduced to ashes, John Walley commented, "Our life is not over because our possessions are gone." The Walleys went on to build a new, albeit smaller, more practical home on the property. Today, although Reverie is gone, it has not been forgotten by many enthusiastic locals in the region.

CHAPTER THREE

# The Carolinas

I was born and raised on a Carolina sea island and I carried the sunshine of the low-country, inked in dark gold, on my back and shoulders.

*—Pat Conroy*, The Prince of Tides

Remove not the ancient landmark which your fathers have set.

*—Proverbs 22:28*

First explored by the Spanish in the first half of the sixteenth century, both North Carolina and South Carolina stemmed from permanent settlements that were first established by the British. Prior to this, in present-day North Carolina the earliest English-speaking colony in the Americas was established at Roanoke Island by John White. After a trip to England for provisions, White returned to find that the entire settlement and all of its inhabitants had vanished, leaving only the word "CROATOAN" mysteriously carved in a tree.

By the second half of the seventeenth century, permanent settlements had been established, and the single Province of Carolina had been given to the eight Lords Proprietor by King Charles II of England. The colony was named for the king's father, Charles I (Carolus being the Latin form of Charles). Even at this early date, agriculture flourished. The proprietors' first settlers included many Barbadians, and in the southern part of Carolina a plantation economy similar to that of the West Indies emerged. By 1691, a deputy governor was appointed to oversee the northern half of the province, and by 1712, the split between North Carolina and South Carolina was complete.

After colonists revolted against proprietary rule, the Lords Proprietor sold their interest, and South Carolina became a royal province in 1719. North Carolina followed suit ten years later, becoming a crown colony in 1729. Agriculture continued to thrive in South Carolina where sugar and indigo were grown, but rice had become the principal cash crop. Rice in many ways defined the landscape and plantation economy of coastal South Carolina and Georgia. A nearly continuous line of rice plantations could be found along rivers, near creeks, and in the swamps from the southernmost end of the Georgia coast through the South Carolina Low Country and into the southern coast of North Carolina. Tobacco estates overflowed from Virginia into the northern parts of North Carolina.

South Carolina became a busy hub of the slave trade. Early on in its history, the colony's slaves originated from the West Indies, but later, hordes of enslaved people were brought directly from Africa across the abominable Middle Passage. As early as 1720, the majority of South Carolina's population was enslaved, and this demographic trend continued most of the time until the Civil War. These enslaved people faced hardships and horrors that are unimaginable by today's standards, and work in the swampy rice fields, which involved being knee deep in putrid water, was especially grueling. Death rates among these slaves were astounding, and it is said that two out of three slave children on rice plantations died before their sixteenth birthdays.

While slaves toiled in the fields, their white masters sought freedom of their own from Great Britain. In 1788, South Carolina became the eighth state to ratify the U.S. Constitution, and North Carolina followed suit one year later, becoming the twelfth state to enter the Union. The following year, in 1790, North Carolina ceded its westerns lands to the federal government, and in 1796 these lands became Tennessee.

Not long after these two states joined the Union, the invention of the cotton gin, coupled with an increased demand for cotton in European mills, created an economic and cultural boom that fueled the creation of cotton plantations throughout the inland Carolinas. Greek Revival homes reminiscent of ancient temples were constructed, adding to the milieu of already existing colonial houses with their stringent Georgian styling and West Indies influences.

But, as elsewhere in the South, the building boom was cut short by the onset of the Civil War. South Carolina played a forefront role in the conflict, being the first state to secede from the Union on December 20, 1860. On April 12, 1861, the first shots of the war were fired in South Carolina at Charleston Harbor, and two days later, the federal garrison at Fort Sumter surrendered to rebel forces. North Carolina reluctantly seceded on May 20, 1861, but became the state that provided more men and materials to the Confederate cause than any other. It also counted the largest number of losses during the war.

Woodlawn Plantation. The mansion in a decayed state only shadowed its prior elegance. The ruined house was destroyed along with many other important South Carolina plantations with the creation of the Santee Cooper Hydroelectric and Navigation Project.

After the war, both of the Carolinas were in shambles. Many plantations had been destroyed, and many others were badly damaged. The economy was in ruins and the slave workforce was free. But planters picked up the pieces of their lives and carried on, albeit in a much different manner than before the war. In much of North Carolina and South Carolina sharecropping took hold as former slaves and their descendants continued to work the land.

Over the years, as the economic dominance of agriculture dwindled, plantations began to fade. Some, like North Carolina's Devereux Plantation, were lost to fire, and some were destroyed by other forms of natural disaster, but, interestingly, two dozen of South Carolina's most important plantation estates drowned at the hands of men. In what has come to be known as one of the greatest single acts of southern plantation destruction since the Civil War, twenty-four historic plantations were inundated between 1939 and 1942, when the South Carolina Public Service Authority, funded largely by federal grants and loans provided by Roosevelt's New Deal administration, dammed the Santee and Cooper rivers, flooding 160,000 acres of the state. Known as the Santee Cooper project, this created a waterway transportation system linking Columbia to Charleston, two beautiful lakes (Marion and Moultrie), and a hydroelectric project that still provides electricity today. It also displaced more than a thousand families and destroyed many historic structures and estates.[1,2]

Several of the flooded plantations are featured in this chapter; others include such historic sites as Belvidere Plantation, the home of the Sinkler family near Eutaw Springs that featured a historic master house constructed in 1786. It was significant for its asymmetric plan and for providing an example of architecture that influenced the design of other important houses built later in the region. Ophir, six miles northwest of Pinopolis, was one of the ancestral homes of the powerful Porcher family. The plantation mansion was an impressive raised two-story structure with a broad covered porch that ran the length of the house and a tall roof with three front dormers. Here the Porchers built a large church for their slaves to use. Woodlawn, built by Stephen G. Deveaux, was arguably the most fabulous of all the drowned plantations. Its complex plan boasted eight massive rooms and two large halls on the first floor alone. Above the mansion, a handsome balustrade once encircled the rooftop garden. Even before, this architectural gem was threatened by neglect, having sadly fallen into disrepair and decay. Alongside these impressive estates, the ruins of many more historic plantations now sit silently at the bottoms of Marion and Moultrie lakes, their important architecture lost forever.

Other significant lost plantations that could not be featured in this chapter include Eden House in Bertie County, home of North Carolina governor Charles Eden, which has recently been the site of much archeological excavation and study, and Point Comfort Plantation, also once located in Bertie County, which was originally part of the Brownrigg estate. In South Carolina, besides those submerged under Lake Marion and Lake Moultrie, a number of other important plantations have been lost, including Altamont Plantation, the home of Col. Thomas Pinckney, Jr., the son of Revolutionary War hero and South Carolina governor Gen. Thomas Pinckney. Altamont was razed in the 1940s, and only the fine Italian marble mantels were saved. Another South Carolina plantation home lost in the 1940s was the Tom Seabrook Plantation of Edisto Island. The noted master house survived precisely two hundred years before it burned in 1940.

Of course, both North Carolina and South Carolina are home to many plantations whose architectural glory is still in existence. Many of these serve as private homes, but others are open as public museums. Among the most popular in South Carolina are Drayton Hall, the oldest preserved plantation house in the U.S., which is open to the public, Mansfield Plantation—one of the most well-preserved rice plantations in the nation—which serves as a bed and breakfast, and Middleton Place, which claims America's oldest landscaped gardens. North Carolinians and visitors to the state enjoy such estates as Somerset Place on the shores of Lake Phelps, which serves as a state historic site, and Latta Plantation in Mecklenburg County, a cotton plantation that is open to the public.

Scholarship on the Carolinas' lost plantations is limited, but a few fine published sources do exist. Mills Lane's volumes on North Carolina and South Carolina, both part of his *Architecture of the Old South* series, provide much information. *Plantations of the Carolina Low Country* by Samuel Gaillard Stoney was originally published in 1938, but has subsequently been reprinted on several occasions, most recently in 1989 by Dover. This work details several dozen important plantation homes and other structures, both standing and demolished. Douglas Bostick's recent publication *Sunken Plantations: The Santee Cooper Project* provides a visual and historical journey of plantations lost under Lake Marion and Lake Moultrie. Thomas T. Waterman's 1939 report, *A Survey of the Early Buildings in the Region of the Proposed Santee and Pinopolis Reservoirs in South Carolina,* for the National Park Service, likewise provides much important information about these estates. And Frances Benjamin Johnston and Thomas Tileston Waterman's *The Early Architecture of North Carolina*, published by the University of North Carolina Press in 1941, is also a useful source.

Much primary source material about the Carolinas' plantation past can be found in various repositories. At the University of North Carolina's Southern Historical Collection in Chapel Hill, original source matter regarding plantations across the South is maintained. The university has made a portion of these materials available online through its "Documenting the American South" project.

The South Carolina Department of Archives and History maintains records on many estates, and, of course, the Library of Congress's Historic American Buildings Survey holds a large variety of photographs, measured drawings, and historical documentation about plantations from both states.

The stories of South Carolina's and North Carolina's lost plantations—pieced together from old primary sources and well-documented secondary materials—provide rich interlaced histories of an era gone by, a people forgotten, and a grand architectural legacy that has faded into the past.

## Pooshee

At one time the Ravenel family home—Pooshee Plantation—was one of South Carolina's finest estates. Today, like an Atlantean dream, its lands lie motionless at the bottom of Lake Moultrie in Berkeley County. Pooshee was among a number of historic local plantations whose fates were sealed with the creation of the Santee Cooper Hydroelectric and Navigation Project, a massive public program that functioned to spur transportation and development, while destroying historic properties.

The property, originally one thousand acres, was granted to Pierre de St. Julien de Malacare in 1705. St. Julien sold the property to his brother, Henry Le Noble, who passed it on to his son-in-law René Louis Ravenel. The first house built on the plantation was constructed in 1716, but it was replaced in 1804 with a fine wooden mansion.[3]

The house was a raised two-story structure with a hipped roof and two gabled dormers from the attic. The original structure followed the standard central hall plan with two large rooms resting on both sides of the central passage. Between these, on either side, was a fireplace. Later, an additional wing was built on one side of the house, and another room was constructed on the back. A large basement under the raised first floor was divided into storerooms, including a room for diary products, another for meats, and a room for wood. The in-

terior of the house was decorated with a variety of wooden embellishments and filled with mahogany furniture. Hand-painted window shades echoed a variety of familiar local scenes.[4]

Outside the main house, a variety of outbuildings could be found. At opposite ends of a large, broad lawn the carriage house and stables rested, "the two elements bound to come together put, apparently for convenience sake, as far apart as possible."[5] There were also the usual barns, kitchens, and other outbuildings so ubiquitous on the southern plantation estate.

Eventually this grand house and its surrounding plantation property were passed into the hands of Dr. Henry Ravenel, a physician. He was described by his grandson in the following way: "He was truly a typical gentleman of the old school, though in appearance more that of a statesman than of an unpretentious country gentleman . . . I never saw him dressed otherwise than in a blue broadcloth full dress suit, with polished brass buttons and the customary standing collar and high black silk stock."[6]

Ravenel abandoned medicine to devote himself fully to planting and his family. His son, Henry William Ravenel, considered studying medicine, but instead took up botany. In 1852, he went on an exploratory expedition of Aiken and parts of Georgia with Professor Francis S. Holmes and Dr. William Porcher Miles, who was also a lawyer and congressman. Here he became enthralled with natural history and the study of local flora. He became one of the most celebrated and well-published botanists of his time.[7]

But, even with Henry William intensely focusing on his scientific work and his father concentrating on his agricultural operations, the family still found time for fun. One of the greatest historical treasures remaining from Pooshee is a complete description of antebellum Christmas celebrations held there. It is perhaps one of the most detailed descriptions of Christmas celebrations from any lost plantation of the South. The typewritten manuscript was composed by Samuel Wilson Ravenel, grandson of Henry Ravenel, the physician. He describes the jovial holidays at Pooshee, noting that

The front façade of Pooshee Plantation House. The broad, raised porch dominated the front of the old mansion. The side wing was a later addition.

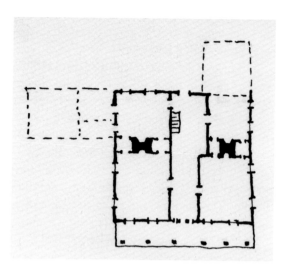

This rough sketch of Pooshee Plantation's master house from Waterman shows that the original first-floor plan conformed to the standard central hall configuration found so prominently in the South. The dotted lines represent the side wing and rear room which were added later.

Christmas celebrations there lasted from December 25 through New Year's Day.[8]

During this jolly time, more than fifty family members and friends packed into the plantation to enjoy food and frivolities. Practical jokes were much the order of the day. Samuel wrote that if one was not careful on Christmas morning, his toothbrush would be so bitter with quinine that he would hardly know at breakfast that his coffee or tea was spiked with salt and pepper.[9]

Samuel described many of the jokes. Most illustrate the formal gender roles that were defined through the nuances of frolicsome play. For example, while children and adults all took part in these games, they "never overstepped the bounds of respect and decorum." He also noted that even little girls were shown "due regard and deference," as one day any one of them might grow up to be the "mistress of the house."[10]

Strict gender division is exemplified in nearly every joke described in the manuscript:

What fun and revenge it was to go to bed, knowing that at day-break those . . . frolicksome [sic] and mischievous girls were to be kept awake by the crowing of that miserable old rooster you had bribed the poultry woman and the chamber-maid to lock up in the closet of the young ladies' room . . . Yes, it was very laughable, until that night when you, in your triumphant glee, discovered that the same chamber-maid had turned traitor and sold you out, and horrors, every possible part of your night garment had been stitched and stitched, around and together . . . until nothing but patience and a sharp knife could extricate you from your difficulty . . . and when you jumped into bed, you found that they had . . . filled your sheets with flour, cracked corn and sticky holly-leaves, that you were compelled to get rid of before you could sleep, even if you did try to beat their robe-de-nuit joke by dispensing with the superfluous night garment.[11]

The practical jokes were a constant at these holiday celebrations at Pooshee, but these seemingly random pranks were actually guided by a set of strict rules and mores that reveal much about the Old South and its social constructs. For example, Dr. Henry Ravenel, the family's patriarch, was never on the receiving end of a practical joke. Nor was the mistress of the house. It was assumed that she had much to do in overseeing the house servants and the cooking, and practical jokes would impede her in these duties. She did, however, act as the ultimate confidant. Each individual prankster was required to confide in the mistress, explicitly explaining the details of each joke. She ensured that proper social boundaries were maintained and that each joke went off smoothly.[12]

The most notorious of these pranks was known to the family for generations as the "joke of the boots and the ball." It was the custom of the day that each man place his boots outside his chamber door each night and a slave would pick them up. That night, the enslaved house servants would polish the boots and replace them near the doors by morning. One night, the women of the house stole all of the gentlemen's boots, including those of the young bachelors who all stayed in another house beyond the mansion known as the "lodge." The next morning each man simply thought the slaves were running late or that his boots had been forgotten. It wasn't until they saw all of the women going for breakfast (without any of the other men) that everyone realized what had happened.[13]

The following year, in order to get back at the women, the men plotted to invent a grand ball that was never to happen. They issued phony ball invitations from the Saracens, who were neighbors. For days all of the women primped and prepared for the ball while the men went out hunting. The night of the ball, the women were all dressed in their finery, coaches at the ready, waiting anxiously for the men to return from the hunt. They were going to be late for the ball. The men finally returned. One wore a paper fool's hat on his head and another beat a tin can as a tambourine. Together they chanted, "Boots . . . boots . . . boots . . ." And the women of the house realized they had been fooled. Grave disappointment rose up in the ranks of the women, but they were determined to attend a ball. They called for the slave fiddlers, Israel, Ellison, and Caesar, and had a "regular frolicing [sic] country dance right there."[14]

The celebrations and occurrences at Pooshee give much insight into the lifestyle of a planter and his family before the war. They show the inhabitants of this plantation as real people, many with a great sense of humor. They also suggest that the Ravenels had much leisure time, as well as excess monies to fund such lavish celebrations. In fact, a Christmas tree would always be set up during this time. Under and around it were found many thousands of dollars' worth of gifts, ranging from tin toys to full silver services. It was also not uncommon, according to Samuel Ravenel, that deeds to slaves be hung on the tree as gifts for adult children of the plantation master.[15]

Of course, Christmas was also a time of celebration for most of the slaves. But one must wonder how those slaves who were given as gifts off the Ravenel Christmas tree must have felt. In his accounts, Samuel notes that field hands were allowed certain indulgences during this time. They were given three days off, and three fatted cows were slaughtered and shared among the enslaved community. The carriage house was cleared, and its wooden floors were dusted with sand, creating a dance hall for the slaves. Their dances started about two or three in the afternoon and lasted until dawn the next morning; this went on for three nights. Often these dances were preceded by a slave wedding, performed by a slave preacher and attended by the Ravenel family, who were invited as guests. The Ravenels always received a large basket of warm food after the ceremony, and they retreated to the master house, while the slaves' dance commenced.[16]

For the enslaved house servants and kitchen staff, the holidays must have been a dreadful time. While their field hand counterparts were enjoying themselves, they were quite literally slaving away, creating huge dinners for an expanded household of fifty or more guests, polishing every man's boots all night long, and generally seeing to all the cleaning, washing, transportation, and service needs for this huge crowd. Their plight must have been one of exhaustion and extreme labor.

But even for weary house servants Christmastime came to an end, annually, with a New Year's fireworks display. The Christmas celebrations at Pooshee lasted until the war, during which time the Ravenels, like all other planter families, faced great changes and difficulties. The slaves were freed, the economy collapsed, and the plantation system (even the extravagant Christmas week festivities) faded into history.

The mansion at Pooshee Plantation was partially damaged by fire sometime after the turn of the century, but structurally it still stood strong. It was in 1940, when the Santee Cooper company built a dam that flooded the Pinopolis basin, that the plantation was finally finished. The floods from the dam created current-day Lake Moultrie and Lake Marion, which swallowed up many plantation homes and other historic structures. Today the Ravenels' great estate is submerged deep below the still waters of Lake Moultrie, and the great Christmas celebrations are but a dim memory scrawled across the parchment of time.

# Millwood

Today, all that is left of the Hampton family's great Millwood Plantation are a few crumbling columns. These represent for Columbia and all of South Carolina a bygone era and a past often forgotten.

The Hampton family has lived in South Carolina since the mid-1700s, when Anthony Hampton moved to Spartanburg from Virginia. He and his family established a farm, but were distraught to find themselves constantly under the threat of nearby bands of Native Americans who resented the encroachment upon their hunting grounds. While five of their sons were away from the farm, Anthony, his wife, another son, and a grandchild were murdered by the Cherokees.[17]

Their sons recovered from this great tragedy, carving out lives for themselves in South Carolina's economy and society. One of Anthony's five sons, Wade, fought in the Revolutionary War. Distinguished by his bravery and ability, he was promoted to colonel. Shortly after the war he settled onto the Millwood property near Columbia in Richland County. He operated a toll bridge across the Congaree River until it was washed away in 1791, the same year his son, Wade Hampton II, was born. The elder Hampton built a cotton gin in 1799, and began to produce a large amount of the crop.[18]

As the colonel grew old, his son took over much of the operations of the plantation. He constructed a fine house there in 1817. Originally, its plan was simple: a center stair hall flanked by a single room on each side, and a matching floor plan above on the second story. The house was raised, with steep stairs leading to a large yet simple front porch that traversed the width of the house. A year after constructing the house, Wade Hampton II became a father. His son, Wade Hampton III, was born in 1818.[19]

The house was later renovated to accommodate the growing Hampton family. The front of the home was redone entirely. The original one-story porch was removed. Four giant Grecian columns were added across the front, and flanking those on the ends were two large square pillars with sunken panels and molded bases. The Corinthian columns topped the house's two stories, supporting a massive entablature and cornice. Elements of Greek Revival style were added to the door and windows, and a balustrade was installed across the porch.[20]

Additionally, two-story wings were added to each side of the house; these wings greatly expanded the width of the original house. In front of these wings builders constructed one-story porches that were continuous with the large central two-story Grecian veranda. These smaller porches were supported by one-story-high columns that were identical to the square-end columns of the larger central porch, only smaller. Cumulatively, these architectural renovations and additions gave the appearance that a much larger new house had been constructed. It is said that when one opened the large folding door dividing the four front rooms, a giant ballroom was created, extending a width of 104 feet.[21]

Col. Wade Hampton I died in 1835, as his family's empire continued to expand. At the height of their wealth, the Hamptons owned over a dozen plantations across the South, including the 148,000-acre Houmas Plantation[22] in Ascension Parish, Louisiana. The family also owned thousands of slaves, who labored in the vast fields of these estates.[23]

Wade Hampton II took over operations of the family fortune, spending lavish amounts of money on horses. He became an avid sportsman and famous horseman, commissioning many expensive paintings of his prized steeds. Hampton II had served in the War of 1812, carrying the news of vic-

The ruined columns of South Carolina's Millwood Plantation are all that remain of the estate. These represent an antebellum modification of the original house that included four giant Grecian columns, which were flanked on the ends by two square pillars with sunken panels and molded bases. Each was set atop brick pedestals. The ruins attract many visitors today and hold a special place in the hearts of local citizens.

tory at the Battle of New Orleans to Washington, D.C. He died in 1858, leaving the famed Millwood mansion to his daughters.[24]

Hampton II's son, Wade Hampton III, did not reside at Millwood, but he considered it "home." He visited his sisters there often, before continuing his family's legacy of renowned military service. Hampton III joined the ranks of great Civil War generals. He also single-handedly outfitted and funded Hampton's Legion, which was made up of six infantry companies, four cavalry companies, and an artillery battery equipped with six field guns. After the war, Hampton III served as governor of South Carolina and in the U.S. Senate; he was, however, penniless. He died in 1902, having survived the last years of his life on charity.[25]

In 1865, as Union forces rode through Columbia, Sherman decided to burn Millwood. The house represented the seat of the Hampton family empire, and it was seen as a bastion of Confederate ideals and wealth. Before the tragedy the family was able to save a few pieces of silver, china, crystal, and some of the paintings from the house. They hurriedly ripped the heavy red silk damask draperies from the windows, using them to wrap the fragile items for transport.[26]

The items saved from the plantation eventually made their way to the Hamptons' house in town at Columbia, known as the Hampton-Preston Mansion. These objects can still be seen on display there today, as the residence is now a house museum.

Additionally, the site of the old plantation mansion is now open to the public. Ruins of the great columns that once supported the historic structure are all that remain, echoing a past of splendor and privilege that has long since disappeared. These columns gained particular interest among South Carolinians around the turn of the century, when their likeness appeared on everything from opera curtains to postcards. They represented for these people the often romanticized ideals of the powerful economic system of antebellum times, as well as the grace and grandeur associated with the lifestyle of the planter elite. The ruins still stand, representing for the generations of today an intriguing and meaningful past.

## Prospect Hill

Prospect Hill Plantation house in Halifax County, North Carolina, was noted for its elaborate embellishments and unique architectural elements, but its historic legacy came to an end after the estate's destruction.[27]

The plantation was owned by William Williams Thorne, the son of Samuel Thorne and Martha Williams of Halifax. He began constructing the wooden-framed house there shortly after his marriage to Temperance Williams Davis in 1820. The house was completed in 1828. Account books recall expenses related to the construction. In September 1828, Thorne paid $1,800 to an architect/builder named Burgess from Boydton, Virginia. Prior to this, he paid for various supplies and labor, including: $21.25 to a man named Peter for mauling rock, $100 to sawyers, $122 to stonemasons, $92 for oil paint, $12 for brass locks, and $395 for plastering to a decorator from North Carolina.

It is clear that a large portion of money funded decoration and embellishment of the house, and this could be observed by anyone who saw the mansion. Every fireplace, doorway, and window dripped with intricate, almost gaudy ornamentation. Scrolled, carved, reeded, and applied motifs covered many surfaces and trimmed nearly every nook and recess. Ironically, however, the elegant winding staircase was quite simple, with only a modest scalloped design on the brackets.

The mansion's overall plan was as unusual as its eclectic embellishments. A large central hall that ran the length of the mansion was divided into two separate spaces by a massive, high, decorated arch. The rear space served as the stair hall. To one side of this hall the house gave way to one giant drawing room that opened onto the rear two-story loggia, under the main roof. This loggia was supported by three incredibly slender Tuscan columns. The opposite side of the main hall opened to two rooms within the main structure of the house, and beyond these another room jutted out from one side

The principal façade of the Prospect Hill house brought high style to colonial tradition. The central Greek Revival porch was flanked by Palladian-type windows.

A log slave cabin on North Carolina's Prospect Hill Plantation is now only a memory.

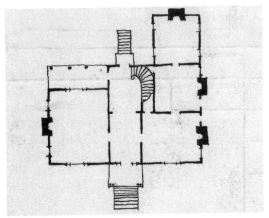

A rough sketch (not to scale) showing the asymmetric and unusual first-floor plan of Prospect Hill's master house. The large drawing room opened onto the rear two-story loggia.

of the rear. All in all, these unique elements collectively functioned to create one of the most distinctive plans for any southern plantation house of the time.

Adding to the home's uniqueness was its façade. A one-story Greek Revival porch was the center point of three bays. This porch was supported by a set of double, fluted Doric columns, and had an intricate entablature complete with dentil features. The front windows were all triple windows, and the lower ones included a detailed arch in the center, flanked by elaborate embellishment, creating a Palladian-type effect.

Eventually, the plantation was inherited by William Williams Thorne's son of the same name, who later passed it along to his own son, also of the same name. The plantation was significant not only for its unusual architecture and because it served as a centerpiece of local agricultural production, but also because it was the birthplace of several notable citizens, including Walter McKenzie Clark in 1846. Clark, a noted author and editor, served as chief justice of the North Carolina Supreme Court.

Prospect Hill survived the Civil War and even the two world wars, and it remained well into the twentieth century, only to be destroyed sometime after the 1940s. In many respects it has been forgotten, although ghostly images of the estate can be found in the Historic American Buildings Survey and in a few old books.

## Eutaw

The Sinklers' Eutaw Plantation was once nestled in a swampy, low-lying area on the Santee River in Upper St. John's Parish. Remarkably, the plantation was owned by one and only one family throughout its long existence. Like many of its neighbors, Eutaw Plantation was a victim of progress; when the Santee Cooper dam project flooded its fields, water enveloped its built environment.

Captain James Sinkler, the son of an early Scottish immigrant, was one of the region's first settlers.

He was a Revolutionary War hero who received a land grant in the St. John's vicinity. It was here that the captain constructed Belvidere Plantation in the early eighteenth century. He also owned Old Santee Plantation in St. James Parish, where the family found much success in growing indigo.[28]

The site of Eutaw was about three miles east of Eutawville and one mile west from the battlefield of Eutaw Springs. Originally, it was accessible only via the Santee River and Cooper Canal. The plantation house at Eutaw was built on an isolated bluff overlooking a creek that flowed from nearby Eutaw Springs. It was constructed for James Sinkler's son, William, upon his marriage to Elizabeth Allen Broun in 1810.

The house itself was situated at the end of a long avenue amid Spanish moss–draped trees. It stood atop a large raised basement and was supported by a beautiful brick arcade below. The arcade was said to have been made of bricks salvaged from the ruins of the house that the British had earlier used as the center of their line during the Battle of Eutaw Springs. A broad piazza, perhaps a later addition, sat atop the arcade encircling the front of the house, while three neat dormers peeked through the steep gable roof. All in all, the home's components melded to provide a beautifully proportioned façade.

Originally, the house corresponded to a modified central hall plan, with the central stair hall extending only midway through the rear half of the first floor. The first floor was nearly square in plan, and it contained four large rooms, with the largest extending upon what would have been the front portion of the central stair hall had it continued to the front of the house.

There were fireplaces serving each of the four principal rooms, two each back-to-back sharing a chimney. Later, when the house was expanded, wings were added to both sides. Above the central portion of the house, a half story nestled in the steep gable provided additional living space for the family, and dormers illuminated this area of the master house.

Remarkably, an original contract between the

The plantation house at South Carolina's Eutaw was raised above a large basement. A distinctive brick arcade provided a pleasantly proportioned base at the ground level.

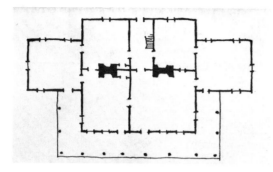

This early rough sketch details the floor plan of Eutaw's principal dwelling. The central portion of the plantation house was of a modified central hall plan, with the front parlor encompassing the area where the central hall would have traditionally been placed. The rear of the house had a central stair hall. The symmetrical side wings and the wraparound piazza were probably added later.

Eutaw's intricately embellished fireplaces complemented the home's equally detailed moldings, doorway trims, wainscotings, and other finishes.

The Sinklers' home at Eutaw Plantation showcased an inviting façade, with a broad, wraparound porch and three symmetric dormers peeking through the roof.

builder, Benjamin King, and the Sinklers still exists. For the total sum of $450, the builder was to provide:

> [A house] forty feet in length, and thirty nine feet in breadth, one and a half story high, the first story to be twelve feet in the clear . . . The two front rooms are to be finished with flat paneling chairboard high, beaded within, with capping & molding above, and wash boards below, with double architraves to the doors and windows, and a chimney piece and breast work suitable thereto . . . The Piazza to be the length of the house and ten feet wide in the clear, to have a neat floor tongued and grooved, five columns and two half columns against the house . . . and to have a flight of steps at each and descending to the grounds with newels, rails, ballisters.[29]

By 1842, William Sinkler's son Charles had married Emily Wharton of Philadelphia. A navy man, Charles spent much time away from his wife. He established her at Eutaw Plantation with his family, and she quickly became accustomed to life on the plantation. Her letters—mostly to her family in Philadelphia—provide a fascinating glimpse of antebellum life in this isolated estate.

Of the plantation house itself, Emily wrote: "You cannot think how nice every thing is here. The house is very pretty outside. Down stairs is the dining room and drawing room. On the left wing is my room and Mr. Sinkler's dressing room [Emily always referred to her husband as 'Mr. Sinkler'], and on the right wing is Eliza's room and her father's. I am sitting now in the drawing room with a little table drawn before a large oak fire with two tall spermaceti candles writing on a perfect sandal wood desk which came out in the Columbia from Charleston."[30]

Outside the mansion, there were numerous outbuildings and slave cabins. One particularly interesting structure was known as the Lodge. It was a small cabin that sat in front of the house facing the broad alley of trees leading to the mansion. The Lodge, a wood frame building, was designed in the pattern of a small Greek temple, with a beautiful four-columned portico and crowning pediment. Its original use was said to have been as a workplace for a planter-physician member of the family who used the building as a medical office.[31]

Life for the Sinklers was one of great privilege and luxury on their plantation. Emily provided a vivid view of daily life at Eutaw in a letter written to her family in Philadelphia on December 5, 1842:

> Breakfast is from half-past 8 to quarter of 9. I get up after 7. Mr. Sinkler five mornings out of seven gets up at four or five and mounts a horse and goes off to shoot wild ducks or deer or foxes. All the family assembles at 9:30 for family prayers. There is a great variety of hot cakes, waffles, biscuits. I don't take to all these varieties however and always eat toast for breakfast and supper. They make excellent wheat bread and toast it very nicely by the coals. Hominy is a most favorite dish. They eat it at all three meals. It is what is called grits in Philadelphia. We take breakfast in the hall and sit there all the morning.
>
> Soon after breakfast our little carriage comes to the door and we set off to take a drive. The whole equipage is quite *comme il faut*. The carriage is perfectly plain just holding two persons. The horses are very dark brown with plain black harness. When we set out the dogs come running up so we have a cortege of two greyhounds and two terriers generally, one a perfect creature looking like a little horse; not much esteemed by the family. I have named him Spry. We are always preceded by Sampson on horseback to open gates. We are home at 12 or 1 and I then read and sew etc. until dinner time.
>
> Mr. Sinkler goes off with his brothers to hunt and shoot partridges until dinner. They are always as you see on horseback. But you would be surprised to see how different Mr. Sinkler looks. He has grown fat already and has an excellent color.
>
> We dine between half-past 3 and 4. Eliza is an excellent housekeeper. The ice cream here is really the best I ever tasted. After dinner I go out and feed the poultry which are now very well acquainted with me and are exceedingly obstreperous if I am late, stand-

ing at the foot of the steps and calling vociferously. I have a great favorite among them, the frizzly fowl. Its feathers are all put on the wrong way, which gives it the most ridiculous look. We have supper at 8 or half-past which is very much like breakfast except we have cold meat and after the cloth is removed wine and cordials. In the evening we have music, both piano and guitar.[32]

Emily's letters also provided vivid descriptions of the Christmas events that took place at Eutaw. Specifically she describes how the family would gather at the plantation mansion and allow the slaves three full days of leisure away from the grueling work in the fields. During this time, the family allowed the slaves from all of the Sinkler plantations the use of the master house's large piazza as a dance hall. Fiddlers and other slave musicians would provide entertainment and all the slaves would dance tirelessly. Inside, the Sinkler family exchanged numerous, expensive presents. The entire holiday season was a time of great celebration and rejoicing. Emily wrote:

> Early on Christmas morning before break of the day the Negroes began to arrive from the different plantations of Mr. Sinkler and I was soon awakened by loud knocking on my door and then "Merry Christmas Masse Charles, may you have a many many years. Merry Christmas Miss Emily, long life and prosperity to you." They went to every door in the house and made some such speech . . . As soon as I came out of my room I was surrounded by all the House Servants eager to catch me. That is to say Merry Christmas, etc. first. Such laughing and screaming you never heard. Before breakfast everyone takes a glass of egg-nog, and a slice of cake . . .

The Christmas holidays were not the only times of jovial celebration. The Sinklers quite regularly celebrated the racing victories of their many steeds. Like some other southern plantations, Eutaw was a landmark site of horse racing. Here famed horses were bred and trained by a black trainer called Hercules. Interestingly, Hercules has gone down in South Carolina equestrian history as one of the most well-known and successful trainers to date.

But the celebrations and gaiety the Sinklers so enjoyed were not to last forever. The Civil War changed everything. During the war, Colonel Alfred Stedman Hartwell marched his troops upon Eutaw. He took the plantation mansion as his headquarters, allowing the frightened women to reside in the attic. Hartwell transformed one of the plantation's outbuildings into a hospital for his wounded soldiers, and it is said that two of these soldiers were buried on the plantation property.

Hartwell, newly elected to his high rank, found favor among his troops by exercising little discipline and allowing much freedom among them. It is said that the troops camped on both sides of the broad alley leading to the plantation. Here, accompanied by the newly freed, former slaves of the plantation, the enlisted men drank much, fought amongst themselves often, and generally caused as many disruptions and problems as they could. Nightly, the Sinkler women watched from the high dormers of their mansion as the soldiers' band played loud, jovial music and former slaves danced in the avenue of oaks.

Despite the change of culture and economics that came with Reconstruction, the Sinklers maintained ownership of their plantation home. Without their enslaved labor force, they never again realized the massive profits that they enjoyed before the war, but they managed to keep Eutaw agriculturally and economically lucrative.

The Sinklers continued to live at Eutaw until the early 1940s, when the South Carolina Public Service Authority implemented the Santee Cooper hydroelectric project, inundating over 160,000 acres of land with waters from the Santee and Cooper rivers. The plantation mansion was destroyed in anticipation of the project, and today the plantation property and its historic cemetery lie silently submerged in the dark floor of massive Lake Marion.

# *Springfield*

Springfield Plantation House, built 1817–1818, was at one time a landmark of Upper St. John's Parish and was renowned for its intricate woodwork. It was once the seat of the Palmer family, who retained ownership of the estate throughout nearly all of its history. Like its neighbors, Springfield was submerged by Lake Marion during the construction of the Santee Cooper project.[33]

The Palmer family of Berkeley County, South Carolina, traces its American origins to ancestor Thomas Pamor, an English immigrant who left four children: Joseph, David, John, and Elizabeth. Thomas's son John settled Gravel Hill Plantation in St. Stephen's Parish and made a fortune in the turpentine industry, so much so that he became known as "Turpentine John." In his will, Turpentine John instructed that his progeny would change the spelling of their family name to "Palmer." Interestingly, the children complied, but retained the pronunciation of the original surname.

One of Turpentine John's sons, Thomas Palmer, along with his business associates, Isaac Couturier, obtained a land grant destined to become Springfield Plantation. Later, Thomas's brother Captain John Palmer purchased this property, although he never resided upon it. Instead, the captain lived at Richmond Plantation in St. Stephen's Parish. Although absent from the plantation, Palmer was active in its development. His journal contains many entries regarding "Springfield," including one as late as 1783, in which he notes that his workers were "planting indigo at Springfield."

The captain remained at Richmond Plantation until his death in 1817. At this time, Springfield Plantation was inherited by his son Joseph. This same year, on October 20, 1817, construction of a new plantation house began. There was apparently an older house at Springfield, but the exact dates of its existence are unknown. It was clear, however, that the new house that was to replace this older domicile would be grander in scale and ornamentation. The new plantation house was built by George Champlin and completed on June 17, 1818.

The plantation house was a two-story structure set atop a tall basement. The central portion of the house had five bays with a triple window in the center, above the elaborate double front door. A steep gabled roof above was pierced by two chimneys with decorative plaster necking. A one-story portico stretched the length of the central portion of the house. Its roof was supported by narrow turned columns. On either side of the house there were small one-story wings with front porches supported with square shafts.

The plan of the house was simple yet elegant. Two large front parlors abutted one another. Each one was accessible from one of the two closely placed double front doors. Behind each of these large parlors a slightly smaller room existed. Between these smaller rooms there was a stair hall with a large closet. These back rooms led to a back porch that spanned the length of the home's central portion. One-story, one-room wings flanked the main house. These wings were connected to each side by doorways in both the front parlor and back room. There were six fireplaces on the first floor, with those in each parlor sharing a chimney with the fireplaces in the associated smaller back rooms.

The interior of the main house—covered with intricate woodwork and carvings—was noted among local plantation houses for its exquisite attention to detail. Dentil cornices, richly detailed wainscoting, and elaborate doorframes adorned the inside of the dwelling. Especially celebrated were the fireplace mantels and overmantels with their meticulously crafted pilasters and multiple sunburst motifs. The house's ornate interior provided an amazing example of the high-quality workmanship of skilled slaves in the antebellum South.

Outside the master house, the usual outbuildings were found. Shops, barns, and slave cabins dotted the plantation landscape with fields beyond. A kitchen building was located a few hundred feet from the main structure. It contained a large brick

Springfield Plantation, home to the Palmer family of South Carolina, boasted a handsome master house with a broad front porch and a variety of detailing. The house was raised above a brick basement, and the side wings, especially, boasted intricate embellishments around the exterior doors and windows.

An example of the elaborate and ornate fireplaces found at Springfield Plantation.

The ruins of an old brick oven at Springfield Plantation.

oven, whose ruins were still extant at the time the plantation was destroyed.

The Springfield Plantation house became one of the many icons of local agricultural success, and it owner, Joseph Palmer, grew to be one of the most well-respected citizens of the area. It is noted that few individuals served as executor of so many wills. Palmer was assiduous, exacting, and trustworthy, and friends, family, and acquaintances put their trust in him to administer the enactment of their last wishes.

After Joseph Palmer's death, his children inherited the plantation. The Palmers continued living at Springfield until the construction of the Santee Cooper Hydroelectric and Navigation Project, which flooded the plantation, creating Lake Marion and submerging the house.

## Stoney-Baynard

Sandwiched between Baynard Park Road and Plantation Drive on South Carolina's Hilton Head Island, the ruins of Stoney-Baynard Plantation attract many visitors. Also known as Braddock's Point, the plantation was once home to the Stoney family, until it was acquired by William Eddings Baynard, in a poker game, local legend says. Today, the tattered tabby remains of the estate have been made into a public park in honor of the plantation's illustrious history.[34]

The land that later made up the Braddock's Point Plantation was originally owned by John Bayley, but was confiscated and auctioned in 1782. It was purchased by a popular Beaufort merchant, John Mark Verdier, and Thomas Fergusson, although the Bayley family may later have regained control of the property. It is thought that sometime around the beginning of the nineteenth century the estate was acquired by Captain John Stoney and Captain James Stoney, both Charleston merchants.

At some point in time—likely between 1800 and 1815—the Stoneys constructed a large dwelling house on the plantation property. This was the height of Beaufort's first cotton boom that would likely have coincided with much new construction in the region as profits were made and fortunes swelled.

Through careful examination of the vestiges of the main house and thorough archeological study, researchers have pieced together what the house was like. It is clear that the master dwelling was rectangular in form, measuring 40.5 by 46.5 feet, with the exterior walls being constructed of tabby measuring nearly two feet wide. The house was thought to have been built atop a raised basement, and probably stood about seventeen feet tall. A hipped roof likely topped the sturdy structure, while nine-foot-wide porches surrounded at least three (and likely all four) sides. The exterior of the house was covered with at least two coats of oyster shell lime stucco, with the outer coat being scored to resemble stonework. Inside, a central hall was flanked by other interior spaces, but the exact layout of the rooms is unknown.

Several generations of the Stoney family lived in the large master house, including Dr. George Mosse Stoney, who apparently willed the estate to his eldest son, known as "Saucy Jack." Local legend claims that Saucy Jack lost the plantation to William Eddings Baynard in all-night poker game; however, the accuracy of this is questionable. In information compiled by the Chicora Foundation, it appears that the Stoney family lost the house under financial duress from creditors, when it was acquired by the Bank of Charleston in 1842. It was sold to William E. Baynard in 1845, according to Chicora. At this time, the plantation encompassed approximately twelve hundred acres.

William Baynard died four years later, and the plantation was inherited by his son, Ephraim. By this time, maps of the plantation clearly illustrate that while the master house and its dependencies were largely unchanged, the plantation's slave village had diminished in size, then including a total of ten cabins in two discontinuous, parallel rows. The map also shows seven larger structures in a scattered cluster, likely representing barns and shops, etc.[35]

During the Civil War, the Stoney-Baynard Plantation fell into Union hands at the Battle of Port Royal in 1861. It was sold for unpaid taxes equaling eighty dollars plus penalties in 1863, and was said to be valued at that time at four thousand dollars (over eighty-two thousand dollars in 2007 dollars).[36]

The plantation was purchased at auction by the United States government for a sum of $845. It is likely that the plantation was the victim of much looting at this time, as neighboring estates were being ravaged for any valuables they might contain. The house was used as a dwelling house for soldiers who likely furthered its decline.

The master house fell victim to fire in 1867, and was never occupied again. The plantation property was subdivided and sold in 1893, and by the 1950s, the site of the ruinous master house was acquired by the Hilton Head Company. It was later passed to the Sea Pines Plantation, which planned a recreational area around the storied plantation ruins.

Today, the ruins are open to the public and provide a popular local attraction, complete with interpretive signage and other amenities. Also, in recent years, much archeological investigation has been undertaken at the ruin's site, supported by the Chicora Foundation, a Columbia, South Carolina, nonprofit heritage preservation organization founded in 1983. The Chicora Foundation has also created publications based on their findings of this important historical site. Through research, archeology, and public involvement, the memory of the Stoney-Baynard Plantation lives on even as the majority of the historic estate's built environment has been lost to time.

## White Hall

Another historic plantation submerged under Lake Moultrie during the construction of the Santee Cooper Hydroelectric and Navigation Project was White Hall, home to several families over the years including the Porchers and the Whites.

White Hall was located on the south side of Ferguson Swamp between Hanover and Ophir plantations in Berkeley County, South Carolina. The first extant record of the plantation comes from 1774, when owner Blake Leay White transferred eight slaves to the commissioner of high roads. The estate, however, was likely much older, and it is thought that White was probably born there in 1748.[37]

In addition to the usual agricultural enterprises, there was also a tavern at White Hall that served weary travelers along the Congaree Road. Similar taverns could be found in colonial days along roads at more or less regular intervals between Charleston and the so-called "Upcountry."

Blake Leay White was eventually elected commissioner of high roads for St. John's Parish, a position in which he played a prominent role in local affairs. His son, John Blake White, found much distinction as an artist—today several of his paintings hang in the Senate wing of the U.S. Capitol.

The plantation was eventually sold to Thomas Porcher, of Ophir Plantation, who built a mansion there for his son, Thomas. The original house was a raised two-story with a gable roof and eighteen large windows. The windows on the front of the house were embellished with paneled shutters, while those on the side had louvered ones. The exterior of the house was covered with weatherboarding. Inside, the plan of the original block was simple. A wide central stair hall was flanked by large parlors on either side. The second story likely boasted a similar arrangement.

The house was situated in the middle of a very large yard punctuated with numerous and massive oaks. A tranquil pond rested to one side of the mansion. Beyond, fields blanketed the horizon that was dotted with slave cabins, barns, and production buildings.

Finding success with an estate of his own, Thomas Porcher married Catherine Gaillard, the daughter of Captain Peter Gaillard of The Rocks, another lost plantation once located near Eutawville. Their daughter, Elizabeth, married Dr. Charles Lucas, who expanded White Hall's mansion greatly. Dr.

White Hall Plantation master house. Here Dr. Charles Lucas's large perpendicular addition can be appreciated.

White Hall Plantation master house. Dr. Charles Lucas's expansions can be seen, including the perpendicular addition and the front porch. The house sat atop a raised brick basement.

White Hall Plantation master house. Intricate woodwork surrounded doors throughout the home.

White Hall Plantation master house. This is a fine example of the detailed hand-carved fireplace mantels and moldings that could be found in the house.

Lucas undertook his expansion in 1854, adding a large, perpendicular wing to the main house. The new wing contained a large entrance hall, which abutted and opened onto the stair hall at a right angle. Opposite this, the new entrance hall gave way to an enormous dining room or ballroom with a great bay window at the end.

Outside, Dr. Lucas built a one-story, raised piazza around the front of the new wing and the exposed front of the older one. The piazza was supported by four stout square pillars. It is said that the home's expansion was undertaken with such care and attention to detail that it was impossible to locate the seams that melded the new wing to the older construction.

Inside, the new wing contained what was said to be the finest and most exquisite woodwork found in the region, equaled only by that found in the double parlors at nearby Ophir Plantation. It has long been thought that these interior spaces were crafted by the same artisan, especially considering the similar motifs. This would seem likely as it was the Porcher family who commissioned both houses.

The plantation and its agricultural enterprises faced great upheaval during the Civil War. Of particular concern for the family was the fear of former slaves rebelling against the woefully outnumbered white masters. In her diary, Charlotte Ravenel recounts: "March 10, 1865. We received notes from White Hall and Sarazins and also a letter from Alice Palmer. Quite a treat. The White Hall negroes behaved shamefully; they rushed into the house, tore down the curtains, carried off the bedding and blankets and trunks, and are grumbling now that they have not enough. We hear that one man asked Cousin Marianne [Miss Marianne E. Porcher] to step out and take a dance, that they were all equal now."[38]

Obviously, status changes brought by freedom represented huge social shifts for the Porchers and surrounding families, as former white masters relinquished their paternalistic and dictatorial roles. Former chattels were now free men, and the concept of equality seemed too much for the Porchers.

Despite the vast changes wrought by the war, descendants of Elizabeth Porcher and Dr. Charles Lucas remained at White Hall until the early 1940s, when the plantation and its physical structures were inundated by the waters of Lake Moultrie during the creation of the Santee Cooper Hydroelectric and Navigation Project. Today, the fine woodwork and craftsmanship of the plantation house is remembered in faded photos and a few brief lines found in old books; otherwise, White Hall is but a memory, its legacy largely lost under the murky waters of time.

## The Rocks

Built in the first years of the nineteenth century by Peter Gaillard, the mansion at The Rocks Plantation near Eutawville was threatened with destruction like many others by the Santee Cooper project, but was narrowly saved when J. Rutledge Conner moved it, along with several other plantation buildings, about a mile and a half away. Sadly, while it survived inundation by the waters of Lake Moultrie, the house was destroyed by fire in 1992.

The conflicts of the American Revolution and postwar economic shifts left Captain Peter Gaillard and other indigo planters largely broke. In 1794, in an attempt to reestablish his wealth and feed his dozens of slaves, Gaillard purchased lands in Upper St. John's Parish that would later be home to The Rocks. He initially sought to plant crops for consumption, but soon after the invention of the cotton gin, Gaillard became the first planter in the area to successfully produce cotton.

By the beginning of the nineteenth century, Gaillard was reaping a handsome profit and had paid off all of his debts. With his agricultural enterprises flourishing, the captain began construction on his plantation mansion, which was built between 1803 and 1805. Gaillard kept a meticulous journal of his activities at the plantation. It can be found today microfilmed in the Peter Gaillard Plantation Records at the University of North Carolina at Chapel Hill. Here the planter notes that on September 1, 1803, he began to make bricks for his home, and in May of the same year he was overseeing the production of shingles from cypress. One large tree yielded some sixty-five hundred shingles. On November 21, 1803, Gaillard hired a "Mr. Walker" as carpenter for $1.50 per day. And, by February of the next year, the first bricks of the foundation were laid. On April 4, 1804, the workmen began to raise the house, while other materials were being made in the "North." In July 1804, the second coat of paint was added, and finishing touches were completed in early 1805.

The finished house was quite a showpiece. It was a two-story structure with a broad front porch that spanned the width of the home's five bays. Six Tuscan columns rose from the porch to the one story overhang covering it. Two large chimneys framed the tall hipped roof. Inside, the first floor featured side-by-side double front parlors with side-by-side twin front doors (one opening into each parlor). The parlors opened onto a central stair hall that was flanked by two smaller rooms on the side. The rear of the stair hall opened to a rear entrance hall which was likewise flanked by two even smaller rooms. This rear entrance hall and two back rooms likely represented a later addition.

The erection of the house and the affairs there were also dutifully recorded by the owner. And, as with the meticulous documentation in his journal, Captain Gaillard approached nearly every aspect of his life and work with precision, impeccable organization, and poise. It was said of Gaillard in the memoirs of Frederick Augustus Porcher: "His reputation as a planter was immense. As long as I lived in the country I heard his opinion quoted, even by those who never had known him, and it was considered presumptuous in any one to act in opposition to his practice."[39]

Peter Gaillard married Elizabeth Porcher, daughter of Peter Porcher of Peru. Together they had eight children. As the children grew up and Gaillard grew wealthier, he gave each of his five sons a plantation and each of his three daughters a house in Charleston. Of the sons, Peter received Heyden Hill (also known as Iron Head), James was given Laurel Hill, Thomas was given Walnut Grove (Thomas and James later traded their plantations), David was given Belmont, and Samuel was given The Rocks, when his father retired to Charleston.[40]

Samuel, however was not to be master for long, dying unexpectedly at the young age of twenty-nine. His daughter Elizabeth inherited the house and she and her husband, James Gaillard, Jr., of Walnut Grove Plantation (also her cousin) ran the estate.

Despite all of the family's holdings, The Rocks was always the flagship of the Gaillard clan's homes. It was here that the family gathered for important occasions and for festive events. Christmas was a very special time at the plantation, as noted in the memoirs of a Gaillard family member, Mrs. A. P. Leise Palmer Gaillard. She writes of the feast:

> At one end of the table, a turkey stuffed with spinach (the housegirl or cook plucked a huge dishpan of spinach and washed it thoroughly, then as much butter as was conveniently spared probably a half pound or maybe a little more was put in a big frying pan on the stove, the spinach dumped into it and as many eggs as you could muster stirred into that, and then stirred and stirred until that mass of spinach and egg made a gigantic pile of green scrambled egg, and you stuffed the turkey). At the other end of the table another turkey stuffed with the more usual bread crumbs, egg, etc. At various places along the table were a boiled ham, a large one, a huge roast of mutton, leg and loin, from four to six boiled chickens big ones with a very rich sauce with hard boiled eggs stirred up in it, dishes piled with snowy rice. I asked Mary once how much rice did she have cooked for that dinner, and she said a peck of raw rice, and a negro from the negro quarters cooked it out in the yard in an iron wash pot. In addition there were big pans of macaroni, sweet potatoes, Irish potatoes, creamed artichokes sometimes, glass dishes of whole artichoke pickles, a decanter of whiskey and two or three decanters of wine. Then for dessert; Charlotte Russe, wine jelly and Syllabub, and always four kinds of pie coconut, lemon, mince, and sweet potato. I don't remember whether there was cake or not, perhaps I was just too full to be impressed by it.[41]

The Rocks Plantation House was saved from the floodwaters of the Santee Cooper project, only to be destroyed by fire in 1992.

Another important social aspect of life at The Rocks revolved around the various tilts and tournaments held there in the decades following the Civil War. It was here that young men showed off their skills at horsemanship and sport, while, of course, attempting to impress young women. A competitive cavalry company known as the Eutaw Light Dragoons annually competed on the plantation grounds against the Charleston Light Dragoons. The teams competed for a silver cup, and after the exercises and competitions were over, there was always a large ball held in the master house. The "knight" who earned the highest score on the mock field of battle had the distinction of crowning the queen of the ball.

An article in the December 31, 1892, edition of the *News and Courier* recalled: "A delicious dinner was served and eaten by the Dragoons, the air and exhilarating exercise having given their appetite as keen as edge as their saber . . . The ball was a brilliant affair and was successful in every particular. It took place at Mr. James Gaillard's residence and was well attended. Charleston sent some of her loveliest daughters who were much admired by the Eutaws, and the graceful and beautiful daughters of St. John's captured the hearts of the Charleston soldiers."

The history of these games sheds light onto the structured social life of the region, but it also speaks of the general economic condition of the area in the decades following the war. Conditions may have been relatively difficult compared to the antebellum era, but there was still time and resources afforded for competitive sports and elaborate social gatherings.

A few decades later, in 1900, the plantation was damaged by a destructive storm. At this time, boards on the front of the house were replaced and other repairs were made. Soon after, a rear addition—including an attached kitchen, bath, and porch—was built.

James and Elizabeth Gaillard sold the plantation to T. L. Conner in 1907. He later gave it to his son, J. Rutledge Conner. In 1927, the younger Conner added modern plumbing and electricity throughout the house.

The Rocks Plantation. Interior staircase.

The interior of the Rocks Plantation House was elegant and refined, as seen in this beautiful hand-carved mantel.

The Rocks Plantation. Double slave cabin.

The smokehouse at the Rocks Plantation was one of the many outbuildings that was moved in order to be saved from inundation by the waters of the Santee Cooper project.

In the years that followed, the 1930s and early 1940s, The Rocks, like many other historic estates in the area, was greatly threatened by the Santee Cooper project. The hydroelectric and navigation project eventually inundated the plantation lands, and would have similarly flooded the plantation house had it not been for J. Rutledge Connor, who at great personal expense had the plantation house, slave quarters, smokehouse, and several other plantation buildings moved to nearby Belmont Plantation, approximately 1.6 miles away.

Decades later, in 1976, portions of the plantation grounds that were spared from the Santee Cooper flood along with bodies of water created by it were opened as the Rocks Pond Campground, a successful enterprise that is still operating today.

Fifty years after The Rocks plantation house was saved from inundation by floodwaters of the Santee Cooper project, the historic home caught fire and was destroyed. The 1992 conflagration brought with it an end to the hopes for preservation that had been enacted by J. Rutledge Connor, and the beloved family home of the famed Gaillard clan was gone. The plantation house was officially removed from the National Register of Historic Places in 2000.

# Devereux

Devereux, also known as Runiroi (Uniroy or Runiroy) Plantation once was the principal plantation of the Devereux and Pollock families of North Carolina. Today, after the destruction of the master house by fire, the estate is largely a fading memory.

The estate, which was situated in Bertie County exactly 2.25 miles from Hill's ferry on a road that led to Woodville, was originally owned by Thomas Pollock III and his wife, Eunice Edwards. She was the daughter of famed New England preacher Jonathan Edwards and Sarah Pierrepont.[42]

Thomas Pollock III died in 1777, leaving Eunice a widow. She eventually moved to New Bern and married Robert Hunt. Runiroi passed to Thomas and Eunice's daughter Francis, as all of their sons had died at a young age before having children. Francis Pollock married John Devereux. The estate later passed to John Devereux, Jr., and his wife, Margaret Lane Mordecai.

Margaret recorded much of the history of Runiroi, which became known as the Devereux Plantation, in her recollections, originally meant to be a few scattered memoirs that she hoped to read to her grandchildren. The writings, however, were so engaging that they caught the attention of many, including Arthur Winslow, who decided to publish them. In the introduction to the book Margaret Devereux writes:

> TO MY GRANDCHILDREN. As the "New South," with all its changes and improvements, rises above the horizon, those whose hearts still cling to the "Old South" look sadly backward and sigh to see it fade away into dimness, to be soon lost to sight and to live only in the memory of the few. Hoping to rescue from oblivion a few of the habits, thoughts, and feelings of the people who made our South what it

was, I have drawn from memory a few pen sketches of plantation life, based upon actual events, in which are recorded some of the good and even noble traits of character which were brought forth under the yoke of slavery.[43]

The Devereuxs were quite successful planters, having amassed some seven or eight large plantations and well over fifteen hundred slaves. The plantations included such estates as Conacanarra, Feltons, Looking Glass, Montrose, Polenta, and Barrows, among others. The Devereuxs made their summer home at Conacanarra, but Devereux Plantation was their principal estate. Margaret describes seeing the plantation upon their return following the family's summer absence: "From Kehukee bluff, which we usually visited while waiting for the ferryman on our return journey after the summer's absence, the plantation could be seen stretching away into the distance, hemmed in by the flat-topped cypresses. From there we had a view of our distant dwelling, gleaming white in the sunlight and standing in a green oasis of trees and grass, all looking wonderfully small amid the expanse of flat fields around it."[44]

The master house at Devereux was a rather simple dwelling, considering the family's great wealth. It was a plain symmetrical and boxy five-bay structure with virtually no ornamentation or adornment whatsoever. The two-story master house was topped by a simple gable roof and was framed by two chimneys. There were no porches, no columns, no eaves or overhangs at all. Margaret describes the house in her book: "The house at Runiroi was a comfortable, old, rambling structure, in a green yard and flower garden, not ugly, but quite innocent of any pretensions at comeliness."[45] Surrounding the house, the large variety of outbuildings could be found:

> Every plantation had a set of buildings which included generally the overseer's house, ginhouse, screw, barn, stable, porkhouse, smokehouse, storehouse, carpenter's shop, blacksmith shop, and loomhouse, where the material for clothing for each plantation was woven,—white cloth for the underclothes,

and very pretty striped or checked for outer garments. At Runiroi, the weaver, Scip, was a first-class workman, and very proud of his work. I often had sets of very pretty towels woven in a damask pattern of mixed flax and cotton. The winter clothing was of wool, taken from our own sheep.[46]

Our dairy was very pretty; it was built of immense square logs, with a paved brick floor, and great broad shelves all around. The roof was shaded by hackberry trees . . .[47]

The dwellings of the negroes were quite a distance from the "Great House," as that of the master was called, and were built in two or more long rows with a street between. This was the plan upon every plantation. Each house had a front and back piazza, and a garden, which was cultivated or allowed to run wild according to the thrift of the residents. It generally was stocked with peach and apple trees, and presented a pretty picture in spring, when the blue smoke from the houses curled up to the sky amid the pink blossoms, while the drowsy hum of a spinning-wheel seemed to enhance the quiet of the peaceful surroundings.[48]

The Devereux slaves enjoyed a lifestyle that, while restrictive, was not as severe as those of some of their counterparts on other plantations. Slaves on the estate were allowed to use their free time to trap otter, raccoon, and mink. They sold the skins from these animals to make supplemental income. Other slaves kept beehives—some as many as thirty—and sold honey and beeswax to generate extra money. All of the slaves were given the basic necessities of life, and additionally the Devereuxs provided sweet potatoes and other foodstuffs to supplement the slaves' diet.

Religion was an integral part of life on the Devereux estate, and the plantation had its own large church. Here slaves and white family members gathered each Sunday to worship. A large bell that hung from a branch in an oak tree outside the church beaconed the faithful. Every other Sunday, a chaplain from town would come to lead the service, but on alternate Sundays, Jim Carpenter, a trusted slave, gave the sermon. It is said that the slaves much preferred the services led by one of their own.

Life on the plantation revolved around work for the slaves, but the white masters enjoyed more leisure. Margaret Devereux recalls the lazy days spent upon the "fishing porch":

> One of my pleasant memories is connected with our fishing porch. This was a porch, or balcony, built upon piles driven into the river upon one side, and the other resting upon the banks. It was raised some eight or ten feet above the water and protected by a strong railing or balustrade and shaded by the overhanging branches of a large and beautiful hackberry tree. It made an ideal lounging-place, upon a soft spring afternoon, when all the river banks were a mass of tender green, and the soft cooing of doves filled the air. We usually took Minor [young slave boy] with us to bait our hooks and assist generally, and often went home by starlight with a glorious string of fish.[49]

Life for the Devereuxs changed in dramatic and positive ways with the boom in steamboat traffic in the early nineteenth century. Steamers opened lines of commerce and communication beyond the dreams of the family. Goods could be purchased, crops could be shipped, and much trade could commence. The family placed a standing order with one reputable bookseller who would regularly select and send a variety of books and printed materials to them. They also placed special orders for books. The steamboat opened new worlds for the family, socially, materially, and financially.

But within a few short decades the prosperity and plenty brought by the steamboats would crumble. As the Civil War encroached, the Devereaux family fled to Raleigh, where they sought refuge from the conflict. After the war, the family was devastated financially, but the plantation persisted. The master house escaped destruction by the Union forces and went on to survive more than a century longer as a private home and beloved cultural treasure in Bertie County. Sadly, the house was destroyed by fire in the second half of the twentieth century, leaving little behind but memories.

# CHAPTER FOUR

# Georgia

You have to know the past to understand the present.

—*Carl Sagan*

The events of human life, whether public or private, are so intimately linked to architecture that most observers can reconstruct nations *or individuals* in all the truth of their habits from the remains of their public monuments or from their domestic relics.

—*Honoré de Balzac*

The earliest foundations of Georgia rest in the philanthropic ideals of its notable founder, James Oglethorpe. Oglethorpe, a military leader and member of the English Parliament, visited a friend who was imprisoned for debts, and there he found conditions to be quite atrocious. He petitioned for parliamentary investigations and later pressed for debtors to be freed. He envisioned a colony that would provide homes for such debtors, along with persecuted Protestants and other disenfranchised subjects. Because his colony would serve doubly as a populated barrier protecting the northward colonies of the British from the Spanish in Florida and the French in Louisiana, it gained widespread support.

In 1732, Oglethorpe and his colleague John Percival secured a royal charter to establish the colony, which was named after King George II. They assembled a board of trustees to govern it. The next year Oglethorpe arrived with the first settlers and soon after established Savannah. Initially, Oglethorpe and the trustees sought to create silk and wine industries in their colony. Early settlers were provided land to cultivate, along with livestock and equipment. They were also provided with mulberry trees, silkworms, and grapevines. Unfortunately, silkworms did not proliferate in the Georgia climate, and the grapevines wilted.

Originally, the trustees forbade slavery, but when they relinquished control of Georgia in the early 1750s, much changed. James Wright was appointed governor and heralded a period of unprecedented economic and agricultural growth. By this time, restrictions on slavery had been lifted, and rice plantations flourished on Georgia's Atlantic coast on the great Sea Islands. Similar estates were actively farmed in tidewater regions along the Savannah, Ogeechee, Altamaha, and St. Mary's rivers. Wright himself operated some dozen rice plantations, so he was naturally a strong advocate for the thriving rice plantation economy. Inland, other planters found much success with indigo.

With rice and indigo thriving, most colonists were quite content in Georgia. But, even as British

sentiment was quite high, the colony sent representatives to the Second Continental Congress and joined the other colonies in the American Revolution against England. British troops attempted to seize Savannah in 1778, but local guerilla forces prevented them from doing so. In 1782, the British evacuated Georgia, and new economic and agricultural opportunities abounded under a new nation.

The turn of the nineteenth century brought even greater change. Eli Whitney invented the cotton gin on Nathanael Greene's Mulberry Grove, and his revolutionary machine became widely popularized. Cotton planting swept through central Georgia, and plantations proliferated. The forced removal of the native Creeks and the Cherokees by the federal government later opened up more cotton lands, spurring the industry forward even more.

Of course, the Civil War meant ruin for many of the great estates, their fields and architecture. As elsewhere in the South, with agriculture giving way to industry the built environments of plantations were forsaken for factories, and farm plots gave way to paper mills. Seven of Georgia's most notable lost plantation estates are featured here, but many more plantations were lost.

North End Plantation on Ossabaw Island was once home to Jim Morel, who established an indigo plantation there. All that is left are three slave cabins made of tabby, a mixture of lime, oyster shells, sand, and water. Today, archeologists are excavating large areas in and around the cabins and making remarkable physical and intellectual finds. For example, researchers found French-made gunflint near one cabin, indicating perhaps that trade with the French was more common than once realized.

Cannon's Point Plantation, the home of John Couper and his family, was found on St. Simons Island. Couper built his plantation mansion in 1804, and he lived there for many more years. Couper, an avid horticulturist, excelled in various experimental enterprises with exotic plants. On the urging of Thomas Jefferson, he acquired olive trees and soon produced fine olive oil. Couper died at the age of ninety-one in 1850, and his beloved plantation mansion burned to the ground about a half century later. Today, only a few brick ruins remain.

Edward Swarbeck built Chocolate Plantation around 1820 on Sapelo Island. He purchased the tract earlier from French royalists. The plantation, legend hails, got its distinctive name from a nearby Native American settlement called Chucalate. Later the plantation was purchased by Charles Rogers, and its master house burned in 1853, while being occupied by Randolf Spalding. Today, only the ruinous remains of fifteen of the plantation's tabby buildings can be seen.

Wormsloe Plantation, once the home of Noble Jones, on the Isle of Hope near Savannah, served as an important colonial fortification and agricultural estate. The tabby ruins of the original master house are preserved today in a state park.

Some of Georgia's plantation estates and mansions remain in good states of preservation, thanks to the proper stewardship of caretakers. Pebble Hill Plantation, near Thomasville, partially burned in 1934, but was swiftly rebuilt. Today, it operates as a house museum and hosts special functions. Jarrell Plantation, outside of Macon, was once a moderately sized six-hundred-acre estate that was worked by thirty-nine enslaved men and women. Planter John Fitz Jarrell built a simple house, sawmill, cotton gin, gristmill, shingle mill, sugar cane press, syrup evaporator, workshop, barn, and other outbuildings. In 1974, his descendants graciously donated these buildings and the plantation estate to the state of Georgia for the establishment of the Jarrell Plantation State Historic Site. Today, the public can tour the site and explore architecture and life on a medium-sized antebellum plantation.

Georgia's lost plantations, like those of all southern states, collectively have been neglected and forgotten by historians and the public alike. Their stories weave a rich tapestry of life and labor in the South that creates a fuller, more accurate description of antebellum history. The accounts of their decline likewise contribute to the understanding of the role of preservation or lack thereof in southern culture.

# Casulon

The white-columned Greek Revival mansion at Casulon Plantation in Walton County, Georgia, survived many trials in its nearly 180-year history. Imminent threats endangered the notable home numerous times throughout its long saga. But, unfortunately, it was in 2002, after a bitter struggle with a company determined to undermine the area's heritage, that this great landmark—the site of a Georgia governor's historic wedding—was reduced to ashes in a highly "suspicious" fire.

Casulon Plantation's history can be traced back to 1824, when it became one of the first structures to be built in Jones Woods. Joseph Moss commissioned James W. Harris[1] to oversee the construction of the plantation mansion. Enslaved people provided the bulk of physical labor during the construction. About fifteen years later Moss sought to move west, selling the plantation to Harris, the builder.[2]

The house itself was originally built with a plain front. A Greek Revival–style portico with six large columns was later added to the front, giving the house its characteristic façade. The house was built on a brick foundation, but the structure itself was of a wooden frame of heart pine with a metal roof.[3]

The interior of the house included a large entrance hall. In the moldings above this hall, the builders carved twelve stars representing the original colonies—all except Georgia, whose star could be found embedded in the stone walk leading to the gazebo in the garden. The house was surrounded by a number of support structures: a well house, root cellar, slave cabins, slave cemetery, tenant house, caretaker's house, blacksmith shop, corn crib, carriage house, and log house; remarkably, all survived into the twenty-first century.[4]

Casulon became the seat of a great agricultural empire, and at the helm of this operation was James Harris, who became a successful planter.

The Greek Revival mansion at Casulon Plantation, seen here peeking through lush formal gardens, survived many trials and tribulations, only to be destroyed in a highly "suspicious" fire in 2002.

C A-1110

By 1860, he owned over 130 slaves, and eventually commanded over ten thousand acres. Harris died on January 21, 1864, leaving his wife, Sarah Strong Thompson, and their two adult daughters, Susie and Mary, to administer the plantation during the ravages of the Civil War. Later Susie inherited the plantation. She married Georgia governor James S. Boynton[5] at Casulon in 1883. Boynton had been president of the state senate when Governor Alexander H. Stephens died in office. Boynton assumed the office, but later lost the governorship with the election of Henry D. McDaniel. Days after the election the magnificent wedding of James Boynton and Susie Harris commenced at the plantation.

The wedding itself was described as one of the grandest, most memorable in Georgia history. An article in the *Atlanta Constitution* about the wedding described the plantation: "The residence of the bride was a handsome country house in the midst of a grove of beautiful and stately oaks."[6]

Another article proclaimed, "The proverbial hospitality of the old home was displayed at its best in the royal bridal supper. The tables were decorated with flowers of the rarest and sweetest varieties and bore the most substantial charms of delicious viands . . ."[7]

The ceremony was preformed by Rev. Clement A. Evans and Rev. G. A. Nunnally. After their wedding, Susie and the governor boarded a train, making their way towards Atlanta for their honeymoon at the famed Kimball House hotel.[8] It is said that at every station along the way crowds of well-wishers gathered to glimpse the governor and his new bride.[9]

Eventually, the plantation passed into the hands of Sallie Maud Jones, the daughter of Mary Harris (Susie Harris's sister) and Dr. Daniel Chandler Jones. Sallie was a wealthy woman in her own right, who never married but remained at the house until she grew elderly and ill. During her years on the plantation she employed a chauffeur, who drove her around in a large black Cadillac. She also employed an African American woman called Aunt Sis Thompson, who lived in a former slave cabin. Sallie became well known throughout the area for her generosity and philanthropy. It is said that she funded the college education of many local students.[10]

During her tenure as proprietor, Jones saw the plantation dwindle both in size and economic might. The magnitude of property shrank from ten thousand acres to six thousand, while cotton production and sales wavered. Sallie Maud Jones died in 1948, and her nephews, Harris and Bannon Jones, inherited the estate. During the 1950s, the Jones brothers invited A. L. and Lauriee Williams to move in as caretakers of the estate. The Jones brothers sold Casulon to Armstrong Cork Company in 1968, who then scheduled the mansion for demolition.[11]

Hearing of the historic mansion's plight, the neighboring Morgan County Historical Society decided to take action. The group successfully negotiated for the donation of the property and fifteen surrounding acres. Having been long abandoned in rural isolation, the house was attracting a number of visitors, who caused great damage. Historical society member Colonel Zender Dean and his wife actually moved a small trailer near the home, camping out to discourage unwanted visitors. The society began renting out the house in the 1970s to a group of "hippies" who opened it up for tours, charging fifty cents for admission. But the society abandoned this practice when the renters threw one too many "wild parties."[12]

Having taken the fifty-cent tour, Wil and Janice Burrell Sommer fell in love with the house, and, after months of talks, persuaded the society to sell it. The society was reluctant to do this, but the house was becoming too much for the small organization of elderly citizens to manage. The new owners immediately began restoring the house to its previous grandeur; they were, however, oblivious to the coming trials ahead.

The couple's trouble started in the early 1990s, when Davidson Mineral Properties sought to begin a mining operation very near the plantation mansion. Afraid of the effect such a harsh industry would have on the plantation, the Sommers convinced the state environmental protection agency to deny a mining permit. This protection was overturned, but because the unique mansion was recognized as one of the most significant and historic in the state, the Georgia legislature modified the State Surface Mining Act to preserve this important piece of architecture.[13]

Davidson Mineral Properties was then bought by Hanson Aggregates of England, who began to aggressively renew efforts to start a quarry operation near the historic landmark, being all too aware of the blockade Casulon represented to their multimillion dollar efforts. As Hanson filed paperwork for the permits, the Sommers were facing a divorce. They placed their beloved plantation home on the market, asking $1.85 million for it. On March 25, 2002, while the Sommers were both out of state, a highly "suspicious" fire occurred at the rurally isolated mansion. Investigations determined the fire began near the back door of the mansion. The historic home went up in flames, being destroyed completely, along with several equally important outbuildings. Walton County sheriff Al Yarbrough said, "We're looking at this as a very suspicious fire." Who or what may have started the fire was never fully determined; however, another nearby historic home was also burned down not long before Casulon, while its owner, Mary Ellen Singleton, was away in Florida. Of the fire at Casulon, owner Janice Burrell said, "It's an enormous loss to me personally as well as the state of Georgia. It was an historic treasure . . . And if it were set deliberately, I'm appalled."[14]

Of course, these "suspicious" fires were extremely convenient for Hanson Aggregates officials, who were standing by to advocate ever more aggressively for their intrusive quarry. They eventually secured the final permits necessary to build their quarry, but as they did Janice Burrell and her neighbors fought even harder against the industry. "The fire has only strengthened the group's resolve," she said. Together the local citizens founded Walton-Oconee-Morgan Environmental Group Inc., an organization devoted to preserving the environment of the region while actively campaigning against the proposed Hanson Aggregates quarry.[15]

While the destruction of Casulon fuels the fiery rage against a big business seeking to invade a community, the memory of this historic house also echoes an era long lost. Many lessons can be learned from the rise and fall of this historic estate, and it is to be hoped that, for the citizens of Georgia, its tragic and "suspicious" loss will not be in vain.

# Mulberry Grove

About twelve miles from Savannah is the site of one of the most historic plantations in the country. It was at Nathanael Greene's Mulberry Grove Plantation that Eli Whitney designed and constructed the first cotton gin. This simple machine ushered in an economic boom that led to the "golden years" of the antebellum South, a time when wealthy planters ruled their estates like sovereign princes, slaves labored and suffered in fluffy, white fields, and the cash crop cotton was crowned "king."

Although it was cotton that gave Mulberry Grove its fame, it was the plantation's first major crop—silk—that gave the estate its name. In the mid 1730s, the property's first owner, Captain John Cuthbert, established a mulberry nursery on the site in order to cultivate silkworms. Cuthbert, along with several other Scottish gentlemen, began to improve this tract and some surrounding lands. Collectively, this settlement was known as Joseph's Town.[16]

By 1739, Cuthbert's Mulberry Grove contained thirty acres of crops, barns for cattle, several additional farm buildings, and a home for the captain and his sister. The plantation's growth was halted that same year when Captain Cuthbert died unexpectedly. His sister, Ann, inherited the plantation, and a year later, she married Dr. Patrick Graham. Ann Cuthbert had been a patient of Dr. Graham's. William Stephens reported the marriage to the trustees of the colony in the following manner: "Mrs. Cuthbert (Sister to the late Capt. Cuthbert, deceased) found his Patient dangerously ill in a Fever, at that Time a Lodger in his House; the Doctor

took the Opportunity of prescribing Matrimony to her, as a Specifick [sic] which he was sure would compleat [sic] her cure; and on consenting to take his advice in it, they were married at her late Brother's Plantation."[17]

Under Dr. Graham's administration the plantation flourished, earning a great profit for its owners. He continued cultivating mulberry trees on the estate, not only using them in his own cultivation of the silkworm, but selling the trees to his neighbors as well. He also profited from the woodlands surrounding the plantation, selling large amounts of timber for construction in Savannah. But Graham's most profitable enterprise was probably the rice he planted, of which he sent samples to London.

Interestingly, at this time slavery was prohibited in Georgia, so plantations like Mulberry Grove relied on the labor of white indentured servants. As the plantation economy expanded in the colony and the demand for a steady labor source grew, rules were changed to allow slavery. This represented an enormous shift for the plantations. At Mulberry Grove and elsewhere, the institution of slavery provided the needed labor to expand rice cultivation. Mulberry Grove's black slaves went to work building a massive system of drainage canals and irrigation channels for the rice fields. The cultivation of rice was exhausting, arduous labor, but as the economy surrounding this crop swelled, so did production.

As Graham led his plantation into the lucrative world of rice, his property and profits grew, as did his popularity. Throughout his tenure as planter, Dr. Graham was awarded various political appointments and offices. He served on the Governor's Council, as an official agent to distribute "presents" to the Indians, and as an "assistant" in the civil government. In 1755, at the very height of his political and entrepreneurial success, Graham died.

Three years later, Ann Graham married James Bulloch, a classics scholar and planter from South Carolina. He continued the agricultural operation at Mulberry Grove that Anne's first husband had so eagerly nurtured. Anne Graham Bulloch died in

1764; a few years later James Bulloch sold his wife's plantation to his own son-in-law, Josiah Perry.

Less than a year after his purchase, Perry sold Mulberry Grove, along with adjacent lands he had purchased, to John Graham. Graham, who was not related to Dr. Patrick Graham, was a member of the King's Council, later serving as lieutenant governor of Georgia. Under his care, Mulberry Grove was greatly expanded. Graham added new lands, purchased more slaves, and increased production significantly.

Newspapers from the era give a glimpse into the slave culture of the plantation. In 1775, Graham published advertisements for runaway slaves in the *Georgia Gazette.* Cuffy, Stepney, and Robin were male runaways for whom Graham offered rewards. They were described as wearing white jackets and pants with white metal buttons. The advertisement stated, "They have not been above five months in the province, cannot speak English and will probably not be able to tell their Master's or Overseer's name."[18]

In 1776, John Graham was forced to abandon his plantation. He was a loyalist, and, as a revolutionary spirit filled the hearts of many who longed for independence from Britian, Graham fled. He returned to Georgia in 1779, in order to take his place as lieutenant governor and president of the council. Mulberry Grove, however, was in shambles and all the slaves had run away. As the Revolution mounted and the patriots' success was evident, Graham was stripped of all his property and forced to flee again.

It was not until the Revolutionary War had ended that Mulberry Grove once again became a thriving plantation. The property was presented to war hero Major General Nathanael Greene for his honorable service. By this time the plantation totaled 2,171 acres. In a letter Greene wrote: "We found the house, situation, and the out buildings, more convenient and pleasing than we expected. The prospect is delightful, and the house magnificent. We have a coachhouse and stables, a large out-kitchen, and a poultry-house nearly fifty feet long, and twenty feet wide, parted for different kinds of poultry, with a pigeon-house on the top, which will contain not less than a thousand pigeons."[19]

By 1786, Greene had the plantation back in order and planting was under way. At that time he wrote: "We have got upwards of sixty acres of corn planted, and expect to have one hundred and thirty of rice. The garden is delightful. The fruit trees and flowering shrubs form a pleasing variety. The mocking birds surround us evening and morning . . . We have green peas almost fit to eat, and as fine lettuce as you ever saw . . . We have in the same orchard apples, pears, peaches, apricots, nectarines, plumbs [*sic*] of different kinds, figs, pomegranates and oranges. And we have strawberries which measure three inches round."[20]

The same year, Greene died after a bout of sunstroke, which he suffered during a visit to a neighbor. Greene's widow, Catherine, took up management of the plantation. She received two visits from George Washington in 1791. He came in grand style with carriages and wagons commanded by drivers, coachmen, footmen, and a valet all dressed in fancy red and white uniforms. These visits are said to have inspired Catherine Greene to continue her efforts to profit from the plantation. She appointed Phineas Miller, her children's Yale-educated tutor, as her plantation manager, undertaking day-to-day operations of the estate.

In 1793, the widow Greene received a young visitor who would change everything. His name was Eli Whitney. He was a native of Connecticut and a recent graduate of Yale. While at Mulberry Grove Whitney was shown the perplexing dilemma of processing cotton, a tedious task that required manual labor to separate the cottonseed from short-staple cotton fiber that grew in the area.

After being presented with the problem, Whitney immediately took to finding a solution. An upstairs room of the Mulberry Grove Plantation mansion became his workshop, and Phineas Miller became his financial backer. His solution was a machine that consisted of spiked teeth mounted on a revolving cylinder. When turned by a crank, the machine pulled cotton fibers through a series of slots, thereby separating the seeds from the cotton fibers. A rotating brush removed the fibrous lint from the spikes.

Functionally, the machine was a great success, although financially it was not. Greene and Miller set up many of the machines across the South, undertaking an advertising campaign. It was their intention that farmers would bring their unprocessed cotton to these central mills, and that for the fee of two-fifths of their crop, the cotton would be processed. Planters and smaller farmers immediately turned against this idea, citing the exuberant charge for this service. Instead, they copied the simple design of the machine and built their own. Versions of the cotton gin sprouted up all over the South, in time producing a new economic boom that would boost plantation culture and the institution of slavery in the South like no other. Whitney and Miller spent decades and many fortunes trying to defend their patent; however, the efforts never yielded profits in their lifetimes.

In the meantime, Catherine Greene continued running her plantation along with Miller. She married him in 1796, with a prenuptial agreement granting her all rights of ownership of the plantation. Although she continued trying to profit from Mulberry Grove, the debt from her late husband, General Greene, finally caught up with the new bride.

The family moved to Dungeness, a Cumberland Island plantation, and Mulberry Grove was eventually sold to Major Edward Harden. In his role as plantation master, Harden played an active part in politics, much as his predecessors had. He served as an alderman, was elected to the general assembly, and was made a justice of the inferior court. Harden died in 1804, but during his tenure he improved the status of the plantation, successfully turning a profit.

After Harden's death, Mulberry Grove was divided between two of his sons, Edward and John. John retained most of the plantation's original lands, while Edward took the more western property that had been added through various expansions. Under John's tenure, the plantation deteriorated, due in part to an embargo on rice. John Harden died

sometime before 1819. The plantation eventually passed through several owners until it reached the hands of James Wallace, who also purchased the adjoining Drakies Plantation. Once again the plantation was re-created and renewed, until being sold to Henry McAlpin in 1838 and then again to Philip Ulmer just two years later.

Ulmer continued to expand the plantation and its agricultural operations until his death in 1856. At this time, fifty-seven individuals were enslaved on the plantation, and the estate possessed a steel rice mill and two stone mills. His wife retained a portion of the property along with a summer residence, but the majority of the plantation was auctioned.

In December of that year, 617 acres of Mulberry Grove along with 31 acres from Drakies was sold to Zachariah M. Winkler, one of the greatest rice planters in the state, for fourteen thousand dollars. Under Winkler's care, the plantation soared to its greatest heights, but it all came to an abrupt end when the Civil War broke out.

Union troops pillaged the estate and burned the great mansion to the ground. Winkler died shortly after. Following the war, two of Winkler's sons, Zachariah and Van, continued planting rice at Mulberry Grove, despite poor economic conditions and a lack of slave labor. Zachariah died, but Van continued planting rice into the twentieth century, until it became economically impossible to do so. He continued to reside at Mulberry Grove, attended to by a young African American boy, until his death. His heirs profited from the plantation's timber.

Over the years, ownership of the plantation continued to pass through various hands, but no major agricultural efforts were undertaken. Today, little remains of what was once one of the most important estates in the South. A few buried bricks hint at where the foundations of buildings used to be. Fortunately, commemorative signage has been erected on the site, and a foundation has been established to promote and preserve the estate's legacy.

# *Hamilton*

The ruins of two slave cabins are all that remain of Hamilton Plantation, once a thriving estate on Sea Island off the Georgia coast. The property was originally owned by Captain James Gascoigne, and it was known as Gascoigne Bluff. The captain commanded a ship called *Hawk*, which transported settlers to the area in the 1730s. He was also in charge of various military ships docked on the coast. These ships aided in the defense of the colony. Gascoigne spent much time and effort developing his plantation, but in 1742, it was destroyed by invading Spaniards. Disheartened by this, the captain returned to England.

In the 1780s, the plantation was revived by Major Alexander Bissett and Richard Leake, who cultivated cotton there. They also utilized the property's extensive live oaks for timber. Much of this timber was purchased for the construction of the United States' first naval ships, and it was even used in the creation of the famed vessel the USS *Constitution*, which came to be known as "Old Ironsides."

Scottish businessmen James Hamilton and John Couper relocated from North Carolina to St. Simons Island in 1793. Hamilton purchased the plantation at Gascoigne Bluff and renamed it after himself. Couper purchased Cannon's Point Plantation. In a very short amount of time both men prospered from their investments. Hamilton was producing a fine quality of cotton, spearheading an economic boom for "Sea Island cotton." He often fetched a higher price at market for his product, as its quality was so remarkable.

In the midst of this success, Hamilton constructed a mansion on his plantation. The house was a two-story frame structure raised high off the ground. It was designed in the colonial style, with a large piazza out front. Of course, he commissioned formal gardens to accent the building. These gardens contained a variety of plants, including yucca. There were also herb gardens and a rose garden, all delineated by picket fences and boxwood hedges.

Support structures surrounding the house included detached kitchens, barns, and slave cabins, among others. Most of these were made of a unique material called tabby. Thought to have been introduced by the Spanish during early colonial times, evidence of tabby construction is found along coastal Georgia and the Carolinas. This substance was a type of cement made by combining lime that was extracted from burnt oyster shells with sand, shells, and water. This thick mixture was poured into great wooden molds in order to make walls, pillars, and other elements of architecture. Mortar, often mud mixed with Spanish moss, was used to seal joints and otherwise caulk the structures. And it was from these tabby buildings that much of the work of the plantation was done.

Hamilton's years at the plantation were certainly prosperous ones, but after many successful crops, in the early 1820s Hamilton retired to his Phildelphia mansion. He gave up planting cotton, but retained ownership of his plantation in Georgia. He died as one of the nation's wealthiest men in 1829.

Hamilton's daughter Agnes Rebecca Hamilton and her husband, Francis P. Corbin, of Paris, inherited the plantation. During this time, John Couper's son, James Hamilton Couper, acted as the administrator of the estate. John Couper's daughter, Ann, and her husband, Captain John Fraser, operated the plantation on a day-to-day basis and lived in the mansion. It is said that they hosted some of the area's most elegant and memorable balls and soirees.

Some time later, plantation operations passed to Ann's brother, William Audley Couper. In 1852, he witnessed the explosion of the side-wheeled steamboat *The Magnolia* just off the Hamilton Plantation wharf. Many passengers and members of the crew were killed or maimed. The survivors were brought to the plantation. Couper immediately converted the spacious second floor of his barn into a makeshift hospital. Bales of cotton were opened to make beds, and many of the injured stayed for weeks until they were stable enough to return to their own homes. Survivors commissioned a large engraved silver pitcher to thank Couper and the entire plantation for their hospitality and care.

Later, James Hamilton Couper, now a successful planter, purchased the plantation from the Corbins. The Civil War brought much ruin to the plantation and to the economy upon which its success was founded. The property was auctioned for debt and was interestingly acquired again by the Corbins of Paris.

Without slaves to tend the lands and with the owners away in Europe, the plantation slowly declined. In 1868, a merchants group from New York City purchased the estate. They founded the Georgia Land and Lumber Company and quickly developed Hamilton Plantation. Soon, the once untended plantation was again bustling, as four mills were constructed and large wharves were built. By the 1880s and 1890s, the lumber industry in the area began to be replaced by the tourist trade. Resorts sprang up across the island, and, by the turn of the century, the area had become a favorite destination for travelers.

With all of this expansion and change, the plantation's properties and built environment declined, and architectural remnants of antebellum times were lost to neglect and development. Today, all that is left of Hamilton Plantation are the tabby ruins of two slave cabins, which themselves still attract visitors.

# Hampton

The Sea Islands off Georgia's coast were home to numerous important plantations. St. Simons Island was the site of Hampton Plantation, among others. Hampton was also known as Butler's Point, once part of the empire of the Butler family. It served as a refuge for an exiled U. S. vice president and later inspired a British actress's poignant pleas against slavery. The plantation mansion burned in 1871, and the estate later returned to wilderness.

The site of Hampton Plantation was first occupied by Europeans in 1738, when General Oglethorpe stationed nineteen soldiers and their families there to guard the seaboard against a Spanish attack and ensure the general security of the inland regions. At this time, the settlement was known as Newhampton, but its name was quickly shortened to Hampton.[21]

Within a decade, the political situation had changed, the troops were disbanded, and the settlement at Hampton was virtually nonexistent. Before the beginning of the nineteenth century, the property was acquired by Major Pierce Butler, who transformed the estate into a proper plantation.

Butler was born in County Carlow, Ireland, on July 11, 1744, and came to America in 1766 as a British military officer. He was originally stationed in Boston. He later moved to Charles Town (now Charleston), South Carolina, where, in 1771, he married Polly Middleton, a wealthy local heiress. Major Butler resigned from the military and became a colonist, active in public life. He served as a delegate to the Congress of 1787 and was elected to the U.S. Senate multiple times.[22]

Polly Middleton Butler died in 1790, and it was after this event that Major Butler began acquiring properties in Georgia. In addition to Hampton, he also acquired Butler Island in the Altamaha River and nearby Woodville Plantation.

Although Butler never considered Hampton his primary home, he spent time there supervising the management of the estate. As a former British officer, Butler ran Hampton and his other holdings with military strictness and precision. Every aspect of life on the Butler properties was administered efficiently and stringently, from agricultural production and the manufacturing of goods to the personal lives and affairs of the slaves. One method by which Butler sought to control his slaves absolutely was via their extreme isolation. Although enslaved individuals from other neighboring estates were allowed to visit between plantations, Butler's slaves were never given this privilege. He demanded that all of his slaves remain on his property at all times and severely limited any contact they had with fellow slaves from adjacent or nearby estates.

The profound authoritarian aspects of Major Butler's personality could also be seen in his hospitality, which was said to be rigidly formal and decorous. In their history of St. Simons, R. Edwin Green and Mary A. Green note that visitors to Hampton were required to meet a warden at the dock and formally state their name and business before being ceremoniously escorted to the main house. Despite his formality and stiffness, Butler entertained extensively at Hampton. He also offered his residence at Hampton to various business associates, political colleagues, and friends when he was away at other plantations or at his homes in Charleston or Philadelphia.

One of the most prominent guests to reside at the plantation during Butler's absence was Vice President Aaron Burr, who took refuge there after killing Alexander Hamilton in a duel. Burr was essentially exiled after the famous shooting and sought sanctuary in the South where dueling was less frowned upon. He traveled to Mississippi, where he was arrested in Natchez, and took residence at Windy Hill Manor while awaiting trial.

During his extended absences from Hampton, Butler relied on Roswell King and his son Roswell King, Jr., to manage Hampton. Although they followed his strict regimens for agricultural production and slaves, much routine maintenance was neglected in order to show larger annual profits. The plantation and its environs ultimately suffered.

Major Butler died in Philadelphia on February 15, 1822. He was buried there in Christ Churchyard. He willed his three Georgia estates to his two grandsons, John and Pierce Mease, under the strict condition that they change their surname to Butler.[23] The brothers agreed and became the new owners of Hampton, Woodville, and Butler Island.

In 1832, Pierce Butler met the famous British actress Fanny Kemble, who was on a two-year theater tour of the United States.[24] After seeing Fanny perform, Butler became infatuated with her. He began to pursue her and eventually sought her hand in marriage. The couple was married in 1834.

Fanny was an extremely independent-minded individual who was fond of reading, outdoor activities (including horseback riding and vigorous exercise), and music. She was strong willed, opinionated, and often quite vocal, all traits that Butler assumed she would politely curb after the wedding ceremony. He soon realized his assumption was in error. Fanny's strong personality quickly unnerved

Butler, who envisioned an ideal wife to be quiet, docile, and subservient to her husband.

Soon, Butler's young wife began to question him about his fortune. She wanted to know where the funds to support their lavish lifestyle came from. He enlightened her as to the source of his wealth, and she expressed her horror of the fact that she now shared in the ownership of over seven hundred slaves!

Fanny adamantly demanded a trip to Georgia to visit the plantations. Both John and Pierce were reluctant to bring her to any of the estates, but she stubbornly persisted with her demands, and Pierce finally gave in. In December 1838, he traveled with her to the rice plantation at Butler Island, along with their two small children, Sally and Fanny. The family stayed on the plantation for several months, and they then moved to Hampton for a while.

Fanny was horrified by the conditions she found, especially as they related to slaves. While on the plantations, she unceasingly advocated for the slaves to her husband, whose frustrations with her only grew. She kept a meticulous journal of her experiences on the estates and later published them as *Journal of a Residence on a Georgia Plantation*.

Of her arrival at Hampton, Fanny wrote: "At the end of a fifteen miles' row we entered one among a perfect labyrinth of arms or branches, into which the broad river ravels like a fringe as it reaches the sea, a dismal navigation along a dismal tract, called 'Five Pound,' through a narrow cut or channel of water divided from the main stream. The conch was sounded, as at our arrival at the rice island, and we made our descent on the famous long staple cotton island of St. Simon's [sic], where we presently took up our abode in what had all the appearance of an old half-decayed rattling farm-house."[25]

She aptly noted the poor conditions on the plantation; obviously, years of absentee ownership had taken their toll at Hampton. Fanny also noted that a new overseer's house was being constructed, although she called both the location of the abode and its architecture "hideous." However, she did note that on future visits she would reside in this new building.

Of the slave cabins at Hampton, she wrote: "All

the slaves' huts on St. Simon's [*sic*] are far less solid, comfortable, and habitable than those at the rice-island. I do not know whether the labourer's habitation bespeaks the alteration in the present relative importance of the crops, but certainly the cultivators of the once far-famed long staple sea-island cotton of St. Simon's [*sic*] are far more miserably housed than the rice-raisers of the other plantation. These ruinous shieldings, that hardly keep out wind or weather, are deplorable homes for young or aged people, and poor shelters for the hardworking men and women who cultivate the fields in which they stand."[26]

Fanny became disillusioned and cynical about the horrors of slavery she found at Hampton. She also became frustrated as her suggestions and pleas on behalf of the slaves were being more and more ignored by both her husband and his overseers. Nonetheless, the slaves realized her empathy regarding their situation, and they flocked to her for aid. Upon departing the plantations she wrote: "At every moment one or other of the poor people rushed in upon me to bid me good-bye; many of their farewells were grotesque enough, some were pathetic, and all of them made me very sad. Poor people! how little I have done, how little I can do for them."[27]

A few months after they left, the Butler family returned to Philadelphia. Pierce vehemently refused to allow Fanny to subsequently return to any of the plantations. She moved out of his house in 1846, and two years later, they were formally divorced. Fanny moved to Massachusetts, and then returned permanently to England.

Later, Fanny's published journal played a major role in public opinion in Britain. It has been suggested that her volume was one of the major reasons why England did not support the South in the Civil War, thereby indirectly aiding the Union cause.

The story of Pierce Butler and Fanny Kemble's union and their trip to the Georgia plantations is so well known and appreciated that it was made into a television movie in 2000 called *Enslavement: The True Story of Fanny Kemble*. The famed British actress was played by Jane Seymour, a popular British actress in her own right. The role of Pierce Butler was played by Keith Carradine.

Shortly prior to the Civil War, Pierce Butler decided to abandon the plantations for financial reasons. He liquidated his Georgia properties, including 429 slaves that he auctioned in Savannah. The slaves alone netted him $303,850 (over $6.9 million in 2007 dollars).[28]

After the war, the plantation was devastated. Although sharecropping was attempted at the estate, it was not a success, and Hampton was soon abandoned. The plantation house was destroyed by fire in 1871. The land slowly returned to wilderness. During World War II, the site served once again as a lookout for soldiers who guarded the coast from invasion. In recent times much of the property has been redeveloped for residential use, and little trace of this once-famed plantation can be found.

## The Hermitage

Once located three miles east of Savannah, the Hermitage, previously known as Exon, was an elegant estate with a long, storied history. The plantation's graceful master house was purchased by one of world's first billionaires and demolished so that he could use the bricks to construct another building.[29]

Between Musgrove and Pipemaker's creeks, land was set aside in the earliest days of the colony for the exclusive use of natives from the Creek nation. Depletion of this tract left it deserted until it was claimed by the Crown in 1750. The first colonist to own the property was Joseph Ottolenghe, a former Jew who had embraced Christianity. He was excited at the prospects of culturing silk in the area and began planting mulberry trees. He called his estate Exon. It originally encompassed some one hundred acres.

Soon, Ottolenghe became a resident expert regarding silk, and when the colony's director of the silk industry, Pickering Robinson, returned to England for health reasons, Ottolenghe was asked to take his place. By 1753, the silk industry had lost

McAlpin's mansion at the Hermitage Plantation featured a keenly proportioned façade with Greek Revival–style columns above a stately arcade.

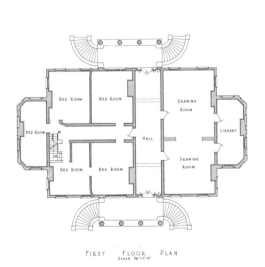

FIRST FLOOR PLAN
SCALE ⅛"=1'-0"

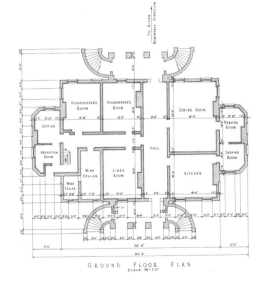

GROUND FLOOR PLAN
SCALE ⅛"=1'-0"

The principal floor of the the Hermitage Plantation House was raised above the ground floor. It contained a broad off-center hall that ran from the front of the mansion to the rear. The hall connected to a cross hall that led to the bedroom wing on one side and the double parlors on the opposite side. The double parlors both opened onto the elegant library at the side of the house. The original scale does not apply to this reproduction.

The ground floor of the mansion was largely set aside for service functions and storage. It also contained an office with a reception room offering a separate exterior entrance for business associates. And the level was the setting of the dining room and kitchen. The original scale does not apply to this reproduction.

This plot plan of the Hermitage Plantation showcases the general layout of buildings on the estate. The incredibly long avenue of oaks must have been an amazingly beautiful, impressive, and intimidating entrance for visitors. The opposite side of the house fronted the Savannah River, thereby providing access from both land and water. The inset image provides a closer view of the mansion and its immediately surrounding structures. (Not to scale)

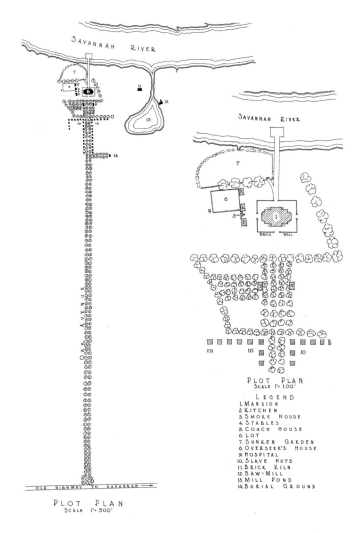

SAVANNAH RIVER

SAVANNAH RIVER

OLD HIGHWAY TO SAVANNAH

PLOT PLAN
Scale 1" = 500'

PLOT PLAN
Scale 1" = 100'

LEGEND
1. MANSION
2. KITCHEN
3. SMOKE HOUSE
4. STABLES
5. COACH HOUSE
6. LOT
7. SUNKEN GARDEN
8. OVERSEER'S HOUSE
9. HOSPITAL
10. SLAVE HUTS
11. BRICK KILN
12. SAW-MILL
13. MILL POND
14. BURIAL GROUND

A few of the brick slave cabins at the Hermitage. Two of these were later disassembled by automotive magnate Henry Ford and reassembled in Dearborn, Michigan, at his museum.

much of its allure, and even Ottolenghe began planting rice at another location.

As the leader of the silk industry he had gained notoriety in the settlement, despite the industry's problems. In 1755 and 1756, he was elected to the colony's house of representatives. He became a justice of the peace in 1759, and in 1762 he joined the general assembly.

Sometime prior to 1762, William Grover purchased the Exon tract from Ottolenghe. Grover, the chief justice of the province, established residency at the plantation, where it is thought he built a comfortable house and was probably engaged in the timber industry.

Unfortunately, Grover was an unseemly type, and his "dishonourable, partial, arbitrary, illegal, [and] indecent," behavior resulted in his dismissal as chief justice in 1763.[30] The same year, he sold Exon to Captain Patrick MacKay of Joseph's Town. It was MacKay who renamed the plantation Hermitage. An announcement published by MacKay in the *Georgia Gazette* in 1763 stated:

> Whereas the subscriber's plantation lately, Chief Justice Grover's, now named Hermitage, is grievously and unsufferably [*sic*] annoyed and disturbed by negroes, who come there by land and water in the night-time, and not only rob, steal, and carry off hogs, poultry, sheep, corn and his potatoes, but create very great disorders amongst his slaves . . . some are so audacious as to debauch his very house wenches: These therefore are to give notice to all proprietors of slaves, that . . . the subscriber is determined to treat all negroes that shall be found within his fences, after sunset, and before sunrise, as thieves, robbers, and invaders of his property, by shooting them.[31]

Obviously, at this time, MacKay had established residency on his plantation. He was planting corn and potatoes and raising livestock and poultry. Also, he had house servants in addition to his field hands.

By 1765, MacKay had abandoned the Hermitage, taking up residence on another tract that he held. He sold the former Exon tract to David Murray for four hundred pounds on June 17, 1765. Mur-

ray owned fifty slaves and over a thousand acres of property elsewhere, but chose the Hermitage as his home, probably because of the fine house that had been built there for the chief justice. He brought with him his wife, Lucia, and daughter, Charles. He also brought a variety of furnishings that were mentioned in his will.

In 1775, after Murray's death, his plantation was auctioned to pay certain debts and obligations. It was purchased by John Murray, probably a brother of the deceased, for the sum of three hundred pounds. The latter Murray, the new owner, produced firewood on the estate, which he advertised in the *Georgia Gazette*.[32]

By 1776, John Murray had to abandon his plantation. He was a loyalist, and revolutionary sentiments by his neighbors and the activities of such groups as the Sons of Liberty forced him to flee. Later, in 1781, the property was seized and auctioned.

It was purchased by Major Thomas Washington for only three hundred thirty-five pounds. Washington had fifty slaves on the estate, but due to debts incurred he had to sell the estate. Dr. Samuel Beecroft, a popular surgeon, became the next owner, purchasing the property for a thousand pounds. He enthusiastically operated the plantation, planting orchards and cultivating gardens. He also started a brick-making operation on the tract, a business that would later be very important in the plantation's history.

Dr. Beecroft sold the plantation in 1798 to Samuel Wall for $2,785. At this time the Hermitage encompassed 230 acres. Wall advertised the plantation for sale a year later. An advertisement in the May 25, 1798, issue of the *Georgia Gazette* described the property: "Too well known for its beautiful situation, (Commanding from its bank a full view of Savannah), good soil valuable wood, large handsome convenient buildings, gardens, and peach orchards, to require a more particular description."

That year the estate was purchased by a young French aristocrat, Jean de Berard-Mocquet-Montalet, Chevalier Marquise de Montalet, who came from Santa Domingo. Montalet was somewhat of a social butterfly, and as a French nobleman he was quite a rarity in Georgia. He had been raised in fashionable circles in Paris before crossing the Atlantic, and succeeded in charming most of Savannah with his exotic charisma and wit.

Montalet continued the brick-making trade on the plantation, and also planted cotton. He brought with him many slaves, probably from Santa Domingo. He called his slaves by French names, among them Mathurin, Antoine, Gustin, Dominique, Prene, and St. Foix. In 1801, three slaves belonging to Montalet's brother, William Polycarp Montalet, were baptized as Catholics at the Church of St. John the Baptist in Savannah.

Montalet married Angélique Servanne Charlotte de Picot-Boisfeuillet in 1804. The next year, at the age of eighteen, she was dead. Montalet died a decade later at the age of forty-nine. The Hermitage was sold for fifteen hundred dollars to William I. Scott, who purchased it for his friend Henry McAlpin, an architect.

McAlpin greatly expanded the brickworks on the plantation, in order to fuel his career as a builder and architect. He also expanded the plantation property, purchasing farm and timber lands that bordered the Hermitage and even a twenty-acre island on which he raised hogs. He planted rice, and built a rice mill, a sawmill, and a new brickyard all along the river.

In January 1820, McAlpin built one of the nation's earliest railroads, which transported fresh bricks to the kiln from the clay and sand pits, some distance away. Fort Pulaski on the Savannah River was constructed of bricks from the Hermitage. McAlpin also opened an iron foundry at the plantation. In 1821, *The Georgian* published an advertisement regarding the foundry:

> Cast Iron Foundary, Where Castings of all descriptions are done in the neatest manner & at as short a notice as the nature of the work wanted will allow, and of the very best materials. I can with confidence recommend my castings to millrights and engineers, as the Iron is soft and good, and can be fitted without much trouble: Any size Castings can be done from one to four thousand pounds. Persons wishing any Blacksmith's work, Turning, or Brasses for their Castings, can be supplied, if requested.[33]

With all of his success in planting and in the many industrial enterprises upon his estate, McAlpin set out to replace the old manor house at the Hermitage with a fine plantation mansion. The house, thought to have been designed by McAlpin's close friend, the architect William Jay, was a graceful and beautiful structure.

The house was rectangular in structure with small six-sided wings added to the two sides. The front and back of the home were identical and featured centrally raised porches meeting the elevated main floor. Three well-proportioned arches centered two elegantly curving marble staircases in front of each porch. Above, slender fluted columns supported a heavy entablature, giving the house a sophisticated, delicate feel.

A large ground-floor basement contained an off-center hall extending from the front to the back of the mansion. There was also a dining room and kitchen, as well as rooms for house servants, a linen room, wine cellars, and an office with a reception room.

The main floor above had a corresponding off-center hall with double drawing rooms and a library to one side and an intersecting cross hall opening to five bedrooms on the opposite side.

Outside, an impressive mile-long alley of oaks led from Augusta Road to the house, which itself backed up to the Savannah River. Between the house and the river, McAlpin constructed a sunken garden. All of the outbuildings and associated structures, including a two-story kitchen, stables, and smokehouses, were built of brick, which, being manufactured on the plantation out of indigenous materials (i.e., sand and clay) and fired by flames fueled from plantation timberland logs, cost the owner practically nothing but the labor of his chattel.

Two villages of slave cabins could be found on either side of the avenue of oaks, near the house. Each of these villages had a single row of cabins, lining a large rectangular central court (these are partially shown in the plot plan). The cabins themselves were among the finest dwellings offered to slaves on a plantation. Each brick structure contained a kitchen with fireplace and two sleeping chambers. Given that only one family was usually assigned to each cabin, the slaves on the Hermitage were housed in much more hospitable quarters than most of their contemporaries.

Between the villages of slave cabins and the main house, there was a two-story overseer's house and also a two-story brick hospital with separate quarters for men and women.

Through the 1830s until the time of his death in 1851, Henry McAlpin greatly expanded his land holdings, the built environment of his plantation, and industrial enterprises along the Savannah River. At the time of his death, the Hermitage consisted of over six hundred acres. His will also noted sixteen carts, carriages, and buggies, thirty-two wheelbarrows, forty-two horses, twenty-one mules, twenty-three oxen and cows, thirty-eight sheep, and thirty-two hogs. There were also one hundred seventy-two slaves. In addition, there were nearly four hundred thousand bricks and four hundred thousand feet of timber and lumber.

The Hermitage was inherited by six of McAlpin's children.[34] His oldest son, Joseph, had no interest in this claim, as he was bequeathed a separate plantation in Upson County. It came under the direction of McAlpin's son Angus, who was said to be the most appropriate person to take over operations.

By 1854, when all of the children had reached twenty-one, the plantation properties were divided into six equal shares. It was agreed that three of the brothers, including Angus, would take the portions of the plantation containing the main house, slave cabins, brickworks, and timber and lumber mills, as well as 185 slaves. They incorporated their enterprise as "A. McAlpin and Brothers," and Angus and his family took up residence in the plantation mansion, along with his brother Donald who never married.

A few years later when war broke out, both Angus and Donald joined Confederate forces in fighting to preserve their way of life. Angus's wife fled with her children, including a two-week-old infant, to a pine tract sixteen miles away after a stray cannonball landed in the garden. It is said that because the trusted nanny was too obese to fit into a carriage, they were forced to take a young slave girl with them instead, to care for the baby.

Prior to their escape, Mrs. McAlpin buried the family silver and jewels under a nearby tree. Later, after the war, a trusted former slave helped the family find their buried treasures.

During the war, troops badly damaged the mansion, using fine furnishings for firewood and smashing the windows. After the war, the McAlpins lost the estate to foreclosure. It came into the possession of Aaron Champion, the father-in-law of Angus's brother James Wallace.

Champion allowed his son-in-law and his family the right to remain at the plantation, providing a life estate for his daughter; however, they chose instead to reside in a town house on Orleans Square that Champion had also provided for them. The plantation remained deserted.

Upon the death of Mrs. James McAlpin, her five children inherited the estate. Eventually, by 1903, three of them had come into full possession of the estate, including Judge Henry McAlpin. He married Isabel E. Wilber of Pennsylvania, and they lived for a short time at the Hermitage with his daughter Claudia (from a previous marriage). The two female socialites preferred city life to isolated agrarian existence, and the family soon moved to Orleans Square. This was the last occupation of the mansion.

Over the years industry encroached as a railroad and chemical company, among others, occupied the land. All the while, the house fell into decay. There was some talk of saving the mansion as a historical treasure, but it mostly fell on deaf ears.

Judge McAlpin and the other heirs set up a company, called the Hermitage Corporation, to manage their interests in the estate. In 1919, the Diamond Match Company purchased nineteen acres of river frontage for a hundred dollars, and industry encroachment continued.

Judge McAlpin died in 1931, and his daughter

Claudia and his third wife, Mary Young of Augusta, inherited his interests in the estate. By 1935, the plantation had passed into the hands of the city of Savannah and its port authority.

At this time there was again a weak cry to save the mansion. One of the most prominent people to get involved in the discussion was Harold L. Ickes, secretary of the interior, who wrote the mayor of Savannah in 1935: "As the Hermitage mansion in Savannah is one of the finest sites in existence illustrative of Southern history prior to the Civil War, it would be highly desirable not only to preserve this fine old building from complete destruction, but to keep it on the site it now occupies."[35]

Ickes obviously understood the importance of historic preservation even at this early date, but his requests were quickly ignored. The city sold the buildings on the property to automotive magnate Henry Ford for a total sum of ten thousand dollars.

Ford demolished the mansion and had the famed grey bricks transported to Bryan County, Georgia, where he used them to construct a new house, reminiscent of a plantation mansion but significantly different from the Hermitage. The new house is still standing at the Ford Plantation in South Bryan. Ford had two of the brick slave cabins meticulously disassembled and shipped to his museum in Dearborn, Michigan, where they were carefully reassembled. Today, both are part of Greenfield Village, a component of The Henry Ford, a living-history destination that includes the Henry Ford Museum.

In 1935, the Hermitage property was leased by the Union Bag and Paper Company, which constructed a massive paper plant near the site of the demolished mansion. The paper company also utilized buildings that had been erected there earlier by the Diamond Match Company.

Today, the paper plant is still in operation under the direction of International Paper. It has been greatly expanded and updated and employs seventeen hundred local residents. The scope and fervor of this current industry occupying the site would certainly impress Henry McAlpin, who spent his life promoting industrial endeavors side by side with agricultural operations on the Hermitage Plantation.

# Retreat

Retreat, another plantation on Georgia's great Golden Isles, was one of the first sites where famed Sea Island cotton was grown. It was on this St. Simons estate that the Page and King families ruled their plantation empire, and it was upon this "Retreat" that Anna Matilda Page King, isolated and abandoned, was forced to courageously manage her family, her slaves, and her properties. Today, all that remains of this storied lost plantation are a few crumbling, tattered ruins of its agricultural and architectural past.

In 1736, James Oglethorpe stationed John Humble at the south end of St. Simons Island on the Georgia coast. Humble became the first pilot of the harbor, and he established his home on this property. Some time later, Humble's lands were granted to John Clubb in reward for his service to Oglethorpe's regiment. Clubb sold the estate to Thomas Spaulding in 1786. Spaulding, a Scotsman, received a variety of cottonseed from a loyalist friend who was harboring in the Bahamas during the Revolution.[36]

Intrigued, Clubb cultivated this cottonseed, some of which had been developed on Anguilla in the West Indies. Surprisingly, the Anguilla seed produced very fine quality cotton, which came to be known as "Sea Island cotton," and was soon prized for its silkiness, luster, and long staple. As its reputation grew, Sea Island cotton quickly began to fetch a much higher price than standard varieties of the crop.

Clubb eventually moved on to larger plantations, purchasing Sapelo Island and selling his St. Simons holdings to Major William Page and his wife, Hannah Timmons Page. Major Page was a native of South Carolina who had served under General Francis Marion in the American Revolution.

The Retreat Plantation House. Note Grasshopper Hall, the two-story building behind the house where the young, unmarried men in the family resided. Courtesy of the Coastal Georgia Historical Society.

A masonry shell is all that remains of the slave hospital at Georgia's Retreat Plantation.

The tattered ruins of Retreat Plantation House pictured here included this brick chimney.

Page and his wife moved to Georgia in the 1790s, first living in Bryan County. While there, they had visited their friend Major Pierce Butler at Hampton Plantation on St. Simons Island. They noticed during this visit that their only living child, an ailing daughter who had survived all of her siblings, grew healthy in the fresh sea air. The family decided to remain on the island, and Page took the responsibility of managing Butler's properties (including Hampton Plantation), especially during Butler's lengthy absences. The Page family remained at Hampton until 1802, when Butler hired Roswell King. It was after this that Page purchased Retreat from Clubb and began cultivating this plantation of his own.

Page continued growing Sea Island cotton on the estate and also cultivated rice in the lowlands, far enough from the sea to avoid much of the harsh saltwater, but close enough that his fields were flooded with the movement of the tides. Page expanded and developed his plantation into one of the most successful in the region. At a time when standard cotton sold for forty-two cents per pound, Page's much-prized variety sold for a whopping fifty cents per pound.

The plantation house had been built by Spalding, after the estate's original residence had been destroyed in a coastal storm. The newer house was a replica of Orange Hall, Oglethorpe's West Indies–style house in Frederica. This raised cottage was one and a half stories, with a full basement and shuttered porches. A two-story building called Grasshopper Hall was connected to the rear of the main house by a breezeway. It served as the residence for the five King boys, and, like the *garçonnières* of French Louisiana, allowed the young men to have a great deal of freedom while still being within the realm of the plantation and near its services and conveniences.

A number of buildings were constructed around the main house, including a schoolhouse, guesthouse, cotton barn, corn barn, and greenhouse. Numerous tabby slave cabins were lined in rows. The cabins each contained four rooms with a central chimney and fireplaces serving each side of the

divided structures. Sets of stairs on either side of the house led to wide sleeping quarters in the attic. Most certainly, these structures were built to house at least two families. The plantation complex also contained a large slave hospital made of tabby, with ten rooms. Rooms on the first floor were reserved for men and those on the second floor for women; the third-floor attic contained quarters for two full-time nurses.[37]

While he developed his plantation, Major Page carefully taught his daughter, Anna Matilda Page, who was then growing into a healthy young woman, all he knew about planting, managing an estate, construction, and other such arts that would later serve her well.

She grew into a lovely young lady, who was the object of many suitors' efforts and affections. Anna fell deeply in love with Charles Molyneux, and her heart was broken when his father could not come to an agreement with her father regarding the dowry. In December 1824, she married Thomas Butler King, a successful attorney from Massachusetts who, like Anna Matilda's father, had come to coastal Georgia for a visit and had decided to move there.

Two years later, both Page and his wife were dead, leaving Anna Matilda and her new husband as the sole owners of the Retreat property. King had very little interest in the estate, except for the huge profits that he reaped from its crops, so he actively pursued interests outside of Retreat. He was soon elected to the Georgia senate and later moved on to the U. S. Congress. He served as the collector of the Port of San Francisco and was heavily involved in the promotion of the transcontinental railroad. He was quite frequently far away from Retreat, leaving his wife alone to attend to matters at home.

Abandoned and disappointed, Anna Matilda was forced to use the skills and knowledge she had learned from her father in order to manage the estate. In her many letters, some of which have been compiled into a book by Melanie Pavich-Lindsay, Anna Matilda expressed her deep disappointment in her absentee husband and recounts her many struggles in maintaining her family, her plantation, and the large community of individuals she enslaved.

In various letters she spoke of her adverse situation. In a letter to her son Lord she wrote, "I am getting painfully anxious to have another letter from your dear father it now over three months since he left us—and 2 months & 8 days since his last letter written . . ." In another letter she wrote, "Could you my children only know the loneliness the pain I suffer—you would each one strive to repay me by your doing all in your power to improve."[38]

Her writings reveal that Anna Matilda would have wanted nothing more than to be the stereotypical plantation mistress and wife. But her husband's repeated absences and her resulting isolation forced her into a role few women of her time assumed, that of plantation master. She recounts having to attend to many various functions on the plantation—overseeing the slaves, attending to the health of her family and the slaves, managing agricultural operations, and even personally disposing of decayed human corpses that strangely often washed ashore.

In a letter to her daughter Florence written on February 11, 1852, she stated: "This morning before breakfast Peter found the body of another white man just opposite the last negro house. It was in a far worse state then the others were—I have had real trouble to get it buried . . . I actually had to attend to it myself. The body was in such a state I would not let the negros put their hands into the pockets—consequently we do not know who it is. The face was gone & the little hair left was red . . ."[39]

In addition to simply maintaining Retreat Plantation and dealing with the difficult issues that arose each day, Anna Matilda also expanded cultivation, laying so-called "New Fields" to the north of the estate. She had one of her husband's friends lay out a large drainage ditch, which was dug by slaves in 1836. Between 1848 and 1849, a public road was built to the New Fields by the Retreat slaves, and five hundred trees were planted along it.

Anna Matilda died in 1859, on the eve of the Civil War. Her sons Henry Lord Page King and R. Cuyler King both served in the Confederate army.

Lord, as he was commonly known, brought his faithful manservant, Neptune Small, along with him. After Lord was killed at the Battle of Fredericksburg delivering a dispatch to a distant line, Neptune Small risked his life that night to retrieve Lord's body amid violent gunfire. Small delivered Lord's body to Retreat and attended to its burial there. He then returned to battle to serve Cuyler, the youngest son of Anna Matilda. He was later rewarded with a tract of the Kings' lands that is today a public park named in his honor.[40]

Before his death in 1908, Small told reporters of the fateful night when he found Lord King's body. A transcript of his statement appeared in a local newspaper article by J. E. Dart:

> He cum an' eat he supper, but don't talk like mos' de times; w'en he thro' he look in de fire a long time. I ben busy washin' de dishes w'en all a sudden he say: Neptune, a big fite to-morrow mornin'; good mens will eat deir las' supper to-nite . . . Well, de nex' day I see de canon gwein by, an' de solders marching by, an' de gen'rals ridin' by, an' I known'd trouble wus comin' . . . [the] gentlemans, "war broke loose on dat day"; . . . Nite cum, but no Mas' Lord. I stir up de fire to keep he supper warm, but no Mas' Lord . . . Well, after it git good dark I lef' de supper by de fire to go look fur Mas' Lord. I met a' officer on a hoss. I ask him if he see Mas' Lord. He say not since 2'clock. I makes no answer, but my heart cum up in my thro't, an' I know'd den he mus' be hurt. I gone towards de Confederate line wher' dey ben fiten all day . . . I crawl down de hill; de mens was ev'ry wher', but none look like Mas' Lord. At las' it wus very dark. Den I cum to a' ofier layin' on he face. Som'body had pull off he rite boot an' lef' de lef', cos it wus so blody . . . an' I put my han' in he hair but de blod was clot, and de hair didn't fell like Mas' Lord's; but I turn he head over wére the blod was not so t'ick. I turn he face up so he could look in old Neptune's face, an' I say, "my young master—Mas' Lord, dis is old Neptune; supper is ready; I ben waiting fur you—is you hurt bad?" But he never answer he old nigger—he, he, he Gen'mens, wate on old Neptune a little w'lle—I can't talk now. Genl'mens—he, he, Lord have mercy—he was ded![41]

During the war, Retreat was ransacked by sailors from the gunboat *Ethan Allen.* Among the many items they took was a mantel clock wrapped in a black shawl. Ironically, in 1930, these two items were sold at an auction in Attleboro, Massachusetts. While making repairs to the clock, collector Edmond H. Gingrass discovered a small slip of paper on the back of the dial—it read: "This clock was taken from the Thomas Butler King Plantation on St. Simons Island, Georgia, January 10, 1863, by members of the United States gun boat Ethan Allen."

When word spread about the clock, arrangements were made to return it to descendants of the King family. The old plantation had been sold by the King family in 1926, and it had been transformed into the Sea Island Golf Club. With great pomp and circumstance, politicians from the North and South gathered with hordes of citizens in one of the few remaining buildings on the plantation: the old slave hospital. The shawl had also been found, and both items were returned to the King descendants with great ceremony.

The clock remained on the former plantation, being displayed in the golf clubhouse, but unfortunately, the building burned in 1935, destroying the clock. The Retreat Plantation House had also earlier burned in 1905, and today all that remains of the plantation are the tattered ruins of the house, a large barn, and ruins of the slave hospital, which can all be found on the golf course. A single slave cabin from Retreat that now houses an antiques store can be found at the intersection of Frederica and Demere Roads.

In addition to the published works about the plantation and its people, Retreat and its families have been memorialized and remembered in a variety of different ways. For example, the King family is recognized in local streets named after the children of Anna Matilda and her husband, Thomas King; among them are Mallery, Georgia, Virginia, Lord, Butler, Floyd, Cuyler, and Florence. Also, besides the many written historical accounts of Retreat and its inhabitants, the plantation's history has also been highlighted in exhibits by historian Melanie Pavich-Lindsay and artist Lisa

Tuttle. In "Retreat: Palimpsest of a Georgia Sea Island Plantation," and a companion installation called "A Slave Speaks of Silence," Tuttle and Pivach-Lindsay focused on the vibrant slave community at Retreat.

Whether on the written page, on street signs, in a park, in museums, or even simply in the minds of local citizens, the memories of this intriguing lost plantation and all of the people who contributed to the estate over the decades certainly have affected many, engraining themselves in multiple ways into a collective consciousness of the lost South.

# Horton House

Once the principal estate of Jekyll Island, Major William Horton's Horton House Plantation was the home of an early American brewery. It later became the antebellum dominion of the du Bignon family, at which time the last slave ship in America landed there. Later still, it was used as an exclusive resort by the nation's wealthiest men. Today, only a few ruinous tabby remnants remain, providing scant physical evidence to the sea island's most interesting past.

William Horton came to Georgia with James Oglethorpe in 1736, when the first settlers for Frederica were brought to the colony. It is said that Horton had been undersheriff of Herefordshire prior to his arrival in the New World. Horton served originally as a captain in Oglethorpe's regiment, but was later promoted to major.[42]

He brought with him to the colony ten indentured servants and was granted five hundred acres on Jekyll Island. His initial embankment onto the island was recorded in a 1744 book called *A Voyage to Georgia Begun in the Year 1735* by Francis Moore: "Mr. Horton, who had five hundred acres of land granted by the Trustees, went to take possession of it, being on the other side the branch of the Altamaha, and about six miles below the town. Mr. Oglethorpe ordered one of the scout boats to carry him: . . . he found the land exceeding rich."[43]

Horton House ruins.
The tabby shell of Major
Horton's once-proud
plantation home.

Horton House ruins. The
remains of a brick fireplace
and chimney.

Here he built a two-story home made of poured tabby, as well as a variety of other structures, including a massive barn. He established a brewery there and began planting rye and hops.

On November 13, 1745, James Pemberton of Philadelphia and his associate William Logan visited Frederica and Jekyll Island. Pemberton noted that he "saw the largest barn he ever beheld at Major Horton's plantation on Jekyll."[44]

Logan wrote in his journal: "[We] were gentiely [sic] entertained by Capt. Horton and after dinner Horton took us out about a mile to see a field of barley which is an uncommon thing in this Colony, but he having a particular inclination to farming hath made many good improvements on this Island and has one of the largest barns I have ever seen."[45]

In 1746, John Pye, an early settler, wrote: "I had ye pleasure to see Major Horton's improvements on Jekill [sic]. He has a very large barnfull of barley not inferior to ye barley in England, about 20 ton of Hay in one Stack, a Spacious House and fine garden; a plow was going with eight horses, and above all, I saw 8 acres of Indigo of which he has made a good quantity and two men are now at work. They told me the Indigo was as good as that made in the Spanish West India's."[46]

Over time, Horton not only gained a reputation as one of the greatest planters in the colony, but he also became one of Oglethorpe's most trusted officers. He was placed in charge of Georgia when Oglethorpe was away from the colony. And, in 1740, the founder of the colony sent Horton to England to lobby for munitions and men. After many meetings and an appearance in Parliament, he successfully secured the needed resources.

Major Horton's beloved plantation house was burned when the island was attacked by invading Spaniards. Horton himself died only a few years later on January 23, 1748. He was in Savannah at the time, and it is said that he caught a fever of some sort. It is thought that Horton's friend Raymond Demere managed the estate on behalf of the widow Horton and her son, but neither ultimately retained the estate.

Clement Martin, the secretary of Georgia's

# CHAPTER FIVE

# Alabama and Florida

. . . the murmuring stream sings, perpetually, its gentle requiem.

—*Charles Wickliffe Yulee*

The American South is a geographical entity, a historical fact, a place in the imagination, and the homeland for an array of Americans who consider themselves southerners. The region is often shrouded in romance and myth, but its realities are as intriguing, as intricate, as its legends.

—*Bill Ferris*

The adjacent states of Florida and Alabama share similar pasts and in some areas similar geographies. The Spanish were the first to extensively explore these contiguous areas, which they claimed as a singular "Florida." Ponce de León traveled there in 1513, and later conquistadors, including Pánfilo de Narváez and Hernando de Soto, continued surveying the region, confirming that Florida was a large peninsula instead of an island as earlier thought. Soto also explored several rivers of present-day Alabama, while the English claimed areas of what today is north Alabama as part of their Carolina and Georgia colonies.

The first settlers of Spanish Florida, mostly French Huguenots, arrived in the mid-sixteenth century. Later, French settlers claimed areas along the Gulf Coast and constructed forts along the Mobile River and near the present-day city of Mobile. These settlers were faced with a variety of hardships, most notably aggressive natives, with whom they, along with future settlers, had numerous violent interactions.

By the time St. Augustine, America's oldest city, was founded by the Spanish in 1565, colonists were actively involved in agriculture, planting citrus as well as other familiar crops. But these early agricultural efforts were largely limited for the next two hundred years.

When the British gained control of Florida in 1763, agriculture flourished. Most enterprises centered on Sea Island cotton, rice, indigo, and oranges. Spain regained Florida, including Mobile and other coastal areas of present-day Alabama, in the 1783 Treaty of Paris, which successfully terminated the French and Indian War and ended French occupation of Alabama. Great Britain came into possession of the region between the Chattahoochee and the Mississippi rivers, while portions of present-day Alabama below the 31st parallel were integrated as part of West Florida. Lands northward became parts of the Illinois Country. With Spain in control of Florida, again agrarian ventures floundered under the complex bureaucracy and politics of the ailing empire.

After the war of 1812, the United States came into possession of present-day Alabama, which became a territory in 1817. Alabama was admitted to the Union as the twenty-second state on December 14, 1819. Agriculture thrived in the Black Belt region of the state, with large numbers of cotton planters establishing substantial estates.

The United States later gained control of Florida by the 1821 Treaty of Adams-Onis. Shortly after, General Andrew Jackson received his commission as military governor of Florida. Jackson's political enemies chose him for this position as much for his knowledge of the area as for the opportunity to isolate their foe in the largely uninhabited wilderness of the region.

The acquisition of the Florida Territory by the United States was politically perilous, given that many congressmen feared the large land mass would be divided into two southern slave states, thus upsetting the delicate balance of equal numbers of slaveholding and nonslaveholding states in the Union. From an agricultural perspective, Florida's new affiliation with the U.S. was like the opening of a dam of opportunity for southern planters and smaller farmers.

Entrepreneurial planters, many from nearby Georgia, Alabama, and Carolina, poured into Florida, where they found abundant, unpopulated, and cheap lands. An area of rich soil between the Suwannee and Apalachicola rivers in middle Florida became a hotbed of plantation development. By 1825, two out of every three African Americans lived in the five cotton-growing counties of this region.

In both Alabama and Florida, yeoman farmers were forced to the periphery as wealthy planters vied for the best lands. Although there was much tension between the pretentious large slaveholders who quickly gained political control of both states and the humble yeoman settlers, all agreed in their support of the institution of slavery, confirming the essentiality of the South's "peculiar institution."

Planters developed extensive cotton plantations and produced other cash crops including indigo and sugar in smaller quantities. Many of these plantation owners were from neighboring states, having extensive personal, family, political, and business connections with the leading planter aristocracy of the older established South. This facilitated the importation and confirmed the solidity of the Old South's predominant plantation culture.

Soon, plantation mansions and wider complexes were constructed in Alabama and parts of Florida that would have been at home in Virginia, Georgia, or elsewhere. Like planters from other areas, members of Florida's new aristocracy constructed the built environments of their estates from materials found around them. From the British reign through the American periods, plantation structures were mainly made of timber, often from native pines and hardwoods. On coastal plantations like New Smyrna and Bulowville, porous coquina rock, an incompletely consolidated sedimentary rock containing shells or coral that is often associated with marine reefs, was used as the principal building material. Other nonmarine stone was rare, and it was not used abundantly in construction projects of the region.

Plantation estates and their built environments played a great role in life and labor in Florida and Alabama. By the dawn of the Civil War, in 1860, nearly half of both Alabama's and Florida's populations were enslaved. Ironically, of the white half of the population, only a small number owned slaves. In Florida, about 3.6 percent, a little over five thousand individuals, were slave owners. Of these, a smaller number still were considered large slaveholders or planters (owning twenty or more slaves). This tiny, elite, and ultrapowerful minority dominated and largely controlled the state's marginalized majority, both free whites and enslaved African Americans.[1]

Of course, the Civil War wrought great change for both Alabama and Florida, as it did for all of the Confederate states. The economics of agriculture was devastated, and the great slave labor force that made plantations profitable was now gone. Like everywhere across the South, plantation architecture representing a bygone era—from grand mansions to proud slave cabins, from well-worn mills to various outbuildings—began to fade.

This chapter details the rise and fall of eight of Alabama's and Florida's lost plantations. There are hundreds, maybe thousands, of others that are now gone and more or less forgotten. Most of Florida's greatest plantation houses have fallen victim to industrial or residential development, both urban and suburban. Certainly the commercialization of Florida's natural beauty and culture and the rapid growth of the tourist industry have both helped and hindered matters. Besides the few mentioned in this chapter, there were also plantation homes like that of Augustus H. Lanier in Gadsden. The handsome five-bay mansion was built on the Lanier Plantation in 1837, but was lost in the 1970s. There was Rosetta Plantation, once located near present-day Moultrie, which was established in 1770 by Florida's lieutenant governor John Moultrie. Here, seventy slaves labored on two thousand acres, until 1783, when the British ceded Florida back to the Spanish and the plantation was abandoned. Neglect and fires destroyed the plantation completely.

In Alabama, estates such as that of Alexander McGillivray's plantation have been lost over time. McGillivray, the son of a Scottish trader and his French Creek wife, became a successful planter, Creek leader, and commissioned officer in both the U.S. and Spanish militaries. Another mansion, Montpelier Plantation House, near Tuscumbia, was maliciously demolished by the Southern Railroad Corporation to make way for a switchyard.

But there are some antebellum plantation houses still standing in the two states, and a notable few have been fully restored. In Florida, the columned Gamble Mansion, the seat of Robert H. Gamble's sugar empire, was abandoned for years until 1925, when the United Daughters of the Confederacy saved the mansion, restoring it and donating it to the state. Today, it serves as the Judah P. Benjamin Confederate Memorial and State Historic Site, honoring the Confederacy's secretary of state, who took refuge there after the war, until his passage to England could be secured. It is open for public tours. Likewise, Great Oaks, the plantation home of Hamilton Bryan, was fully restored and has the distinction of being one of the few surviving plantation mansions in Jackson County. In nearby Calhoun County, Willoughby Gregory built an unusual brick plantation house with a full foundation, rather than piers, which were more customary for the region. The house still survives in largely unaltered form.

As in Florida, a small portion of Alabama's antebellum plantation architecture still exists. Most notably, Gaineswood, in Demopolis, provides an extant example of a beautiful and complex plantation mansion that is said to have been built around a traditional Alabama dogtrot cabin. Belle Mont in Hillsboro provides a perfect example of Jeffersonian style, with its two-story columned portico flanked by symmetrical one-story wings. Several Alabama plantation estates have been turned into hunting resorts, such as Hamilton Hills, in Minter, where guests can lodge in the original plantation house. The white-columned mansion at Kirkwood Plantation in Eutaw has been meticulously renovated as a bed and breakfast establishment and was given the National Trust for Historic Preservation Honor Award. Of particular note is the Turner Saunders mansion, located about halfway between Florence and Decatur, whose triple pediment façade represents one of Alabama's most extraordinary examples of the Greek Revival aesthetic. This famed house, once owned by the father of Rocky Hill Castle's master, sits in disrepair, and may soon join the list of those lost if decisive action is not taken.

Limited research has been published regarding the lost plantation estates and architecture of Alabama and Florida. Alice Strickland's *Ashes on the Wind: The Story of the Lost Plantations,* which was published in 1985, provides well-documented thumbnail histories of nearly two dozen lost plantations in Volusia County, Florida, once an early hub of agriculture. *Florida's Antebellum Homes* by Lewis N. Wynne and John T. Parks, published in 2004, beautifully illustrates the rich and varied architectural legacy of the state, while detailing histories of both extant and lost plantations. Lula D. Appleyard's unpublished master's thesis written in 1940, "Plantation Life in Middle Florida, 1821–1845," also provides much insight into the lost legacy of Florida's antebellum plantation past. Alabama's antebellum architecture is detailed in part in Robert Gamble's *Historic Architecture in Alabama,* published in 1990. *Ante-Bellum Mansions of Alabama,* a 1951 book by Ralph Hammond, also explores the state's built plantation heritage, and Chip Cooper's *Silent in the Land* pairs poignant photographs and text expressing the quickly deteriorating plantation landscape of Alabama. Mill Lane's volume on Mississippi and Alabama, in his *Architecture of the Old South* series, also gives much insight into Alabama's antebellum architecture, while Ann Boucher's Ph.D. disseration, "Wealthy Planter Families in Nineteenth-Century Alabama," provides additional depth regarding the history of this diverse region.

What follows are accounts of a handful of Alabama's and Florida's many lost plantations. They represent for these two proud states and for the entire South broken links to the past, a lost architectural and built legacy that can never be replaced, and knowledge of our American story that is fleeting and faded.

## Rocky Hill Castle

One of Alabama's most interesting lost plantations, both architecturally and historically, is the famed Rocky Hill Castle once located near Courtland, in Lawrence County. The plantation house was built by James Edmonds Saunders, a fascinating character himself. Saunders was born on May 7, 1806, in Brunswick County, Virginia, the fifth of ten children. He was the son of Rev. Turner Saunders, the founder of LaGrange College. A bright young man, James attended the University of Georgia, but withdrew from his studies at age eighteen, after marrying fifteen-year-old Mary Watkins. Three years later he began practicing law independently, having worked in the offices of Foster and Fogg in Nashville.[2]

By the mid-1820s, Saunders and his wife had moved to Alabama, where he later opened a law practice with John P. Omron, was elected to the state legislature, and was appointed a trustee of the University of Alabama. He also served as collector of customs for the Port of Mobile. After arriving in Alabama, Saunders soon began construction of his plantation home. He commissioned the mansion on a tall hill with a commanding view of his property, 640 acres in all.

The structure was designed and built under the direction of Hugh Jones, a Welsh carpenter. The main house was built in the Greek Revival style with Italianate detailing. The plan contained a basement, two main floors, an attic, and above, a cupola that was surrounded by arch windows. The front elevation of the house was nearly identical to the back, both having large porticos with four columns each, which supported a second-story balcony. The walls of the structure were eighteen inches thick and were built of bricks produced by the slaves of the plantation.

The inside of the house, like the outside, was a tribute to Jones's attention to detail. Impressive stairways boasted walnut banisters, Italian marble mantels embellished the fireplaces, and elaborate moldings decorated the interior. An especially unusual and striking element of the design was the doorway linking the double parlors. While such twin parlors were quite common in plantation mansions throughout the South, the pocket doors at Rocky Hill made these rooms truly unique. An incredibly thick arch was supported by four intricately carved half-columns, making an impressive passage between the chambers. Certainly, numerous balls and parties were held in these rooms. The construction of the house cost Saunders an estimated sum of forty-eight thousand dollars, a fortune at the time.

Later, one-story wings were added to the sides of the house, and, finally, Saunders built the structure for which the house would become most well known—an adjoining gothic castle tower. The tower itself contained six rooms and, on the very top, an observatory that Saunders used to survey the fields and keep an eye on his slaves at work. The other rooms of the tower were actually the domicile of enslaved individuals. Here, it is said, Saunders nightly imprisoned the slaves to keep them from fleeing their bondage in the cloak of night. The tower was designed and built with this purpose in mind, with few windows or other means of escape. It was perhaps one of the strangest and cruelest slave dwellings on any plantation in the antebellum South.[3]

As tensions rose over the evils of slavery, and the debate over secession grew louder and louder, Saunders took an important leadership role. Despite being a strong advocate of slavery, he strongly opposed the dissolution of the Union and voiced his opinions as president of the Stephen A. Douglass Convention held in Montgomery. It eventually became evident, however, that Saunders's view was not in line with majority opinion. With secession certain, Saunders acknowledged defeat and joined the Confederate cause. He enlisted in 1861, joined by his three sons. Saunders was appointed a colonel and served as a staff officer in Middle Tennessee.

While Saunders and his sons were away at war, their plantation home was being utilized to further the Confederate cause. The mansion at Rocky Hill, and even the infamous tower, some sources say, became a hospital for injured and ill rebel soldiers. Two of these soldiers died there and are buried in the family cemetery on the plantation. The tower was also used to hide valuables such as family jewelry. Such items were placed under floorboards and recovered long after the war. Furthermore, the house was also used as a factory for weapons. "Shot for the war was even made in the Castle. Hot lead was poured from the top floor through holes to tubs of water on the ground to chill and moulded [sic] into bullets that were used in the war."[4] Rumor abounds that the plantation was also utilized as a hub for illegal slave trade during the war. It is said that an underground tunnel connected the basement of the mansion with the banks of the nearby Tennessee River. Supposedly, slaves were trans-

Rocky Hill's mansion combined classical Greek Revival elements with Italianate detailing. The symmetric side wings were added later as was the unusual Gothic slave tower. The male figure near the front steps provides a sense of the home's enormous scale.

The interior pocket doors separating the Rocky Hill master house's double parlors were especially unusual. The incredibly thick arch supported by four intricately carved half-columns made an impressive and striking passage between the chambers.

ported on river vessels and transferred to the plantation via this passageway.

During the heat of the war the old plantation house hosted a number of important Confederate guests. General P. G. T. Beauregard and his staff dined at Rocky Hill, and General Nathan Bedford Forrest became a regular visitor. In addition the plantation even played host to the Military Court of the Army of Tennessee, whose membership included Saunders's own brother William.

After the war Saunders and his sons returned to their plantation home. Saunders himself had been badly injured at Murfreesboro, when a musket ball passed through his body. He recovered from these extensive wounds, but sadly, one of his sons was not as fortunate. Lawrence, Saunders's youngest son, came home from the war only to die a short time later from complications related to his war injuries.

Saunders's new life after the war was, of course, dramatically different from the one before it. As with most planters, his vast fortune had dwindled down to a meager amount. This didn't stop him,

however, from pursuing agricultural work on the plantation. He enlisted the assistance of Samuel Miller to help him grow grapes, in an attempt to free himself from his reliance on cotton as a main cash crop. Grapes, however, were not a financially rewarding crop for the colonel.

In addition to the agricultural changes on the plantation, one of the greatest revolutions came in Saunders's new role with regard to his former slaves. Many of the formerly enslaved people remained on the plantation; however, now they were free men and women. No longer did Saunders lock these individuals in his tower; instead he donned a more paternalistic character, building them a church on the property and even helping them establish their own independent court of law on the plantation.

It was during this time that Saunders began looking toward the past and reminiscing about the prominent white families that had early on established themselves in the area. He published many of these memories in a series of newspaper articles later to be compiled into a well-known book entitled *Early Settlers of Alabama*. Saunders's daughter, Ellen Virginia, also became known as a great writer after publishing *The Little Rebel*, a popular book that was later made into a movie.

Saunders died in 1896, and he was buried in the family cemetery on the plantation. His granddaughter, Elizabeth Saunders Blair, wrote poetically of him:

> To live parallel with a century is rarely allotted the span of any one human existence; but to have appeared in the dawn, and lingered (with every faculty alert) late into the evening of the present era, in which men have grappled with such titanic forces as our War Between the States, and the intricacies of the age's magic progress, denotes a rare virile ichor coursing the veins—a gift, perhaps, of some heroic ancestor—distinguishing the honored octogenarian, bravely battling with the storms of fate, and militant even with the time—to whom he is the noble hostage from all the ages.[5]

After Saunders's death, the plantation passed through many hands. It was at one time owned by his grandson Dr. Dudley Saunders, but he and his family mysteriously and abruptly abandoned the mansion, leaving behind their personal belongings, the home's furnishings, and even the food on the table. The house was also held by the Wann family, and was later jointly owned by H. D. Bynum and R. E. Tweedy, who purchased it from Dr. Saunders in the mid-1920s, after he and his family fled. Eventually, the house was abandoned and soon began to decay. A familiar scene was set, with treasure hunters and vandals wreaking damage while the faint voices of a few well-meaning preservationists were lost in the mayhem. During the castle's last days, the structure itself was purchased by Gordon McBride and his wife. The plantation property was not included in this transaction. The Gordons salvaged what they could from the mansion—doors, beams, and bricks—and used these materials in the construction of their new home in Decatur. Later the property was purchased by Wayland Cross, and a new, modern home was built on the site.

## Forks of Cypress

The Forks of Cypress Plantation near Florence in Lauderdale County, Alabama, was one of the most important historical and cultural sites in the state. It was engrained in the minds of Americans by Alex Haley's important works, such as the famed book and movie *Roots*. This home of politician James Jackson endeared itself to the hearts of many locals. It was tragically lost in 1966, when, after being struck by lightning, it burned to the ground.

James Jackson was born on October 25, 1782, in Ballybay County, Monaghan, Ireland, to parents of average means.[6] He was educated in Ireland, but fled to Germany along with his uncle because of their involvement in the Irish Rebellion. From Germany, he, along with his sister and brother-in-law, Thomas Kirkman, traveled to Philadelphia. He later settled in Nashville, Tennessee. Here he met and married the nineteen-year-old widow Sarah Moore McCullough in 1810.[7] Soon after coming to the United States, Jackson became close friends with Andrew Jackson and other influential leaders. In 1817, along with General John Coffee and U.S. Supreme Court Justice Andrew McKinley, Jackson founded the Cypress Land Company, which acquired great tracts of property.[8]

By 1820, the young Irishman had secured his wealth via landownership and planting, and he was ready to build his castle. Jackson located the perfect spot about five miles from what is today Florence, Alabama. At the location where a sparkling stream forks into the Little Cypress Creek and Big Cypress Creek, a rising hill—described as an inverted bowl of blue-green grass—luxuriously emerges. This is said to have been the site of the home of Doublehead, a famous Cherokee chief, who may have continued to live on or near the property even after Jackson purchased it from him. This unique fork of the Cypress creeks inspired the Jackson estate's distinctive moniker, the Forks of Cypress.[9]

The Jackson family lived in a log cabin while

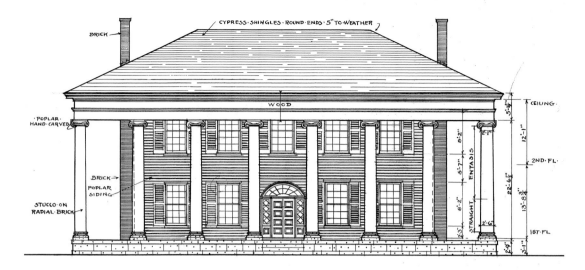

Forks of Cypress, front elevation. Note the symmetrical Ionic columns and arched transom.

James Jackson commissioned his mansion at the very nadir of the grassy hill at the waterway forks. The house melded a number of architectural styles common to regions both north and south of Lauderdale County. The mansion itself was a five-bay structure constructed of wood with two chimneys on each side along the exterior wall. This general arrangement was typical of plantation homes seen in the Upper South, such as in Tennessee or even Virginia. These typical Upper South features were balanced by a surrounding Greek Revival colonnade of twenty-four Ionic columns supporting a heavy entablature, commonly seen in mansions of the Deep South. These columns were plastered with a mixture of sand, molasses, horse hair, and charcoal.[10]

The interior of the house featured a front entrance hall leading to a larger back stair hall. The front entrance hall was flanked by a large parlor on one side and a dining hall on the other. The back stair hall was flanked by two smaller rooms. The second floor had a similar plan, although a linen closet could be found in the upper room corresponding to the lower entrance hall.[11]

From his unique mansion perched on its high hill, Jackson could survey much of his three-thousand-acre plantation below. Surrounding the mansion were four large orchards, two formed exclusively from apple trees and the other two filled with peach trees. Nearby, an alley of peach trees led to the slave quarters, where a large blacksmith shop and carpenter shop could be found. Here, between the two shops, all the farm implements used on the plantation were produced. Expert slave blacksmiths and carpenters worked together to create everything from plows and hoes to wagons. The slaves all cultivated garden plots near their quarters, as was the custom, but it is said that "Captain Jack," a trusted slave, had the most elaborate garden at the Forks. He grew such delicacies as watermelon, celery, asparagus, and even artichokes.[12]

Jackson, like many planters, had multiple interests outside the agricultural work of his plantation. He was involved in politics and served in both houses of the state assembly at various times. In 1831, he became president of the Alabama State Senate, a position he held until 1832.[13]

Jackson was also a prize-winning horse breeder. He became quite well known for his impressively stocked stables. Expensive thoroughbreds such as Leviathan, obtained from Lord Chesterfield of England, and Glencoe, purchased from the Duke of Grafton's stables, made Jackson's horses among the most celebrated in the nation, and he prided himself immensely in his other fine steeds such as Peytona, Iroquois, and Gallopade. The descendants of Jackson's horses are still winning races to this day![14]

In the 1830s, local newspapers such as the *North Alabamian* were filled with advertisements placed by James Jackson. For a fee he would sire out his stallions. The advertisements included extensive genealogies for each horse going back for many generations. Glencoe was sired for the fee of one hundred dollars plus one dollar for the groom. Often a warranty was attached—if no offspring was produced, gratis breeding service was provided for the following season.[15]

James Jackson lived an active life at his impressive plantation, but his days were cut short in 1840, when he died after a brief illness. He was buried in the plantation cemetery. An obituary in a local newspaper recounted the following:

> Mr. [Jackson] had experienced, a week or two before his death, a violent and dangerous attack of fever; but had recovered from it sufficiently to take moderate exercise, and on the fatal morning rode out upon his plantation, as was his custom when in health. It is probable, however, that on this occasion he presumed too far upon his restoration and his naturally robust and stirring habits—he retuned to the house with a chilly, full sensation, and before one o'clock was a corpse![16]

After his death, Jackson's wife took over operations of the estate, and she remained at the mansion until her death on December 24, 1879, at the age of about eighty-eight.[17]

The house passed through various owners, but was eventually acquired by Jessie Allen Dowdy in 1933. In 1945, Jessie's son, R. B. Dowdy of Birmingham, inherited the mansion, and opened it as a tourist attraction. It was an immediate hit. Dowdy filled the house with over a million dollars' worth of period furniture, antiques, and artifacts. His niece, Mrs. A. J. Wallace, was employed to run the estate.

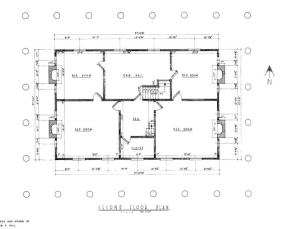

Forks of Cypress, second-floor plan. The narrow stairway in the center hall led to the attic.

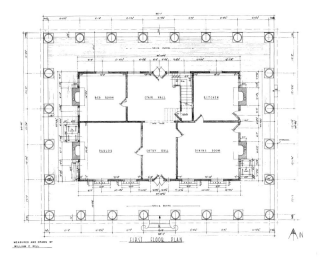

Forks of Cypress, first-floor plan. The house was completely surrounded by twenty-four columns, echoing the symmetry found throughout the plan.

This plantation museum was of great local interest, and community members grew fondly sentimental regarding their distinctive historical treasure.[18]

Unfortunately, the plantation museum at Forks of Cypress was to be short lived. A corner of the sheet metal roof of the plantation mansion was struck by lightning on June 6, 1966, and it ignited a fierce fire that burned the structure to the ground. Mrs. Willie Rhodes lived in a nearby cabin and remembered the event clearly: "I remember the day of the fire somebody came running in during the storm and said the house was on fire. I said, 'Oh, no, that house is not on fire!' But I ran out in the yard and the flames had already run across the back of it. It was gone in thirty minutes."[19]

All that remained after the fire were the brick columns; only one was destroyed. This event was a huge blow to the local citizens. Community leader Billy Warren wrote, "The Forks was such a source of interest and pride among the locals that people who lived here at the time of the fire can tell you exactly where they were and what they were doing when they learned about the fire."[20]

There was much interest at the time of the fire in reconstructing the mansion; however, the estimated cost to rebuild in 1966 topped two hundred thousand dollars, not including the expensive furnishings. Despite local fervor for the plantation, reconstruction was not accomplished then.[21]

It is very interesting to note that in recent years the Forks of Cypress has become quite well known because of its connection to celebrated author Alex Haley. Haley's grandmother, Queenie, was born a slave on the plantation. With Haley's fame from the book and movie *Roots,* the plantation was thrust into the national spotlight. After the program *Queenie* premiered on television, visitors from across the nation besieged the site of the mansion. Sadly, many took with them souvenirs, including bricks and other remaining pieces of the ruined plantation.[22]

In 1997, a group of local preservationists formed Heritage Preservation, Inc., an organization which raised over eighty thousand dollars in private contributions to stabilize the still-remaining twenty-three columns. They also completed restoration work on the columns. The stabilized ruins became the property of the Alabama Historical Commission. It has since been a site of much local interest and has even hosted weddings and other events.[23]

Over the last few decades since the mansion's demise, there have also been strong efforts with regards to researching the plantation's cemeteries. The white cemetery, although somewhat eroded by time and vandalism, still contains many large marble monuments, including several towering obelisks. The overgrown black cemetery contains several hundred gravesites, including those of Alex Haley's ancestors. Both cemeteries have been the topic of research papers.[24]

In addition to the local preservation efforts regarding the ruins and the research on the cemeteries, the AmSouth Bank's main office in Florence, which was completed in 1983, was modeled as an exterior replica of the Forks of Cypress mansion. These efforts—from the copying of the plantation mansion's façade for modern use and the stabilization of remaining ruins at the historic site to the celebration of the plantation's slave community and culture in the works of Alex Haley—provide examples of how a southern community has come to terms with its past, while successfully preserving and integrating plantation history into modern life.[25]

## Umbria

Located about ten miles from Greensboro near Sawyerville, Alabama, Samuel Pickens's Umbria Plantation at Hollow Square showcased a great U-shaped mansion that was home to Pickens and his large family. The house was a landmark of the area for over 140 years, until it burned in the early 1970s.[26]

Samuel Pickens, the son of Captain Samuel Pickens and Jane Carrigan, was born in North Carolina in 1791. He married Mary Everard Meade on February 4, 1830. It was around this time that Pickens constructed his plantation mansion at his Alabama estate.

The house was a large, raised structure that was designed to provide maximum airflow and circulation in the sweltering southern heat. The central portion of the U-shaped house contained a basement with a central hall and four rooms in a single row. The portion of the lower level corresponding with the broad side wings upstairs was an open area of pilings and supports.

The main level of the house, which was raised to a second-story level, contained a large parlor measuring over thirty-two by nearly twenty feet. This room opened onto a large almost square dining room. Both of these rooms opened in the front to an over twelve-foot-wide covered porch and in the back to the central portion of the covered rear gallery.

On either side of the main portion of the house, two bedroom wings formed a wide U shape. It is thought that these wings were built c. 1850s, some twenty years after the central portion of the house. The wings contained in total five bedrooms and, in the wing adjacent to the dining room, an attached kitchen—a rarity in most southern plantation homes, which usually had separate, disconnected kitchens. The kitchen at Umbria had its own entrance stairway, porch, and adjacent service room, providing a separate passage and work area for slaves. Both parallel wings had interior galleries that connected with the rear gallery of the central portion of the structure. Together these formed an enclosed, private three-sided court that opened to a central flower garden below.

Unfortunately, Samuel Pickens's wife, Mary, did not have the opportunity to enjoy the house. She died in 1831, and likely never saw the central portion of the house completed. Pickens remarried, to Selina Louisa Lenoir, the daughter of Colonel Thomas Lenoir and Selina Louisa Avery Lenoir. Together the couple had one child, Thomas Lenoir Pickens. Sadly, Selina also died young, leaving Samuel Pickens twice a widower. He remarried again, to Mary Gaillard Thomas of South Carolina. She bore him many children, including James (Jamie), Samuel, William, John, Mary, Louisa, and Isreal.

As the Pickens family continued to grow, so did their wealth. In addition to their flagship estate, Umbria, the family also acquired other plantations, such as Canebrake and the Goodrum Place. Samuel Pickens died June 23, 1855, leaving his wife an enormous fortune. The U.S. census of 1860 notes that the Widow Pickens owned assets valued at nearly a half million dollars (roughly $11 million in 2007 dollars[27]), including over two hundred slaves.

Life on the plantation was good for the widow and her children. Two of her sons, Samuel and Jamie, left detailed dairies that recount the activities of their daily lives at Umbria and later their military service. In 1862, as war loomed for the family, Samuel wrote of the agricultural operations on the various Pickens estates:

> Jamie and I got up about 5 O'clock this morning. He went to Hol. Sq. before breakfast and got the paper. After breakfast I started on horseback to the Canebreak Plantation. Stopped at the Goodrum Place and took dinner. The early corn [is] generally pretty good. The late corn is very poor, except in the low, rich places in the Mead tract. The fodder on the high-thirsty land is almost all burnt up. There are about 40 acres of Pease [sic] which look flourishing and seem to stand the long & severe droughth [sic] better than any thing else. Cotton was planted only on such poor spots as would not bring corn and consequently is very small and looks badly. But Cotton is beneath notice this year & you never hear it spoken of or see it noticed in the news papers. Every one gave up Cotton and turned his attention to raising an abundant Grain Crop for home consumption and the support of our Armies, except a few avaricious men . . .[28]

In addition to their agricultural operations, the Pickens family invested in other industries, including a brick factory. Young Samuel Pickens wrote: "The weather is very dry & hot. Jamie & I rode to the Goodrum Place, & after dinner went to Port Royal, where we are making brick. The yard is for Professor [indecipherable] house. A Mr. Doug. Patterson is employed to supervise until we get the hang of the . . . operations, and he will return & burn the kiln when we shall have made enough. We propose making a hundred thousand if the weather remains favorable."[29]

Samuel and Jamie both enlisted during the Civil War in Company D, Greensboro Guards, Fifth Alabama Infantry Regiment, which served in the Army of Northern Virginia. Their extensive personal diaries have been published in a compilation of journals edited by G. Ward Hubbs. Both brothers had attended Henry Tutwiler's Greene Springs

Umbria's front façade was highlighted by six Ionic columns. The raised basement consisted of a central hall and four flanking rooms. The remainder of the elevated house was supported by pillars.

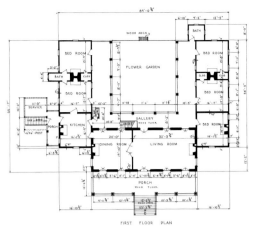

FIRST FLOOR PLAN

NOTE:
ORIGINAL USE OF BASEMENT ROOMS UNDETERMINED

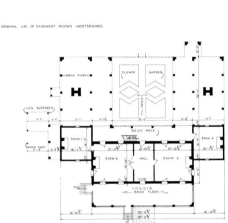

FOUNDATION & BASEMENT PLAN

Umbria Plantation, principal floor plan. The side bedroom wings are thought to have been constructed later than the central portion of the house, which corresponds with the raised basement. The U-shaped house enclosed a courtyard and flower garden below.

Umbria from the rear.

Umbria Plantation. The photograph was taken from the raised back gallery, looking onto one of the bedroom wings.

School near Havana and both later attended the University of Virginia. Their writings reveal that although the brothers had similar upbringings at Umbria and comparable educations, their temperaments could not have been more different.

Samuel relished army life and made a great success of his service, while Jamie tried ardently to get out of his responsibilities to serve. Under the Confederate Conscription Act of 1862, all healthy white males between eighteen and thirty-five years of age were required to serve in the military for three years. Jamie Pickens sought to exercise a loophole in the law by hiring a substitute to replace him, but none could be found. When Jamie was finally forced into service, he spent much of his time in the military hospital with various illnesses and ailments. He abhorred the war and did not remain in service long. While lying in a hospital bed he wrote:

> There were a large number of Yankee prisoners which we captured yesterday, which passes to the ear whilst I was at the provost guard's last even'g. Also a quantity of wounded men, both of ours & the Yankees—mutilated & shot in almost every imaginable manner. The sight was shocking to behold. There was a considerable number of wounded at the hospital to-day when I got there, & ambulances were constantly arriving with them. Amputation is going on & there are several who have died of their wounds & been buried near by the hospital. Oh the horrors of war! no one knows until he sees for himself how much suffering & distress there is in battle. [Wish] to God the strife were over & that peace again blessed our land![30]

Jamie left military life as quickly as possible, and in 1870, he married Juliet Damer, with whom he had three daughters. Samuel Pickens remained in the Fifth Infantry Regiment until the end despite being captured twice and wounded once. He was finally forced to take an oath to the Union after his army surrendered. He never married and died in 1890.

Umbria saw vast changes after the war. The Pickens children were grown, many with lives of their own away from the struggling farmlands. Remarkably, the plantation stayed in the family for several more generations, and was extensively renovated in the mid-twentieth century. The main house was tragically destroyed by fire on December 30, 1971.

A one-room schoolhouse from the estate survived the fire and was donated to the Gulf States Company, which moved the building to Tuscaloosa where they displayed it along with the two-room Greek Revival Gainsville Bank, an antebellum structure where Confederate money was once printed. The company later donated the schoolhouse to the Tuscaloosa County Preservation Society.

Today, the original plantation site is surrounded by a fence and brick foundations, and crumbling outbuildings can still be seen.

## New Smyrna

New Smyrna Plantation, which once thrived in what is today Volusia County, Florida, is said to have been the largest single settlement in the North American English colonies prior to the Revolution. Here, Dr. Andrew Turnbull led a grand experiment in agriculture and plantation organization, successfully producing the highest quality indigo by exploiting indentured Mediterranean laborers. The scheme ultimately failed, and today the massive ruins of a structural foundation along a Florida beach and a few other obscure remnants of the plantation's extensive built environment are all that remain of this intriguing and vast estate.[31]

The area destined to become this great and unusual plantation was originally called Los Mosquitos because of its abundance of the pesky insects. It was located about seventy miles south of St. Augustine, and it was originally granted by the Spanish to Joaquín de Florencia. He called the property Santa Ana de Afafa, and may have used it for cattle ranching. Later, workers cut trees there for shipbuilding.

Florida fell under British control in 1763. Its colonial rulers hoped to make great improvements upon their new lands while supporting the regional economy and their own pocketbooks. Among the British elite who saw great potential in Florida was Dr. Andrew Turnbull, a Scottish physician who had established his medical practice in London. He was joined by two of his associates, William Duncan and Prime Minister George Grenville (who acted through his agent Sir Richard Temple), in establishing a Florida agricultural operation on the grandest scale. Together they secured collective land grants totaling over one hundred thousand acres, including the forty thousand acres set to become New Smyrna.

Turnbull traveled extensively, visiting many foreign lands. He married Garcia Dura Bin, the daughter of a wealthy Smyrna merchant. Turnbull had been exposed to Greek workers and understood the hardships they faced under the rule of the Turks. He embarked on an expedition, traveling for almost a year through the Mediterranean region, recruiting laborers for his plantation. He enlisted Greeks from Corsica and some from the areas of the Peloponnesos and the Greek islands and over a hundred single men from the Italian peninsula. He also secured over a thousand workers from English-controlled Minorca, an island off the coast of Spain. These individuals were to be indentured laborers who were to share the fruits of their labor in exchange for the promise of land at the end of a specified term (five to ten years). Along with these workers came Father Pedro Camps, a Catholic priest whom Turnbull agreed to pay three hundred pesos a year, and Father Bartolemeo Casasnovas, a monk. Together, over fourteen hundred embarked on eight ships bound for Florida.

The voyage was long and arduous, and by the time they arrived 148 of the workers had died. Making matters worse was the fact that provisions had only been obtained for 400 to 600 people. The governor of East Florida commented that the arrival of these individuals represented the "largest importation of White inhabitants that ever was brought into America at a time." The governor sent some provisions for the new settlers, but still food, clothing, and housing were in short supply. The workers fished and grew vegetables to supplement their few rations. They initially lived in small palm huts, but soon they constructed buildings and other works on the plantation.

The entire plan of the plantation from the importation of workers to construction of the built environment was devised step by step in an organized plan. Turnbull was to be the on-site administrator of the plantation, and as such was ultimately responsible for turning a profit. He established a smaller private cotton plantation of his own adjacent to the larger New Smyrna enterprise.

New Smyrna, named after the birthplace of Turnbull's wife, initially wavered as the bills mounted and profits faltered. The huge workforce was demoralized, and the other investors were very unhappy. Turnbull's two associates punished him for this apparent failure, reducing his share of the company from one-third to one-fifth, while each retained two-fifths. At this point Turnbull was inspired to make the enterprise work.

But the doctor's most pressing matter was his indentured workforce. As food became scarcer and the death rate rose among the workers, a rebellion was organized. The Italians along with some of their fellow Greek laborers—three hundred in all—stormed the plantation's warehouses and commandeered a ship. They threatened to kill any Minorcan who stood in their way, and dismembered the chief overseer. Because the rebels took three days to load their loot onto their stolen ship, there was enough time to send word to the governor in St. Augustine, and soon troops arrived to quell the uprising. Two of the ringleaders of the rebellion were put to death.

There were other uprisings on the plantation. When Antonio Stephanolpoli was captured after an escape attempt he was punished with 110 lashes and for sixteen months was forced to wear a fifteen-pound chain. Such resistance efforts were understandable given the cruel conditions the settlers faced. Not only was the death rate rising while the birth rate plummeted, but the workers faced harsh treatment under Turnbull's administration. For example, when ten-year-old Guillermo Vens was too sick to work he was beaten and forced into the fields anyway. Once in the fields, he was still unable to toil the crops, so the driver made the other boys stone him to death. And when pregnant Paola Laurance refused to submit to a driver's sexual advances in the fields, she was beaten so badly that her unborn child died.

Despite the fact that the workforce was abused and dissatisfied, the plantation still continued to grow. South of his own plantation and the waterfront lots of the workers, Turnbull commissioned a large central complex that contained three dormitories for young single men, warehouses, craft shops, storehouses, a church and convent, military barracks with a powder magazine, a stone wharf, a jail, and storage facilities.

Another grand aspect of the built environment which Turnbull spearheaded was the creation of a network of canals to provide drainage and irrigation. During his extensive travels, Turnbull had marveled at ancient Egyptian canals. He brought this design to New Smyrna, lining the waterways with native coquina. Many of these are still visible in the landscape of the present-day community.

During his time as planter, Turnbull also began a variety of agricultural pursuits, from planting mulberry trees for silkworms to raising cochineal insects to make red dye. None of these schemes was successful. It was indigo that would become the so-called "blue gold" of New Smyrna. The Florida climate was well suited to the cultivation of indigo, and once the crops matured, production of dye began immediately. Such production consisted of processing harvested plants in large vats filled with water. Urine, lime, or barilla may have been added to hasten the process, and wooden paddles were used to beat the soaked plants. Later the water from these vats was transferred to smaller containers to dehydrate. The sludge was hung in cloth sleeves to drain and dry. Eventually, solid blue bricks were cut and shipped for the world market. By 1771, the plantation was producing nearly twelve thousand pounds of processed indigo dye, and Turnbull was

turning quite a profit. The quality of Turnbull's indigo was remarkable, only furthering his success in this enterprise.

But his agricultural and economic accomplishments were to be short-lived. Besides the inherently complex workforce issues at play on the plantation, the settlement also faced threats from Seminole Indians who believed the Mediterranean workers to be their Spanish enemies. Despite reassurance that the workers were not Spanish conquistadors, the Indians persisted in terrorizing the plantation. Furthermore, Patrick Tonyn, a man Turnbull despised, became governor of the colony, leading to much political unrest within New Smyrna. "Governor Tonyn did everything to undermine the plantation and nothing to encourage its survival."[32]

In addition to the these setbacks, the area faced severe draughts in 1773 and 1775, badly damaging crop production and causing many of the workers to starve as their kitchen gardens were empty. The final straw came with the American Revolution. The governor asked Turnbull to send men to fight for the British cause, but he adamantly refused this request, preferring his workers to remain on the plantation and salvage what they could of the once-successful enterprise. The governor, angered, sought to indict Turnbull for illegally trying to obtain Indian lands. Turnbull then fled to England to avoid arrest.

Turnbull's twenty-year-old nephew, also named Andrew Turnbull, took control, but his lack of experience and poor management sent the plantation to its final death. In 1777, the plantation workers were relieved of their indentures by the government. Together these proud people walked seventy-five miles down the King's Road from New Smyrna to St. Augustine, where many of their descendants still reside today. Turnbull eventually returned to North America, setting up a very successful medical practice in Charleston. Today, ruinous remains of the great plantation are still visible in the New Smyrna Beach community.

# Bulowville

Bulowville, another great Florida plantation whose existence was threatened by problems with Native Americans, now exists only as a few scattered ruins in a wooded state historic site in Flagler County. This grand plantation's history can be traced back to 1812, when James Russell, his family, and a hundred slaves landed ashore from the Bahamas. They came aboard a schooner called *The Perseverance*, which they traded for twenty-five hundred acres of land from the Spanish crown. Russell established a plantation there that he called Good Retreat, but he died shortly thereafter.[33]

The land was acquired by Major Charles Wilhelm Bulow, a planter from Charleston, who enlarged the holdings to some six thousand acres. He cleared fifteen hundred acres for the production of sugar cane, a thousand for cotton, and set aside smaller areas for indigo and rice. Bulow brought more than three hundred slaves from Charleston. Upon their arrival, these individuals were put to work constructing a variety of buildings, clearing more lands, and cultivating the crops.

The slaves used widely available timber and porous coquina, a friable variety of limestone made mostly of shell fragments, in the construction of several wells, a spring house, a sugar mill, and, of course, the grand master house. The house itself was a board structure that contained a large and well-stocked library. The establishment was finally coming into full fruition when Bulow died at the age of forty-four. He was buried in St. Augustine, leaving behind a widow and two young children, John Joachim and an adopted daughter, Emily Ann.

At some time, John Joachim was sent to Paris, where he was formally educated, and upon his return, he took over day-to-day operations of the plantation. He managed to increase the family fortune significantly as he increased production and profits from Bulowville.

John J. Bulow became one of the principal planters of the region and as such was a noted personality in local society. In 1831, he entertained famed naturalist John James Audubon at Bulowville. Audubon writes in a letter to his wife: "Mr. J. J. Bulow, a rich planter, at whose home myself and party have been for a whole week under the most hospitable and welcome treatment that could possible [*sic*] be expected, proposed three days since that we should proceed down the river in search of new or valuable birds, and accordingly the boats, six hand and three white men with some provisions, put off with fair wind and pure sky."[34]

Audubon's journey led him to find many fine specimens of birds, but the weather was harsh and he returned to Bulow's plantation. "Well, through this sand we waded for many a long mile . . . until we reached the landing place of J. J. Bulow. Now my heart cheers up once more for the sake of my most kind host, trouble as he is with rheumatic pains, I assure you I was glad to see him nearing his own comfortable roof, and as we saw the large house opening to view across his immense plantation, I anticipated a good dinner with as much pleasure as I ever experienced."[35]

Bulow, especially in his younger days, was much accustomed to journeys down the Halifax River, such as Audubon undertook. Accounts note that he often took along with him numerous oarsmen, servants, and cooks, as well as tents, foodstuffs, and other supplies.

Soon the life of privilege and favor Bulow enjoyed would be threatened because of his relationship with the local Native Americans. Bulow worked closely with the Seminoles, who supplied him with much fresh meat. When authorities began forcing these indigenous people west, Bulow expressed his strong disapproval. When Major Putnam and his band of "Mosquito Roarers" came to the plantation, Bulow fired a cannon at them. Not taking kindly to his aggression, the major and his troops swarmed upon the plantation and took Bulow hostage. They forced him into their service and turned his home into their camp.

The major took bales of cotton worth twen-

Bulow Plantation ruins, now a Florida state park. Courtesy of the Florida State Parks.

ty thousand dollars and used them to construct breastworks. He commandeered Bulow's boats into his own service, and refused to let the planter eat at his own table. He even denied Bulow the use of his own possessions on his own property.

This campaign against the Native Americans did not go well for Putnam. His poorly trained men suffered from lack of coordination and even more so from illnesses such as dysentery and yellow fever. Eventually, all the settlers of the area and many slaves were all brought to the camp at Bulow's plantation. They were subsequently transported to St. Augustine some forty miles away.

After Bulowville and the other plantations had been abandoned, the Seminoles took their revenge. They burned the great plantations to the ground. When Bulow returned to his beloved estate, little was left but coquina ruins. Disheartened by the destruction and memories of his imprisonment at his own home, the young man returned to his beloved Paris. There he died a bachelor before reaching the age of twenty-seven.

Today the ruins of Bulow Plantation are opened to the public as a state historic site. Each year they receive many visitors who come to gaze at the walls, the lovely stone arches, the remnants of the sugar mill, and even the foundations of the once-famed plantation mansion that John Joachim Bulow called home.

## Yulee Plantations: Cottonwood and Margarita

Florida's David Levy Yulee, one of its more prominent leaders of the antebellum era, was owner and/or manager of much plantation land. Among his holdings were Cottonwood Plantation near Archer and Margarita Plantation at Homosassa. Today, Cottonwood is remembered only by a highway marker, while the significant ruins of Margarita's sugar mill serve as a historical state park.[36]

Yulee traced his lineage to Spain, where his Jewish ancestors were expelled by edict of King Ferdi-

nand and Queen Isabella in 1492 because of their religious beliefs and practices. The family fled to northern Africa, where Yulee's grandfather, Jacoub Ben Youle (or Youli), served as grand vizier under the Muslim sultan in Morocco. Youle married Rachel Levy, a young Jewish woman from England. After the sultan's death, the couple and their children fled, as Youle found much disfavor with the new Moroccan ruler. The ultimate fate of the former vizier is disputed, but it is clear that his wife and two children, Moses and Rachel, escaped to Gibraltar. Here the children took their mother's surname and freely practiced their Jewish faith. Later, as a young man, Moses immigrated to the West Indies, where he found success as a lumber merchant and married Hannah Margarite Abendanone. Moses and Hannah had four children; the youngest, David, was born on June 12, 1810.

At the age of five, young David Levy learned of his parents' imminent divorce; his siblings were sent to school in England while he remained with his mother on St. Thomas. Four years later, David's father sent for his son to join him in the United States. David was then placed with Moses Myers, an old family friend in Norfolk, Virginia. He attended Norfolk Academy, where he excelled for many years, until 1827, when his father abruptly ceased his education. David moved to one of his father's Florida plantations near Micanopy, and here his life in planting began.

David's father had purchased a great deal of land in Florida, including large parts of the Arredondo land grant in north-central territorial Florida. Moses Levy keenly appreciated the great profits that could come from sugar cultivation and became a very early sugar producer. Upon his father's plantation, David played a supervisory role under the tutorage of the plantation overseer. Here he became filled with agricultural knowledge and was skilled in the art of planting sugarcane. He fell in love with the untamed wilderness surrounding him, spending long days fishing, hiking, and insatiably reading.

After several years of enjoying agrarian life, David left the plantation to become the deputy clerk

on the former senator's behalf. On his release, Yu-lee worked tirelessly, promoting the Florida Railroad and leading the development of Fernandina. In 1881, he and his family retired to Washington, where they constructed a mansion on Connecticut Avenue which later served as the Austrian embassy.

David Yulee died on March 16, 1885, and was buried in Oak Hill Cemetery in Washington. According to Dollie Nattiel, Cottonwood was occupied by Dr. Carew, after the slaves were freed. It was purchased by Monroe Venable in 1906, and operated as a tobacco farm. His daughter Ethyle Venable Crevasse built a new brick house in 1966, near the site of the old plantation house. The original home was destroyed in the late 1970s or early 1980s. Today, the site of Cottonwood is remembered by a highway marker.

At the former site of Margarita, ruins of the old sugar mill still remain, including a large chimney, a forty-foot-long structure that houses the boiler, and grinding machinery. The historic site was granted to the Citrus County Federation of Women's Clubs in 1923, and was later deeded to the state of Florida in 1953.

Since that time, the site has been operated by the Florida Park Service, and today comprises the Yulee Sugar Mill Ruins Historic State Park, which includes interpretive signage and areas for picnicking. In 2006, the ruins were stabilized with lime and sand mortar in original mix proportions. In addition, archeological work has been undertaken at the historic site, which functions as a true connection between local Floridians and their colorful past.

## Mount Oswald

The cluster of settlements and agricultural developments developed by Richard Oswald and East Florida governor James Grant, located between the confluence of the Tomoka and Halifax rivers, flourished prior to the American Revolution.

Known collectively as Mount Oswald, these estates grew quickly, but their success was cut short when Washington's army defeated the British and Spain regained control of Florida. The plantation and its associated developments were abandoned, allowed to revert to nature, and largely forgotten.[40]

Richard Oswald, a British diplomat and businessman, was born in Scotland in 1705. He excelled in business and became the owner of Bance Island, an important facility at the mouth of the Sierra Leone River, where slaves were processed and exported to the North American colonies. Oswald, therefore, had access to a virtually endless source of cheap labor.

Oswald and Grant became business partners in a planting venture around 1765, when Grant agreed to supply twenty thousand acres of the best land in the colony and provide periodic on-site supervision, while Oswald would provide funding and slaves. The site of this large enterprise was chosen at a place called Nocoroco by natives.

The initial settlement of the site was delayed, as the owners awaited the arrival of Marmaduke Bell, a noted overseer from South Carolina who had previously worked for Francis Kinloch, a well-known rice planter. Bell finally decided to begin his own plantation and declined the job at the Oswald estate, again delaying development. Another overseer, Samuel Hewie, was chosen and arrived in June 1766. Grant sent him, along with twelve male slaves, to the Mount Oswald site to begin the arduous tasks of clearing and planting.

Hewie soon proved to be a hot-headed drunkard who often abused the slaves, but despite his cruel behavior, the plantation flourished under his leadership and productivity was high. However, in less than a year, Hewie drowned in what was either an accident or a failed rebellion. He was succeeded as overseer by a Native American man known only as "the Indian Johnson."

Henry Laurens,[41] a planter, business associate of Oswald's, and later American Revolution leader, wrote of the incident at Mount Oswald: "The catastrophe of the wretched [Hewie] & the poor Negroes is affecting. He might have been, according to his credentials a good Servant, but I see clearly that he was unfit for the sole management of a Plantation. His successor the Indian Johnson must behave above the rank of common Caroinian Fugitives, to save his Scalp a whole year. He must be discreet & carry a steady command otherwise the Blacks will drown him too . . ."[42]

Much like his predecessor, Johnson ran the plantation successfully for only a short time. He disappeared a few months after assuming his position as overseer, and whether foul play was involved in his departure was unclear. He was replaced by a man known to history only as "Mr. Parry."

By 1767, Mr. Parry was successfully running the plantation, and Oswald sent the ship *St. Augustine Packet,* carrying seventy Africans who were intended for Mount Oswald. He also sent a carpenter, Phillip Herries, to teach the slaves the craft of carpentry.

By the late 1760s through the early 1770s, Oswald had sent several plantation managers to supervise overseers. Lt. John Fairlamb, a former artillery officer, served as general superintendent of Mount Oswald and the nearby estates of Thomas Thoroton. Oswald also sent Fredrick Robertson and Donald McLean, two of his employees from England and Germany, to Mount Oswald to manage affairs as well. They successfully integrated a hundred additional African slaves into the plantation.

Miscommunication led to Fairlamb's abrupt departure in 1772, when he was incorrectly informed that he was to be replaced. He was succeeded as principal estate administrator by Fredrick Robertson, ushering in an era of continued agricultural success. By 1774, the estate produced four thousand pounds of indigo along with large amounts of sugar and cotton.

It was around this time that carpenter John Brown constructed a large sugar mill for the plantation. The controversial mill was seen as a progressive project by some, but one contemporary account noted, "Oswald's wheel which was contrived by the mad ship carpenter is good for nothing."[43]

Sugar was an innovative crop, and experimentation in sugar cultivation and refining were common on large estates. Oswald grew various types of cane seedlings at his hothouse in Scotland and shipped them to his Florida plantation to be replanted. Swamp Settlement, one of the divisions of Mount Oswald, was often the site where experimental sugarcane was cultivated under the supervision of a cane expert from Jamaica.

In total, there were five main "settlements" of the Oswald plantation, each with specialized and defined agricultural purposes. In their prime, each settlement included large houses for overseers and managers, villages of slave cabins, barns, stables, shops, warehouses, and manufacturing complexes. One observer noted that at one settlement there was "a very good Dwelling House . . . 40 feet by 20 framed and weather boarded Shingled & Glazed, a large framed Barn about 60 feet by 30, floored Weather boarded and shingled. A shell framed Overseers House, Kitchen and Negroe Houses."[44]

Oswald's successful estate may have flourished for decades, but the tensions between colonists and British officials that sparked the American Revolution would also have longstanding effects on the history of the Mount Oswald enterprises. In 1776, Oswald sent his nephew to Florida to oversee his plantations, fearing that the rebellion would spread toward the South. For the next few years, however, life went on virtually unscathed by the battles northward. Anderson successfully expanded rice cultivation on the plantation and turned a sizeable profit.

But, despite financial and agricultural success, Mount Oswald was surrounded by political upheaval and violence. By 1780, Bernardo de Gálvez, the governor of Spanish Louisiana, had captured Baton Rouge, Natchez, and Mobile from the British, and was preparing for an attack on Pensacola. The Spanish also controlled Cuba, and Spanish troops had already plundered the plantations surrounding Mount Oswald. To the north, fierce battles still raged between the freedom-hungry colonists and Britain's mighty army.

Oswald instructed his nephew to move his slaves and property from Mount Oswald to a vacant estate near Savannah, Georgia. Over 240 slaves, along with much property, were loaded onto a ship, which, during the voyage was attacked by American privateers. More than 70 slaves were abducted, and many died during the attack. Those surviving traveled with Anderson to the estate of John Graham, the lieutenant governor of Georgia, who was also a close associate of Richard Oswald.

With the remainder of his slaves and property safe on the Graham estate near Savannah, Oswald went on to lead a peace delegation with the Americans on behalf of the British government. He met with Benjamin Franklin, John Jay, and John Adams, and it was in Oswald's hotel room in Paris where these legendary gentlemen signed the preliminary peace treaties in 1782.

As the brutal violence of war desolated North America, John Graham arranged for Oswald's remaining slaves and property to be transported back to Florida. Meanwhile, James Anderson moved to South Carolina, where he established his own rice plantation. Lt. Col. John Douglas became the manager of the Mount Oswald estate, which he ran from his post in St. Augustine. Less than two years later, in 1784, after the resurrection of the plantation, East Florida was transferred from Britain to Spain. Oswald again ordered that his slaves be boarded on a ship, which transported them to South Carolina where they labored on Santee River rice plantations. Richard Oswald died this same year at the age of eighty.

Mount Oswald was abandoned, and its fields slowly returned to their natural state. The buildings scattered about the massive plantation's five settlements were allowed to gradually succumb to the elements and lack of care. Today, parts of the plantation site are included in Tomoka State Park, where ruins of the plantation's famed sugar mill and a rum distillery can still be seen. Archeological investigations have commenced in and around these sites, resulting in the recovery of interesting artifacts and fascinating information about the settlements. In recent years, a historical marker has been erected at the park to commemorate the history of Richard Oswald's mammoth Mount Oswald Plantation.

## Verdura

Verdura Plantation, once home to the grandest plantation mansion in Florida, was built by Benjamin Chaires, Sr., fittingly, as he was one of the state's wealthiest and most successful planters. The celebrated house burned in 1885, and the estate was abandoned. Today, the charred remains of the structure and nearby family cemetery just southeast of Tallahassee provide a hidden, overgrown shadow of Verdura's illustrious past.

Benjamin Chaires, Sr., was born in Onslow County, North Carolina, and later moved to Milledgeville, Georgia, and then Florida. He was instrumental in planning the development of Jacksonville in the early 1820s, and he was later successful at establishing a bank and railroad in Tallahassee.[45]

He and his brothers established themselves in Leon County and began acquiring great sums of land. Benjamin lived at The Columns in Tallahassee, while his brother Green Chaires founded Evergreen Hills Plantation on two tracts totaling sixty-seven hundred acres. Another brother, Thomas Peter Chaires, owned Woodlawn Plantation, a sprawling estate that produced 225 bales of cotton and 7,000 bushels of corn in 1860.

Benjamin Chaires eventually sold The Columns to move to Verdura, his cotton plantation located ten miles east of Tallahassee. Benjamin constructed what was said to be Florida's finest plantation home at Verdura. The mansion, which was built in the early 1830s, sat on a hill encircled by a stream. It was a three-story building constructed of clay bricks, which were each handmade on the plantation by one of the estate's sixty slaves. The front and rear entrances were approached by broad staircases. On the east and west sides of the house there were verandas supported by great Tuscan columns. The mansion contained some thirteen to fifteen rooms, and for grand parties and balls the great rooms of the lower level could be thrown open to create a flowing eighty-foot-wide space. Inside,

An artist's conjectural elevation of Verdura Plantation mansion based on existing architectural and archeological evidence. Courtesy State Archives of Florida.

The tall ruined columns of Florida's Verdura Plantation House still stand proud on their lofty plinths. Courtesy State Archives of Florida.

double stairways led to the upper floor, and above, in the attic, one could see to the Gulf of Mexico on a clear day.

Benjamin Chaires died in 1838, and his family inherited the plantation. At the time of his death, he had expanded Verdura to over nine thousand acres of prime plantation land and acquired other estates. In fact, when his holdings were divided among his three children—Martha, Charles, and Thomas—each still rivaled the largest planters in the county. The family was further fractured by the great yellow fever epidemic of 1841, which claimed several family members among its victims. The grave markers in the nearby family cemetery record a cluster of dates on which several members of the Chaires family succumbed to the disease within a time frame of a few brief weeks.

The plantation was in full operation on the eve of the Civil War. The 1860 U.S. census records that there were sixty-three slaves laboring on Vendura, and that the estate produced one hundred sixty bales of cotton that year. In addition, twenty-five hundred bushels of corn were grown and over forty-two hundred dollars' (nearly ninety-six thousand dollars in 2007 dollars) worth of farm animals were raised.[46]

The Civil War and its aftermath wreaked great havoc at Verdura as elsewhere, as the slave labor force was freed and the cotton economy crumbled. The final blow came in 1885, when Verdura's grand mansion was consumed by fire. The plantation was abandoned, and the site was largely allowed to return to nature.

Today, amid an overgrowth of hardwoods and brush, one can still find the charred remains of ten towering brick columns atop lofty square bases. They form an impressive and important, yet largely hidden, reminder of Florida's antebellum past. And a few hundred yards away, fenced and largely obscured by wild plants, the little Chaires family cemetery remains, its markers fighting to defy the harsh elements and wounds of time. Sadly, despite its relatively remote locale, the cemetery has been the victim of vandals more than a few times. Still, the ornate urn that marks Benjamin Chaires's grave remains in place, peeking through a thicket of vines and weeds.

The Verdura Plantation site has been recognized by local authorities as one of Florida's most important archeological sites. In 2000, Florida State University anthropology student Sharon Heiland wrote an acclaimed thesis on her archeological work at the site. Her work, "The Verdura Place: A Historical Overview and Preliminary Archaeological Survey," broke new ground and confirmed the importance of the plantation site as a scientific, educational, and cultural treasure.

# CHAPTER SIX

# *Mississippi*

. . . let us, while waiting for new monument, preserve the ancient monuments.

—*Victor Hugo*

In every conceivable manner, the family is link to our past, bridge to our future.

—*Alex Haley*

MISS. I

Natchez's Longwood Plantation still stands in all of its unfinished glory. The octagonal mansion is misleadingly complete on the outside; its construction was abruptly halted at the onset of the Civil War. Inside, unfinished rooms house workers' tools that were left on the site and still sit untouched today.

The lands that now compose the modern-day state of Mississippi were first explored by Hernando de Soto in 1540. More than 150 years later Pierre Le Moyne, Sieur d'Iberville, founded the first settlement at Old Biloxi near Ocean Springs. Natchez was founded in 1716 as Fort Rosalie and quickly became the principal development and trading hub of the region. The region's agricultural expansion that led to the rise of a cash crop, slave-driven economy and the development of complex plantation systems did not come for yet another 100 years.

The Mississippi region was claimed by the Spanish, British, and French, but was officially deeded to the British after the French and Indian War under the terms of the 1763 Treaty of Paris. It was later again controlled by the Spanish, but eventually was ceded to the United States. During this time, settlement in the area was sparse and crops were grown on mostly a small scale and largely for consumption. Although slavery could be found in the region, it was not particularly common, and few were large slaveholders.

The Mississippi Territory was organized in 1798, from territory ceded by Georgia and South Carolina, and it was later incrementally expanded. Around the same time, Eli Whitney invented the cotton gin. This occurred fortuitously as a massive increase in the demand for cotton was spurred by new mechanizations in textile production. In particular, the demand for baled cotton in new British textile mills was especially high. This combination of factors—the sharp increase in the demand for cotton brought about by new industrial innovations coupled with the increase of supplies via the cotton gin—boded well for the Mississippi Territory.

Statehood came for Mississippi on December 10, 1817, when it was admitted to the Union as the twentieth state. And with statehood came great economic growth. Mississippi land was fertile and cheap, and speculators from the North and from older slave states flooded the region in hopes of finding fortune in the cotton industry. The three decades prior to the Civil War were particularly robust, as treaties with Native Americans opened more land and cotton profits rose.

From the turn of the century to the eve of the Civil War, Mississippi was transformed from an unsettled territory to a bustling center of agricultural production and economic activity. The population of Mississippi grew from 5,179 in 1800 to 353,901 in 1860 (an increase of nearly seventy fold in only sixty years); likewise, cotton production expanded from zero pounds in 1800 to over 535 million pounds in 1859.[1]

Although the majority of Mississippi farmers were nonslaveholding whites, a robust plantocracy emerged. It was the large plantation masters, owning many slaves and great sums of land, who dominated the economic, political, and social systems of the day. These planters lived varying lifestyles, but as the years passed it became increasingly popular for them to communicate their wealth and power through the construction of large, sophisticated mansions and intricate plantation complexes.

Between 1830 and 1860, the majority of Mississippi's great plantation mansions were built, with a seemingly unceasing array of competitiveness; each new mansion was bigger and grander than the previous one.[2] Most were designed in the popular Greek Revival style, many with soaring columns and ornate embellishments. Extant examples include Rosswood near Lorman, the home of Dr. Walter Ross Wade, which was used as a hospital during the Civil War, and Waverly in Columbus, with its enormous cupola and thin Ionic columns. In other instances, planters constructed Italianate master houses or Gothic Revival homes such as Airliewood, which still welcomes visitors in Holly Springs.

The plantation building boom ceased abruptly upon the outbreak of the Civil War. Nowhere in the South can this be seen more clearly than at Longwood Plantation in Natchez. Longwood's unusual mansion, planned by Philadelphia architect Samuel Sloan for cotton planter Dr. Haller Nutt, was an eclectic array of Moorish design with elements of Italian, Greek Revival, and other styles. Its magnificently complex, octagonal plan was topped by a sixteen-sided cupola with a dominating, Byzantine style, onion-shaped dome. While the outside of the house appeared misleadingly nearly complete, the interior was still largely unfinished. Workers dropped their tools and unfinished architectural elements, abandoning the project for the battlefields. Haller's descendants occupied the unfinished basement rooms for more than a hundred years, until the home was presented to the Pilgrimage Garden Club in 1970. Today, visitors can still see the untouched workers' tools, the bare brick walls, and the rambling unfinished cupola that all echo the sudden reversal of fortune and economy that the war represented.

Longwood's fancy façade but hollow interior provide a solid metaphor for the entire postwar plantation South. While on the outside much of the architectural glory and mystique of southern plantations remained long after the war, the interiors of the estates—the more obscure production mechanisms that, fueled by slavery and a bustling economy, created the wealth which allowed for such built splendor—were decimated and empty.

The years after the war were difficult, as planters tried to pick up the pieces of their plantations and their lives. Eventually, many estates were abandoned, as the economic reason for their existence was gone. The 1930s WPA guide recalls the "sagging porches and rotting pillars" of these once-grand, then forgotten estates. Other plantations were sold to outsiders, while some remained in the same families. Many succumbed to various fires or other natural disasters over the years, and memories of their existence began to fade.

This chapter details the history of eight of Mississippi's lost plantations. But, for each estate noted in this volume, there were literally hundreds of others that have been lost. Some are well remembered and documented, such as the Johnstones' Ingleside and Annandale plantations, both exquisite Italianate mansions, as well as Bowling Green, the home of Col. Edward McGehee that was destroyed by the Federals during the Civil War. Others are barely known and some have faded completely into the past, leaving no trace or remembrance of their existence whatsoever.

Many of Mississippi's lost plantation homes have been expertly documented by Mary Carol Miller in her *Lost Mansions of Mississippi*. Miller's acclaimed work is among only a very few studies that exclusively document lost domestic architecture specific to a single state or region. Another rich source of documentation on the lost plantation architecture of Mississippi can be found in *Mississippi: The WPA Guide to the Magnolia State*, a source touted by Miller and other researchers. The Work Projects Administration, a New Deal program, provided work for writers and photographers, along with many others, during the Great Depression. State travel guides were among the many works produced by these professionals. The Mississippi guide provides histories and fascinating descriptions of many places now lost to time. The Historic American Buildings Survey, the only WPA project still remaining active today, also provides a wealth of documentation on the lost buildings of Mississippi, as well as the rest of the country.

Today, a small portion of Mississippi antebellum plantation mansions do still stand, and several have been restored, among the most notable being Beauvoir, which faced near destruction during Hurricane Katrina. This historic home of Confederate president Jefferson Davis is now undergoing extensive reconstruction and renovation. Dunleith, a columned, Greek Revival home, was built c. 1856, on the site of the burned Routhland Plantation; it now serves as a popular bed and breakfast and is also home to the acclaimed Castle Restaurant and Pub. Mount Locust, on the historic Natchez Trace, is believed to be the oldest building in Mississippi. It served as a popular inn for travelers, as well as a fully functioning cotton plantation. It remains today, the only surviving inn of more than fifty once found on the Trace.

As we shall see in the coming pages, Mississippi was for many a realm where their greatest aspirations could be realized, fortunes made, and palaces erected. For others, it was quite the opposite, a place where individuals were exploited for their forced labor by a system of active enslavement that fueled the vast agricultural economy. Today, Mississippi is a vibrant place where citizens struggle to honor their fading past, while coming to terms with the unsettling realities of the plantation South. By documenting those estates now lost to time and by endeavoring to preserve those few that still remain, future generations may be ensured the privilege of exploring Mississippi's distinctive and multifaceted plantation past.

## Goat Castle

Goat Castle, also known as Glenwood, was a large and very beautiful mansion in Natchez whose antebellum history has been mostly forsaken for its sensational turn-of-the-century through the depression era legacy. The estate and its neighboring property, Glenburnie, were associated with a murder mystery that made headlines worldwide. Because the incident involved four individuals from the very highest pinnacles of society who had spiraled down, intertwining whirls of eccentricity and even outright insanity the story grew even more thrilling for readers.

The home at the center of this fiasco—Glenwood—was a two-story building made of wood with a large front veranda and balcony that spanned the entire width of the house. Six very slender Tuscan columns held up the balcony that covered the front veranda, while six matching columns above supported a thick paneled cornice. Two large, ornate identical doors in the center of the veranda and balcony were enhanced with surrounding sidelights and fanlights. Flanking each of these doors, on either side, were two shuttered windows. Above the cornice and entablature, which surrounded the entire structure, a large hipped roof enveloped two chimneys and dormers with arched windows.[3]

The house was owned by Fredrick Stanton,

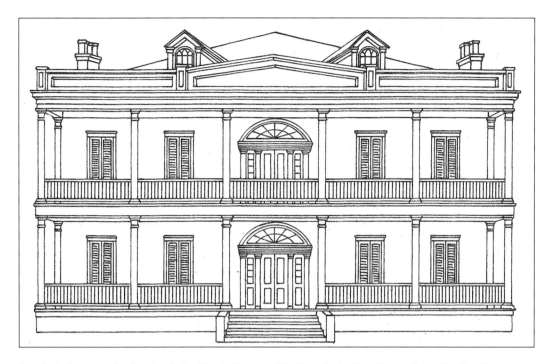

Goat Castle, front elevation. Drawings by Fred Daspit. Courtesy of the Center for Louisiana Studies, University of Louisiana at Lafayette.

Goat Castle, side elevation. Drawings by Fred Daspit. Courtesy of the Center for Louisiana Studies, University of Louisiana at Lafayette.

builder of Stanton Hall, who later sold it to Richard Henry Clay "Dick" Dana. Dana was the son of Rev. Charles Backus Dana, the rector of Natchez's Trinity Episcopal Church. The reverend was such a close friend of General Robert E. Lee that the Dana family was given many Lee family antiques and a fifteen-hundred-volume library from Robert E. Lee himself. Dick Dana earned a degree from Vanderbilt University and later studied piano in New York, aspiring to be a concert pianist. Unfortunately, two fingers of his right hand were injured when a window fell on them. Thus, his dreams of finding fame as a pianist were devastated. He returned to Natchez, where he filled Glenwood with the Lee family's finest furnishings.[4]

At some point Jennie Merrill, daughter of Ayres P. Merrill, the U.S. ambassador to Belgium, moved into Glenwood, but later settled at Glenburnie. Merrill, like Dana, was a wealthy southerner of the highest social standing. She and her siblings had even been presented to Queen Victoria at the court of St. James. During her years at Glenburnie she was visited each night by her companion Duncan Minor, who rode a horse between his home, Oakland, and Merrill's residence. Minor, like Merrill herself, was a southerner of high social standing and wealth, although he was notoriously stingy. It is said that the couple had been in love for decades, but were forbidden to marry because they were distant cousins. Other sources note that a feud between the two households is what actually prevented the couple from marrying. Regardless, the love affair transcended these boundaries, thriving under the cloak of night.

Dick Dana was joined at Glenwood by Octavia Dockery, a true socialite with equally impressive lineage and imposing family connections. She had attended the prestigious Comstock School for Girls in New York City and at age sixteen was escorted to a fashionable New York ball by none other than President Grant himself. She was a well-known writer and published extensively. She brought with her to Glenwood a number of priceless antiques and papers that had belonged to Confederate president Jefferson Davis, a distant relative. Although they lived together for many years, both Dana and Dockery denied any romantic nature to their relationship.

As years passed, all four of these elite southerners became more and more eccentric—none more so, however, than Dana. On one occasion he was accosted by local young people who wanted to play a practical joke on him. So disturbed by this was he that he climbed to the roof of Glenwood and stayed there for two days. When he descended the mansion, it was obvious his sanity had remained behind. He began acquiring a menagerie of farm animals, including cows, pigs, chicken, ducks, geese, and most of all goats. These animals were allowed to freely roam the property both inside and outside the mansion. As the collection of animals grew, so did the deterioration of the mansion. Animal droppings covered the floors, and goats eagerly ate Robert E. Lee's books and Jefferson Davis's furniture.

Community members were shocked by the filthy condition of Glenwood and crowned it "Goat Castle." Octavia Dockery seemed to disapprove of her surroundings; however, she was obviously unable to overcome her situation. As the animals took over her bed, Dockery slept on an old mildew-covered mattress supported by straight-back chairs turned end to end. Dana slept in another room on the floor. Soon, the unkempt Dana became known as the "Wild Man," and Dockery took the nickname of "Goat Woman."

The goats of Goat Castle often roamed to nearby Glenburnie where they regularly destroyed Jennie Merrill's fine formal gardens. She grew angrier and angrier and eventually purchased a shotgun. She became an excellent marksman, killing many trespassing goats. This greatly enraged Dana, so much so that the entire town knew of their great goat feud.

On August 4, 1932, while arriving for his nightly visit with Jennie Merrill at Glenburnie, Duncan Minor discovered a horrific scene. The mansion was covered with blood, and Jennie Merrill was missing! He called the sheriff who immediately thought of Dana and Dockery. When the police arrived at the squalid Goat Castle, they found Dana upstairs washing a bloody shirt. Analysis of fingerprints at Glenburnie revealed that whoever had been there had a deformed or injured right hand, just like Dick Dana. Police immediately arrested Dana and Dockery.

Later a young man assisting with the search for Merrill found her body in a thicket. She had been shot to death. The story was a sensation, making headlines across the world. Readers were fascinated by the high society crime and the eccentric individuals involved. One person who read these headlines was the chief of police of Pine Bluff, Arkansas. He immediately called the Natchez sheriff, explaining that the night before one of his officers had shot and killed a man named George Pearls, after Pearls had pulled a gun on the officer. Pearls's gun matched the one described in the article, and the police chief had reason to believe that Pearls had recently been in Natchez.

Pearls's gun was sent to New Orleans criminologist Maurice B. O'Neill, who concluded it was a perfect match for the bullets that killed Merrill. Upon further investigation it was found that the bloody fingerprints were a match for Pearls, who, ironically, also had a deformed right hand like Dick Dana. The blood on Dana's shirt was determined to be pig's blood from an animal he had slaughtered. And, after a grueling interrogation, Emily Burns, the owner of a local boardinghouse in Natchez, confessed that she had accompanied George Pearls to Glenburnie in order to rob Jennie Merrill. When Merrill pulled her famed shotgun on Pearls, he killed her.

The notoriety that surrounded the case, along with Dana's and Dockery's eccentricities, brought them much fame, as did their squalid mansion. People came often to peer in their windows and watch them from afar, but the odd pair didn't realize the financial reward this fame might bring until 1932, during the first Natchez Spring Pilgrimage. During the celebration, a train from Hattiesburg carried six hundred curious sightseers to Glenwood.

The next year, Dana and Dockery planned to put on a show. They passed out flyers all over Natchez advertising an open house at Glenwood.

For twenty-five cents individuals would be admitted onto the grounds, and, for another additional quarter, they would be allowed into the mansion itself. Once inside, visitors were greeted by Dana himself, clad in a white suit, who played the piano for them. Dockery hosted poetry readings during the event. The two even sold Goat Castle souvenirs. But what many visitors marveled at the most was the mess. Goats and other farm animals wandered through the great house, which, at that time, was more a decrepit trash dump than a home.

Dick Dana and Octavia Dockery made enough money from the pilgrimage and other such public events to sustain themselves, but they didn't have the money to pay a long-forgotten mortgage. They were eventually evicted from Glenwood, but in true Dana and Dockery style, they ignored the eviction and refused to budge. Eventually, after fighting the two for years, the mortgage holder died!

In 1948, Dick Dana died of pneumonia. Octavia Dockery followed him in death the next year. Soon, a massive auction was held that attracted hundreds of curious people from many states. The remaining documents and antiques from Robert E. Lee and Jefferson Davis that had survived the goats were sold to the highest bidders. The next year, the mansion caved in, having been neglected and abused for years. Developers cleared the remains of the once-great home and plotted out streets—Glenwood Drive and Dana Road among them—for a new subdivision. Glenwood, the famed Goat Castle, is now gone, only a strange, fading memory in the minds of local Natchez citizens. Duncan Minor's Glenburnie still stands proudly, a testament to an earlier era.

## Brierfield

One of the most important lost plantations in the South is that of Jefferson Davis, the first and only president of the Confederate States of America. It was here that Davis and his wife, Varina, spent many happy times, but political obligations pulled the couple away from the isolated estate again and again. Remarkably, the commodious master house survived the Civil War only to burn many years later.

Davis, born June 3, 1808, was the tenth and last child of Samuel Emory Davis and his wife, Jane Cook. He was educated at the United States Military Academy at West Point, and it was shortly after his graduation from this institution in 1828 that he first visited Davis Bend, the future site of his Brierfield Plantation. Davis's oldest brother Joseph, who was twenty-four years his elder and was much more like a father to the future politician than a sibling, had earlier purchased about seven thousand acres along a remote bend in the Mississippi River where he established his own Hurricane Plantation.[5]

Joseph encouraged young Jefferson Davis to make a career of military service, and it was in the pursuit of this vocation that Davis met and fell in love with Sarah Knox Taylor, the daughter of Zachary Taylor, then a colonel and later U.S. president. Taylor abhorred the idea of his daughter wedding a soldier, but later blessed the union after Davis agreed to pursue planting instead. The couple was married on June 17, 1835.

Joseph Davis was happy with his brother's decision and sought to aid him in establishing himself as a successful planter. He gave his young brother over two thousand acres of Davis Bend near Hurricane Plantation. The property, uncleared and full of brambles, came to be known as Brierfield.

The two brothers traveled to Natchez, where Joseph arranged the purchase of twenty slaves to begin clearing and cultivating Davis's portion of the bend. Davis's most trusted slave and longtime personal companion, James Pemberton, oversaw operations of the new estate. Sadly, during this busy time, both Davis and his young wife were stricken with malaria. They traveled to St. Francisville, Louisiana, to convalesce at Locust Grove Plantation, the home of Davis's sister Anna, but unfortunately, Sarah grew weaker and died on September 15, 1835, only three months after her wedding. She was buried at Locust Grove.

Grief-stricken and ill, Davis returned to Davis Bend to continue the agricultural work of his plantation. Aided in great part by James Pemberton, Davis oversaw the clearing of land, the planting of fields, and the construction of plantation buildings.

Amid the demands of his plantation estate, Davis's existence was enlivened with his marriage to Varina Howell, the nineteen-year-old daughter of William B. Howell and Margaret Kempe, on February 26, 1845. Varina reminisced about her days at Brierfield as a newlywed: "We passed many happy days there, enlivened by daily rides, in which we indulged in many races when the road was smooth. The game was more abundant than chickens are now. Wild geese in great flocks, made fat by the waste corn in the fields; wild ducks by the thousand, and white and blue cranes adorned almost every slough, standing on one leg among the immense lily pads . . ."[6]

Of their wilderness existence at Brierfield, Varina further noted: "Sometimes a calf was missing and then my husband went to hunt the alligator that had probably taken it. Once he had a very remarkable success in punishing one that had killed two calves. The negroes found its hole, and Mr. Davis put a long cane down it until the creature seized it in its mouth. He then put the gun on a line with the cane and shot the alligator in the mouth. He was an immense animal and a postmortem examination justified the killing, for the last calf was found in part."[7]

In addition to his pursuits as a planter and hunter, Davis became keenly interested in politics. He was elected to Congress in 1845; however, he left his post a few months later after being appointed colonel over the Mississippi Regiment in the Mexican-American War. After returning home in 1847, he was appointed a U.S. senator to fill the vacancy created by the death of Senator Jesse Speight. He later won the seat after this partial term ended.

All the while, in Davis's absence both at war and in politics, agricultural operations at Brierfield continued. In October 1846, James Pemberton reported that over 170,000 pounds of cotton had been picked and that 300 bales would be put up for sale.

With success in planting and politics Davis decided to construct a plantation mansion that would fit his newly found stations in life.

Many years later, Varina Davis recalled of the mansion the following: "The building was one of my husband's experiments as an architect, and he and his friend and servant, James Pemberton, built it with the help of the negroes on the plantation. The rooms were of fair size, and open on a paved brick gallery, surrounded by latticework . . ."[8]

Davis contracted with a carpenter named Marcy and his fourteen-year-old apprentice, W. H. Zeigler, who were to oversee the construction project. While some of the materials were purchased from outside the plantation, the large framing timbers were cut from Brierfield's own swamps.

The finished house was a sprawling one-story raised mansion, with a U-shaped plan. The central portion of the mansion was of a standard central hall plan with both front and rear rooms flanking the hall on either side. The two front rooms served as a formal parlor and library. The two rear rooms served as bedrooms. Flanking this central portion on either side were two rooms to the west, a dining room and bedroom, and to the east a study and an additional bedroom.

Outside, each of the side wings had a symmetrical porch with three columns that balanced the wide central portico with its massive yet plain pediment and six heavy columns. In all, the central portico and the flanking wings created an impressive façade of twelve columns running the entire length of the front of the mansion. Interestingly, the columns themselves were not of solid brick or wood as was common, but instead were hollow, constructed of various pieces held together by pegs to create what appeared to be solid shafts. The exterior of the house was painted bright white with dark green shutters providing a stark contrast.

In the back of the mansion, a wide back porch with straight, square columns ran the length of the house and curved around the smaller rear wings that formed a U shape. The wings each contained a separate kitchen and pantry, as the house was originally designed to accommodate two families—that of Jefferson Davis and that of his sister; this, how-

ever, never occurred and the house always served only Davis and his immediate family.

Inside, the Brierfield mansion was unusually plain with nearly no ornamentation or architectural embellishment whatsoever. There were scarcely any moldings, no ceiling medallions, no wallpaper, and except for two white Carrara marble fireplace mantels—one in the front parlor and the other across the central hall in the library—and two chandeliers in the dining room, the interior of the mansion was bare. The stark arrangement was said to mirror in some way the firm, no-nonsense personality of the house's owner.

Surrounding the mansion, a variety of traditional plantation structures could be found: a tall bell stand, a pigeonnier, a commissary with supplies and goods for slaves and other plantation residents, a number of large production buildings and sheds, and a village of slave cabins. There was also a unique octagonal cistern house built of lattice walls and boasting a peaked shingled roof with small spire. Immediately surrounding the house, a fence adorned with running roses provided both beauty and a pleasant pastime in flower gardening for Davis and his wife.

Happy in the plantation mansion, Davis again turned his attention to his political aspirations. In 1851, he resigned his Senate post to run for governor. During the campaign, however, he was again struck with malaria, and was bedridden. He lost the election.

Jefferson and Varina Davis were surprisingly content with the outcome of the election. They both were happy to have a sojourn away from political life and relished their roles at Brierfield, spending much time tending a variety of exotic plants in their garden, working with livestock, and overseeing slaves and their agricultural work. Away from the stress and strain of government, Davis and his wife had their first child, Samuel, in July 1852. The year was marked with sadness, however, upon the death of Davis's most trusted companion and servant, James Pemberton.

Davis's vacation from politics was brief. On 1853, President-elect Franklin Pierce convinced Davis to accept the office of secretary of war. He found much success in the position, and when his term ended, he was again elected to the Senate.

Davis's large amount of time in Washington took its toll on Brierfield. Without James Pemberton to oversee operations, the plantation declined physically, but still continued to generate a profit.

After Lincoln's election to the presidency in 1860, Jefferson Davis fought diligently in the Senate and beyond in an effort to preserve the fragile union. However, his efforts were in vain as South Carolina withdrew from the United States on December 20, 1860. Mississippi followed a few weeks later, and Davis had no other choice but to resign from the Senate on January 21, 1861. He was commissioned as the general of the Mississippi Volunteers, but returned to Brierfield before taking his post.

While at Brierfield for only three or four days, on February 10, 1861, Davis and Varina were gently tending their roses when a rider on horseback approached to deliver the most important telegram of Davis's life. Varina recalled the event vividly: "The messenger . . . found him in our garden assisting to make rose cuttings; when reading the telegram he looked so grieved that I feared some evil had befallen our family. After a few minutes' painful silence he told me, as a man might speak a sentence of death."[9]

The news, of course, was that Davis had been elected the first president of the world's newest nation: the Confederate States of America. The plantation's great bell was rung, summoning all the slaves. Davis delivered an "affectionate" farewell speech to them, and he left promptly for Montgomery the next morning where he was inaugurated on February 18, 1861. Davis sent a copy of his inaugural address to Varina, and after she read it aloud to her father and Davis's brother Joseph, the two men cheered so loudly and wildly that the Brierfield slaves ran to the mansion from the fields, fearing a house fire or some other great tragedy had befallen their white masters.

Soon thereafter, Joseph Davis purchased two small inland plantations where he felt the family and slaves would be safe from Union forces. He moved his brother's books, papers, and other important possessions to one of these estates, Fleetwood Plantation.

In June 1863, Union soldiers descended upon Brierfield and Hurricane and pillaged and plundered the plantations. Furniture from the mansion at Brierfield was largely destroyed, but the house was preserved for some unknown reason—perhaps as a symbolic trophy. Hurricane, however, was destroyed. The U.S. took formal possession of Davis's estate on Independence Day, July 4, 1863, incorporating it as a possession of the Freedmen's Bureau. It was purchased by the Montgomerys, former slaves of the Davis brothers.

Interestingly, after the war, as if signaling the herculean transformation of southern reality, the massive Mississippi River unexpectedly shifted its course, cutting off the plantation lands and making Davis Bend into Davis Island.

After the war, Joseph Davis, who had never actually given his brother Jefferson deed or title to the Brierfield property, argued that the plantation was actually a subdivision of Hurricane, and therefore his property. Having in no formal way been involved with the fight for southern independence, Joseph petitioned President Andrew Johnson for the return of his property, and his request was granted.

Joseph arranged for his former slaves to continue cultivating the old plantation, and he set a purchase agreement with them. However, the former enslaved men and women were faced with unusual, devastating flooding that destroyed their crops, and when they were unable to make payments, Brierfield reverted to Joseph and eventually back into the hands of Jefferson Davis.

Davis eventually retired to Beauvoir, his waterfront estate on the Mississippi Gulf Coast at Biloxi. He returned to Brierfield only a few times. He died in New Orleans on December 6, 1889, at the age of eighty-one. A massive funeral was held that included a continuous march from New Orleans to Richmond, Virginia, where he was entombed.

The mansion at Brierfield was occupied by a

farm manager, and rooms were converted into a post office and school for those remaining on the island. In 1922, a great flood caused irreparable damage to the house when water rose halfway up the columns. Davis's grandson had the entire house raised on ten-foot pillars, an act that saved the mansion from another great flood in 1927.

In 1931, a young girl was assisting with heating irons in the fireplace, and placed wood shingles on the fire. Unfortunately, a strong wind carried the smoldering shingles through the chimney and onto the roof, where they set the dry wooden roof aflame. Despite efforts to extinguish the conflagration with buckets of water, the house was ultimately destroyed, leaving only the tall pillars upon which the elevated mansion had stood. A small cabin was built on top of the pillars shortly thereafter; however, it burned within a year.

On April 3, 1953, Jefferson Davis's heirs transferred the Brierfield property to William E. Parks and George D. Hayes of Louisiana. A year later, the two men sold the plantation to John Dale, Jr., and Lessley D. Dale, also of Louisiana, who maintained the property as a game preserve.

Today the remote lands are only accessible by boat. Through thick weeds and snake-infested overgrowth, the decaying remnants of stone foundations, brick cisterns, and bits and pieces of other faded architectural miscellany can be found. These rusty relics pay homage to a built past that has long since given way to time and nature, much as the society and people did that created them.

## Hurricane

Near the Brierfield tract on Davis Bend, Jefferson Davis's brother Joseph constructed Hurricane Plantation, with its unusual mansion and well-known garden structures. The master house was destroyed by Union forces during the Civil War.

Joseph E. Davis was born on December 10, 1784, in Georgia, and grew up to be a famed attorney in Mississippi. He was a member of the convention of 1817 that produced the constitution for the state of Mississippi.[10]

Joseph purchased much property near what would later be the city of Vicksburg. At the height of the property acquisitions he held nearly seven thousand acres on what would come to be known as Davis Bend, where he cultivated vast amounts of cotton.

Aside from planting, Joseph Davis continued to be active in the legal profession. He banded together with other Mississippi legal professionals to form the Mississippi Bar Association, the first in the nation. He served as the group's president in 1824.

During this time, Joseph Davis was busy constructing his plantation mansion on his Davis Bend property. In the middle of construction a harsh tropical storm caused great damage to the plantation and to the house. A portion of the house collapsed, crippling Joseph's brother Isaac and killing Isaac's infant son. Isaac and his young wife were greatly distraught by this event, moving from the plantation at once. In remembrance of this occurrence Joseph called his plantation Hurricane.

The mansion was finally finished around the time forty-three-year-old Joseph married sixteen-year-old Eliza Van Benthuysen of New Orleans in 1827. The house itself was described as quite unusual. It was a three-story structure with many tall, turret-like dormers. The main portion of the house was laid out in a traditional plan, with a large central hallway flanked by two rooms on both sides. A large annex, which measured twenty-five by forty-three feet, was added to the west of the house. The annex contained a massive dining room downstairs and a portrait-lined, upstairs music room with an arched ceiling.

The house contained striking modern conveniences such as indoor plumbing. A large tank rested in the attic, and each morning slaves pumped water into it. This supplied the master house bathrooms with all the water they needed for the day.

Outside the house, a detached kitchen and

laundry building included upstairs living quarters for slaves. In the garden, a large columned "garden house" served as a French *garçonnière*, or bachelor's quarters, and possibly also as a library. And one of the most unusual outbuildings was a structure known as the "hall of justice," which functioned as a slave court. One can only imagine how Joseph's legal experience melded with his status as slaveholder when he acted as judge in pseudocases he brought against his own slaves. Certainly, it suggests that Joseph was a man who valued order in a social sense and who probably treated his chattel stringently and meticulously.

And although the slave court brings to mind harshness and discipline, we know that Joseph Davis did harbor some compassion for slaves. In 1836, when a slave named Benjamin Thornton Montgomery escaped and tried to return to the plantation, he was not punished, but instead the Davis family agreed to let him freely read and write if he would agree not to run away again. Reading insatiably, Montgomery became so adept at business that both Davis brothers allowed this slave to oversee their plantations' accounts and business operations. Later, Montgomery's son Isaiah Thornton Montgomery served as Joseph's private secretary.[11]

By the time his brother was sworn in as president of the Confederate States of America, Joseph Davis had become one of the wealthiest planters in Mississippi. The 1860 slave schedules, a supplement to the U.S. Census that year, shows that Joseph owned a total of 365 slaves.[12]

Although he took little part in the new government, Joseph's position as a member of the Confederacy's first family would have dire consequences. On June 24, 1862, Union soldiers on their way to Vicksburg burned the mansion at Hurricane Plantation to the ground. The troops stole much of the china, crystal, and glassware, which they shattered with muskets. The books from the famed Davis library were hauled to the lawn and used to fuel bonfires.

After the war, the Hurricane Plantation lands ended up in the ownership of their former slaves,

including the Montgomerys. Here the former slaves set up a remarkable utopian experiment, which they administered successfully and profitably, becoming the third-largest cotton producers in the South.[13]

Joseph Davis and his descendants, unhappy with the arrangement, undertook a years-long battle to regain their property. Joseph wrote President Andrew Johnson, "I took no part in the war. I did not bear arms. I was not a member of the legislature nor of the convention nor attended any public meetings. I contributed nothing, subscribed nothing, made no investments in Confederate bonds or securities."[14] Eventually, the property was restored to Joseph Davis and his family. The former slaves were forced to move from their happy home.

In 1887, Isaiah T. Montgomery and his cousin Benjamin T. Green, along with several of their fellow freedman from Hurricane Plantation, founded the all-black community of Mound Bayou about halfway between Vicksburg and Memphis. The community still exists today.[15]

Joseph Davis's granddaughter, Mary Elizabeth Hamer, lived in the columned garden house for many years. This structure became known as the Hurricane Plantation House itself. It burned in 1913. Over the years the Mississippi River has moved, and the peninsula of Davis Bend has become Davis Island. Little, if any, physical evidence is left of the isolated plantation.[16]

# *Windsor*

The history of Windsor Plantation in Claiborne County, Mississippi, defines tragedy in its most astute form. Smith Daniell spent three long years building his remarkable mansion, only to die a few short weeks after its completion. The house itself shared a similar disastrous fate—thought to be fireproof, it was consumed in a great conflagration only thirty years after its birth.[17]

Smith Coffee Daniell II was born in Mississippi

Windsor Plantation mansion. The ruined columns partially stripped of their finish provide insight into their construction. The brick bases and curved brick columns (over which stucco was laid) are clearly visible in this photograph.

in 1826. He married Catherine Freeland, and together the couple had three children. Daniell became a prominent planter, producing large crops of cotton, and as his empire grew, so did his family's prominence in the state.

Windsor Plantation stretched across twenty-six hundred acres of Claiborne County, although Daniell's total landholdings topped twenty-one thousand acres in Mississippi and Louisiana. In 1859, he set out to build a massive plantation mansion that would rival any other in the state. The house was a four-story, seven-bay structure with a four-bay annex. Crowning the central part of the mansion was a large, handsome observatory.

The house was constructed of bricks that were produced on the plantation by slaves, a common construction material found in antebellum plantation mansions. The millwork and finishing touches were added by contractors from New England. The elaborate columns were brick and plaster, standing thirty feet tall. And their crowning, massive capitals were of cast iron. These, along with the fancy iron balustrades and four staircases, were manufactured in St. Louis and are said to have been floated down the Mississippi River to Windsor via a barge.

The massive Corinthian columns lined the building, enclosing wide galleries. Each column rested on a large paneled plinth, themselves one story tall. The plinths framed the home's ground level that functioned as a basement, containing a schoolroom, a dairy, a doctor's office, a commissary, and storage area for supplies.

Above, the elevated first floor contained a central hall dividing large living spaces, including a double parlor and library. A master suite, complete with a bedroom, study, and bath also occupied the first floor of the main structure. A spiral staircase led to the second floor, which contained bedrooms and an additional bath. Large tanks in the attic provided water for the interior baths, a rare luxury in antebellum times.

In all, there were twenty-three rooms and twenty-five fireplaces, each framed by a marble mantel. The observatory that topped the roof of the central core of the house offered a view of the river and of Louisiana on the other side, as well as much of the plantation lands. Certainly this would have been an ideal place to survey agricultural operations and the slaves.

The completed mansion and its fine furnishings cost Daniell a total sum of $175,000 (a sum equal to approximately $4 million in 2007 dollars). He lived in his master house only a few short weeks before his death in 1861, at the age of thirty-four.[18]

Soon, the nation was divided in Civil War and Windsor played host to both Confederate and Union troops. Catherine Daniell was fond of recounting the story of how the Union overtook the Confederate officers at Windsor. Apparently, one evening Windsor was the scene of a lavish party thrown for socialites from all around. In attendance were three Confederate officers who were stationed nearby. Union leaders, having closely monitored this situation, presented themselves to the party in full formal, nonmilitary attire. They were immediately invited in. They spotted the Confederates in their dress uniforms and proceeded to arrest them. One of the Union officers described the scene in a letter:

> So we entered and there in the parlor of the house was quite a party, singing and laughing and having a fine time generally. Among them were three Confederates dressed in their gray uniforms. I walked in and went up to the one that seemed to be in command, touched him on the shoulder and inquired, "Are you a Confederate officer?" He promptly replied, "Yes, I am." At this the singing stopped, and the ladies present came around and insisted that we Yankees were not gentlemen and that we should not spoil their evening by arresting and taking prisoners these three Confederates. The ladies grew very boisterous and attacked us with their fists and fingernails, and refused to allow the arrest . . . The lieutenant (posted at the rear of the house) and his detail came in from the rear and we then took the three rebels prisoners and marched them down to the river edge from Windsor to where our yawls had been left . . . they were placed in prison.[19]

After the Battle of Port Gibson in May 1863, the Federals used the basement at Windsor as a hospital, and it is believed that this may be the reason it survived the Yankee torch.

On February 17, 1890, less than thirty years after the mansion's completion, a house guest flicked a lit cigar into a pile of dry sawdust left over from a repair project. Instantaneously, the house was aflame and in no time at all the entire structure, brick walls and all, was reduced to a rubble pile. The only things left standing were twenty-two of the large columns, complete with some of the fancy iron banister work from the gallery still attached.

These columns survive today, along with some of the attached ironwork. Some of the fancy railing was stolen by workmen and installed in a house in Houston, while the elaborate iron steps were used to adorn Oakland Memorial Chapel at Alcorn State University.

The columns themselves are today mostly unchanged from their condition after the fire. The state of Mississippi acquired the property, along with the ruins, in 1974, from Sam Magruder, who was said to be a descendant of the original owners. Today, the Mississippi Department of Archives and History's Historic Properties Division is charged with the preservation of the ruins and the maintenance of the site.

These almost Grecian silhouettes have cemented themselves into the hearts of locals and the culture of the region. They receive frequent visitors and have been featured in several films, including *Raintree County* (1957) and *Ghosts of Mississippi* (1996). Additionally, images of the ruins are popular commodities for locals and tourists alike. Photographers and artists produce and sell likenesses of the columns with great fervor, and visitors come from far and wide to explore the site and gaze upon this lost plantation's few remaining vestiges.

## Prairie Mont

Prairie Mont, the home of Dr. Cowles Mead Vaiden, was a columned landmark of Carroll County, Mississippi, for nearly 120 years until it was demolished in 1958 to make way for a modern home.

Cowles Mead Vaiden was born on April 25, 1812, in Charles City County, Virginia, and was named after Cowles Mead, a distant cousin who served as the secretary of the Mississippi Territory and as acting governor of the state. The young Vaiden was educated locally, but at the age of seventeen, he moved to North Carolina where he became a schoolteacher. He later studied medicine at the University of Pennsylvania, where he graduated as a physician in 1836.[20]

The next year, Vaiden married Elizabeth Whitfield Herring in Lenoir County, North Carolina. A year later, in 1838, the couple moved to Mississippi, finally settling in Carroll County. Vaiden purchased many tracts of land, and accumulated three thousand acres that he formed into Prairie Mont, his plantation estate located east of the tiny community of Shongalo.

Upon a high hill overlooking his vast property, Vaiden constructed a mansion from which to rule his empire. Designed by James Clark Harris in the 1840s, the house blended Greek and Italianate styles. The front of the five-bay mansion was dominated by a large two-story portico with its four slender Ionic columns that supported a heavy bracketed cornice and balustrade above.

A large crowning cupola featured arched windows on each side. The windowpanes were tinted in four hues to symbolize the four seasons. The cupola itself was topped with a bracketed cornice, echoing the roofline below.

Inside, the first floor featured seven large rooms and cross halls. A spiral staircase led to the five rooms of the second story and continued to the attic, which contained a storied windowless room where Cowles Vaiden stored his trove of whisky. From the attic another staircase led to the cupola. The interior of the mansion was finished with heavy woodwork, including carved cornices, moldings, door frames, and baseboards. Marble mantels graced the fireplaces throughout. It is said that an artist from New Orleans executed frescos upon the principal walls and ceilings of the mansion.

Happy with his finished home, Vaiden sought success outside his plantation. He allowed the right-of-way through his plantation to the Mis-

The mansion at Prairie Mont Plantation was an impressive sight with its slender Ionic columns and large, dominating cupola.

Prairie Mont mansion. Side view. Note the Italianate brackets supporting the roofline and the detailing around the windows.

This interior photograph of Dr. Cowles Mead Vaiden's Prairie Mont Plantation home suggests that the house was probably expanded at one time or built around a smaller structure. The photograph, taken from the home's central hall, looks across the cross hall into the rear stair hall beyond. The entrance to the stair hall was very likely once an exterior door. It was flanked by sidelights and full windows beyond, suggesting that this wall was once the front of the house and was later incorporated into an expansion.

sissippi Central Railroad (which later merged into the Illinois Central Railroad). Soon, Vaiden became one of the company's directors. The railroad later established a station on his property, naming the post after him. Interestingly, the few townsfolk of Shongalo all abandoned their little village and moved to Vaiden, which is still today a quaint little hamlet on the Mississippi map.

Dr. Vaiden found further success in politics, serving several terms in the Mississippi state legislature. He later supported and survived the Civil War, as did his plantation. In the twilight of his life, fighting illness, Vaiden, who was childless, devoted himself to the support of higher education. At the time of his death on February 6, 1880, it is said that seventy-four young men were attending the University of Mississippi with his financial backing.

Local newspapers lamented Vaiden's demise:

> Though the health of Dr. Vaiden had been bad for years and disease had wasted his frame, he had resisted its gradual encroachments with so much resolution and borne his afflictions with so much unfailing fortitude, that few of his friends realized that he was for a long time on the brink of the grave, and when at last his physical forces succumbed to the destroyer, they were unprepared for the melancholy announcement that his brace and gentle spirit had indeed passed through the shadow of the dark valley and entered into life and immortality beyond.[21]

Prior to his death Vaiden had commissioned a ten-thousand-dollar life-sized statue of himself for his grave. The statue was carved in Italy and narrowly escaped being lost at sea, as the ship it was transported across the Atlantic on sank.

After Vaiden's death, Prairie Mont Plantation passed through various hands. It was acquired by Roger Jones. WPA photographs from the 1930s show the house in fair condition, with paint peeling and shutters sagging. It was described by journalist George M. Moreland at this time as follows: "I saw the marble mantels imported from Italy. I saw the fine frescoes on the high walls and ceilings made by the New Orleans artist long before

the Civil War. Although not in the best of repair, Prairie Mont is in better condition than the average ante-bellum home in Mississippi. In the upper rooms some plastering is crumbling, but the wide halls, the spacious rooms and even the cupola on top are yet in good condition."[22]

The mansion later sold to W. M. Lowrey, Sr., in the late 1940s. It became the victim of much neglect. By the 1950s, a visitor described a sad scene: "You will see how woodpeckers have drilled holes for droning bees to swarm into four tall columns. Broken window panes stare at you vacantly. You can hear the drip of a leaking roof into a battery of pots and mason jars . . . You can see where the imported Italian mantels have been ripped from the walls, and a fresco medallion in the twelve-foot ceiling shows where sparkling chandeliers once hung."[23]

By the late 1950s, the mansion was dilapidated. Lowrey's son demolished the house in 1958. He incorporated some of the bricks from the chimneys into a new home that he built on the site. Furthermore, the mansion's massive paneled doors were used as scrap wood to build a storage shed. Dr. Vaiden's plantation is no more, its few remnants now unrecognizable.

## Malmaison

The striking home of famed Choctaw chief Greenwood Leflore, a unique mansion at Malmaison Plantation, was almost as illustrious and remarkable as its controversial owner. The great house remained in the Leflore family throughout its existence, but was destroyed by fire in the 1940s, and today little remains of the historic estate.[24]

Greenwood Leflore, who has been described as "one of the most pivotal yet least studied characters in Mississippi history,"[25] was born on June 3, 1800, the son of Louis LeFleur, a French-Canadian trader, and Rebecca Cravat, a full-blooded Choctaw princess. Greenwood was the fourth of eleven children.

MISS 110

Choctaw chief Greenwood Leflore's striking mansion at Malmaison Plantation expertly blended elements of Greek Revival and Italianate design.

The elder LeFleur moved to Mobile prior to Greenwood's birth and later settled in present-day Jackson, Mississippi, where he established a trading post. Prior to being chosen as the state's capital and obtaining the name Jackson, in honor of the seventh president of the United States, the area was known as LeFleur's Bluff. LeFleur also established a trading post and inn on the Natchez Trace, and this is likely where he and his family encountered Major John Donly, who ran a mail coach along the storied Trace. During his interactions with the LeFleur family, Donly was very impressed with young Greenwood's intelligence, and convinced the LeFleurs to allow him to take the boy to Nashville and supervise his education.

Greenwood was twelve at the time, and he devoted himself fully to his tutors. It was probably in Nashville that he changed the spelling of his name from LeFleur to Leflore. After five years of studying, at the age of seventeen, young Leflore fell in love with Rosa Donly, the major's eldest daughter. The Donlys frowned upon the union because of the young age of both parties, but Greenwood and Rosa eloped, and were subsequently accepted by the family.

In his early twenties, Greenwood Leflore was democratically elected chief of the Choctaws, leading twenty thousand indigenous people.[26] He succeeded his great-uncle, Chief Pushmataha. As leader, Leflore sought to improve the lives of his people, encouraging education, marriage, and clean living. He also supported the Christianization of the Choctaws.

In 1830, Leflore engaged in one of the most important and controversial aspects of his life when he negotiated the Treaty of Dancing Rabbit Creek with agents of the U.S. government. The treaty, which ceded Choctaw lands to the United States, guaranteed the rights of Native Americans to remain in their homes; however, government officials ignored that clause of the agreement. Thousands of Choctaw tribe members were forced to move west of the Mississippi, mostly to present-day Oklahoma. This forced removal of the Choctaws has been

Malmaison Plantation mansion. The interior of the mansion was dominated by a traditional broad central hall that served as an impressive entrance.

Malmaison Plantation mansion. This interior photograph shows one of the staircases that dominated the symetical cross halls off the main central hall.

This crimson and gold front parlor exemplified the ornate and impressive design once found inside Malmaison Plantation's master house.

Malmaison's expansive formal dining room was dominated by a large central table and a fireplace with a black marble mantel.

Malmaison Plantation mansion. This view showcases the long galleries that ran along the deep sides of the house.

called a precursor to the infamous Trail of Tears saga that would soon follow.

For his work on the treaty, the U.S. government gave Leflore a thousand acres of land in northern Mississippi, near his ancestral homelands, where few of his people were allowed to remain. Negotiating the treaty was a pivotal point in Leflore's chiefdom. He was seen by his own people as a traitor who befriended U.S. officials and squandered the Choctaws' sacred lands for his own personal gain, ultimately leading to the forced removal of his people. Most whites viewed Leflore quite differently, as a hero—a noble, savvy, and wise man.

Aside from his responsibilities as chief, Leflore found much success in planting. He amassed over fifteen thousand acres of lands in various tracts, but his principal plantation was Malmaison, named after the estate of the Empress Josephine, whom he greatly admired. At the height of his agricultural empire, he owned over four hundred slaves whose labor created great wealth from his property.

In the mid-1850s, Leflore set out to build a plantation mansion at his estate. Designed by James Clark Harris, the architect responsible for the mansion at nearby Prairie Mont Plantation, the house blended Greek Revival and Italianate elements. The front of the mansion was a five-bay structure, dominated by a two-story portico boasting four square pillars. The roofline was marked by a heavy bracketed cornice. The roof was topped by a widow's walk with balustrade that encircled a small cupola. The bracketed cornice of the roofline was echoed in the decorations below the balustrade and above the cupola. Two-story side porticos supported by two square pillars each flanked the west and east sides of the house.

Inside, the mansion was of a typical central hall plan, but was modified by the addition of a sixty-five-foot cross hall that created a central Greek cross. Large rooms occupied each corner of the cross, and both sides of the cross hall boasted magnificent staircases. An enormous dining room off the back of the house with associated service rooms gave the house an L shape. A porch with covered gallery above surrounded the exterior of the dining room.

The interior of the mansion was embellished with exuberant decoration, from the black marble mantels to the crystal chandeliers. One especially celebrated aspect of the home's furnishings was an elaborate parlor set that had been custom designed and imported from France. It contained several types of chairs, sofas, and divans all of French hickory overlaid with gold and upholstered with crimson silk damask. Legend has it that a French noblewoman saw the set in Paris and wanted to buy it. Because it had been custom-made for the Leflores and was not for sale, she settled for having replicas made for her own château.

The famed furniture set was the highlight of Malmaison's front parlor and was complemented by matching crimson silk damask drapes, crowned with elaborate gold valences. The room's four window shades were hand-painted with images of four famous French châteaux: Versailles, Fontainebleau, St. Cloud, and, of course, Josephine's original Malmaison.

The parlor's black marble mantel was topped with a pair of intricate candelabras and in the center a fine clock of gold and ebony representing a crusader on horseback. A table of ebony inlaid with mother-of-pearl rested in the center of the room atop a crimson and cream carpet of seamless tapestry decorated with roses.

Across the central hall the mansion's library was a testament to its owner, housing not only Leflore's many rare books but also several important political treasures such as an original copy of the Treaty of Dancing Rabbit Creek. Other items included a sword and belt given to Leflore by the president of the United States and a great silver medal awarded to a previous chief by Thomas Jefferson.

The lush interior of the house was contrasted by the more functional structures outside. A two-room kitchen building and separate smokehouse, both outside the main residence, served the nearby dining room, while two traditional *garçonnières* with associated cistern houses flanked the mansion on either side. There were two carriage houses that, along with the *garçonnières,* marked the corners of a square that enclosed the large curving front drive. The entire residential complex of the estate was set in such a way as to communicate the success and importance of its owner.

Confident in his accomplishment as a planter, Leflore went on, as many of his fellow planters did, to serve in a public capacity, twice winning seats in the Mississippi House of Representatives and serving one term in the state senate. One notable story about his service in the senate notes that he was infuriated by the way some of his colleagues interjected Latin phrases and terms into their speeches. The last straw for Leflore was when one of his younger colleagues made an entire speech in Latin on the senate floor. In turn, Leflore gave an hour-long address in Choctaw, despite the disdain of the perplexed senators.

As Leflore's empire grew and success swelled, so did his family. His wife, Rebecca Donly, died after bearing him a son and a daughter, and he soon married Elizabeth Coody, the niece of noted Cherokee chief John Ross. Unfortunately, Coody died shortly after her marriage. Leflore's third wife was Priscilla Donly, the sister of his first wife. She bore Leflore a daughter.

When the nation polarized in the grapple of the Civil War, Leflore steadfastly clung to the Union, supporting the federal effort despite his neighbors' apprehensions. During the war, Malmaison was visited by troops, and some outbuildings were damaged, but the house survived untouched, due largely to Leflore's support of the U.S. federal effort.

Leflore died on August 31, 1865. During his funeral ceremony, per his requests, his young grandchildren held an American flag over his coffin. His patriotism and support of the U.S. was unwavering: he had consistently aligned with federal officials during treaty negotiations, supported the Union efforts during the Civil War, and even remained true to the stars and stripes in death.

He was buried at his plantation's cemetery, and an impressive marker bearing the words "The last chief of the Choctaws east of the Mississippi" was erected in his honor. Leflore was memorialized in surrounding areas in many ways, including in the names of the city of Greenwood, Mississippi, and Mississippi's Leflore County. The now extinct town of Point Leflore in Leflore County was also named in his honor. Today, the Greenwood Leflore Hospital and the Greenwood-Leflore Airport both bear his name, as do many agencies and institutions in the region.

Remarkably, Malmaison Plantation remained in the possession of Leflore's heirs until its physical demise. The house became a landmark of the area and topic of literary and historical works, inspiring poems and various writings.

At the time of its destruction, Malmaison was occupied by two of Leflore's great-granddaughters. They owned the house in part with two of Leflore's other great-granddaughters, who both lived out of town. On the evening of the fire, March 31, 1942, the two residents were entertaining a female friend and her daughter. They discovered the fire, which was thought to have been caused by a defective chimney, and immediately sounded the alarm with gunshots. Five African Americans responded to the gunshots, and successfully saved a silver coffee pot, a pitcher, some glasses, and a few chairs. Everything else, including the house itself, was completely destroyed.

Outside, a carriage house also burned, but the carriage that Leflore rode to Washington in was saved. Over time, the remaining structures on the plantation decayed due to disregard and abandonment, and they were all eventually demolished by neglect. Remaining stone cisterns and foundations were overtaken by kudzu, and even the plantation's cemetery faced utter obliteration.

Besides encouraging weeds and other vegetation, the cemetery was the victim of grave robbers and vandals. Urns were stolen from Leflore's monument and, in March 1964, two Boy Scouts discovered that the grave had been disturbed. Upon court order, the grave of Greenwood Leflore was unearthed, but the only thing remaining was a small piece of pine. Rumor has it that around the same time, a young boy brought a human skull to his Greenwood school for "show-and-tell." Supposedly, he told his classmates that the artifact was the head of an "Indian chief." Though battered and overgrown, the Leflore cemetery remained partially intact, and Leflore's grand grave marker survived, even if his remains did not.

The memory of Greenwood Leflore also survived, as did the community's recollection of and fondness for the lost Malmaison. There was even talk of rebuilding the plantation at one time; however, the state chose to build Florewood Plantation instead. Today Florewood serves as a living history museum and state park in Greenwood.

The plantation lands were eventually purchased by the Belmont Shook Partnership of Memphis, a land and lumber investment group who owned the property for many years. In 2001, Greenwood attorney A. Lee Abraham, Jr., obtained an option to purchase an 896-acre tract containing parts of the former plantation, the cemetery, and what little was left of the mansion site (mostly overgrown cistern remains and partially buried foundations).

He approached Phillip Martin, long-time chief of the Mississippi Band of Choctaw Indians, about developing the property. Martin was intrigued since the land had such historic importance to his people. Among many other business successes, the chief had previously overseen the creation of the Choctaws' Pearl River Resort, which includes the Las Vegas–style Golden Moon Hotel and Casino, the Silver Star Hotel and Casino (with over a thousand hotel rooms between the two properties), and the Dancing Rabbit Golf Club. Abraham and Martin both envisioned a tourist destination at the Malmaison site, although the chief made clear his intentions to preserve the property's heritage, suggesting that a museum or cultural center be constructed there.

The Mississippi Band of Choctaw Indians purchased the land from Ann Shook Canale, a partner in the Belmont Shook group, for $1.7 million. Abraham noted at the time that the purchase of the property by the Choctaws was "probably one of the most significant economic events for Carroll and Leflore counties that I can remember . . . because of the potential for investment and development—historical and economic."[27] He further noted that he planned to work with Martin and his administration to pursue three goals, mainly the reconstruction of the Malmaison mansion, economic development and job creation, and an expansion of educational opportunities though the creation of a school of excellence.

Hearing of the Choctaws' acquisition of the property, local protestant ministers abhorred the thought of gambling in their region. Rev. Archie Goodwin of the North Carrollton Baptist Church immediately put together a group of concerned citizens to formally oppose any casino project. Goodwin was quoted as saying, "The problem we have is [Martin] also said they were doing feasibility studies and looking for a quick return on their investment . . . You hear that, and red flags start going up. A museum? We're not located in Jackson or Memphis. We're in a rural area. We are giving him the benefit of the doubt, but we are still going ahead with our organization."[28]

Chief Phillip Martin responded in a letter to the people of the region: "There is no master plan or hidden agenda for the property . . . We have no plans to build a casino . . . The demographics, infrastructure, supporting businesses and other economic criteria are not favorable for such a project . . . The only way that I would do it would be if the people of Carroll County voted for it . . . As many of you know, all of what is now Carroll County was once home to the Choctaws, and Malmaison was the home of Greenwood LeFlore, a Choctaw chief who played a pivotal role in the tribe's history."[29]

Despite Martin's assurances, the local residents, spurred by their religious leaders, were still fearful that the Choctaws would attempt to introduce gambling to their conservative rural community. Development of the property failed to flourish amid this stifling environment, and the property's decline continued.

Today, the site of Malmaison is still overgrown, isolated, and largely unremembered. The plantation itself, however, has been memorialized in some ways. A highway marker was placed some nine miles from the plantation site to commemorate the estate. And today, the Cottonlandia Museum in Greenwood, Mississippi, has a room devoted to Malmaison where original plantation artifacts, images, and some surviving furnishings are on display. The heritage of Chief Greenwood Leflore's remarkable life and estate lives on in the region he once dominated, a tribute to his sometimes controversial and always fascinating memory.

# Homewood

Once one of the Natchez area's most stunning showplaces, Homewood Plantation was part of David Hunt's vast plantation empire and later home to the Balfour family. This plantation mansion survived the Civil War and other threats to sit in quiet, dignified splendor until January 1940, when the house caught fire and burned to the ground.

David Hunt was born on October 22, 1779, in Hunterdon County, New Jersey. At the age of 22, he moved to Natchez, Mississippi, to work for his uncle, Abijah Hunt, who had found great success in the mercantile business. While working for his uncle, young David Hunt was notoriously miserly, and he saved nearly every penny he earned to invest in real estate, purchasing lands along Coles Creek in Jefferson County and elsewhere.[30]

In 1800, Hunt married Margaret Stampley and started a family. After receiving a promotion and a raise from his uncle, Hunt founded Woodlawn Plantation near his uncle Abijah Hunt's own Huntley Plantation in Jefferson County. Woodlawn later served as the flagship estate of Hunt's empire and as his private home until his death.

In December 1808, Hunt married Mary Ann Calvit, the daughter of Colonel Thomas and Zepha Calvit of Calviton Plantation (an estate which adjoined Woodlawn). It is not clear how his first marriage to Margaret Stampley ended. A few years later, in 1811, David Hunt's beloved uncle Abijah was killed in a duel with George Poindexter, who later served as governor of Mississippi. David inherited much of his uncle's sizable estate and bought out other heirs.

David Hunt married his third wife, Ann Ferguson, in 1816 when he was about thirty-seven years old. She was the daughter of David and Jane Dunbar Ferguson of Oakley Grove Plantation, in Adams County, Mississippi. A few years later, David dissolved his uncle's mercantile business, shutting down the general stores and using the liquidated assets to purchase plantations. It was also around this time that he inherited Calviton Plantation and its slaves from his former in-laws. Through the years, David Hunt's vast empire of plantations grew, eventually earning him the mocking moniker of "King David." In all, Hunt owned some twenty-five plantations, including the vast Homewood estate, which was located about a mile or two north of Natchez.

Two WPA slave narratives give a good glimpse of what life was like for enslaved people on Hunt's plantations. Peter Brown remembered the following: "I was born on the Woodlawn place. It was owned by David and Ann Hunt. I was born a slave boy . . . My remembrance of slavery is not at tall [sic] favorable. I heard the master and overseers whooping the slaves b'fore day. They had stakes fixed in the ground and tied them down on their stomachs stretched out and they beat them with a bull whoop [cowhide woven]. They would break the blisters on them with white oak paddles that had holes in it so it would suck. They be saying, 'Oh pray, master.' He'd say, 'Better pray fer yourself.' I heard that going on when I was a child morning after morning."[31]

Cyrus Bellus recalled the following:

I was born in Mississippi in 1865 in Jefferson County. It was on the tenth of March. My father's name was Cyrus Bellus, the same as mine. My mother's name was Matilda Bellus . . . My father's master was David Hunt . . . The slaves had to weave cotton and knit sox. Sometimes they would work all night, weaving cloth, and spinning thread . . . They used to have tanning vats to make shoes with too. Old master didn't know what it was to buy shoes. Had a man there to make them . . . My father and mother were

The front façade at Homewood Plantation's mansion was an impressive sight, with its four well-proportioned Ionic columns, broad dentil-detailed entablature and pediment, and five symmetric bays.

MISS.149

Homewood Plantation mansion. The sides of the mansion featured fancy cast-iron filigree, reminiscent of the Spanish-style architecture of the New Orleans French Quarter.

The rear of Homewood Plantation's master house had a most peculiar appearance. A recessed central area was created by peripheral rooms that jutted out from the main structure, and these protrusions were surrounded by galleries that were completely covered from the base of the porch floor to the crown of the roofline with rows of thick wooden louvered shutters, which provided both privacy and cross-circulation of air.

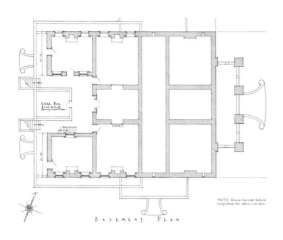

A

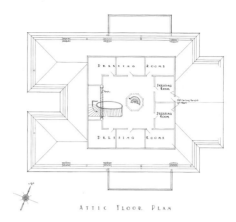

D.

B.

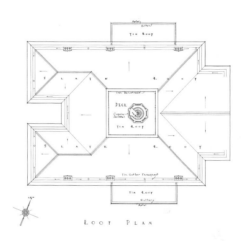

E.

Homewood Plantation
House Floorplans.

A. Ground floor (basement).

B. Principal floor plan.

C. Second-floor plan.

D. Attic floor plan. Note
central spiral stairs (to
observatory and widow's
walk) and surrounding
dressing rooms.

E. Plan of observatory and
widow's walk.

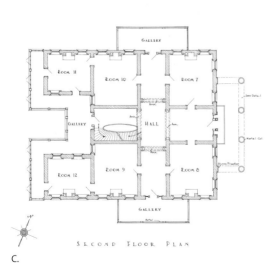

C.

Homewood Plantation House. Attic. Spiral stairs to observatory and widow's walk.

The main staircase on the second floor at Homewood was identical to the one on the first. This staircase led to the attic.

both field hands . . . They were supposed to pick—the man, four hundred pounds of cotton, and the woman three hundred. And that was gittin' some cotton. If they didn't come up to the task, they was took out and give a whipping. The overseer would do the thrashing . . . The slaves were allowed to get out and have their fun and play and 'musement for so many hours. Outside of those hours, they had to be found in their house. They had to use fiddles. They had dancing just like the boys do now. They had knockin' and rasslin' and all such like now . . . So for as serving God was concerned, they had to take a kettle and turn it down bottom upward and then old master couldn't hear the singing and prayin'. I don't know just how they turned the kettle to keep the noise from goin' out. But I heard my father and mother say they did it.[32]

The former slaves' recollections shed light onto what daily existence was like on David Hunt's plantations, Homewood and many others. Both narratives agree that Hunt was a harsh master, requiring overseers to regularly whip the slaves. Bellus's account is further remarkable for several reasons. It illustrates how self-sufficient the Hunt properties

were, from producing thread and cloth for slave clothing to making leather for shoes. It also gives a glimpse into active slave resistance, from participation in games and amusements as a method of transcending a bleak existence to organizing banned religious gatherings. The strong image of the upturned pot or kettle amid clandestine worshipers is a theme found in plantations across the South. The origin of the practice traces back to Africa where it was thought an upturned vessel would protect covert conversations from being heard.[33]

Life on the Hunt estates was obviously difficult for enslaved people. In drastic contrast were the privileged lives of David Hunt and his white family. His children and his wives lived in want of nothing. Despite his tightfisted reputation, Hunt was fond of giving a plantation or two as wedding presents to his children. His daughter Charlotte, for example, received Lansdowne Plantation, a six-hundred-acre estate neighboring Homewood, along with another small plantation in Louisiana, upon the occasion of her marriage to George Marshall, the son of Levin Marshall of Richmond Plantation in Adams County.

Homewood itself was given to daughter Catherine in 1850, when she married William Suggs Balfour, the son of William Lovett and Elizabeth Davis Gartley Balfour, who themselves owned a plantation empire. The newlyweds lived initially on a Balfour plantation in Issaquena County until their mansion at Homewood was complete.

Their Homewood mansion was designed by James Hardie, a noted architect from Scotland. It was not completed until 1860, and the Balfours only lived there for a brief time before the war. The house itself was magnificent. In front, the five-bay structure was dominated by four massive iron columns of the Ionic order. These supported a heavy entablature with dentil styling and a lofty pediment. The front door was a richly carved conglomeration of sidelights of pink Belgian glass and Corinthian pilasters supporting a weighty entablature. Above, a similar door on the second story opened to a small iron balcony. On both of the sides, the house was adorned with porches and covered balconies, which were surrounded by lacy cast-iron filigree, reminiscent of the Spanish-style architecture of the New Orleans French Quarter.

The interior of the house was quite elaborate. In her 1937 book *In Old Natchez,* Catharine Van Court described the plan of the house as follows: "There are four entrances to the main corridor, each entrance facing one of the four points on the compass. These open into lofty hallways which form a perfect Maltese cross and are connected by a series of elliptical arches."[34] Entering from the front door one would have been in the front entrance hall which was flanked by large parlors with massive pocket doors. Straight back was the central cross hall, flanked by two side halls which led to the side entrances and porches. Straight from the center hall, a stair hall with an elegantly curved staircase sat at the rear of the house. There were two rooms on either side of the great stair hall and behind each of these a smaller room jutted out, creating a small court at the central back porch.

Of the principal floor, Van Court noted: "On the first floor there are six rooms. The library, reception hall and drawing room may be thrown into one salon, seventy-two feet long. The sliding doors here are of mahogany, three inches thick, rubbed to a dull luster. All doorknobs and hinges on this floor are of solid silver . . . In the library, the hand-carved mantel is of pink marble delicately veined in gray. The mantel in the drawing room is of white marble and in the dining room, of pink marble mottled with oxblood."[35]

The house in total was five stories high. A full basement with many rooms formed the base of the mansion and supported the principal floor, actually the second level of the house. Above the main floor, the "second" story mirrored the plan of the first, with tall ceilings and strong, graceful archways. A curved stairway identical to that between the first and second stories led from the second story to the massive attic. A tall central room in the attic was completely surrounded by lower cedar-lined closets and dressing rooms. This central attic room was surrounded above by a line of horizontal windows that encircled the top of the room where the uppermost portion of the walls met the ceiling. In the very center of this central room a small staircase tightly spiraled around a slender pillar. This led to the hexagonal observatory, which opened to a lofty widow's walk.

Outside the rear of the house, the two back rooms projected out, forming a recessed area at the entrance to the back stair hall. A porch and balcony above surrounded these protrusions continuing from one end of the house to the other. The portions of the porch and balcony that projected outward—flanking either side of the central recessed porch—were completely covered from the base of the porch floor to the crown of the roofline with rows of thick wooden shutters, giving the back of the house a most peculiar appearance. These shutters would have provided both privacy and protection from the elements, while still allowing for cross-circulation during the sweltering summer months.

Beyond the mansion, a number of ancillary buildings dotted the plantation landscape. Among them, the usual stables, barns, shops, and slave cabins could be found. Notable, however, among the structures were two prominent buildings flanking the master house on either side in the rear. These structures were both two stories tall and built of brick. They each had wide porches in the front with covered balconies above. The function of the two structures is unclear, but one probably served as a kitchen with servant quarters, and the other could have served as an office, school, additional servant quarters, or as a home for bachelor sons.

Shortly after the completion of the mansion and its grounds, family life and agricultural production at Homewood were disrupted by the onslaught of war. William Balfour left Homewood to serve the Confederacy, leaving his wife and children behind on the plantation. There, Catherine mourned as she watched four of her beloved children die over the next years. After the war, the Balfours retained ownership of the plantation, and the family remained there until 1907.

After the Balfours left Homewood, the plantation passed through many hands. The plantation fields, once snowy white with cotton, gave way to the new industry of oil, as "black gold" was found on the property. The Homewood Oil Fields were created around the house. Throughout the years, the old mansion stood proud, a poignant example of an era gone by, until the night of January 2, 1940, when firefighters were summoned to the site. The house was ablaze in a fire of unknown origin, and, despite great efforts, by morning all that was left were blackened brick walls and scorched iron columns. Today, all that remains of this once-massive plantation is one of the two-story brick dependencies, now converted into a private home.

## Windy Hill Manor

Windy Hill Manor, the plantation home of Benijah Osmun and later of a governor of Mississippi and his daughter, was the site of Aaron Burr's reclusion after his arrest for treason. The plantation mansion fell victim to neglect in the twentieth century and was demolished for wood in 1965.

Located several miles from Natchez along Liberty Road, Windy Hill Manor was founded by Rev-olutionary War veteran Benijah Osmun. It was Osmun who constructed the first master house on the property. The original house was little more than a simple dwelling with a few rooms, but would later be enlarged to become a proper southern mansion.[36]

The house was a one-and-a-half-story structure with a wide front porch. There was a broad central portico that dominated the front of the house; it consisted of four thick Tuscan columns supporting a broad pediment with a central vertical window. The pediment was flanked by dormer windows on each side. Later, symmetrical wings were added on each side of the house. These smaller wings were ornamented with Greek Revival–style pilasters and topped with steep pediments, which, like that of the central portion of the house, also contained vertical windows.

The interior of the house was noted for its beautifully crafted front staircase that spiraled up, completely unsupported, to the second-floor bedrooms. Outside, the house was surrounded by moss-draped oaks, and a long avenue of cedar trees formed the front drive. Near the back of the house, a large detached kitchen building provided for the dietary needs of the household and its many guests.

One of these guests, Osmun's good friend Aaron Burr, became the estate's most famous and reviled visitor. Burr, who in 1801 became the third vice president of the United States, had much political discord with founding father Alexander Hamilton. In 1804, the two men met in a duel upon the very site where Hamilton's son Phillip had died in a duel three years prior. Burr was victorious, shooting Hamilton, who died the next day. As news of the event surfaced, citizens wide and far were outraged. Although charged with multiple crimes related to the duel, Burr was never tried for Hamilton's death. He finished his term as vice president and then made his way to the Southwest, largely in exile. He networked with leaders there and is rumored to have devised a conspiracy to establish a new, large nation out of the territories there.

Burr later traveled to Mississippi, where he was

As the twentieth century progressed, the master house at Windy Hill Manor fell into grave disrepair. Here the rear of the house shows not only signs of age but evidence of partial structural collapse.

The Greek Revival–style mansion at Windy Hill Manor was dominated by its broad central portico of four thick Tuscan columns and pediment with a central vertical window.

Windy Hill Manor's gracefully curving staircase was an unsupported wonder.

chez's Stanton Hall, a renowned Greek Revival mansion that still welcomes visitors today.

Windy Hill Plantation was home to the Stanton family for more than a century, but by the first half of the twentieth century, only three unwed sisters remained. Elizabeth, Maude, and Beatrice grew old together in the plantation mansion, but refused to make repairs to the house. They struggled financially, but their pride forbade them from selling off land or furnishings to finance much-needed repairs. By the mid-1940s, only Maude remained, the other two sisters having died in their nineties. During that time Harnett Kane visited, and was appalled at the deterioration he found. Kane wrote:

> Windy Hill Manor stood among the dark, shifting shadows of its trees. One of the small temple-like side wings was gone; its counterpart, with its peaked roof, huddled at the opposite end, under the protection of the porticoed main building. At the back two or three brick chimneys raised themselves forlornly out of the grass; the rooms that they had served had long since fallen . . . Under a lean-to waited the remains of the carriage in which the sisters once drove to town. Its shaft had broken, and tendrils of green had laced themselves about the unused wheels. Down the forgotten "lover's walk" of Aaron Burr and Madeline Price we could make out the passageway near the broken terrace where the Stanton children had once played.[37]

The mansion sat, decaying for another twenty years, until 1965, when it was demolished for wood by a local cabinetmaker. The dismantling of the house had been a rather simple job, until the man came to the staircase. It refused to budge. Unsupported, it stood strong even as it was tied to a truck. Finally, it was disassembled by hand, board by board. The remaining foundation was pushed into a bayou, as Windy Hill Manor faded into the past forever.

regarded with much mistrust. He was eventually arrested in Natchez on charges of treason. While awaiting trial, Burr resided at Windy Hill Manor with his old friend Benijah Osmun. It is said that, while staying at Windy Hill Manor, Burr met and fell in love with Madeline Price of Halfway Hill Plantation. Shortly after their whirlwind romance, Burr realized that he needed to escape, fearing rumors of an angry mob coming for him. He forfeited his five-thousand-dollar bond and pleaded for Madeline to run away with him. But she refused. He later wrote to her, releasing her of her obligation to wait for him, and she married an English nobleman.

Colonel Osmun died in 1816, and Windy Hill was purchased by Gerard Brandon, who later served as governor of Mississippi. Brandon passed the plantation to his daughter Elizabeth, who married William Stanton. Stanton's brother built Nat-

# CHAPTER SEVEN

# *Louisiana*

On this important acquisition, so favorable to the immediate interests of our western citizens, so auspicious to the peace and security of the nation in general, which adds to our country territories so extensive and fertile, and to our citizens new brethren to partake of the blessings of freedom and self government, I offer to Congress and the country, my sincere congratulations.

*—Thomas Jefferson,*
January 1804, speaking on the occasion of the Louisiana Purchase

But, Alas!, it is all gone now. Its beauty has vanished like some fair dream, leaving what can now be seen, a wreck of former days.

*—Laura Lacoul Gore*
(for whom Laura Plantation was named), describing the fall of Petit Versailles

It has been said that the history of Louisiana flows through the Mississippi River, and certainly this is often the case. In 1682, René-Robert Cavelier, Sieur de La Salle, claimed the entire Mississippi and the lands through which its waters flowed, from present-day Minnesota and beyond to the Gulf of Mexico, in the name of Louis XIV of France, the Sun King. During the early years of the colony, France established stronghold settlements at New Orleans and Natchitoches.

Agriculture was relatively limited at first. Small family farms partially provided for the needs of the colony, while smaller numbers of larger plantations, worked by slaves, attempted to produce cash crops like tobacco and indigo. But neither crop was very successful in Louisiana.

Early German settlers began populating a region known today as the German Coast, and their successful family farms fed the colony. They were joined by the resourceful Acadians (later Cajuns), exiled French settlers from Nova Scotia, who began arriving in Louisiana in 1764. Both groups spurred agriculture, but still production was small scale.

Louisiana had been ceded to Spain in 1762 by the secret Treaty of Fontainebleau. The French rebelled against their Spanish rulers, but eventually order was established, and agriculture improved. It wasn't until the end of the eighteenth century, though—when methods of converting cane juice to granulated sugar were popularized in Louisiana—that plantation culture truly flourished. Sugar plantations developed quickly along both banks of the Mississippi River, the principal transportation route of the region. In time, a seemingly endless parade of stunning white-columned, Greek Revival mansions and colorful Creole master houses could be seen bordering the river's edge from Natchez to New Orleans. Other large plantations were carved out of lands to the west along bayous and in the pinelands to the north.

In 1801, France regained control of Louisiana by the Treaty of San Ildefonso. Napoleon sold the entire colony to the United States in 1803, in an event known as the Louisiana Purchase. Many have argued that the transfer of Louisiana, which was vast at the time, was the most significant event in the history of the United States. It doubled the size of the country and opened the doors for westward expansion. It also created new opportunities for planters, who were ever eager to sell their sugar and other crops.

While cotton and rice were grown in Louisiana, especially in the North, neither was ever as successful as sugar, which gained the label "white gold." When Norbert Rillieux, a free man of mixed race, invented the double and triple vacuum pan systems for refining sugar during the 1830s and 1840s, the industry boomed. By this time thousands of steamboats were navigating the perilous twists and turns of the "Mighty Mississippi," further expanding the industry and fueling the demand for sugar.

All the while, planters continued developing and improving their plantations. Most of these were rather modest estates, but quite a few were large, nearly self-sufficient operations. Here, planters built villages of cabins for their slaves, large sugarhouses for their refining equipment, and a variety of other buildings. Regarding their mansions, many of the most successful planters built grand Greek Revival temples, with tall columns and wide verandas. There were also many Creole-style homes, noted for their bright, colorful exteriors, lack of central hallways, and characteristic exterior stairs.

Many of these plantation homes and the agricultural enterprises that surrounded them were greatly threatened during the Civil War. Of those that survived America's bloodiest conflict, like plantations everywhere, none was unchanged. With the emancipation of their labor force and the collapse of the entire southern economic system, planters were forced to embrace a new way of life.

As the years passed, agriculture gave way to industry, especially along the Mississippi River, where chemical plants and oil companies developed massive enterprises. Encroaching industrial development, natural disaster, and pure neglect catalyzed the loss of hundreds of Louisiana's fine plantation homes—many representing the greatest quintessential examples of southern antebellum architecture.

In preparing this chapter, the most difficult

task was choosing which of several dozen potential plantations to include among the entries. Ultimately, those that appear in this work were chosen because of their historical and architectural significance. Those great houses that could not be included due to space limitations, but which certainly warrant further study and recognition, include, among many others: Belmont in St. James Parish, which survived the great crevasse of 1888, only to succumb the next year to fire; Helvetia—also in St. James parish—which was destroyed by Hurricane Betsy in 1965, (some of its architectural elements were incorporated into other structures, and two of its slave cabins survive at the popular Cabin Restaurant in Burnside, Louisiana); Three Oaks near New Orleans, which was swiftly and secretively demolished by the American Sugar Company in 1966; Linwood, an impressive mansion designed by James Gallier, which was considered irreparable and demolished in 1939; Chatsworth, a massive mansion built on the site of an Indian village, which was the location of wild fraternity parties in the 1920s—it was demolished in 1930, when the levee was moved; Cabahanoce, the home of Governor Andre Bienvenu Roman, which was swallowed by the river; and Ellington Manor, another Classical Revival gem in Luling, which was demolished in 1950 by Lion Oil Company and is today the site of a public park.

Still other lost Louisiana plantations include: Belle Chasse, the home of Confederate secretary of state Judah P. Benjamin, a Jewish slave owner who also served in the U.S. Senate; Tchoupitoulas, the home of the Soniat family, which was a fine colonial plantation—its master house was used as Colonial Country Club, until the organization destroyed the mansion to make way for a larger clubhouse; and Tezcuco, located in Darrow, which was built in 1855 by Benjamin F. Tureaud and served as an impressive tourist attraction during recent years until 2002, when it burned to the ground. Some of Tezcuco's outbuildings still survive and have been moved to Whitney Plantation, in St. John the Baptist Parish, which is being restored. There are many, many other lost Louisiana plantations, whose histories could undoubtedly fill numerous volumes.

Some scholarship has already been undertaken regarding the changing face of Louisiana and her lost plantations. Among the most notable recent works is John B. Rehder's *Delta Sugar: Louisiana's Vanishing Plantation Landscape*, which chronicles the swift loss of plantation lands and associated improvements through the stories of six estates. Mary Ann Sternberg provides a sociocultural history and a mile-by-mile travel guide in *Along the River Road: Past and Present on Louisiana's Historic Byway*. From an architectural perspective, Fred Daspit's volumes, *Louisiana Architecture, 1714–1820*, *Louisiana Architecture, 1820–1840*, and *Louisiana Architecture, 1840–1860*, provide excellent thumbnail histories and architectural studies of both demolished and standing plantation houses as well as other structures. A few individual Louisiana plantations have been discussed in various articles or chapters, but few lost plantations have been studied in depth. Notable exceptions include Seven Oaks, once the crown jewel of Westwego. Its history, including its turbulent demise, was featured in this author's *Lost Plantation: The Rise and Fall of Seven Oaks*, the book that served as the impetus for the current volume. Likewise, Belle Grove, the largest and most complex antebellum home in the South, was meticulously documented in an unpublished thesis by Robert Mark Rudd, "Apocryphal Grandeur: Belle Grove Plantation in Iberville Parish, Louisiana." As elsewhere, most current scholarship focuses on plantation structures that are still standing, often totally neglecting the majority of estates that once existed.

While the great majority of Louisiana's plantation mansions are gone, there are fortunately a significant number that still exist. Some are held by private companies, families, or individuals, but others have been successfully restored by community groups. For example, in the late 1960s and early 1970s the River Road Historical Society persuaded American Oil Company (Amoco) to donate Destrehan Plantation for renovation. Today the society operates the plantation as one of the state's busiest tourist attractions. Likewise, the Louisiana Landmarks Society saved the Pitot House, an early colonial plantation manor that was home to a mayor of New Orleans. The Pitot House is also operated as a museum.

By increasing recognition of Louisiana's lost plantation past, a more realistic history that includes both extant and vanished estates is ultimately created. Greater appreciation for demolished architectural landmarks and destroyed agricultural landscapes, along with appreciation for how and why such losses occurred, will surely contribute to future preservation. What follows are the stories of seven of Louisiana's greatest lost plantations. Their storied histories hold lessons for all.

## Le Petit Versailles

Le Petit Versailles was the home of one of Louisiana's most famous planters, Valcour Aime, whose legendary successes and excesses are still widely recounted to this day. His unusual mansion at Le Petit Versailles Plantation was the crown of his plantation empire, which included many properties. And the flagship estate's gardens were among the most elaborate ever conceived in the South. The plantation mansion burned in the twentieth century, leaving but a memory of a man and a plantation that truly defined Louisiana's "Golden Age."

Valcour Aime was born in 1797, in St. Charles Parish, Louisiana, to François Aime II and Marie Felicité Julie Fortier. He was christened François Gabriel, but a nurse called him Valcour, the name he would be known by forevermore. He and his brother Michel moved to New Orleans after their parents' deaths, and the two boys lived with their maternal grandfather. At the age of sixteen, Aime served under René Trudeau in the Battle of New Orleans.[1]

Aime married Josephine Roman in 1819. Her family was among the most prominent in Louisiana, and their business and political connections were seemingly endless.[2] The couple moved to St. James Parish. There, Aime owned the plantation that would come to be known as Oak Alley, perhaps the most recognizable and photographed plantation in the South today. He transferred this estate to his brother-in-law, Jacques Télésphore Roman, and took possession of the old Roman family estate. This Roman plantation measured thirty arpents along the Mississippi River and extended eighty arpents back. Aime filled its fields with sugarcane and began turning an annual profit between twelve thousand and twenty-three thousand dollars.[3]

By the 1830s, Aime's family had grown, consisting of five children: four daughters and one son named Gabriel. By this time, the family needed more space. The Romans' old French Colonial house where the Aime family lived was integrated into the new mansion. The new house was built in the shape of a U with a large central courtyard facing the rear. Massive columns surrounded the plantation house and also lined the courtyard, creating a very remarkable rear façade. Twin staircases on either side of the courtyard framed the rows of columns within.[4]

In its finished version, the mansion boasted sixteen rooms, including a grand banquet hall and private children's dining room on the first floor, as well as private parlors, bedrooms, and a library on the second floor. The large central hall contained a solid marble staircase and marble floors. Also, marble of various colors was found throughout the house in mantels, wainscoting, and in the rear courtyard floor.[5]

Outside the structure, Aime created what was arguably one of the finest flower gardens in the nation. The gardens were designed on a twenty-acre plot as an English park, although the landscapers were actually Parisians. It has been suggested that Aime was inspired by Josephine Bonaparte's English gardens at Malmaison, and it is said that over 120 slaves were employed in the creation of the botanical wonder at Petit Versailles. A large artificial lake filled with exotic fish was built and a stream known as *La Rivière* was supplied with pumped water from the nearby Mississippi River. Roman bridges spanned the rivulet at various intervals. A large hill was constructed with a grotto below, and on top a crowning Chinese pagoda contained stained-glass windows and chiming bells. A small fort, complete with a cannon, was constructed,

Very early photograph of Petit Versailles Plantation house. Notice the young women in the foreground and man with a hat to the left. Courtesy of The Historic New Orleans Collection.

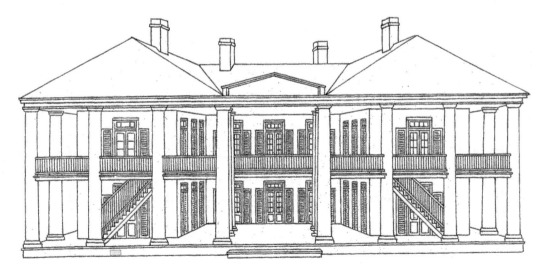

Rear elevation of Valcour Aime's Petit Versailles. Note the large column-lined central court that opened to the rear of the U-shaped home. Drawings by Fred Daspit. Courtesy of the Center for Louisiana Studies, University of Louisiana at Lafayette.

and came to be known as St. Hélène, in honor of the island where Napoleon was exiled. And artificial ruins, some detailed with oyster shells and marble statuary, added a decorative flair to the gardens. Large hothouses were filled with much tropical vegetation, while outside, the landscape artists planted fruit trees, shrubbery, and other plants from as far away as India, China, Korea, Madagascar, Siam, and other distant locations. A small zoo was installed, complete with exotic animals, including many species of songbirds, peacocks, and even kangaroos. In addition, the plantation's internal railroad ran through the gardens to ferry guests around the estate.[6]

When the gardens were finished, one of the landscapers, Joseph Muller, who studied at the famed *Jardin des Plantes*, remained on the plantation to oversee the landscaping. It is said that he had a crew of thirty slaves who worked exclusively in the park.[7] Eliza Ripley visited Petit Versailles and was escorted on a tour by one of Aime's daughters. Ripley wrote of this experience in her book, *Social Life in Old New Orleans*:

Félicie and I, with a whole escort of followers, explored the spacious grounds, considered the finest in Louisiana. There was a miniature river, meandering in and out and around the beautifully kept parterres, the tiny banks of which were an unbroken mass of blooming violets. A long-legged man might have been able to step across this tiny stream, but it was spanned at intervals by bridges of various designs, some rustic, some stone, but all furnished with parapets, so one would not tumble in and drown, as a little Roman remarked . . . There were summer houses draped with strange, foreign-looking vines; a pagoda on a mound, the entrance of which was reached by a flight of steps. It was an octagonal building, with stained-glass windows, and it struck my inexperienced eye as a very wonderful and surprising bit of architecture. Further on was—a mountain! covered from base to top with beds of blooming violets. A narrow, winding path led to the summit, from which a comprehensive view was obtained of the extensive grounds, bounded by a series of conservatories.

It was enchanting. There I saw for the first time the magnolia frascati, at that date a real rarity.[8]

Valcour Aime and his family lived in great splendor on their well-kept estate. His ambitions in planting and vivacious living can be easily seen throughout his life. Aime enjoyed constantly competing with his brother-in-law, Jacques Télésphore Roman, at nearby Oak Alley Plantation. Entries in Aime's personal diary state, "My cane is higher than Jacques'" and "my oranges are much tastier than his."[9]

Aime's many commercial and civic affairs show the breadth of his interests and avocations. He founded the St. James Sugar Refinery on his plantation and was well known for his many scientific experiments perfecting the refining process.[10] He also purchased Jefferson College in 1830, which he restored and enlarged. He gave the college to the Marist Fathers, who operated it as an institution of higher learning for the sons of wealthy planters.[11]

Aime and his entire family were also known for their hospitality. Eliza Ripley wrote of her visit to the plantation:

M. Valcour, tall and graceful, was at that time in the prime of life, and was my (romantic) ideal of a French marquis; Mme. Valcour, inclined to *embonpoint* and vivacious, kissed me and called me *"ma petite,"* though I was quite her height. But the charm of my visit to that incomparable mansion, the like of which is not to be found on the Mississippi River to-day [sic], was the daughter, Félicie, who at once took me under her wing and entertained me as only a well-bred young girl can. She showed me all over the premises, opening door after door, that I could see how adequate the accommodations for the guests who frequently filled the house; into the salon that I might see and listen to the chimes of the gilt clock Gabie [Gabriel] had sent from Paris.[12]

The Aimes held lavish social gatherings at their home, and they prided themselves, as did many planter families, on the self-sufficiency of their plantation. Legend has it that Aime, who came to be known as the "Louis XIV of Louisiana," wagered ten thousand dollars, a fortune at the time, on the premise that he could produce an entire dinner from his plantation without relying on anything brought from outside the estate. It is said that Aime and his friend dined on all manner of meat and seafood, fruits and vegetables, and breads and desserts. They drank expensive wine, and finished the meal with fine cigars and a cup of coffee. Aime's dining partner exclaimed that he had won the bet since coffee and cigars were certainly not produced in Louisiana. Aime then rode with his friend to the plantation hothouses and showed the astonished gentleman the coffee beans and tobacco growing in the carefully maintained artificial environment. And with that Aime won the bet!

When the future king of France, Louis Philippe, visited Le Petit Versailles, legend says that Aime served him dinner on solid gold place settings. He later threw these into the Mississippi River, as no one was worthy to eat after the royal guest. Another version of the story states that Aime threw his solid gold place settings into the river during the Civil War, rather than have Union soldiers steal them. Regardless, if any of these stories are totally historically accurate, they illustrate Aime's vivacious, often flamboyant personality. They also exemplify his position as a planter-celebrity, a status earned during his era but that even today exists in the popular lore of Louisiana.

Aime's generosity was unequalled, especially when it came to his family. He is known to have showered his children with many lavish gifts. He gave his daughter Felicité a plantation (named Felicity in her honor) as a wedding present.[13] Aime's daughter Josephine was given over $110,000 in gifts by her father, including the use of nearby St. Joseph's Plantation. The Aimes lived a life of privilege and power second to none in St. James Parish, but as conflict loomed over states' rights and slavery, the family realized that their lavish way of life was threatened.[14]

When the country divided in the Civil War, Aime supported the southern cause by financially backing the troops. He gave five hundred dollars to each of the eight units raised in St. James Parish, and one of them was subsequently named in his honor (Company D of the 30th Regiment, Louisiana Infantry, was known as Valcour Aime Guards).[15] During the war, the family often sought refuge from gunboat fire in a large underground bomb shelter near the levee.

Aime's grandson, famed Louisiana historian Alcée Fortier, wrote, "I remember seeing cart loads of shells strewn in the yards. I remember also the holes dug in the ground covered with beams and several feet of earth, the inside arranged like a comfortable room and filled with provisions of all kinds."[16] The family later fled to Bayou Teche. Upon their return, they found that the plantation had suffered much damage.

Aime survived the war. He outlived his wife and three of his children, including his beloved son, Gabriel, who had died of yellow fever only two days after returning home from an extended trip to Europe before the war.[17] Valcour Aime never got over the loss of his son. Aime died on New Year's Day in 1867, after a bout of pneumonia.[18] His will stated that his family had to reside on his plantation for four years after his death before dividing the estate. John Burnside, owner of many plantations, including Louisiana's Houmas House, later purchased Le Petit Versailles. Later still, the plantation was abandoned as it passed through the hands of various owners.[19]

The mansion burned to the ground in 1920, a final, physical reminder of the finality of Louisiana's Golden Age. The lavish gardens of Le Petit Versailles that once welcomed a future French king have now returned to a thick, overgrown natural state, but many of the exotic plants can still be found there. The property in the immediate vicinity of the mansion's site has been fenced. The garden property was purchased by a landscape architect, who utilized the rich variety of flora found there. Today, a highway marker briefly memorializes the site's remarkable history.[20]

# Belle Grove

The largest antebellum house built in the American South was found in Iberville Parish, Louisiana, in the heart of sugarcane country. Called Belle Grove, it was one of the greatest and most magnificent plantation homes ever constructed. Today, all that remains are memories and a commemorative marker bordering the modern neighborhood that now occupies the former site of this extraordinary plantation.

The agricultural operation, which became known as Belle Grove, was first envisioned by an industrious Virginian named John Andrews. Andrews, who was born in 1804, arrived in Louisiana in the 1830s, destined to make his fortune. This was a period of great migration to the lower South, as young businessmen and entrepreneurs sought to strike it rich in cane, cotton, and related agricultural enterprises. Andrews was no different. He originally partnered with Dr. John Phillip Read Stone, and together the two men founded the Belle Grove Plantation. This partnership ended in 1844, when Andrews took full ownership of the estate.[21]

Andrews married Penelope Lynch Adams in 1832. Over a few brief years she bore him eight children, five of whom survived. She died in 1848, leaving Andrews a widower. Grief stricken, Andrews poured himself into his work at the plantation, becoming somewhat of a recluse. Interestingly, unlike his neighbors and fellow planters throughout the South, Andrews did not participate in politics, he was not active in local affairs or social circles, and parish records indicate that he was not involved in lawsuits with his competitors or neighbors (as was frequently the case with the planter class). His public life was virtually nonexistent, except in one arena—planting cane. And in this pursuit he was king. By the 1850s, 150 slaves were producing well over a half million pounds of sugar each year from Andrews's seven thousand acres. Andrews's success as a sugar magnate was virtually unparalleled, with a few notable exceptions.

Among those few was John Randolph, a fellow Virginian who also came to Louisiana to make his fortune in sugar. The rivalry that existed between the two successful planters became quite legendary. And their competition extended to their homes. The men sought to outdo each other in the construction of their mansions. Arguably, Andrews won by creating the largest and one of the most magnificent plantation houses ever built in the antebellum

The mansion at Belle Grove Plantation—the largest house built in the antebellum South—was in poor condition in this photograph, yet it still exuded much of the grandeur of an earlier era.

South. Randolph's mansion—called Nottoway—was a close second. It, too, is a massive structure which combined both Italianate and Greek Revival features, and displayed many similarities to Belle Grove, including an asymmetrical plan and façade. Today, Nottoway is the largest surviving plantation mansion in the South and among the most beau-tiful. It is open to the public as a historic attraction, and its famed White Ballroom still serves as a popular location for weddings and other special events.

Andrews's mansion at Belle Grove, which was constructed between 1852 and 1855 (a few years before Nottoway), sought to communicate the wealth

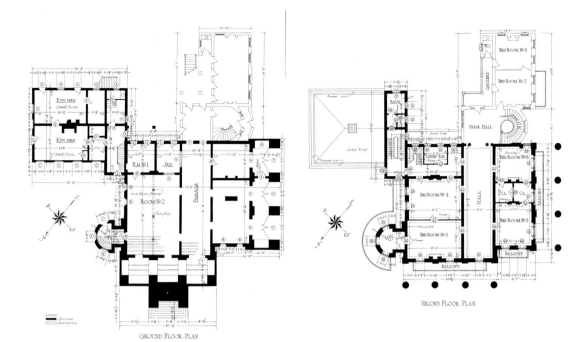

GROUND FLOOR PLAN

SECOND FLOOR PLAN

The ground floor at Belle Grove Plantation House was appropriated for various service functions. Here everything from kitchens and storage areas to a "dungeon-like" jail could be found.

Belle Grove's upper floor was reserved mainly for large bedrooms.

Belle Grove's principal floor was a unique and complex array of spaces that provided varying levels of privacy as one ventured deeper into the mansion. A library wing was connected to the main structure via a grand stair hall, and a servants' wing was reached through the dining room and a separate servants' stair hall.

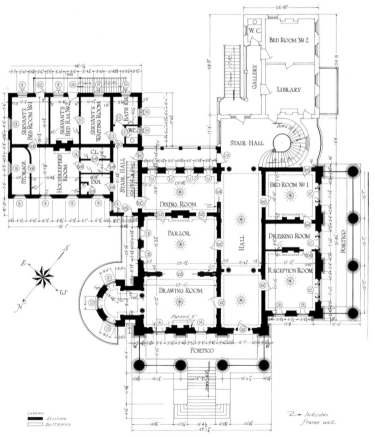

FIRST FLOOR PLAN

Belle Grove Plantation House—exterior column with capital. The image of Belle Grove took on a much greater representative ideal and communicated widely the idea of success in the South. Its memory is still alive today, inspiring everything from needlepoint kits to an Internet discussion group.

and economic status that the Andrewses had attained. While many sources suggest that famed architect James Gallier, Sr., was chosen as the designer of the house, it was actually the relatively unknown Henry Howard who was awarded the top job.

Howard, who was born in Cork, Ireland, in 1818, never formally trained as an architect. He immigrated to the United States in 1836 and arrived in New Orleans the next year. He worked as a simple carpenter and later was employed under noted architect James Dakin and then engineer Henry Molhausen. Despite his lack of formal education, he was an obvious master of his craft. Before completing his principal and defining work, his magum opus at Belle Grove, Howard designed the Ascension Parish Courthouse at Donaldsonville, as well as Madewood and probably Woodlawn plantation houses for the Pugh family, among other important works.[22]

Howard's designs for Belle Grove were among the most sophisticated thus conceived in the United States. The house was an asymmetrical amassing of innumerable design elements plucked from various sources and expertly melded into a magnificent, complementary whole. The house boasted an amazing twenty-six different styles of windows and incorporated numerous and varied porticos, galleries, and balconies. The size of the mansion was equally as impressive as its complex design. The house was 52 feet high, 122 feet wide, and 119 feet deep, including the porticos.

The exterior of the house featured two massive columned porticos, one in the front and one on the southwest side. Each of these porticos had four elaborate fluted Corinthian columns and matching pilasters. These supported a heavy entablature with dentil styling. In the front portico the massive columns supported a crowning pediment, while the side portico omitted this element. There were extensive, discontinuous balconies around the house, but they did not extend fully to meet the columns.

The exterior of the mansion was an exhibition of brilliant colors. In fact, Belle Grove was perhaps the most colorful plantation house in the South.

The shades of white and gray or natural earth tones that were commonly seen on the exteriors of most large Greek Revival plantation homes across the South were not predominant at Belle Grove. Instead, the mansion itself was a soft, rich pink, highlighted by vivid blues and lavender. Architectural elements were delineated with straw yellow, olive green, and bright red trim. The roof was of purple and blue slate. Certainly this eclectic conglomeration of colors made for quite an impressive sight, especially to those passing by on riverboats.

The house had four levels and several distinct divisions. The main section of the structure contained major social areas on the first floor, including parlors and the dining room and bedrooms above. From the rear of the house, the library wing stretched away from the main structure, connected by the stair hall. And, to the left of the main section, a large service wing accommodated house servants and provided for various service functions.

On the ground floor, massive rooms afforded much storage. There was even a dungeon/jail where slaves were punished. The service wing on the ground level contained two large kitchens and there were two water closets for the house servants. The southwest side included areas for carriages, which entered through three sets of large doors beneath the side portico.

The first floor was reached by an impressive twelve-foot-high marble stairway in front. This principal floor was dominated by the off-center hallway that ran through the entire length of the main portion of the house. It was divided by columns about a third of the way through, creating an entrance foyer. The hall ended in a large rear stair hall that housed a large, circular staircase. This stair hall connected the main portion of the house to the rear library wing, which was the business end of the house, with its ground-floor offices and first-floor library.

In his thesis on Belle Grove, Robert Mark Rudd suggests that the more modern rear communicated a message entirely different from that of the stately Greek Revival front of the mansion. The rear was used for business functions, and its modernity, with its water closets and updated design, conveyed that Belle Grove was a technologically advanced, progressive sugar estate, while the front of the house communicated wealth, stability, and in a broader sense connection with the established hierarchy of the Old South.

In the main portion of the house, a reception hall could be found to one side of the hall; here the planter greeted associates, in a private room separate from the other social living spaces of the mansion. On the opposite side of the hall a drawing room and attached half-turret provided a larger, more private, social area for the family and guests. The half-turret was set off with columns and curtains, and is said to have been used as a courting area for Andrews's daughters. The drawing room opened by way of large pocket doors into a parlor that further gave way to the dining room beyond.

A second stair hall attached to the dining room connected the service wing of the mansion. From the exterior this two-story wing looked like an immense formal ballroom, with its arched windows and graceful lines, but inside it was divided into many small rooms, which housed servants on the first floor.

Above, the design of the second story mimicked that of the first, with some exceptions, among them being that the servants' wing was nonexistent on the second story. The second floor mainly contained bedrooms and gave access to the immense attic above, which housed massive copper tanks that supplied the home's progressive baths and water closets.

Rudd noted in his thesis that the entire plan and layout of Belle Grove was conceived with various layers of social exchange, intimacy, and privacy in mind, in ways that had never been devised before. For example, on the first floor there were sequential spaces, open to more and more private areas, such as a hall leading to the drawing room, opening to the more private parlor and finally the innermost dining room towards the rear. In many ways, this notion of privacy reflected John Andrews's own state as a highly private and reclusive individual. Certainly, the home's design also incorporated var-

ious security measures to ensure both safety and privacy, as entrances and accesses were much more limited than in other plantation mansions.

While the interior of the house was an amassing of opulent spaces cloaked in various levels of privacy, the outside was ironically designed to widely and publicly broadcast a clear meaning. The Belle Grove mansion's message of wealth and domination was undeniably apparent. It quickly became a well-recognized symbol of the formidable success of sugar in all its excess. In 1858, an image of the house crowned Marie Adrien Persac's famous map of the plantations along the Mississippi from New Orleans to Natchez. Robert Mark Rudd notes that an image of the house was engraved on a silver sugar bowl included in a coffee and tea set ceremoniously presented to the collector of the Port of New Orleans in recognition for his service. The implication was obvious; the house epitomized the affluence and accomplishments of cane culture.

Outside of the famed mansion, a variety of buildings could be found. The sugarhouse was the most obvious of these. It was designed as a functional center of productivity, as well as to communicate the economic status of the estate and its owners. It was a massive brick structure with soaring smokestacks that could be seen for miles around. Other structures surrounding the mansion and sugarhouse included a large slave hospital, a massive warehouse for sugar, a steam-powered sawmill with attached gristmill, a brick blacksmith's shop, and a brick overseer's house.

The slave cabins, twenty in total, stretched downriver from the mansion in two symmetrical rows. Each of these double cabins contained two rooms, each measuring ten by sixteen feet. An additional two-story structure contained six more quarters for slave families or unattached slaves. It was from these simple dwellings that enslaved people gazed at the monumental master house, a clear reminder of who reaped the rewards of their grueling forced labor.

John Andrews lived a privileged life with his family at Belle Grove, garnering handsome profits off the backs of his slaves. Although he wasn't known for his social involvement in the area, the wedding of his daughter Emily to Edward Schiff of Paris, France, at the plantation was an event long remembered and celebrated in the annals of the elite. The exterior of the house was hung with thousands of lights for the grand event. A famous New Orleans chef named Imbert, along with his staff, came a week in advance to begin preparing the feast, which included such delicacies as daubes glacés, pyramids of nougat, elaborate salads, savory bouillons, oyster dressings, and intricate confections in the shapes of swans, steamboats, and even the mansion itself. It is said that fifty house guests stayed a week for the affair, and an additional five hundred guests, along with their personal servants, came for the ceremony and festivities. This occasion generally functioned to cement Andrews's superior position among members of Louisiana's plantocracy and gave him some additional foothold in the social affairs of the day.[23]

John Andrews and his family lived sumptuously and bountifully at Belle Grove until the outbreak of the Civil War. At that time, he fled to Texas. His daughter stayed behind to manage the estate. The war left Andrews devastated, and in 1868, without laborers to farm his fields, he was forced to cede his beloved Belle Grove. He sold the plantation to his associate Henry Ware for twenty-five thousand dollars cash and an additional twenty-five thousand dollars secured through two deeds to lots in New Orleans.

Ware, a native of Georgia, had moved to Alabama with his wife, Martha Ann Everitt, after their 1837 marriage. The couple later moved to Texas, where they owned Oak Grove Plantation near Marshall. After the war, Ware lost a political election in Texas, and he moved to New Orleans. He resided on St. Charles Avenue for about three years until he purchased Belle Grove.[24]

The Wares operated the plantation, and rather than go into a decline immediately after the war, as did most other estates, Belle Grove flourished in many ways. The Ware family, including descendants of Henry, lived in Belle Grove and operated the plantation for sixty-five years.

The Wares lavishly filled the plantation mansion with many antiques and other fine furnishings. The socially vibrant family hosted innumerable balls and extravagant parties in the house, and even built a successful horse racetrack on the estate. Two of Henry Ware's sons, James Andrew Ware and John M. Ware, eventually acquired the estate. James Andrew married Mary Eliza Stone, the daughter of Dr. John P. R. Stone, a physician and planter. The couple eventually gained full ownership of the plantation.

Mary Eliza flourished in the role of postbellum plantation mistress. She brought the family's social status to the highest levels, hosting ever more opulent and lavish parties. She spent a fortune on superfluous gowns and jewels, and it is said that she hired two young African American boys, whom she dressed in Middle Eastern garb, including turbans, to accompany her, following her every footstep during her famous balls.

Mary Eliza and James Andrew had only one child, John Stone Ware, known invariably as Stone Ware. Harnett Kane interviewed Ware years later, and he told of his isolation and loneliness at Belle Grove. He noted that he was "a spoiled brat, hardly fit to live with. I had, I guess, anything a kid could ask, except maybe companionship. I eventually learned to get along without that."[25] As a boy, Stone Ware would play in the immense mansion, using the turret as a lookout for his spyglass. He was well educated at the mansion by a host of private tutors and later attended Tulane University.

One observer noted, "Somebody clattered along the road on a handsome horse, a fellow with all the composure in the world. He drew up sharp before the bar, tossed the reins to a Negro, and strode in. He took several drinks, and he was affable, yes, and nodded to several people. But he drank alone. After he rode off, I was told he was Stone Ware, just back from college. Lord, how I resented him!"[26]

Stone Ware traded his horse for an automobile, a speedster that he rode in wearing a tan jacket, goggles, and gloves. He eventually bought several vehicles, and hosted races at Belle Grove. He married Carmelite Gourrier, and they became the last residents of the mansion. The 1920s brought crop failures and bankruptcies to many sugar planters, and the Wares were not immune. John Stone and his wife left in 1924, and they sold Belle Grove the next year.

The plantation passed through various hands, and was generally allowed to decay through the Great Depression. The library wing completely collapsed. In 1940, after reading of the mansion's impending demise, brothers John and William Wickes, both Michigan architects, purchased it. They owned the property only two years.

In the winter of 1940–1941, the *Louisiana Conservation Review* published an article regarding the state of Belle Grove. The opening paragraph read:

Twenty-five miles from our State Capitol at Baton Rouge the most elegant plantation house ever built in America is crumbling to ruins. Abandoned as a place of residence, it has been, for a score of years, the shrine of a few faithful dreamers; it has been an inspiration for several artists and writers, but in its state of decadence it has failed to stimulate motivation on the part of more prosaic men and women who are in position to do something about it. Painters have gone there and attempted to reincarnate its living spirit upon canvass; writers and photographers, historians, architects and artisans still journey to the hallowed old house and marvel at its austere beauty. Sentimentalists go there, brush tears from their eyes, and wonder why such a magnificent structure is left to the ravages of time. Many of the bricks have fallen from the walls and are returning to dust from which they were made, all because those of us who appreciate the aesthetic value of such a building have failed in our duty to stimulate definite action through some of our state agencies.[27]

The article further said that the state planning commission intended to purchase the plantation for restoration. The *Louisiana Conservation Review* went on to suggest that the mansion be used as a public library and research facility for housing antebellum books and manuscripts, as well as a house museum with period furnishings. The article suggested that a sports component should be integrated into the plantation property, reminiscent of the horse racing that prominently took place there. Furthermore, it was suggested that facilities for camping should be installed, with Louisiana State University student groups and church groups in mind.

Sadly, none of these grand plans ever took place, as the nation was soon thrust into the Second World War, and preservation rightfully took a backseat to defense. Belle Grove, however, continued to rapidly deteriorate. By 1943, hearing of the house's great decline, Frederick J. Nehrbass purchased the largest mansion constructed in the American South prior to the Civil War along with seventeen surrounding acres for a preposterous two thousand dollars!

The condition of the mansion was described as appalling: "The great wings of this incredible house lie sodden and rotting. The stately Corinthian columns have been cruelly defaced by vandals. Little minds have guided irreverent hands in writing upon the faded, weather-stained walls. Thieves have carried away the marble mantels, and the marble of which the broad steps were made, and the silver knobs of the doors . . . Yet somehow, despite the havoc wrought by the elements and neglect and the vandals, a splendid dignity and stateliness linger about the old ruin."[28]

Unfortunately, Nehrbass was able to do little—the costs were too great and the job was too daunting. The final blow came on the afternoon of March 15, 1952, when the mansion was burned by an arsonist. Residents of Iberville Parish hurriedly gathered on the levee and watched in awe and sorrow as the greatest plantation house was claimed by bright, dancing flames. The massive fire consumed the fine woodwork and plaster, leaving behind only a charred, crumbling brick shell.

A few years later in the mid-1950s, the ruins of the house were bulldozed to make way for the new Belle Grove subdivision. By 1958, developers Ross Campest and Peter Cappo were building the community, laying out streets with names like Stone, Ware, and Grove, which resonated with the memory of those who earlier had called the plantation home.

And, although the structures of this unparalleled plantation are now gone, the memory of it vividly lives on. The story of Belle Grove, albeit often romanticized, can be found in innumerable books. Images are mass-produced in needlework kits, postcards, and fine art prints. And, in recent times, there has been so much interest in the estate that an Internet discussion group with hundreds of enthusiastic members was founded at http:// groups.yahoo.com/group/bellegrove/. On the site of the plantation, a lonely historic marker bounding the suburban neighborhood notes the land's historic past.

## Woodlawn

Woodlawn, on Bayou Lafourche near Napoleonville, was the seat of the Pugh family's vast plantation empire. Here they constructed a large, complex mansion that rivaled the greatest plantation houses of the South. Sadly, as the family fell from greatness so did their mansion—it was allowed to rot away to ruins that were removed in the 1940s.

The Pugh family had been residents along the North Carolina–Virginia border for nearly one hundred years when they made their way to Louisiana in the second decade of the nineteenth century. They originally settled in St. Mary's Parish, where they planted indigo, but later moved to Lafourche Parish, where they made a fortune planting sugar and rice.[29]

William Whitmell Pugh was a young boy when his family moved from North Carolina. He grew up on the estate purchased by his family along Bayou Lafourche and later attended the University of Pennsylvania.[30]

Upon concluding his education he returned to the bayou and sought to build a proper plantation mansion on the family estate. Construction of the house was started in 1835, and was completed in 1839, at a cost of $70,000 (roughly $1.3 million in

2007 dollars[31]), not including slave labor. It is likely that the original home consisted of merely the central portion and that the flanking wings were added at a slightly later date. Many have suggested that this might have been accomplished by architect Henry Howard, who designed a similar house, Madewood (which today still stands not far away), for Pugh's half-brother Thomas Pugh in the 1850s. Howard also designed Belle Grove.[32]

The completed mansion at Woodlawn, with wings and accompaniments, was a great sight to behold. On the outside, six large columns lined the front portico. The two pillars on the end were square with recessed panels, and the center four were fluted Ionic columns which showcased the only known use of marble capitals in Louisiana. The columns supported a massive full entablature with unique parapet that broke above each column to a higher point towards the center.[33]

Outside, on either side of the main structure, two large wings provided balanced visual symmetry. From the front, the one-story wings looked like attached dependencies with framing pilasters at the corners and rather plain pediments. From the side of the house, the full depth of the wings could be appreciated. A central portion of each wing was recessed between two symmetrical pediments providing visual interest. The outside of the mansion conformed to the colorful array so prominently found in plantation mansions of French-speaking areas of Louisiana. Woodlawn was painted a soft pink with white trim and greenish-blue shutters.[34]

Inside, the central portion of the mansion was similar in plan to traditional plantation mansions—with two rooms back to back flanking a modified center hall. At Woodlawn, the standard central hall had been divided into a front foyer and separate back stair hall. The wings made the mansion unique, each containing three main rooms, a bath with a marble tub, and smaller rooms and passages. The wings each enclosed three sides of two open-air brick courts that were as distinctive as they were practical. Each of the courts was further closed in on one side by louvered shutters, creating a totally private space.

The second floor of the mansion was of a more traditional plan. Four main rooms buttressed the standard central hall. In the back, two smaller rooms framed a so-called "cabinet gallery," or balcony enclosed on three sides. There was also a third floor with a similar plan, excluding the rear rooms and gallery. In total, the mansion contained over a dozen bedrooms. It measured approximately 132 x 66 feet, creating a great presence along the bayou.[35]

In addition to the baths, Woodlawn also possessed a number of other early modern conveniences. The construction of Woodlawn is said to mark the first installation of gas in a Louisiana plantation home, and the house also contained a unique speaking tube that ran from the dining room to one of the upstairs bedrooms.[36]

In 1850, an article in *DeBow's Review* described the plantation:

"Wood-lawn" does not belie its name. From the first glance we have of it in the beautiful lawn gently sloping to the Bayou, on both sides, the soil carpeted with suitable grass for purposes of pasturage, interspersed with shade trees, presents a rich appearance. The pasture ground extends the whole length of the plantation, two miles long and several hundred yards wide, embracing quite 200 acres in all, exhibiting a front view from the dwellings, though there is a large body of land beyond, used for farming purposes. There are in this plantation 1,500 acres under fence, 800 in cane. It is in depth more than a mile. There are nearly 100 miles of ditching on this place. It combines all the qualities of a Tennessee farm in relation to raising stock of all kinds and pastures, with every quality which characterizes a sugar-planting interest. There are 300 slaves on this plantation. The quarters are very comfortable houses, supplied with every necessity of life, arranged in proper method, and several rows of shade trees run continuously between these two rows of buildings, presenting in a high degree and aspect of comfort.[37]

As the years passed, the Pughs continued to expand their plantation empire, eventually amassing thirteen plantations. One popular English joke asked, "Why is Bayou Lafourche like the center aisle of a church?" The response was, of course, "Because there are Pughs lining both sides." As Protestants from North Carolina, the Pughs were oddities in many ways to most of their French-speaking Catholic neighbors. Rather than attend Mass, the Pughs supported the growth of Protestantism in the area, even providing the cypress, bricks, and slave labor for the construction of Christ Episcopal Church in the early 1850s.[38]

In addition to his work with the Episcopal church, Pugh became interested in politics. He obviously assimilated into French-speaking society well enough to be elected to public office by his neighbors. He was a member of the Louisiana legislature, earning the distinction of serving as speaker of the house of representatives during the 1850s.

It is interesting to note that Pugh was a guest at the celebrated resort on Louisiana's Last Island on August 10, 1856, when a famed torrential hurricane destroyed the massive hotel, along with all of the buildings on the island, and killed more than two hundred of the four hundred guests. He survived this tragedy, going on to serve with distinction during America's bloodiest conflict.

When the Civil War broke out, the Pughs strongly supported the southern cause. William Whitmell himself served as a colonel, and his young sons—Welman F. Pugh, only fifteen, and his younger brother—also joined the Confederate military. Welman left an interesting journal of his experiences. Far removed from the battles and blood so prominent in the war, he writes that he and his young brother and their friend "went to Donaldson [and] had a grand time." He recounts that they sold a pig for five dollars in silver and "was threatened to be shelled by the Yankees." Like many young men and boys who joined either Confederate or Union units, he found the thought of riding off to war thrilling. Welman wrote enthusiastically, "Rode 50 miles on horseback at night."[39]

The most disrupting thing about the war for the Pughs was the removal of their slaves. In an embit-

This photograph shows Woodlawn Plantation mansion in its latter-day state of decay. Its stately columned portico and expansive side wings can be easily appreciated.

Even in a ruined condition, Woodlawn Plantation demonstrates the opulence of a bygone era.

The Ionic capitals of Wood-lawn Plantation's principal dwelling represented the only known use of marble capitals in any Louisiana plantation house.

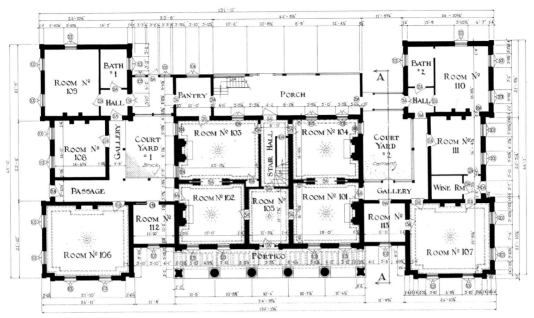

FIRST FLOOR PLAN

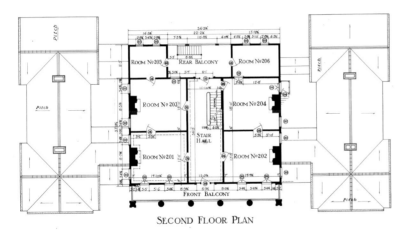

SECOND FLOOR PLAN

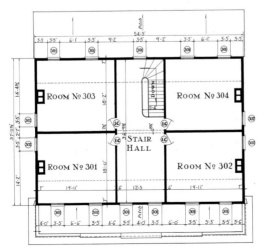

THIRD FLOOR PLAN

Woodlawn Plantation House was noted for its size and its complex plan. The central portion of the house was flanked by private court-yards, and the side wings were accessed by galleries that wrapped around these courts.

Woodlawn Plantation House. The second story above the central portion of the house corresponded to a more traditional plantation plan. A wide balcony ran across the entire front of the house, while a cabinet gallery in the rear provided a cool area for air circulation.

Woodlawn Plantation House. The mansion's third floor featured four additional rooms and a large stair hall.

surrounding the house were dotted by a variety of little marble fish ponds and fountains. The sugar mill, a dairy, slave cabins, stables, and a variety of warehouses and shops could also be found on the grounds.

In 1867, after the Civil War and after the death of his father, Thomas Morgan's son George sold Orange Grove to Louis Fasnacht for sixty thousand dollars. Fasnacht was a Swiss immigrant who had come to the United States in 1844, at the age of twenty-four. At one time he operated the St. Louis Hotel, a famous institution in New Orleans at that time.[51] He later tried his hand at the candy business and then was associated with a brewing company. But one of his greatest ventures was at Orange Grove, where he grew sugarcane, cotton, and rice. He devised a system of pumps and siphons to deliver river water to his rice fields, after he was denied permission to disrupt the levee.

One of Fasnacht's greatest challenges was procuring laborers to work his fields. With the emancipation of the slave labor force came a great need for plantation workers throughout the South, and Orange Grove was no different. Fasnacht provided the freed slaves with a school and books, but they still refused to work his fields.

Finally, in 1871, he contracted with twenty-six Chinese immigrants whom he paid fourteen dollars for every twenty-six days of work. In addition he provided each worker with rations consisting of fifteen pounds of pork and fifty pounds of rice each month. Collectively for the crew, he provided supplies of tea and opium for the month. The signing of the contract with the Chinese at Orange Grove was a ceremonious event. The Chinese consul and his aid attended, both wearing elaborate silk robes. The contracts were signed with fine golden pens. The Chinese saved all of their monies earned from the plantation labor, and, upon the conclusion of their contracts, they left the estate and opened laundries.[52]

In 1874, Fasnacht contracted with eighty-five Italian immigrants whom he paid one dollar per day, but they provided their own food. They were also allowed to maintain vegetable gardens and to fish and hunt in their spare time. After two years, the Italians left to start produce businesses, an industry that is still dominated by Italian families in the area to this day.[53]

Unable to find adequate labor, Fasnacht sold the plantation in 1884 to an English syndicate. At this time the British invested heavily in the area to try to gain some political foothold. Their ventures were short-lived. When the majority of their holdings were destroyed in a 1927 crevasse in the levee, they abandoned Louisiana.

In 1952, the Southern Railway System purchased the plantation. By this time, some vandalism of the property had already begun. The railroad installed a caretaker in the mansion, but he may have done more harm than good. While his presence discouraged vandals, it wreaked havoc upon the house. He used the great hall as a place to raise chickens and dry furs. And when he finally left after many years, the house was filled with his ragged clothes, broken furniture, and trash.

Even at this time, a few outspoken preservationists expressed their disdain with the situation at Orange Grove. The railroad refused to work with any group interested in preserving the property, and the company stated: "We may someday need the property on which [the plantation mansion] stands for other uses."

In the early 1960s, William R. Cullison researched the plantation for his master's thesis at Tulane University. He estimated that restoration of the plantation mansion would cost a mere one hundred thousand dollars at the time. He, along with preservationists including Betsy Swanson and Roulhac Toledano, envisioned the house as a library and community center, where organizations could hold meetings. This idea was quickly rejected by the parish.

The executive of Plaquemines Parish, the commission council president, Chalin O. Perez, came from a colorful and corrupt family that has been called "one of the most audacious and clever political dynasties Louisiana ever produced."[54] Perez ruled the parish with a strong iron will and a stronger iron fist. Of the idea of turning Orange Grove

Orange Grove Plantation mansion, front façade. Courtesy of The Historic New Orleans Collection.

Orange Grove Plantation mansion, rear façade, in poor condition. Image by Clarence John Laughlin. Copyright © The Historic New Orleans Collection.

into a library, he said that the parish "has no interest in saving old houses—we need the money for more important things."[55]

The plantation continued to deteriorate, and press coverage of the preservation effort led many souvenir hunters to further vandalize the site. In 1979, Welham Plantation in St. James Parish was maliciously and secretly demolished by Marathon Oil Company. A deluge of bad press flooded the local media regarding this event, so when Plaquemines Parish officials heard rumors that Southern Railway had similar plans for Orange Grove, action was taken. Parish officials contacted the railroad and reminded them of an ordinance prohibiting the destruction of landmark buildings. However, the parish leaders mostly wanted to avoid negative publicity—they had no real interest in the house, as they refused to put forth any money to restore or stabilize the mansion.[56]

On January 16, 1982, the remaining vestiges of the deteriorated plantation mansion were gutted by fire, said to have been set by an arsonist. Twenty firefighters battled the blaze for more than two hours. They used over two thousand feet of hose because the mansion was so far from the highway. Their efforts were largely in vain. This was the final blow for those who had fought for the mansion; all hopes of saving the historic landmark had literally gone up in smoke.[57]

A few months later, James Hoffman, a public safety officer for the parish, declared that the mansion's ruins were unstable and unsafe. The charred brick walls were bulldozed under the direction of Chalin P. Perez, who paid for the demolition himself. After the machines completed their job, all that remained were two damaged and weathered chimney towers and a massive heap of bricks.

Perez, who had laughed at the idea of saving the mansion and later financed its demolition, had the audacity to try to acquire the bricks for an addition to his own historic plantation home on the east bank of the river. He haughtily said, "It would certainly be more appropriate to use the bricks in the parish on another historic building."

The story of Orange Grove is a cautionary tale.

Few saw the value in saving this unusual piece of history. It was a common opinion that industry would bring prosperity, and few envisioned tourism, especially to historic sites, as a viable and profitable industry. *Times-Picayune/States-Item* columnist John Ferguson wrote: "If there can be such a thing as martyrdom for an inanimate object, then one can say that Orange Grove's death may serve as a rallying point for those Louisianans who are distressed at the loss of yet another of the great houses for which the Mississippi once was so justly famous. Some action on the part of the state government should be taken to prevent any further losses. After all, how many people will travel the banks of the Mississippi to look at an endless line of petrochemical plants and hazardous waste dumps."[58]

Certainly today, many people realize that plantations and other historical attractions provide an economic engine via tourism that is cleaner, safer, and much healthier than the vile, carcinogenic chemical plants that have taken over many historically and/or archeologically significant sites along the majestic Mississippi River. But this realization came too late for Orange Grove and many plantations like it. Still, in the enlightened twenty-first century there are those who would bulldoze our remaining antebellum mansions, those few remaining links to our precious, fading past, rather than slightly inconvenience chemical or railroad corporations.

## Seven Oaks

Directly across the Mississippi River from Uptown New Orleans's famed Audubon Zoo, the bustling community of Westwego mourns the loss of its greatest cultural and historical asset: Seven Oaks Plantation. Once one of the greatest sugar plantations along River Road, the estate was maliciously stolen from local citizens by an incompetent and indifferent railroad company in the 1970s.[59]

Only one year after the founding of New Orleans in 1718, the French minister of state, Monsieur LeBlanc, and three of his associates[60] were granted property—known then as Petit Desert or Little Wilderness—across the river for a plantation. They quickly developed this early plantation into a port and depot for both slaves and goods going to and from LeBlanc's various holdings in the colony.

In 1738, LeBlanc sold Petit Desert and the plantation there to Joseph Assailly and Charles Favre Daunoy. It was passed through various hands until 1794, when it was sold by Alexandre Harang to his son-in-law Michel Zeringue. Zeringue, a descendant of the famed builder Johann Michael Zerhinger,[61] continued agricultural operations on the estate, but it was his son Camille, who inherited the plantation after his father's death in 1811, who truly transformed the colonial farm into a gem of sugar production.

Although sugar had been cultivated in Louisiana for a number of decades, its success as a cash crop was not fully recognized until the end of the eighteenth century and on into the nineteenth century. Camille Zeringue realized the profits to be made and planted his fields with cane. By the 1850s, he was annually producing over three hundred thousand pounds of sugar.[62]

In addition to his agricultural enterprises, Camille Zeringue was a popular politician, serving on the Jefferson Parish police jury of his time. He was also a shrewd businessman. In 1829, realizing the profits to be made as steamboat traffic boomed on the Mississippi, he joined several influential planters in founding the Barataria and Lafourche Canal Company, which sought to provide a major steamboat water route from the Mississippi westward. Camille Zeringue convinced his fellow company officials to construct a portion of the canal on his plantation over an already existing smaller colonial canal. He realized the advantages such a waterway on his property would afford. The canal venture was a grand success, supported liberally by the state (many of the original founders were extremely politically connected), and Zeringue benefited greatly.[63]

Inspired by his successes in politics, agriculture, and business, Zeringue sought to construct a mansion for his family that would properly communicate the family's social standing. The house was constructed around 1830, and family tradition states that it was designed by German architect Valentine von Werner. The house had an unusual plan; instead of the traditional long central hallway running from front to back, the dining room was placed centrally, causing the entrance hall to end near the center of the mansion, rather than continue towards the back.

Also, because the second story had a more familiar plan with a long central hall from front to back, the chimneys from the dining room fireplaces did not meet those in the bedrooms above. Builders constructed the chimneys to twist and turn within the walls in such a way as to meet the fireplaces above. Then, the four chimneys rose symmetrically through the attic and out the roof, framing a central widow's walk (that was replaced with a hallmark belvedere during the Civil War). Although chimneys are routinely built in a similar manner today, this was an exceptionally unusual design for the time period.

Outside, the house was surrounded by twenty-six huge Tuscan columns. The mansion's characteristic feature, of course, were the seven columns that lined the sides of the house, rather than the more traditional eight. Some have argued that the columns inspired the plantation's modern moniker, Seven Oaks, while others speculate that the numerical significance of the number seven was first echoed in the seven large oak trees that surrounded the mansion, providing a most obvious source for the title.

Surrounding the columned mansion was a variety of standard barns, kitchens, and other outbuildings. Nearby twenty-two slave cabins lined up in parallel rows of six to seven. By the 1860s, Zeringue owned over a hundred slaves, who worked in the fields and tended to domestic operations on the estate.[64]

Originally, the sugarhouse was located near the mansion, but when Camille Zeringue replaced his old open kettle type sugarhouse with industrialized vacuum pan apparatuses, the sugarhouse was

The Zeringue family's mansion at Seven Oaks Plantation, here in poor condition, was a showcase of antebellum splendor along River Road. Note that the front of the house (like the back) had eight columns, while the sides had seven. Also note the large cistern that collected rainwater for use on the plantation. The belvedere, which was added during the Civil War, crowned the structure.

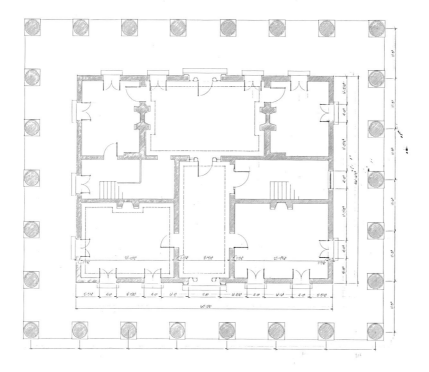

The first floor of the Seven Oaks Plantation mansion omitted the long central hallway so ubiquitous in Louisiana's Greek Revival–style plantation mansions; the dining room was placed centrally instead. A private stairway for the family was accessed off the entrance hall, while the servants' stairway was entered via the gallery outside. Courtesy of architect Davis Jahncke.

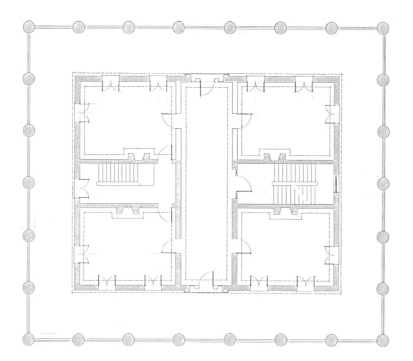

The second floor of the Seven Oaks Plantation mansion was totally surrounded by a broad balcony. The layout of this floor conformed to the more traditional central hall plan, creating the need for the chimneys to twist and turn within the walls in order to meet the fireplaces in the bedrooms above. Courtesy of architect Davis Jahncke.

significantly enlarged and was moved back into the fields. This was probably done so that freshly cut cane could be more quickly transported for grinding, as it quickly loses its sugar content after being harvested, but it also functioned to move production away from the domestic center of the estate and create a separate manufacturing area.

In 1861, life as the Zeringues knew it came to a screeching halt. At first the cause for southern independence was a faraway, idealistic endeavor. Sentiment was almost unanimous locally that the South would easily prevail in any military conflict with the North. Zeringue and his fellow planters rallied troops, even sending their own young sons to war, raised funds and made huge contributions, and generally supported the Confederacy in any way they could. Soon, however, the war was no longer a distant idea, but had found its way into the planters' own backyards. Confederate troops set up an earthen fortification line along the canal at Seven Oaks, not far from the mansion. Zeringue's sons had all ridden off to war, and his wife and daughter fled to their city retreat across the river. He remained at his plantation.

The canal was seized by Union forces, and eventually, the war ruined Zeringue, both personally and professionally. On a personal level, only one of his sons returned home. The others had died during the war. To make matters worse, the remaining son, Jean Fortune, returned home crippled from his war injuries. From a business perspective, Zeringue's empire was in shambles, but ironically, all of his freed slaves remained on the plantation at least for a while.

Later, after the war, the family was further shattered when Zeringue's four daughters left home one by one to become nuns. The Zeringues were devout Catholics, and, before the war, even had a nun residing on the plantation. Sister Marie Jeanne Aliquot[65] wrote numerous letters about her experiences on the plantation, and it was clear that she inspired Zeringue's daughters to join her in a religious profession. As detailed in Matrana's *Lost Plantation: The Rise and Fall of Seven Oaks*, each of the young Zeringue women gained great notoriety in the Society of the Sacred Heart, and earned positions of power and authority within their religious communities and beyond.[66]

With his family mostly gone, Camille Zeringue faced one of the biggest battles of his life. In 1870, Zeringue landed in court with a railroad company who wanted to expropriate a large portion of his property between his mansion and the canal. Before the war, he had given the railroad a right-of-way through his fields with the agreement that no terminal ever be placed on his plantation. However, railroad officials now wanted more, and they wanted to construct a terminal. The Louisiana legislature had given railroads the legal authority to expropriate land in any way they saw fit, so the courts had no option but to award the property to the railroad.

Camille Zeringue remained in possession of the plantation mansion, some fields, and property bordering the canal, but a huge chunk of the plantation between the mansion and the canal became the site of a large railroad facility. Zeringue died only two years later, on January 6, 1872, at age eighty-two. His disabled son, Jean Fortune, tried unsuccessfully to operate the plantation, but lost the estate, including the house, in 1891, after he was unable to pay a mortgage to the Citizens Bank of Louisiana.

The plantation was purchased by a Spaniard, Pablo Sala, who turned it into Columbia Gardens, one of the nation's finest resort attractions. Visitors rode steamboats across the Mississippi to enjoy entertainments at the "pleasure gardens," including famed cornetist Jules Levy, several choirs, sport spectacles, acrobats, and even tightrope walkers. Feasts of food were served and games and amusements were organized. Columbia Gardens was a major hit, hosting over twenty thousand visitors a day on holiday weekends. Under the auspices of Columbia Gardens the mansion at Seven Oaks became the first structure in the region to boast electricity, as its exterior was hung with strings of hundreds of electric lights, much to the amusement and astonishment of the guests.

Concurrently, while his resort was at its zenith, Sala began planning a residential community along the canal. While the lots he subdivided sold slowly at first, when displaced hurricane victims from the coastal community of Cheniere Caminada made their way to the area, "Salaville" grew quickly. It later became the city of Westwego, a name coined by railroad executives who eagerly sought to build their local lines west.

Pablo Sala died in 1894, and the short-lived but vastly profitable resort closed its doors. Seven Oaks Plantation then passed through various hands until 1912, when it was purchased by the Missouri-Pacific Railroad Company. A few years later, during World War II, the commodious plantation mansion served as a barracks for 150 soldiers who guarded the railroad lines. Unfortunately, their stay was a tumultuous one, and although the railroad was reimbursed for damages incurred, they made only futile repairs to the house.

Shortly after the war, in 1919, the railroad offered residence in the house to its local foreman of wharves, William Howard Stehle. The Stehles raised their daughters in the mansion, through the years hosting family weddings and even their daughters' senior proms there. The family remained at Seven Oaks until they were forced to leave in 1954, when the railroad refused to repair a large leak in the roof.

Three years later, in 1957, preservationists prompted the American Liberty Oil Company, which subleased the plantation site as an oil storage facility, to stabilize the mansion and install a new temporary roof. The company, along with the Louisiana Landmarks Society, sponsored a successful public *fête champetre* to raise funds in hopes of one day fully restoring the mansion. Unfortunately, plans failed, and after a brief time the house again fell into disrepair.

The mansion's deterioration was hastened in 1965, when Hurricane Betsy destroyed the belvedere and badly damaged the roof. It soon became a popular spot for vandals, thrill seekers, souvenir hunters, and the homeless, all of whom caused irreparable damage. Even in decline the plantation mansion still held romantic ideals for many. It became a popular spot for artists and young lovers.

In 1973, author Truman Capote visited for a photo shoot, an event that was soon after immortalized in a feature article by John McMillian that appeared in the *Times-Picayune*'s *Dixie Roto Magazine*.[67]

In November 1975, as the deterioration grew, the Westwego city attorney informed the Texas-Pacific-Missouri-Pacific Railroad that it would have to repair the mansion or demolish it completely. The railroad felt the easiest option was to destroy the house, and in 1976, the Westwego Board of Aldermen condemned the ruinous plantation mansion. By this time, preservationists and local citizens were up in arms. The mayor's office filled with letters, and phones rang off the hook at city hall. Public sentiment was unanimous—almost everyone wanted the mansion saved!

Jefferson Parish author and historian Betsy Swanson proposed stabilizing the ruins for a public park. She argued that the ruins were already attracting hordes of tourists, and stabilization would be much less costly than a full renovation. Likewise, the ruins would be preserved for restoration at a later date.

Westwego officials made it clear that they were not interested in saving the plantation, but were concerned about possible liability suits if someone were injured on the property. The board of aldermen did grant preservationists a one-month stay of execution in order to allow them to pursue possible avenues of saving the mansion. Jefferson Parish attorney Bruce D. Burglass said, "We're going to try to do everything we can to preserve it as a tourist attraction. The tragedy of this situation is that once you put a bulldozer to that place, there's nothing you can do."[68]

Parish officials met with railroad executives, who firmly stated that they would not sell the property for historic preservation use nor would they lease it at a token rate. The parish was nearly successful in subleasing a small portion of the property, including the mansion, from the lessee, North American Trading and Import; however, this, too, fell through.

Soon, one voice rose above the angry shouts of frustrated preservationists and politicians. State

Delicate pilasters supported a Greek Revival entablature above the front door, which was flanked by two sets of French doors on each side.

representative John Alario, Jr., from Westwego, tried diligently to push preservation measures through the house of representatives. He even went as far as trying to have the plantation mansion declared a Jesse James memorial site, stating that "the notorious train robber of history perpetrated no worse evils upon the railroads of the country than the Texas-Pacific-Missouri-Pacific Terminal Railroad is perpetrating by its refusal to allow this great historic landmark and symbol of Louisiana's past to be preserved."[69]

By April of 1976, Alario had persuaded Louisiana governor Edwin Edwards to commit $750,000 towards saving Seven Oaks. The state planned to use the home as an office facility, perhaps a driver's licensing bureau. Westwego's officials strongly endorsed the plan. But the Jefferson Parish Council smugly turned its back on Seven Oaks when the state became involved. They purportedly questioned the safety of state offices near oil tanks. Alario quipped, "It appears that if a project is designed to help Westwego and the Fifth Ward, the council can find all kinds of excuses to delay and try to defeat its completion." On the issue of safety, he commented, "The state is going to take every precaution to make sure Seven Oaks is safe for anyone wanting to visit it—even councilmen."[70]

But the Jefferson Parish Council did not budge in their efforts to thwart the state's plans. Alario said, "Taking a preservation project before the Jefferson Parish Council is like having Colonel Sanders baby-sit for your chickens." The lack of support from parish officials, along with their own deep reservations about the project, led railroad executives to question preservation of the plantation house. Railroad vice president Charles Roberts said, "We need jobs a damn sight worse than we need museums. It would ruin a good industrial tract if they went in there and rebuilt it."[71]

Roberts's view of the situation was held in part by many, and this lack of vision complicated issues. Even the strongest preservationists saw Seven Oaks as a crumbling monstrosity from the past, not as the vital economic engine it could become—perhaps surpassing the railroad in its local economic impact.

Today, for example, Oak Alley (the nearest house standing that could compare with Seven Oaks), more than fifty miles from New Orleans, regularly brings in tens of thousands of visitors for special occasion weekends. Combined with the daily tours as well as revenue from weddings, gifts shops, onsite restaurants, bed and breakfast services, etc., this plantation provides a major economic catalyst for the region. Seven Oaks was located minutes away from downtown New Orleans, in an area that would have insured its success. The plantation played host to over twenty thousand visitors a day during special occasions when it was open as a resort in the 1890s. But sadly, no one could truly envision the economic potential of the fading mansion. It was largely viewed as a nostalgic token, not a money-making engine.

By November 1976, the efforts to save Seven Oaks had widely fallen through, partly due to local political tensions, as well as the railroad's outright objections. Alario fought heroically, but the Westwego aldermen were scheduled to meet to again discuss demolition. Preservationists won an additional six-month stay of execution; however, this came and went with no real plans to save the house.

On August 27, 1977, to the disgust and dismay of local citizens, indifferent officials of the Texas-Pacific-Missouri-Pacific Railroad ran a bulldozer through Seven Oaks Plantation. The entire demolition took less than an hour. All that was left was a massive pile of rubble.

Interestingly, across the Mississippi in nearby Kenner, Louisiana, Dr. Henry Andressen, a popular obstetrician and gynecologist, and his wife, Kay, planned to construct their dream home on Lake Pontchartrain. Avid history buffs and collectors, the couple had hired famed architect A. Hays Town to design their house. Town, noted for using original materials in his designs, instructed the couple to "buy everything you can get your hands on" upon hearing of the destruction of Seven Oaks.[72]

He then spent the next seven years working with the Andressens to design and build a plantation home from the rubble of Seven Oaks. The finished house looked nothing like the original Seven Oaks.

It was instead a working 1795 plantation house from Louisiana's Spanish dominion. Town felt it would better suit the Andressens' modern lifestyle than the original 1830s Greek Revival. The couple immediately fell in love with the house, furnishing it with period antiques, Mardi Gras memorabilia, and rare Audubon prints. Today, they have opened their special home to share with the world, operating a bed and breakfast there.

Back in Westwego, sentiments towards the town's history have changed dramatically. With the publication of several books about the city's past by local business and civic leader Daniel P. Alario, Sr., and his wife, Zenobia, the community embraced its heritage. A historical society and commission were formed. And a historical district was created around Sala Avenue, the original street first created by Pablo Sala in the 1890s and occupied by hurricane survivors from Cheniere Caminada (many of their descendants still reside in the community today). A historical museum was also opened there, and, since, a multitude of community enterprises—including a major riverboat landing, performing arts complex, community center, visual arts center, large farmers' and fishers' market, and more—have been developed. The community mourns the lost of the plantation, realizing that it would be the biggest tourist attraction of the entire Westbank region and perhaps one of the most popular in the New Orleans area. John Alario, Jr., has since served several terms as Louisiana's speaker of the house, and was later elected to the state senate. His cousin, Daniel Alario, Sr., who spearheaded the community's historic revival, was appointed mayor of Westwego, after the elected mayor resigned to take over John Alario's seat in the Louisiana House of Representatives.

The site of Seven Oaks Plantation was sold by its railroad owners in 2002 to energy giant Kinder-Morgan, who donated a small portion of the land to the city of Westwego for commemorative purposes. A highway marker has been placed at the site by the Jefferson Parish Historical Commission, and the Westwego Historical Society erected a large granite monument and developed a small roadside park there with monies granted from the Jefferson

Parish Council. Citizens and elected officials are excited about the possibilities ahead. Future archeological excavations have been discussed, and locals hope to preserve this nationally important site for prosperity and for potential reconstruction.

# Uncle Sam

Once the magnificent home of Samuel Fagot, Uncle Sam Plantation, previously known as Constancia, was located just upriver from Convent, Louisiana, on the east bank of St. James Parish. It was renowned as one of the South's most intact plantation complexes, until it was destroyed in 1940, in order to move the Mississippi River levee back.[73]

Pierre Auguste Samuel Fagot, known more commonly as Samuel Fagot, was a native of La Rochelle, France. He traveled to North America, and public records show that he was in the Convent, Louisiana, area by 1828. He married Emilie Jourdain, and had two daughters, Marie Emilie Eugenie Fagot, who later married Jacques Auguste Demophon Tureaud, and Felicie Fagot, who later married Lucien Malus.[74]

Fagot began acquiring property in St. James Parish in 1829. Over the next thirty years, this small, dark-skinned man with a thick black beard became one of the largest landowners in the state. His name appears in the St. James Parish Conveyance Records nearly ninety times, indicating that he was actively acquiring a tremendous amount of property in a gradual, piecemeal fashion.[75]

Fagot centered his plantation empire along the Mississippi at Constancia Plantation, an estate that had been established in 1812, the year Louisiana was admitted to the Union. The celebrated complex that Fagot created on his estate was obviously well thought out. It is said that he first built two small buildings that flanked the main house toward the rear, before laying the foundation for his mansion in the mid-to-late 1830s. It is also said that, prior to the construction of the columned great house, there was another much smaller master house at the plantation that was destroyed by fire.

The master house that Fagot built was a typical Greek Revival temple-style mansion, surrounded by twenty-eight Tuscan columns enclosing a wrap-around veranda and second-story gallery. It supported a large attic and roof with two dormers in both the front and back and one on either side. The house itself was a classic five-bay structure with a wide central hall flanked on both sides by two large rooms. Each of the rooms had a fireplace. The two rooms on the north side of the hall, probably double parlors, were separated by wide pocket doors that could be easily opened to create a great space for balls and other large social gatherings. Behind the back room on either side of the hall were smaller rooms, possibly used for service purposes. Additionally, the main stairway servicing the central hall was tucked behind one of the back rooms, and one of these little rooms also had its own smaller stairwell, most certainly for house servants. The second story of the mansion featured an almost identical plan to the first floor. The total cost of the mansion exceeded one hundred thousand dollars, a sum that did not include plantation labor or bricks and cypress that were both produced on the estate. In addition, Fagot spent seventy-five thousand dollars more on imported furnishings from Europe.[76]

What made Uncle Sam particularly unique was not only the grand house and its contents, but also the overall plan of the plantation house grounds and larger production and slave areas. The main house was flanked by the two smaller buildings that Fagot constructed earlier. Both of these were identical, with a temple-style façade of four columns supporting a full pediment on both the front and back. Between these columned porches, each building had a front and rear room with adjoining fireplaces sharing a central chimney. One of these buildings served as the plantation office, and the other was the kitchen.[77]

Flanking the great house beyond these buildings were larger structures that resembled smaller versions of the main plantation mansion. These were the *garçonnières,* or bachelors' quarters. It was a French Creole custom among planters that once a

Uncle Sam Plantation House was in poor condition prior to its demise. One of the *garçonnières* can be seen in the background.

boy reached adolescence he would no longer sleep in the main house with married men or females, but would instead reside in a separate, nearby house. Life in the *garçonnières* offered boys and young single men a great deal of freedom, away from the immediate scrutiny of their elders in the big house but close enough to enjoy various comforts such as meals with their families and being waited on by slaves. Reassured by their proximity to their families, the boys and young men often took full advantage of their separate bachelors' quarters, enjoying rowdy pastimes that often included gambling and large sums of alcohol. In fact, it has been said that the *garçonnières* at Uncle Sam Plantation saw more money pass hands than any other halls in the state.[78]

Each of the two *garçonnières* was a one-and-one-half-story building that had six Tuscan columns lining both its front and rear façades. The columns supported a wide overhanging attic with dormers identical to those of the main house. This created long front and rear verandas that provided even more living space, especially during the hot summer months. The structures were very similar in plan, both with central halls flanked by large rooms on each side. These large rooms opened to narrow rooms that framed the sides of the structures. At least one of these narrow rooms in each *garçonnière* contained a staircase leading to an attic loft above.

Flanking the mansion and to the rear of the *garçonnières* were tall, symmetrical *pigeonniers* (pigeon houses that were similar to dovecotes). Given that squab, or young pigeons, were a delicacy in French cuisine, hundreds of the little birds were raised in these impressive hexagonal structures that were over forty feet tall. John B. Rehder notes, "The story is told that, whenever the planter's sons misbehaved, the boys would be sent to be locked in the hot, foul, malodorous *pigeonnier* for several hours. Knowing what pigeons do to statues, you can imagine the severity of the punishment."[79]

Several cisterns also dotted the cluster of Greek Revival buildings. These large barrel-like structures held potable rainwater for use in the plantation

The interior of Uncle Sam Plantation House during the demolition. Note the incredibly large wooden beams that supported the floor and the thick brick walls.

house and bachelors' quarters. The cisterns, each well over twenty feet tall, were capped with ornate pointed metal domes, giving these large functional containers the appearance of towers.

To an observer on a Mississippi River steamboat passing by the plantation, the marvelous assemblage of buildings created an amazing sight. Looking at the plantation complex from the front, one would see the central mansion with its eight soaring columns in front and dormers above, flanked by the two little Greek temples (office and kitchen), each with their four front columns and pediments, and the wide *garçonnières*, each with six columns and dormers, and, finally, toward the back, the tall *pigeonniers,* framing this cluster of architecture like two soaring towers. Dotted within this mélange of structures were the cisterns with their bright metal domes. To the observer gazing from the river towards the front of the plantation, the line of structures would appear—with relatively little space in between each building—from *pigeonnier to pigeonnier,* as a conglomerated collection or campus of twenty-eight columns across the fronts of the buildings, soaring towers, and shiny domes. It was undoubtedly a most impressive sight!

Beyond this famed cluster of buildings, Fagot constructed the rest of his plantation with equal linearity. To the north of the residential cluster could be found a large overseer's residence, a carriage house, and a stable. To the south, a large slave hospital was constructed. A line of five slave cabins stretched from the hospital towards the rear of the main complex. Here, a variety of buildings relating to plantation production could be found, including the massive sugarhouse and sugar mill, a blacksmith's shop, a scale house, and more slave cabins. There were also two large ponds centered in the middle of this productive cluster. A few hundred yards to the south, a massive barn and stables building separated the rest of the area from the large slave village beyond. Here, over a dozen more slave cabins were found in neat rows. With the Mighty Mississippi in front, these sprawling clusters of complex buildings were surrounded on three sides by fields of cane stretching over hundreds of acres.

Eventually, Fagot's great plantation earned the designation "Uncle Sam." Boundless stories exist explaining how and why this name was chosen, but among the more popular legends is that when a young male relative returned home from a European tour with a stylish mustache, he was teased mercilessly by his kinfolks and given the nickname "Uncle Sam." Another story recounts that the plantation was among the first to export sugar internationally. These exports were stamped with the seal "U.S." for United States, but plantation residents jokingly said they stood for "Uncle Sam," and thus the name stuck. The most probable account is that the plantation was named for Samuel Fagot himself. Although he was a bit of a recluse among St. James Parish society, Fagot often and enthusiastically hosted countless relatives, friends, and associates at his estate. His numerous nieces, nephews, and other relatives would routinely board steamers at New Orleans or elsewhere in order to spend a few days or even a few weeks at "Uncle Sam's place."[80]

Fagot owned his "place" until his death shortly before the outbreak of the Civil War. The plantation passed to his widow. It was operated, however, by Fagot's son-in-law, Lucien Malus. Fagot's widow died in the 1870s. Despite hard times during Reconstruction, Malus still managed to turn a profit at Uncle Sam, a feat few planters anywhere in the South were able to match at this time. This was due in great part to the many former slaves who agreed to stay at Uncle Sam and continue their previous work under new and dramatically different terms as paid laborers rather than property.[81]

During Malus's tenure as plantation owner, the plantation store, a ubiquitous entity on larger plantations starting at the time of Reconstruction, played a vital role in plantation operations. As employees rather than property, former slaves were no longer provided with food and clothing. Instead they bought these and many other staples and goods at the general stores found on the plantations. It is evident from the data found in the Uncle Sam Plantation Papers at LSU that the plantation store at Uncle Sam was not only an integral part of life for former slaves, but was also an establishment of great importance to the wider community.

Malus died in 1876, and the still successful plantation passed to his two daughters (Fagot's granddaughters), Emilie and Felicie Malus. These young sisters married two brothers, Jules and Camile Jacob. The brothers took over operations at Uncle Sam, and together they continued their late father-in-law's momentum, turning a modest profit. They were also among the first Louisiana planters to embrace the use of tractors on a large scale. At some point, Jules bought out Camile's share of the plantation.[82]

Jules Jacob retained ownership of Uncle Sam until 1915, when he sold it to a New Orleans commission merchant. After this transaction, the master house was never inhabited again, although the smaller more manageable *garçonnières* were occupied until the estate's destruction.

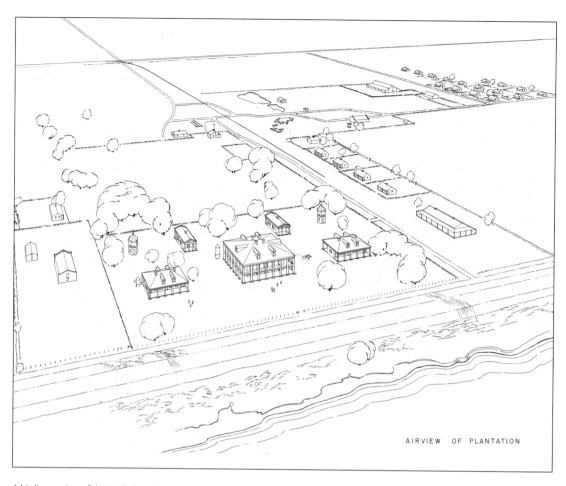

AIRVIEW OF PLANTATION

A bird's-eye view of the Uncle Sam Plantation complex—said to be one of the most complete plantation complexes ever constructed.

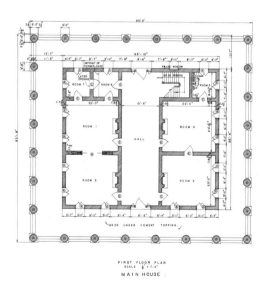

FIRST FLOOR PLAN
SCALE ⅛" = 1'-0"
MAIN HOUSE

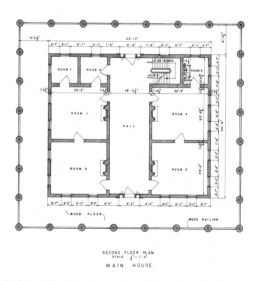

SECOND FLOOR PLAN
SCALE ⅛" = 1'-0"
MAIN HOUSE

Uncle Sam Plantation House. First-floor plan with traditional center hall layout. (Not to scale)

Uncle Sam Plantation House. Second-floor plan. The plan of the second floor corresponded with the first floor below almost identically. (Not to scale)

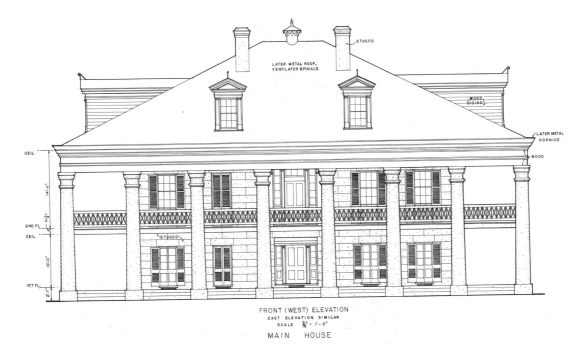

Uncle Sam Plantation House. Front elevation. (Not to scale)

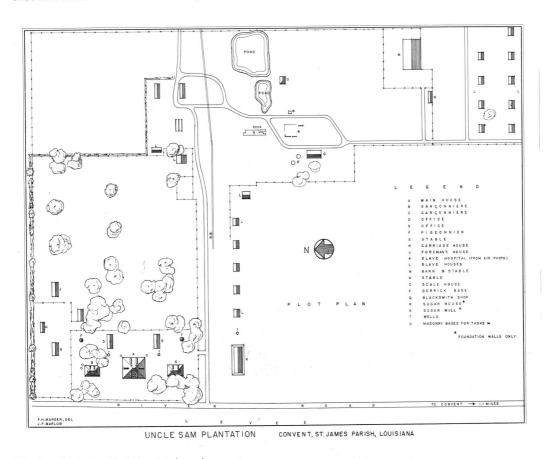

Plot plan of Uncle Sam Plantation. Note legend.

One of the many outbuildings at Uncle Sam. Such structures collectively served many functions, but individually were used for specialized purposes.

Uncle Sam Plantation *pigeonnier*.

Vacuum pans, seen here from Uncle Sam Plantation, brought industrialization onto the plantation landscape. Such apparatuses replaced the old open iron kettle method of sugar production and greatly increased the efficiency of sugar making.

Uncle Sam Plantation.
Plans and elevation of the
*garçonnières.* (Not to scale)

The plantation was operated as an agricultural venture by numerous partnerships and companies; among the most notable were Falgout and Reynaud, and Stebins and Hymel. Moise J. Hymel, one of the owners, designed and developed a "V-type-ditching" machine that is still used in agriculture today.[83]

In the 1930s the plantation's sugarhouse and associated machinery were sold for ten thousand dollars. The new owner demolished the building, and it is said that he not only recouped his investment, but also made a profit from selling the bricks alone.

Around this time, levee officials began realizing that the Mississippi was shifting and a subsequent shift in the levee would be necessary. Considering the mammoth size and power of the river and the bulk of the levee system, this would be no easy task.

There were structural problems in the levees at either end of the Uncle Sam property, and in 1940, the board of commissioners for the Pontchartrain Levee District declared that the new levee would have to be situated on the site of Uncle Sam Plantation! Demolition of the plantation structures—the mansion and all of its accompanying buildings—would be necessary and it quickly commenced.

At the time of its razing, historians and other scholars agreed that the built environment of Uncle Sam represented one of the most complete and unaltered plantation complexes in the South. And, although the plantation structures had weathered nearly one hundred years, they were still in relatively good condition throughout.

Of the demolition, one observer noted: "And as the workmen hurried to demolish the remaining structure[s] to make way for the levee, the mighty Mississippi ate greedily, lazily licked its banks and then, lowering its waves as if in shame, rolled slowly on—an amazing chapter of the South's romantic history closing in its wake."[84]

On March 12, 1940, as most of the demolition was complete, the U.S. engineer office in New Orleans received the following telegram from the director of the National Park Service in Washington, D.C.: "Have learned of the impending demolition of the Uncle Sam Plantation near Convent, Louisiana. Stop. Can demolition be deferred short time pending investigation by National Park Service to determine possibilities for status as a national monument or historic site?"[85]

Sadly, if the telegram had come a few days earlier, perhaps Uncle Sam would still be standing today, the impressive white pillars of its historic buildings lining up like sentinels guarding the "white gold" in the sugar fields beyond. Today, only a lonely historic marker on River Road indicates the site near where Uncle Sam Plantation once stood.

# Elmwood

The colonial and antebellum history of Jefferson Parish's Elmwood Plantation is as complex and curious as the convoluted challenges that preservationists faced in the early 1980s, when they tried to save the plantation's ruinous mansion. Legend and lore surrounded the property, but it wasn't until an archeological dig in 1982 that the plantation's true history was unearthed, both in archives and in the ground. At that time, much of what historians thought they knew of the famed estate was found to be erroneous. What follows is as straightforward an account as one might hope for of the New Orleans East Bank region's great lost plantation.

The land that was destined to become Elmwood Plantation was originally granted to a Monsieur Kolly in the early 1720s, in an area known as the Chapitoulas (later Tchoupitoulas) Coast. This particular concession was known as Ste-Reyne, and it was located upriver from the nearby concession of the Chauvin brothers. The Chauvin property was earlier thought to be the precursor of Elmwood, but evidence to the contrary has since been uncovered. The Ste-Reyne concession soon enveloped a neighboring estate that was originally granted to two brothers, Monsieur Guenots and Monsieur Prefontaine (Trefontaine), and their business partner Monsieur Macy (Massy). The expanded Ste-Reyne estate was developed into a working plantation early in its history, probably growing rice, corn, tobacco, indigo, and vegetables. It is known that by the early 1720s, both the Chauvin concession and the Guenot/Prefontaine estate used plows, an agricultural implement just introduced into the Lower Mississippi Valley a few years before. A 1723 map shows that the Ste-Reyne concession was the largest estate in the area and that even by this early date it was well developed with a variety of structures.[86]

The Ste-Reyne concession was administered by a director named Ceard. In 1724, he and the Chauvin brothers were entangled in a suit brought before the Superior Council. Apparently, in the spring of 1724, the Mississippi River had overflowed its banks and flooded the Ste-Reyne concession, including the indigo fields. Much of the water taken on by Ste-Reyne had been diverted from the Chauvin brothers' estate via a series of dams and ditches they had built. One of the brothers, known by the title Nicolas Chauvin de Lafreniere, noted to Ceard that "he preferred their land to be flooded [rather] than his." The Superior Council ordered that the Chauvins destroy their ditches and dams. It was because of this incident that the first levees were constructed in Louisiana.

Kolly sold the Ste-Reyne tract, and it is clear that Nicolas Chauvin de Lafreniere purchased more land in the area. The future Elmwood site later came into the possession of Jean Baptiste La Grange, an Illinois fur trader and entrepreneur, and his business partner Etienne Marafret Laissard (Layssard). Layssard made his home on the property, along with his wife and six children. There were thirty-eight slaves on the plantation at this time.

Unfortunately, La Grange and Layssard had many financial difficulties, and their plantation ended up in the hands of Nicolas Chauvin the Younger, who was later to be executed in 1769 for leading a revolt against the former French colony's new Spanish leaders in 1768.

Prior to his execution, Chauvin the Younger had sold his plantation to his brother-in-law, Jean-Baptiste Cezaire LeBreton. At the time, the estate was described as follows:

A plantation containing nine arpents front on a depth up to Lake Pontchartrain adjoined on one side by Mrs. Wiltz and on the other by Mr. Desilest about three leagues from the city on the same side of the river ascending on which there is the principal house fifty feet long by thirty-eight wide, elevated two feet from the ground with galleries nine feet wide back and front with a hall, three room with a cabinet and an office placed on the back gallery, brick chimneys, with a kitchen and other outbuildings all in good condition. The vendor, Lafreniere, acquired the property at a judicial sale from Mr. Laissard in partnership with Mr. la Grange.[87]

LeBreton did not own the plantation for long. He was murdered on another of his plantations by two of his slaves in 1771. The slaves were later hanged for the offense. The plantation then passed to Nicolas Lafreniere's son, Alexandro Juan Baptiste Chauvin de Lafreniere, LeBreton's nephew. Alexandro died of a contagious illness in 1778, and the plantation was acquired by one of his creditors, Oliver Pollock, and was later transferred to Francisco Pascalis de la Barre.

By 1783, the plantation had been acquired by Michel Fortier, whose family would hold the estate for more than fifty years. Fortier was L'Armurier du Roi (King's Armorer), and he made a fortune in the arms trade and in commercial shipping. Fortier died in 1785, not long after his purchase of Elmwood. The plantation passed to his wife, Perrine Langlois, who was named executrix of the estate and tutrix of the minor children.

The plantation was damaged in 1780, and sometime after this the new master house was constructed, either incorporating remnants of the old house or from new materials. The new plantation house was of a French colonial design, measuring eighty-eight by fifty-four feet. The first floor was surrounded by a wide gallery that wrapped around all four sides of the house. The gallery was enclosed by a colonnade of short, stout Tuscan columns that supported the wraparound balcony above. The balcony, which corresponded with this lower gallery, was encircled with slender wooden columns, resting above each of the wider Tuscan columns below. These slender wooden columns supported a broad, tall hipped roof with three dormers in the front.

Fortier's son Norbert acquired the adjacent Wiltz plantation, and it is likely that he aided his mother in managing Elmwood. After her death on March 17, 1804, Norbert inherited Elmwood and later acquired a nearby plantation that once belonged to Pierre Denis de la Ronde. In total, he owned thirty-six consecutive arpents on Chapitoulas Coast.

Twelve years after the Louisiana Purchase of 1803, the U. S. government confirmed Norbert Fortier's titles to his three adjoining plantation tracts. After the death of his wife, Genevieve Aimee Hardy de Boisblanc, in 1829, Norbert began dividing and selling much of his property. On March 4, 1836, Norbert sold Elmwood to two of his sons, Charles and Jacques Berthier Norbert Fortier, along with sixteen slaves, with the agreement that his sons assume his debts. The sale was largely in name only as the father retained both use of his former slaves and residence in the plantation master house. Soon thereafter the brothers divided their holdings, with Jacques retaining the original Elmwood Plantation (although his father continued to reside there and retain the labor of the slaves).

In 1839, Jacques sold Elmwood for $150,000 to the noted cartographer Charles Frederick Zimpel, whose famed maps of local plantations are still of great use today. Unfortunately, Zimpel lost his plantation after problems with creditors. It was purchased at auction by William Fredrick Mason, and included thirty-five slaves, twenty-nine heavy mules, six horses, and approximately twenty-nine head of cattle and oxen. Mason successfully ran the estate as a sugar plantation, producing over four hundred hogsheads of sugar nearly every year.

The Civil War had devastating effects on Elmwood, and Mason's annual crop plummeted to below two hundred hogsheads after the war. He sold the plantation in 1872, and it passed through various hands until it ended up in the possession of the Illinois Central Railroad Company in 1908.

By the 1920s, the plantation's great house was in a decayed condition. It was largely restored thereafter by Mr. and Mrs. Jack Lemann and later inhabited by Mr. and Mrs. Durel Black. The plantation master house burned on February 3, 1940, after a defective flue caught fire.

Some accounts note that the mansion's second floor was well preserved following the fire and was moved down to serve as a new main floor for the buildings. Others contradict this, stating instead that the second floor was destroyed, leaving only the first as the principal story. Regardless, in time the burnt-out two-story structure was revitalized, although, after repairs were made, the plantation house had only one story surrounded by short Tuscan columns supporting a broad, commodious hipped roof. Mr. and Mrs. Black continued to reside in the house after these renovations.

The plantation was later purchased by a group of investors who formed Elmwood Plantation, Inc. They turned the refurbished plantation mansion into a restaurant in 1962. The restaurant's owners promoted the establishment by advertising it on matchbooks, ashtrays, and other paraphernalia; soon, it was a smashing success, becoming a local institution of sorts. In 1977, the Louisiana State Tourist Commission graced the house with a historic marker.

Sadly, in December 1978, Elmwood was victim to yet another fire. This time, a faulty water heater was to blame. The principal owners of Elmwood Plantation, Inc., Joseph Marcello and Nick Mosca, members of two local Italian families, successfully sued the manufacturer of the faulty water heater, winning a large sum, which, according to their attorney, was above and beyond the normal sum for such a verdict as the court had taken into consideration the mansion's historic value. Unfortunately, Marcello and Mosca did not use any of this money to reconstruct or repair the plantation. Instead they announced that they wished to dismantle the charred remains of the plantation house and build instead two contemporary condo-office towers at the site.

Hearing of the plan, local preservationists and politicians were up in arms! Marcello and Mosca approached the Jefferson Parish Council with a request to have the property rezoned for their new venture. This set off a whirlwind of talks and negotiations that ultimately led to a compromise. The parish would create a committee made up of pres-

ervationists, historical society leaders, politicians, and other concerned citizens to attempt to purchase the plantation property (including the burnt ruins of the mansion). The owners would give the committee six months to obtain the $3 million they sought for the purchase. In the meantime, the owners would continue to pay their monthly notes on their $800,000 mortgage despite a lack of revenue.

Initially, sights were set high. State representative Quentin Dastugue of Metairie announced

Elmwood Plantation house as a two-story colonial structure prior to the fire of 1940. Courtesy of The Historic New Orleans Collection.

that he would ask the state for $1 million towards the purchase. He noted that perhaps the owners would accept the $1 million initially and then set up an installment plan rather than having to pay taxes on the $3 million total. Dastugue added, "I also think we can look at several ways of funding the purchase and restoration through alternate use for the plantation house. It could serve as tourist or visitor's center in conjunction with a batture park. Perhaps we could get it designated a state park or included in the Lafitte National Park like they did with the plantation house [Beauregard House] at Chalmette Battlefield."[88]

He further noted that the plantation restoration could be tied to the 1984 world's fair (Louisiana World Exposition) improvements.

Elmwood Plantation mansion as a one-story structure after refurbishment following the fire of 1940. Courtesy of The Historic New Orleans Collection.

Elmwood Plantation barn. Note the intricate gingerbread detailing and the elaborate castle-like birdhouse structure near the peak of the gabled roof. Courtesy of The Historic New Orleans Collection.

It soon became clear, however, that the large sum needed to purchase the plantation site might not be easily or readily obtainable. The state did not come through with the money, and the committee admitted raising "embarrassingly little." Although about a thousand people joined the committee's campaign, they gave "mostly moral support."

As the deadline approached, local newspaper and television stations ran numerous pieces on the fate of the historic plantation site. Arthur Ballin, an attorney for the owners, made a statement in July 1982. "Contrary to what people think, everybody is pulling together to the same end. This is not a situation where the owners and preservationists are at odds. The owners would like to see it restored as much as anyone else does."[89] He further noted that regardless of whether the committee could raise the money they could still have the plantation ruins to move elsewhere. He also noted that the twenty-two historic oak trees were protected permanently, having been dedicated to the parish at some prior point.

As the deadline was only weeks away, the local newspaper published an editorial recommending that Jefferson Parish purchase the site for a riverside park, given that the parish had an embarrassing lack of public parks and playgrounds. This idea, too, was never to be.

In July 1982, the deadline passed, but the owners and preservationists still were optimistic. Ballin again made a public announcement, this time noting that the owners were willing to extend their deadline and continue to work with the committee to ultimately restore the house.

With the deadline passed, local historians and preservationists felt that their best effort to preserve the property was to try to place it on the National Register of Historic Places. They felt that this would allow for additional funding sources, as well. The Louisiana Department of Culture, Recreation, and Tourism sponsored an archeological dig at the site in order to promote the National Register drive. A federal grant provided ten thousand dollars in funding, which was matched by the Jefferson Historical Society of Louisiana. Archeologists were amazed by findings, and one of the lead archeologists, Dr. R. Christopher Goodwin, remarked, "I think Elmwood is to Jefferson Parish what Williamsburg is to Virginia." Goodwin and his team found over eight thousand artifacts in their limited study, as well as evidence of built structures. Their archeological excavations, along with archival research, totally rewrote the history of the plantation. The group published their findings in 1984, in a Jefferson Historical Society of Louisiana monograph entitled *Elmwood: The Historic Archeology of a Southeastern Louisiana Plantation.* The archeologists noted that the plantation site was one of the most important archeological sites in the region.

The next year, Joseph Marcello made a major announcement that the plantation house would be fully restored. "It will be restored to the original building . . . What and how and when and by who, we can't get into," he said. "We may do it ourselves or we may do it with people we're negotiating with." Sadly, however, after Marcello's announcement, nothing was done. The historic charred brick walls remained essentially untouched for years, becoming overgrown and decayed as the years passed. The property surrounding the plantation site has been heavily developed, and recently the fragile ruins were cleared in order to build houses.

# CHAPTER EIGHT

# *Texas*

I must say as to what I have seen of Texas it is the garden spot of the world. The best land and the best prospects for health I ever saw, and I do believe it is a fortune to any man to come here. There is a world of country here to settle.

*—Davy Crockett,* 1836

Architecture is the printing-press of all ages, and gives a history of the state of the society in which it was erected.

*—Lady Morgan* (Sydney Owenson)

While often more remembered for longhorn cattle and romanticized cowboys, the Texas frontier was also home to slave plantations, especially in the eastern part of the state, which likewise embodied the independent spirit of the region. These were great agricultural enterprises that brought forth a rich cultural and diverse architectural heritage. Of course, much of the built environment of Texas's plantation system has been lost to time.

The region that makes up the modern-day state of Texas was visited sparsely by Europeans in the sixteenth century, but settlers did not inhabit the region until over a hundred years later when, in 1685, La Salle established Fort St. Louis at Matagorda Bay. The community was short-lived, as the French abandoned their post a few years later after a bloody massacre involving Native Americans.

Shortly thereafter, Spain took control of the region, which became a buffer zone between New Spain and French Louisiana. The Spanish ruled Texas for over 130 years, until they were defeated in 1821, in Mexico's war for independence. Texas became part of the Mexican state Coahuila y Tejas.

Soon after, Stephen F. Austin realized his late father's dream when he established an Anglo-American colony in Texas. When he arrived in the region, Austin understood that the greatest deterrent to American settlement in the area and therefore greater economic development was Mexico's prohibition of slavery. By the early 1820s, Austin and others had convinced the Mexican authorities to allow settlers to bring their own slaves into the region, while still prohibiting the sale of human chattel. Over the next years a variety of compromises were made, and many agricultural entrepreneurs blatantly ignored the law and purchased slaves from Cuba and elsewhere.

Texas gained its independence in 1836, and republic president Sam Houston again tried to limit slavery. Texas was annexed as a constituent state of the United States in 1845, opening the doors to great economic developments and expansion of slavery. In the 1840s and 1850s, as American southerners flooded into the new state, they brought with them large numbers of slaves. These new settlers quickly established plantations and ranches, focusing on cattle and cotton.

The decade between 1850 and 1860 saw a tremendous boom in agricultural production and plantation development in eastern Texas, and the sugar industry became fully established in the region. During this time there was a 314 percent increase in the number of slaves in the state, and the total number of farms tripled from approximately twelve thousand in 1850 to more than thirty-five thousand in 1860. The number of planters (men owning twenty or more slaves) also increased dramatically during the decade.[1]

The plantation landscape of Texas was concentrated along the Gulf Coast and inland along the Brazos and Colorado rivers, in east Texas around the area of San Augustine, and in northeast Texas.[2] The epicenter of plantation development in the state was Brazoria County and surrounding regions that were home to numerous large plantations and architecturally impressive mansions.

Styles of plantation architecture varied widely in Texas, but the Greek Revival style was favored in many mansions scattered throughout eastern and southern Texas. Creole-style houses, often a blend of French colonial and West Indies forms, borrowed design elements from structures throughout the Mississippi Valley. And styles of the older, southern seaboard states—Georgia and Virginia, for example—were also prominently found throughout Texas.

As elsewhere in the South, the Civil War had drastic and lasting effects on plantation economy and life in the state of Texas. Many estates were ruined financially and physically, and dissolution of slavery wrought great labor shortages and social change.

In Texas, convicts—mostly poor blacks who had committed petty crimes—were leased by the state to corporations, plantations, and individuals after the Civil War in order to supply the thriving labor demands created after emancipation. Lake Jackson provides a perfect example of this phenomenon, in which prisoners from Huntsville were "rented" to plantation masters for a number of years. Conditions for prisoners on the plantations of Texas and in other leased arrangements were deplorable, and death rates were high. It was eventually determined that the convict-lease system was a failure, and sharecropping and other labor systems became more common.

As agriculture was replaced by other industries and economic shifts transformed fields into other forms, so, too, did the plantation landscape of Texas fade into the past. Today, there are a handful of antebellum plantation mansions still standing in Texas, and a few are open to the public. Dewberry near Tyler, Liendo in Hempstead, and Varner-Hogg Plantation in East Columbia all welcome tourists.

Although a few fine examples of Texas plantations can be seen in the state today, most are gone forever. The stories of Texas's lost plantations are intriguing and have been explored in several volumes. Willard B. Robinson discusses antebellum plantations and much more in *Gone from Texas: Our Lost Architectural Heritage*, while C. Allan Jones investigates antebellum planting in *Texas Roots: Agriculture and Rural Life before the Civil War*. Abner J. Strobel's "The Old Plantations and Their Owners of Brazoria County, Texas," provides a fascinating look at dozens of nonextant estates. Strobel's work can be found in *A History of Brazoria County, Texas*, edited by T. L. Smith, Jr. An unpublished dissertation by Abigail Curlee entitled "A Study of Texas Slave Plantations, 1822–1865," written by the author as a requirement for her Ph.D. from the University of Texas in 1932, provides much insight into estates now long lost. In addition, much primary source material is held by the Texas State Library and Archives Commission as well as the Center for American History at the University of Texas at Austin.

The following essays detail the history of eight of Texas's lost plantation estates. Each gives a glimpse into a world and culture long forgotten and explores the unique ways in which Texas's built antebellum heritage has been lost.

# Lake Jackson

Major Abner Jackson's Lake Jackson Plantation was famous not only for its antebellum splendor but also for its use as a prison farm after the Civil War. Here prisoners became slaves long after the Emancipation Proclamation had been signed. A century later, after the infamous Galveston hurricane had destroyed the estate's structures, an archeological team went digging for answers to the mysterious plantation's past.

Abner Jackson was born in Virgina in 1810. He moved to South Carolina as a young boy, and later became a close business associate of South Carolina governor James Hamilton. Jackson later married Margaret Strobel, a widow with one son.[3]

Jackson moved to Texas in 1838, where he planted a crop on the Trinity River. He began developing Retrieve Plantation with Hamilton the next year. In 1842, Jackson moved four miles down Oyster Creek, where he began development of an estate originally called Lake Place, but which would later be known as Lake Jackson. He constructed a temporary house from elm and ash logs, but soon had much greater ambitions.[4]

Jackson's palatial plantation mansion was constructed between an oxbow lake formed by a cut-off meander of the Brazos River and a creek. The structure was built of bricks made on the plantation, covered over with one full inch of cement, which gave the appearance of solid stone. Interestingly, Jackson eventually converted all of the buildings on the plantation, including the slave cabins, into brick structures. His mansion did not follow the typical plantation plan, but instead was an I-shaped house with twelve rooms and six galleries.[5]

The sugarhouse was also made of brick. It contained the finest, most up-to-date machinery available at the time. In 1856, Jackson produced 295 hogsheads of sugar at Lake Jackson, and, by 1858, his mill was operating on steam power. This ensured that Jackson was indeed one of the greatest

Shown here in a watercolor painting by Don Hutson, the mansion at Lake Jackson was an impressive sight. Its walls were covered with cement, and a heavy portico with broad columns and a large pediment dominated the façade. A crowning cupola finished the grand estate house. Courtesy of artist Don Hutson and the Brazoria County Historical Museum, Angleton, Texas.

planters in Texas. By 1860, he was the second-largest slaveholder in the state, with 285 slaves. Jackson used his quickly growing profits to continue expanding the plantation.[6]

In the middle of the estate's namesake lake, Abner Jackson constructed an artificial island for a total cost of ten thousand dollars. It can still be seen today. He also planted lavish orchards complete with peach and pear trees, and raised quince, plums, grapes, and strawberries.[7]

Jackson fathered four sons and a daughter on his plantation. His wife died in 1857. He was an advocate of education, sending his children to college. The boys went to different schools, as Jackson believed that if they were all to attend the same one, they would want to "run the place." He also believed that different schools would give the young men different views on life. His daughter, Arsenath, was sent to Columbia, Tennessee, for her education. She later married J. Fulton Groce,

the son of Colonel Leonard W. Groce, and had four children.[8]

Jackson's sons went off to war as the Union divided between North and South. Jackson died at the very dawn of this conflict. Two of Jackson's sons died in the war. During the war, Jackson's son John returned to Lake Jackson in order to manage the estate. Under the circumstances, he did a fine job, moving much sugar and cotton even through embargos.[9]

Unfortunately, on December 8, 1868, John's brother George paid a visit to Lake Jackson to discuss his portion of the estate. The two had words and George shot his brother six times in the chest. George was indicted for this offense, but his case never went to trial. He died a few years later of tuberculosis at a hospital in Galveston. None of Jackson's sons married. They all died leaving no children.[10]

The plantation was eventually sold to William

W. Phelps of New York in 1873. That same year, he sold the property to A. J. Ward and E. D. Dewey for $36,000, turning a $15,200 profit. Ward and Dewey continued cultivating the land as Jackson had done before them, but they lacked the necessary labor needed to get the job done.[11]

The state of Texas began leasing its prisoners to individuals and corporations as laborers after emancipation. Ward and Dewey enthusiastically supported this endeavor, leasing the entire Huntsville State Prison along with all of its prisoners for fifteen years. While this system of leasing prisoners adequately addressed some of the labor shortages left by the emancipation of slaves and created a giant revenue source for the state, it functionally brought back slavery to the state of Texas.[12]

In 1874, an inspection of Lake Jackson was undertaken. Conditions for the prisoners were found to be deplorable. A report of the inspection states:

"I (Inspector J. K. P. Campbell) found sixty five convicts confined in the prison out of a force of one hundred and eighty-five, some of whom were quite sick. These men at the time had no medical attention . . . I at once made the sergeant send for a physician . . . The physician expressed as his belief that two or three of the men were beyond the reach of medicine. The sick occupied the same building with the well convicts, and the attention required of the sick prevented the other men from obtaining that sleep which laboring men needed . . . I found three trusty convicts whose backs were cut into pieces in a most shocking manner. The only offense, so far as I could learn, committed by the brutally treated men, was, they had taken some flour and exchanged it for whisky, and returned to camp intoxicated.[13]

The report went on to state that often the plantation was short of food for the convicts. The sergeant pledged his own personal credit in order to obtain beef for the men. It was also found that the convicts had not changed their clothes in ten weeks.[14]

In 1876, Inspector J. T. Gaines visited Lake Jackson. He found that three of the prisoners had died. One died while being punished in the stocks, one

after an escape attempt, and another from natural causes. As the years passed and the bad reports continued, the number of prisoners at Lake Jackson dwindled. By 1884, there were only thirty-three left.[15]

In 1900, four acres of the plantation, including the sugarhouse, sawmill, and blacksmith shop, were taken over by the Lake Jackson Sugar Company. The same year the notorious hurricane that destroyed Galveston also ravaged Lake Jackson. The mansion and sugar refinery were both badly damaged, along with most of the estate's other structures. Thereafter, the sugar company ceased its short-lived operations there.[16]

Although virtually nothing was left of the plantation above ground, in 1992, Texas archeologists began exploring what lay deep beneath the soil at the Lake Jackson site. Several years of excavation and study revealed much priceless information about the old estate and numerous artifacts. Foundations and structural elements of the sugar mill were unearthed, giving project leader Joan Few and her colleagues a rare glimpse into the world of antebellum sugar production. The archeologists even distinguished between the fine craftsmanship of slaves and the coarse work of convicts when studying the structural and architectural work.[17]

Because of the archeological team's hard work, the history of Lake Jackson and its many people is being preserved for future generations. Today the site is a State Archeological Landmark that is opened limitedly to the public, and, although none of the structures stand in their old glory, the plantation still tells its story.

## Clay Castle

Clay Castle, also known as Ingleside, was a massive and unusual plantation mansion once located a few miles west of Independence in Washington County, Texas. The land on which the estate rested was originally granted to Nestor Clay, a cousin of Revolutionary War hero Henry Clay. Soon Nestor's brother Tacitus Matthew Clay made his way from

The Whartons' mansion at Eagle Island Plantation was a wood-frame, one-and-a-half-story farmhouse with an impressive colonnade of six slender wooden pillars topped with a heavy balustrade. Courtesy of artist Don Hutson and the Brazoria County Historical Museum, Angleton, Texas.

Kentucky to Texas. He acquired lands, including a portion of Nestor's property, and here he began a great agricultural operation focusing on cotton. Evidence suggests that the brothers partnered in many of their farm endeavors.[18]

In 1834, Nestor's wife died. He returned with his children to Kentucky, soon going back alone to Texas. He died shortly after from injuries sustained in an Indian raid. Tacitus also returned to Kentucky around the same time in order to wed. He married Vibella McCreery. Soon after the ceremony, Tacitus and his wife, accompanied by her father, Dr. Harold McCreery, returned to Texas. They brought along with them Jesse L. McCrocklin, a blacksmith, and also ten thousand dollars' worth of supplies, dry goods, medicines, and arms that they shared with the surrounding community.

It was after returning that Tacitus began building his plantation mansion. The house itself was built abutting a hill, allowing for a large basement to be open to the back but be unseen from the front side. This basement included storage rooms for produce and other goods and a large delivery driveway that ran through the center of this level of the house.

Above the basement sat the massive first floor. It was approximately seventy-eight feet wide and over ninety feet long, with a large hallway in the center, running the entire length of the house. On each side of the hallway sat two rooms (four in total on the first floor), creating a typical plantation mansion plan. It was the vastness of the rooms (estimated as thirty-two by forty-eight feet each) that gave the house its most striking feature—its size. A curved staircase in the central hall led up to the second story, which featured a plan very similar to the first floor. Above, the glassed-in third floor was not divided into separate rooms, but instead the entire space was open. This was the famous ballroom that hosted so many of the region's well-documented galas and social events.

One of the most unusual features of the Clay house was the captain's walk, a long glass corridor running the entire width of the mansion that hung off the back of the house over the side of the hill. Here the master of the house walked back and forth with his trusty spyglass surveying his fields and carefully observing the slaves at work.

In 1842, the great house received a long-lost heir when Nestor's son, Tacitus T. "Tas" Clay, then age eighteen, returned to Texas. There he became very close friends with George Seward, and two young men are said to have enjoyed many vivacious debaucheries together. They soon became business partners. In 1854, Tas sent an anonymous valentine to George's sister Bettie, although she immediately knew the identity of her not-so-secret admirer. The couple married on June 1, 1854.

Tas was elected mayor of Independence, Texas, a position he held until Texas joined other states in seceding from the Union. In one of his last official duties, he chopped down the pole in the town square upon which the United States flag flew. Tas became a member of Hood's Texas Brigade and earned the rank of captain.

Captain Clay, as he was known, saw much hand-to-hand combat in the war. He suffered many wounds, which he described to his wife in an 1862 letter: "The wound on my side has filled out even with the surface, and has nearly closed or healed up—and on my back where it was cut out it has been healed up several days. The greatest difficulty now will be my walking—for the shot in the leg has injured some of the nerves, and it will require some time for them to be restored. Should I not get well enough in the next month, or a prospect of my being able soon thereafter to join my Company, I shall make application for leave of absence, and if granted come Home—for you need no assurance to believe I hope that I want to see you and the Children as much as a loving husband and father could . . ."[19]

After the Confederacy's defeat, the captain returned to Texas determined to succeed in agricultural operations at his plantation. As was the case all across the South, the emancipation of the great slave labor force was among the greatest hurdles to rebuilding the plantation economy. The Clays secured eight young indentured servants from the St. Louis orphanage to supplement their dwindling workforce. Unlike black slaves, these children were actually taken into the Clay home and reared like stepchildren. In exchange for their labor they were each taught a trade, so they would be able to support themselves independently once their indenture had expired.

Unfortunately, Tas's many battle wounds did not leave him in good health after the war. He died in 1868. The old Clay Castle stood strong for many more years, but was greatly damaged after the famous Galveston hurricane of 1900. After this the battered structure may have been moved inland, but it suffered even greater damage in 1915, from another notorious hurricane. The famed mansion—irreparably mutilated—faded into history, leaving little physical trace of its existance.

## Eagle Island

Today the site of Eagle Island Plantation on Oyster Creek contains, among other developments, the Restwood Memorial Park Cemetery in Clute, Texas. A lone highway marker near the cemetery entrance commemorates the Wharton family's great estate.[20]

The plantation was originally part of Colonel Jared Ellison Groce's estate, but he gave it to his only daughter, Sarah Ann Groce, upon her marriage to William H. Wharton in 1827. At that time the plantation was poorly developed, and the newlyweds lived in a log cabin with a dirt floor. But as time progressed, William Wharton developed much of the estate, building brick slave cabins and a new sugarhouse for the manufacture of granulated sugar from cane.[21]

The machinery for the sugarhouse was produced in Philadelphia, and, interestingly, Wharton had everything installed in duplicate. This served not only to double production capabilities, but also to ensure that an equipment break would not cause the entire operation of sugar manufacturing to cease for weeks or months during the wait for a mechanical part.

As the plantation grew, the Whartons commissioned a grand mansion to replace their little log cabin. The mansion was a wood-frame, one-and-a-half-story farmhouse with an impressive colonnade of six slender wooden pillars topped with a heavy balustrade. Inside there was a large hall and an important library stocked with rare books. The house was said to have easily accommodated thirty overnight guests.

Outside the house in the yard, Wharton built a multiroom office building where he managed the business of the plantation. He also commissioned a European landscape gardener to create formal gardens in front of the mansion and to beautify the lands surrounding the nearby ponds.

As Wharton rose through the ranks of the planter elite, he assumed various political offices as was usually the case during the time. He served as president of the Convention of 1833, which tackled issues varying from a petition to increase Indian defense to a resolution prohibiting African slave traffic into Texas. Wharton served as judge advocate during the Texas War of Independence from Mexico.

After the war, Sam Houston was elected president of Texas and appointed Wharton as minister to the United States. In this capacity Wharton sought U.S. recognition of the new independent state and potential U.S. annexation of Texas. In 1837, while at sea, Wharton was captured by a Mexican ship, and he was subsequently imprisoned at Matamoros. Legend has it that a Catholic priest, Father Muldoon, visited Wharton in prison and helped him to escape by providing him with Catholic clerical garb (a nun or priest's outfit). Using this disguise, Wharton secured freedom and returned to his plantation.

William Wharton died in 1839, when he accidentally shot himself while dismounting a horse. He is credited, among many other achievements, with giving Texas its distinctive "lone star" flag and its state seal.

After his death, Wharton's son, John Austin Wharton,[22] took over operations of the plantation along with his mother. Under John's tenure

the plantation prospered. By 1860, the plantation exploited 133 slaves, some being employed exclusively in hunting. The estate was producing 185 hogsheads of sugar each year. Other crops included 7,000 bushels of corn annually and 100 bales of cotton.

John A. Wharton married Penelope Johnson, daughter of South Carolina governor David Johnson. The couple had one daughter, Kate Ross Wharton. John was elected attorney of Brazoria County, Texas, and also served as sheriff, before the Civil War.

Once war broke out, John joined the Eighth Texas Cavalry (Terry's Texas Rangers), where he eventually served as colonel. He was later promoted to major general and commanded all the cavalry west of the Mississippi River. Ironically, he survived several serious war wounds, only to be killed by one of his own men, Colonel George Baylor.

John's widowed mother was greatly distraught over the loss of her only remaining son, but took great pride in her granddaughter, Kate. Unfortunately, Kate died in 1871, and her mother also died, and the Widow Wharton was left penniless and alone. She later died at Eagle Island and was buried in the little family cemetery across the lake from the mansion.

The plantation was purchased by William Wharton Groce, a nephew of William H. Wharton, and he sold it to Harris Masterson in 1884. The old house and the estate's many other buildings deteriorated through the years, and now nothing is left of Eagle Island Plantation except for a few documents and images. Today, the plantation site is home to a cemetery, and a simple marker notes the property's substantial past.

# Ellersly

Ellersly Plantation, located along the Brazos River, was a thriving Texas sugar plantation, until the Civil War. It contained one of the finest mansions in the state, until 1890, when it burned. Other plan-

The mansion at Ellersly Plantation, seen here in a watercolor painting, was one of the largest and most impressive homes in Texas. Courtesy of the Brazoria County Historical Museum, Angleton, Texas.

tation buildings were subsequently lost to natural disaster.

The plantation lands were originally granted to John Greenville McNeel and his brother George Washington McNeel by the Mexican government in 1824. They were both members of Stephen F. Austin's "Old Three Hundred," a group of settlers who received early land grants. This property was described as one-half league on the Brazos River, a few miles from the Gulf of Mexico.[23]

On what was to be the mansion yard, the brothers found an immense mast from a large ship that had apparently been thrust into the ground during a hurricane. They tried to dig it up, but it was planted so firmly that removal was impossible. So, the ancient mast became a landmark of sorts on the plantation property.[24]

George McNeel died and John took over full authority of the plantation. Around the great ship mast he built an impressive sugar plantation. In the midst of the cane fields, McNeel constructed a large turreted brick sugarhouse that resembled a castle. The sugarhouse contained a double set of sugar kettles. Here, the precious juice, which was extracted from the cane after harvesting, was boiled in the large cast-iron kettles. These were usually set into a brick edifice, under which a large fire roared. The cane juice would first boil in the largest of the kettles and then at the proper moment it would be transferred to a smaller kettle. A series of smaller and smaller kettles were lined up in the brick structure, and, as the cane sap continued to reduce, it was transferred to consecutively smaller kettles. Lime and other agents were added to aid in removing impurities. And, at the precise time when the juice began to crystallize, it was transferred from the smallest kettle into a hogshead barrel where molasses would drain from the solid sugar crystals for some time. In 1852, McNeel made 408 such barrels, together totaling nearly 150,000 pounds of pure sugar. It was from this product and its profits that McNeel and planters like him throughout east Texas and Louisiana became very wealthy.[25]

Spurred by his success in the sugar industry, McNeel built a plantation mansion that was known as one of the most impressive in the state. It was a large two-story building constructed of hand-made bricks that were themselves produced on the estate. The house contained twenty-one rooms, and a large gallery supported by elegant pillars wrapped around the front and one side. Both the stairs and the banister were of mahogany. The ceilings throughout were elaborately decorated and adorned with intricate medallions. The fireplaces and mantels were all made of marble. And, uniquely, all of the floors were fully carpeted.[26]

One of the most interesting features of the mansion was found at its pinnacle. A laboratory was built at the very top of the house. It originally contained scientific apparatuses and even a telescope.[27] Most planters were interested in botany and weather patterns that related to their agricultural endeavors, as illustrated by the profuse popularity of almanacs at the time, but McNeel obviously had an unusually deep interest in science, especially astronomy.

The house was built in an oak grove between two roads. Visitors were greeted by large hand-hewn wooden gateposts that were decorated with carved spades, diamonds, clubs, and hearts, perhaps an indication that the owner was a card player or enjoyed games of chance.[28]

Other buildings on the plantation property included a large slave hospital, a brick overseer's house, a cotton gin, and a blacksmith's shop. The slave cabins, which housed approximately 175 slaves, were also made of the same handmade brick from which all other buildings on the estate were constructed. The slave cabins were two-room structures with a double fireplace, and each accommodated two families.[29]

McNeel's own family also resided on the plantation, where they were free from much of the labor of agricultural production. Instead the privileged family and their guests enjoyed dancing, riding fine thoroughbred horses, hunting, and fishing. McNeel had three sons with his wife Ann Augusta Westall, and after her death, he married Alma Amelia Blydenburg in 1854. She also died, and he later married Laura V. Roane.[30]

As with all other plantation families, the very foundations of the McNeels' wealth and power were shattered with the emancipation of their slave labor force and the Civil War. While in 1860 McNeel's real and personal properties were valued at over $330,000 (an amount equal to over $7.5 million in 2007 dollars), ten years later, after the war, his property was officially worthless.[31]

McNeel's sons, including Confederate officer John Greenville McNeel, Jr., took the losses associated with the war with much difficulty. McNeel was forced to pay over five thousand dollars to the Negro Bureau agent because his sons refused to stop whipping freed slaves. It was said that they were especially perturbed to realize that they could whip a white man without repercussions, but were fined for whipping former slaves. Of course, these incidents illustrate the huge cultural and social changes that were brought with Reconstruction; such transformations quickly led to the dissolution of the plantation economy in the realignment of life in the South.[32]

McNeel died in 1874. Ellersly Plantation was sold by his heirs to James Marion Huntington, who was married to McNeel's niece. The plantation mansion burned in the late 1880s, and Huntington and his family moved into the on-site slave hospital. This structure was destroyed in the great Galveston hurricane of 1900. The Huntington family moved into the overseer's house where they resided for a number of years. The plantation was sold to the Phillips Petroleum Company in 1974. The overseer's house burned in 1983, leaving little physical evidence of this important Texas estate.[33]

# Wyalucing

Famed for its architecture and for its historic residents, Wyalucing Plantation in Marshall, Texas, later became home to Bishop College, an institution of higher learning for African Americans. After the college moved, the fate of the plantation mansion became the topic of major debate. Although the local government sanctioned the idea of preserving the mansion, they later rescinded the idea, and in 1962, Wyalucing became nothing but a memory.[34]

Beverly LaFayette Holcombe, master of Wyalucing, was born on May 3, 1806, at The Oaks Plantation in Amelia County, Virginia. He was the youngest child of Major Philemon Holcombe, Jr., and Lucy Maria Anderson Holcombe. The family moved to Tennessee, and, while there, Beverly met and married Eugenia Vaughan Hunt.[35]

Beverly Holcombe owned Woodstock Plantation on the Wolfe River near LaGrange, Tennessee, but in the 1840s, he suffered several financial setbacks. He decided that a fresh start farther south was in order; so in 1848, he began construction on a house in Marshall, Texas, and moved his family there in 1850.

The plantation house was located on a tract of one hundred acres, which, rather uniquely, was not contiguous with the majority of Holcombe's farmlands. Instead, most of the crops were grown on nearby properties also in Harrison County. The house was constructed on a natural hill that was heavily forested.

The mansion was of an unusual design and plan. The first floor contained five rooms, three in a row across the front of the house, and a row of two rooms immediately behind. There was no central hall on the first floor, but, instead, the rooms were connected directly to one another. The second floor contained five rooms, but had a narrow hallway (that was likely added later) and two small balconies. Originally, there were no interior staircases, although in later years one was built. Instead, two exterior stairwells connected the first and second floors. It was said that Holcombe preferred exterior stairs in order to avoid a tax on interior stairways, and also because he felt the warm Texas climate would lend itself to such structures.

The exterior of the mansion, which was a striking red brick (that had been fired at the plantation by slaves), was completely surrounded by tall, stark white, square pillars. The dramatic contrast between the dark exterior walls and the bright columns and entablature produced an impressive sight. Holcombe called his plantation Wyalucing, said to be a Native American word meaning "home of the friendless."

The house was surrounded with the customary kitchens, barns, and other outbuildings. Slave quarters were also located on this tract, even though it was not the plantation's primary agricultural lands. Interestingly, another lost plantation house once existed on the property. Known as Westover, the earlier plantation had an unusual raised octagonal cottage that was believed to be the home of the Greers, an allied family.

The Holcombe family lived happily in their mansion, gaining increased social status as the years passed. Of Col. Holcombe's five children, Lucy Petway was certainly the most prominent.[36] She possessed a combination of captivating charm and grace, along with mesmerizing physical beauty that endeared friends, family, and the public to her and earned her the title "The Rose of Texas." In addition to her physical charms, Lucy was also a celebrated author. After the death of her young lover in an expedition in Cuba, she wrote *The Free Flag of Cuba*, her first book published under the pseudonym H. M. Hardeman. Lucy was a voracious social climber and used her social skills and charisma to ascend into higher and higher circles. She was entertained by the governor of Mississippi, John A. Quitman, who presented her before the state legislature in 1850.

On April 26, 1858, Lucy married Francis Wilkinson Pickens, a planter from South Carolina who owned Edgewood Plantation in Edgefield. Lucy was not satisfied with a planter, certainly among

The striking and unusual exterior of the mansion at Wyalucing Plantation was largely defined by its white columns and trim set against the dark red brick of the walls. Note the home's eccentric angles and exterior stairs. The larger balcony had been screened in this photograph, and a white paneled addition (a small bathroom) had been constructed off the second story. Also notice the curved brick walls of the low flower terrace with its braces.

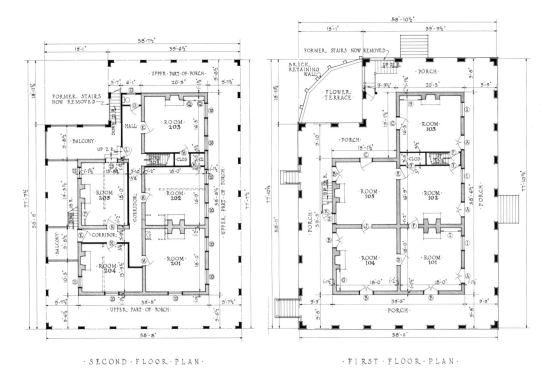

· S E C O N D · F L O O R · P L A N ·                    · F I R S T · F L O O R · P L A N ·

The floor plan of the Wyalucing's master house consisted of two parallel rows of rooms (one row with three and the other with two rooms). The second story shared a similar plan, but was later modified several times to create a corridor and other spaces (both the dark wall lines and the discontinuous wall lines represent former renovations).

the highest social designations at the time, and the marriage proposal had hinged on Pickens accepting a diplomatic position. So, after an elaborate two-day-long wedding reception following the ceremonies at Wyalucing, the newly married couple headed for Europe along with a male and a female slave, both wedding gifts from Lucy's father. There, they toured England and France before retiring to the Russian capital where Pickens took his position as U. S. ambassador.

In St. Petersburg, Lucy used her natural charm in the royal court, and she quickly became very close with Czarina Maria Alexandrovna. She became a favorite dance partner of Czar Alexander II himself. He bestowed upon her many lavish gifts and even had a marble bust of her commissioned. When Lucy became pregnant, the czar and czarina invited her to live with them in the Imperial Palace and kept her under the watchful care of the royal physicians. Lucy gave birth to a daughter on March 14, 1859, at which time palace guards fired a salute and the Imperial Band played in her honor. The child was christened Andrea Dorothea Olga Liva Lucy Holcombe Douschka Francesca Pickens. The czarina served as godmother, and the czar gave his blessings, along with gifts of diamonds, to the child.

A few months later, as news came of the rising tension between the states, the Pickens family decided to return to America. Francis Pickens was elected governor of South Carolina, and he led his state during the war. Lucy sold the jewels the czar had given her in order to outfit the Lucy Holcombe Legion, which contained seven companies of infantry and one of cavalry.

Lucy played an active role in her husband's political affairs and was vocal with Confederate leaders on many various issues. She became known as "Lady Lucy, Queen of the Confederacy," and her picture was printed on Confederate bills of various denominations. The entire family backed her support and aid of the southern cause.

Harrison County historian Eleanor Briggs notes that during the Civil War, the Wyalucing mansion served a number of important purposes. At one time, Wyalucing served as the headquarters for the Trans-Mississippi Agency for the Confederate States of America's Post Office Department, as well as headquarters for the Confederacy's Treasury Department. Additionally, it also served as a temporary office for the surgeon general and command center for various military activities. When Marshall, Texas, became the temporary capital of the state of Missouri, the exiled governor stayed at Wyalucing for a short while.[37] In fact, it was from the steps of Wyalucing that General Joseph Shelby regretfully informed his troops that the Confederacy had fallen.[38]

Beverly LaFayette Holcombe died at Wyalucing on November 16, 1864, at the height of the war. He was entombed in the famed mausoleum at his plantation cemetery. B. H. Greer, a grandson of Col. Holcombe, recounted that the mausoleum was of brick construction, with enough room for chairs and other furniture. He recalled being taken into the structure as a boy and gazing upon his grandfather's corpse through a glass insert in the casket. Holcombe's widow is said to have spent many long days in the mausoleum guarding her husband's body from feared molestation by Union soldiers. In addition, the cemetery later served as a burial site for many paupers and other destitute individuals whom Mrs. Holcombe often aided at the mansion, truly embodying the plantation's title as "home of the friendless."

Holcombe's widow, Eugenia Holcombe, died in 1873, and the Holcombe heirs sold the property in 1880 to a real estate group. It was then purchased by the American Baptist Home Mission Society, a group that formed Bishop College in 1881. The school was named for Judge Nathan Bishop, a New York attorney, whose wife gave several ten thousand dollar gifts to the institution at various times. Its primary goal was to advance the higher education of African Americans.

The college constructed several buildings around the plantation mansion and eventually turned the mansion itself into the C. H. Maxson Music Hall. The officials made few alterations to the historic plantation house, but they did demolish one of the exterior stairwells. The college later used the house as an administration building.

The college moved to Dallas in 1961, and the fate of the campus was flung into jeopardy. Realizing the profound historic importance of the plantation mansion as well as the strategic location of the property, the city of Marshall debated purchasing the college.

Soon after the move, city officials met with leaders of New York's American Baptist Home Mission Society, the group that owned the college. The city offered the society $102,000 for the college campus. The society in turn made a counteroffer of $120,000 for the college campus, including Wyalucing, along with another $20,000 for six additional tracts.[39]

In March 1961, the Marshall City Commission voted three to two to purchase the twenty-three-acre Bishop College campus and the six additional tracts for the asking price of $140,000. At this time, the city made it clear that it would spend no money on actually restoring the plantation mansion, which was still in excellent condition. Instead, Marshall officials would use the college property for a civic center and other city facilities, most likely demolishing those college buildings of little or no historic value. The Harrison County Historical Society envisioned refurbishing the Wyalucing mansion as a historical museum, thereby relieving the city of financial obligation.[40]

Following the vote, a few concerned citizens became extremely vocal regarding the attempts by the city to purchase the college property. They felt an eminent raise in taxes would be necessary to finance the purchase. By April, ads were being placed in local newspapers lambasting the idea. One large advertisement published in the *Marshall News Messenger* on April 16, 1961, asked citizens: "Can you afford to pick up the bill for financing this cultural project when you, as a city tax payer [*sic*], have so many other bills currently due?"

Sadly, the originator of these statements did not see the immense economic potential for the site. It was argued by local preservationists that because of the plantation's proximity to downtown Marshall it would be a great tourist draw. Also, proponents of the plantation saw it as a way to bolster business for the area, while generating profits for both the city and local businesses.

The April 16, 1961, advertisement went on to say, "Culture is nice, but private organizations can assume these cultural projects." Unfortunately, these ill-informed opponents of the plan did not realize the economic potential of the famed estate. They also failed to realize that public financing of historical and cultural projects is as important economically as using tax dollars to finance roads. Few would question the use of federal tax dollars to fund the Smithsonian Institution or the cultural resources of the National Park Service. But, even as their local culture was threatened, these vocal few were afraid that using local funds to save their own historic past might in some way threaten them personally, via higher taxes or otherwise.

Hearing these objections, the Marshall City Commission decided to put the issue before the citizens in an advisory vote. The vote would not oblige the commission in any way, but rather act more as a poll of public opinion. Regarding the vote, Commissioner Cleveland Heard, who supported efforts to purchase the former plantation, stated:

> I have not changed my mind one bit in thinking that purchase of the property is in the best interest of the community. I voted for the purchase thinking that the Commission was acting in the best interest of Marshall's future, which requires long-range planning and investments. I still feel that way.
>
> When confronted with a proposition that the people wanted to vote on that purchase, I did not feel that I should be put in a position that I was opposed to the people voicing their stand. Certainly that is a democratic way.
>
> The Commission frequently spends rather large amounts of money, without such matters being put before the people in a special election, but I shall never oppose the people expressing their views at the polls.[41]

Unfortunately, the voters of Marshall, influenced by the negative rhetoric of a vocal few, became frightened of the prospect of soaring taxes if the city purchased the property. They voted strongly against the purchase. The city commission, in turn, wanting to appease voters, rescinded their previous motion to purchase the property from the American Baptist Home Mission Society

Instead, the Bishop College site, including Wyalucing, was purchased by Price Littlejohn, a local insurance agent. Littlejohn negotiated a deal with Ed Korn, a developer from Dallas, giving Korn the option to purchase the land. Korn envisioned constructing a shopping center on the site.

In the meantime, Littlejohn negotiated the demolition of the campus buildings, including Wyalucing, with two demolition agents. Albert Bishop of the Southwest Wrecking Company of Dallas was to demolish one half of the buildings, and Frank Turney was to demolish the other half, including the Wyalucing mansion.[42]

Turney actually purchased many of the buildings himself, hoping to turn a profit from their salvageable timber and other materials. Harrison County Historical Society president J. Fred Lentz offered five hundred dollars for the remains of the demolished Wyalucing, to be reconstructed at another location. Demolishers quoted a price of fifty-five hundred dollars for the materials themselves, not including the actual demolition work. It was estimated to cost between thirty thousand and seventy thousand dollars to reconstruct the mansion from demolished remains.[43]

Lentz quickly withdrew his offer, citing that a reconstructed version of the mansion on a non-original and less desirable site would diminish its historical value, which is what the historical society ultimately wanted to preserve.[44]

In October 1962, the *Dallas Morning News* reported that the Marshall Historical Society, led by President Seth Walton, would make "a last desperate effort to save Wyalucing." Part of this effort was focused on having the city commission rezone the plantation property under a Texas statute designed for the protection of historic places. A formal request was submitted to the commission by Marshall attorney Franklin Jones, who asked the city to delay or prevent the razing of the structure.[45]

After a lengthy meeting, the city commission released a formal statement: "The city commission met in special session at 5 p.m. Oct. 29 [1962] to consider a request that the city pass an ordinance prohibiting the razing of Wyalucing. The commission, after discussing the matter at length, decided that passage of such an ordinance under the circumstances would be inappropriate and of doubtful legality."[46]

U.S. senator Ralph Yarborough commented that "for Marshall to permit the destruction of Wyalucing would be like San Antonio standing by while the Alamo is torn down . . . [Wyalucing has] a historical connection with the Civil War not equaled by any other building in Texas, perhaps not equaled by any other building west of the Mississippi River . . ."[47]

But stand by is exactly what the city commissioners did, while historical society leaders and other influential community members fought diligently. J. Fred Lentz negotiated a four-week delay in demolition with property holders, one week in order to meet with them to determine a price for the plantation mansion and property and three weeks to raise the money.[48]

After a meeting with option holder Ed Korn and others, Lentz reported in November 1962 that the Bishop College investors would sell the plantation mansion, along with about five acres, to the Harrison County Historical Society for fifty thousand dollars. U.S. district judge T. Whitfield Davidson publicly endorsed this idea, offering "liberal" financial support.[49]

Sadly, even with the pledged support, the historical society was unable to raise enough money in the very brief window of time they were offered. Demolition of the Wyalucing Plantation's great house was begun in December 1962, and was completed before Christmas. Today, the site is occupied by a low-rent housing development. A marker noting the plantation's history, which once stood near the mansion, now resides in the Harrison County Historical Museum, an institution steadfastly devoted to preserving the region's past.

The story of Wyalucing's rise and fall places it among the very greatest of tragic plantation preservation losses in the South. Unlike many of the grand plantation homes lost in Texas, it was not a victim of natural disaster or even neglect. The mansion at Wyalucing was an excellently preserved structure that was a victim of sour politics, of simple-minded elected officials who lacked foresight and vision, and of a poorly informed populace whose ill-founded fears of increased taxation outweighed their responsibility to preserve their rich, multifaceted past for their children and their children's children. Wyalucing is now but a memory, and its economic and cultural potential is lost forever, much like its towering white pillars and deep red walls.

## Orozimbo

Orozimbo Plantation, also known as the Phelps Plantation, was once located in Brazoria County, Texas. This cotton estate was most famous for housing, as a prisoner, the notorious president and dictator of Mexico, General Santa Anna, during the Texas Revolution. Orozimbo was destroyed in the 1930s, by a combination of neglect and natural disaster.[50]

About nine miles northwest of the city of Angleton, Orozimbo was the home of Dr. James Aeneas E. Phelps, a physician and cotton planter. He was one of Stephen F. Austin's famed "Old Three Hundred" colonists, having come to Texas in 1822, aboard the *Lively*. He received a land grant for the Orozimbo properties in 1824.

An 1826 census of the area enumerated Phelps, along with his wife, two sons, two daughters, one personal servant, and fifteen slaves. It was around this time that he constructed a two-story residence on the plantation near a large oak tree.

Phelps was active in community life. In 1835, he helped establish a Masonic lodge in Texas, and in 1836, he was elected a delegate to the Convention of 1836. At the convention, Phelps and his fellow delegates drafted the Texas Declaration of Independence and the Constitution of the Republic of

Texas. They also created a temporary government and named Sam Houston commander-in-chief of the military. A month later, Phelps joined the Texas army as a surgeon. During the war for Texas independence, he established a hospital in Harrisburg.

During the war, the Mexican president and dictator, General Antonio López de Santa Anna, was captured. During his captivity he negotiated with General Sam Houston and recognized that Texas would be granted independence, the Rio Grande being the agreed-upon border. Santa Anna was granted his freedom and passage to Vera Cruz in return for the treaties with Texas. He boarded the schooner *Invincible*, which soon met with a vessel from New Orleans carrying American troops mustered for the war in Texas. With little regard for the Texas government, the American troops decided that Santa Anna should remain a prisoner.

Santa Anna, again imprisoned, was brought to Orozimbo Plantation, where he stayed for months. At times he was chained to the large oak tree near the main house. During one instance there, a guard plotted to assassinate the Mexican dictator. Hearing of the planned atrocity, Phelps's wife went to Santa Anna just as the guard had drawn his gun. She threw herself upon Santa Anna, embracing him and thus preventing the guard from firing. In this act, she saved the general's life.

At another time, despondent and depressed over his imprisonment, Santa Anna tried to take his own life. He ingested a poison, but Dr. Phelps successfully saved him from death by manually pumping his stomach of the toxin. Again, a Phelps of Orozimbo saved Santa Anna's life.

Of his capture, Santa Anna later wrote: "I had been taken to Orazimba [*sic*] . . . a heavy ball and chain was placed on me the 17th of August, and on Colonel Almonte on the 18th. We wore them for fifty-two days."[51]

The Mexican dictator was eventually freed and brought to Washington, where he met with President Andrew Jackson. He was subsequently returned safely to Vera Cruz via a U. S. Navy vessel.

Years later, Dr. Phelps's son, Orlando, was imprisoned while on the ill-fated Mier Expedition, a raiding mission south of the Nueces River. Hearing of the young man's capture and remembering that his own life had been saved twice by Orlando's parents, Santa Anna had him immediately removed to the presidential palace. There he hosted young Phelps as his guest for a number of days. He showered him with good food and fine clothing and provided his passage to New York, giving him a large sum of gold for his trip.

Orlando later returned to Orozimbo, but subsequently moved to Houston. The plantation passed into other hands, and it was allowed to decay. In 1932, the main house was destroyed by a hurricane. In 1936, a black farmer resided in a small cottage there that was made from original timbers of the great house.

Today, little remains of Orozimbo. The little wooden cabin is in total ruin. Rising from the overgrown weeds around the decayed shack, a tall granite marker, not unlike a gravestone, bears the lone star of Texas and the following inscription:

SITE OF "OROZIMBO"
Home of Dr. James A. E. Phelps, a member of "Old Three Hundred" of Austin's colony, hospital surgeon of the Texas army at San Jacinto · Here Santa Anna was detained as a prisoner from July to November, 1836

## Glen Eden

Glen Eden, one of the most famed plantations in Grayson County, Texas, was located along the Red River at Preston Bend. It was the home of a mysterious and vivacious mistress and several of her husbands. When threatened by the eminent creation of Lake Texoma, the historic plantation house was dismantled to be reconstructed at another location. The pieces were damaged, however, and the structure was never reassembled.

Glen Eden was originally established by Col. Holland Coffee. Coffee, born August 15, 1807, was orphaned at age eleven, and he grew up in Tennessee with an uncle. In 1829, he moved to Fort Smith,

Arkansas, where he established a trading post and made contact with Sam Houston. He moved to Oklahoma in the 1830s, and in 1833, he conducted a trapping expedition along the Red River.[52]

Coffee moved to Preston Bend in 1837, establishing a successful trading operation there. The same year, Sam Houston appointed Coffee an Indian agent for the Republic of Texas. Coffee had much interaction with Native Americans through his years operating trading posts, and he became fluent in several Native American languages. The next year, he was elected to the Texas House of Representatives.

Holland Coffee married Sophia Suttenfield Aughinbaugh on January 19, 1839. Sam Houston attended the wedding at Washington-on-the-Brazos. The bride was, at that time, unfamiliar to the area and her secrecy about her past spurred much speculation.

Little is yet known of Sophia's early life, but it is clear that she lived in an area adjacent to Fort Wayne on a military reserve surrounded by Indian lands in present-day Indiana. She was one of only a handful of women in an isolated area populated largely by young men. It is rumored that in this well-suited environment she began a "career" that she would supposedly return to again and again at various times in her life. It is difficult to definitively document that Sophia was involved in prostitution, but correlative evidence suggests that the speculation surrounding her alleged illicit trade may be based on facts.

Sophia married Jesse Aughinbaugh in 1833. Two years later they moved to Texas, and soon after Jesse disappeared. What exactly happened to him was never clear. Whether he abandoned Sophia or was killed or otherwise lost will probably never be known. Certain sources note that after Aughinbaugh was gone, Sophia supported herself by again providing her services to the men of the area.

Shortly after Sophia's 1839 marriage to Holland Coffee, she and her husband lived with Daniel Montague, but they soon began to expand and improve their own land holdings. Together the couple built their plantation home at Glen Eden. Coffee had a large house built on the plantation around 1845. It was located about a mile from the river near the Little Mineral Creek. The house, originally a two-story dogtrot log cabin, was constructed for the Coffees by a Mormon colony led by Lyman Wight. The house had large stone chimneys and an expansive basement.

Throughout their short marriage, Coffee was often away on business, and Sophia used this opportunity to operate a very successful "boardinghouse" for young army recruits. Of course, murmurs regarding her other business with these young men and the reasons for the overwhelming popularity of her lodge reverberated throughout the region.

In 1846, Charles Ashton Galloway, a merchant from Fort Washita (in modern Oklahoma) who married Coffee's fourteen-year-old niece, Eugenia Coffee, is said to have made rude remarks about Sophia Coffee. Several versions of these remarks exist and perhaps they were all said. In one version Galloway commented about Sophia's alleged liaisons with Sam Houston, and in another he noted that she was involved with every young soldier who came through Preston Bend. In yet another version, Galloway noted that Sophia would like to kill Coffee and marry Justice of the Peace Thomas Murphy (who married her sister Frances). In addition to Galloway's libelous comments, Coffee was upset because he felt that the man had taken advantage of his young niece while she visited Sophia. In truth Eugenia had rushed into marriage to avoid going back to her home in Mississippi and back to her mother who was set to wed a strict, elderly man. Coffee's anger with Galloway eventually ended in violence. The two men met in a duel on October 1, 1846, and Galloway took the upper hand, killing Coffee. Sophia had her husband's body interred in an elaborate brick mausoleum she commissioned at the plantation cemetery.

Coffee left Sophia a handsome inheritance of five thousand acres of land in various tracts, nineteen slaves, numerous horses and cattle, several businesses, including his post at Preston, and Glen Eden Plantation. Alone, Sophia continued allegedly to ply her trade and certainly to pour herself

into the management of her estate. She proved herself to be an apt businesswoman. She planted a thousand acres at Glen Eden with cotton, which she shipped to New Orleans via Shreveport. It is even said that she herself accompanied one crop on a barge during a particularly busy season. Sophia hired her nephew J. W. Williams as a manager. He assisted her in running the plantation and managing the slaves. Williams later married Isabel "Belle" Skelly, who became Sophia's seamstress and her closest confidant.

A few years prior to the Civil War, Sophia met and married Major George W. Butt, a Virginian. Major Butt was said to have been an arrogant, egotistical, and short-tempered man. He was often involved in lawsuits, including a 1849 suit in which he was accused of assault with the intent to murder a man. These charges were later dropped. Butt was fascinated by railroads and invested heavily in them. He also served in the 1853 convention that formulated railroad policy in Texas. As a plantation master, Butt was a success. He purchased many additional acres of farmlands and also obtained more slaves for Glen Eden.

In the early 1860s, Butt expanded the plantation house at Glen Eden. In addition to making other improvements and expansions, he covered the structure with siding from Jefferson, Texas, and added long front and rear galleries that were supported by eight slender columns in both the front and back. He also added a wine cellar and a kitchen. Later, a brick kitchen was added in a rear wing, and two ends of the wide rear upper gallery were enclosed as bedrooms.

Sophia, who loved gardening, oversaw the creation of a rock garden on one side of the house and a pit-style greenhouse on the other. She also managed a large orchard of over a hundred fruit trees. It stretched from the master house to the plantation cemetery.

The Butts filled the newly renovated house with fine furnishings from New Orleans, and they raised a large flock of peacocks that served as living, strutting lawn ornaments. The couple hosted lavish parties and banquets that often went on for days.

George Butt's days at Glen Eden transformed the plantation physically, economically, and socially. But, like most of Sophia's marriages, this one, too, would end abruptly. In early February 1864, Butt had gone to Sherman on business, probably to sell cotton. He never returned. A week later, a search party found his body along the Sherman-to-Preston road. His money was gone. Later, Sophia spotted a Confederate guerrilla, Fletch Taylor, wearing Butt's watch. She alerted authorities, and Taylor admitted to murdering Butt. Robbery, it seemed, was the motive. Major George Butt was buried in the West Hill Cemetery in Sherman, and Sophia was once again, for the third time, a widow.

It was during the Civil War that Sophia's heroic efforts earned her the title of "Confederate Paul Revere." She got wind that federal troops were on their way to the area. When they arrived she invited the officers to her home, an invitation they readily accepted, especially considering Sophia's scandalous reputation. Legend has it that Sophia wined and dined the men until they were quite drunk, discussed with them their plans and strategies, and then invited them for a tour of her famed wine cellar. Once there, she locked the men in her cellar, and quickly rode off to warn the rebel forces. Several sources agree that she crossed the Red River and then found Confederate officers, including Col. James G. Bourland, in whom she confided the battle plans and information she had learned. Some sources recount that she returned to her plantation and released the federal officers, while others suggest that she held the men captive until Confederate troops came to pick them up.

Sophia traveled to Waco, along with her slaves and tar buckets filled with gold, hoping to flee the devastation of war. There, she met James Porter, a Confederate officer who had served as a judge in Missouri. Porter was on his way to Mexico to join Emperor Maximillian's army, but he was cut short by Sophia's captivating beauty and charm. On August 2, 1865, the couple was married by Rufus Burleson, the president of Baylor College.

Sophia's holdings, especially at Glen Eden, were harshly affected by the war. Her slaves were freed, but she still had land. She and Porter sold, traded, and purchased much land, often selling old properties at a profit and using the money to purchase cheap, undervalued land at sheriffs' auctions. They held steadfast to Glen Eden, where they lived happily for many years.

In the latter years of her life, Porter convinced Sophia to "get religion," and she attended a camp meeting hosted by the Reverend John Witherspoon Pettigrew McKenzie, the founder of McKenzie College. Sophia, dressed in a bright orange dress, ran down the aisle and threw herself upon the reverend's feet. Knowing well of her sordid past, McKenzie was not convinced by Sophia's conversion. He remarked that she would have to do good works for twelve years before he would allow her into his church, and that even then he wasn't hopeful, as the "the sun, the moon, and the stars," all aligned against her becoming a Christian.

The Reverend J. M. Binkley of Sherman's First Methodist Church wasn't so judgmental, and he welcomed Sophia into his church. She and her husband became great supporters for several local churches and devoted themselves to various causes. Porter died in 1886, and Sophia continued to reside at Glen Eden until her death on August 27, 1897. A large funeral was held at the plantation and she was buried next to her fourth husband in Porter Cemetery.

In 1979, the *Sherman Democrat* published an account by ninety-year-old Denison resident Minnie Jackson Blake, who vividly recalled Sophia's funeral: "She was carried in a fancy black surrey pulled by black horses covered in black net. She was dressed in pink satin covered by black net or lace and just looked beautiful. I remember sayin' that when I died I wanted to have them haul me in a hearse just like that one; it was just beautiful."[53]

In *Red River Women*, Sherrie S. McLeRoy notes that local papers competed to publish the most glowing eulogies for the woman who was once shunned as the town whore. Reporters called her "an aged saint," "an ornament to society," and even "a magnificent example of the Spartan mothers of the old South."[54]

Much of Sophia's wealth was divided between one of Coffee's surviving nieces and plantation manager J. W. Williams. Other properties went to support education, including 337 acres that was donated to Southwestern University in Georgetown, Texas, and other benevolent causes.

Glen Eden passed through many hands, but was finally purchased by Judge Randolph Bryant, who opened the plantation house as a historical attraction in 1936, during the Texas centennial celebration. Three years later the U.S. Congress appropriated $5.6 million to build the Denison Dam and Lake Texoma. The lake would flood a great deal of property, including Glen Eden Plantation.

In 1942, in anticipation of the coming deluge, the master house at Glen Eden was meticulously disassembled for later reconstruction at a more appropriate site. Bryant envisioned reassembling the home on the banks of the Red River reservoir. Unfortunately, while in storage waiting to be restored, some of the materials from the plantation home were damaged, and the mansion was never rebuilt.

Some of the undamaged logs and beams were acquired by the Grayson County Frontier Village and were used in some of the exhibits and buildings that make up the historic attraction. The brick mausoleum that Sophia had built for her second husband, Holland Coffee, was destroyed and his body was interred in the Preston Cemetery.

In 1965, a historic marker was erected in honor of Texas's "Confederate Paul Revere," Sophia Suttonfield Aughinbaugh Coffee Butt Porter. A 1979 issue of the *Denison Herald* included a feature about several items from Glen Eden, including one of Sophia's dresses, images of her, and furnishings from the plantation house, which were acquired by the Sherman Historical Museum for display in their Taliaferro Room.[55] Today, nothing is left of Sophia's plantation. Most of Glen Eden's fertile lands now lie on the bottom of Lake Texoma, and the remainder makes up several resort communities on the shores of the lake. But the story of one of Texas's liveliest plantation mistresses is still widely recounted and recognized by locals, even if her beloved plantation home has long since withered away.

# Peach Point

Peach Point Plantation, the estate of James and Emily Perry, was the only home in Texas that Emily's famed brother, Stephen F. Austin, ever claimed. It was Austin, in fact, who convinced his sibling and her mate to join him in Texas, and it was he who was largely responsible for the development of Peach Point. Portions of the plantation have remained in the possession of the family to the present day, but the majority of the antebellum architecture—except for two historic rooms—is utterly obliterated.[56]

In 1821, Moses Austin received a land grant from the Mexican government to establish an Anglo-American colony of three hundred settlers in Mexican "Tejas." The original grant covered some two hundred thousand acres. But Moses died before his plans were enacted, so upon his last request the responsibility of establishing the community fell on his sons, Stephen F. Austin and James E. Brown Austin. The two men diligently devoted themselves to their father's visionary task, but in 1829, tragedy stuck when James suddenly died hours after experiencing slight pains in his stomach and head.

Distraught, Stephen pleaded for his sister, Emily Margaret Austin Bryan, and her second husband, James Franklin Perry, to move to Texas. He had previously suggested that the couple settle in the colony, but now insisted that they come, desperately wanting to reunite the few remaining pieces of his family. In 1829, he wrote, "I have never been so thoroughly convinced as I now am of the future rapid rise of this country—you have no idea of it, or you would be here before April, family and all . . ." Two weeks later, he urged his family further, writing, "In a year or more this colony will be filled up, now then is the time, if you remove soon you must make a fortune . . . I can do something for you now but after my colonizing business is done, the door will be closed . . ." He later stated, "You may be sure that I would not urge your removal in so positive a manner if I was not convinced that you will be greatly benifitied [sic] there is no time for hesitation or delay." Austin's subsequent letters went on to inform his family that he was dying "rapidly" and that they must leave "immediately" so that he might see his sister and her children "before I die." In fact, he did suffer from ailments throughout his life, but in regard to the assertion that he was near death, exaggeration, rather than illness, was responsible.[57]

At Austin's urging, the Perrys eventually decided to move to Texas, and Austin obtained eleven leagues of land to be owned equally by his sister and her husband. He explained that Emily's portion of ownership was to be for her children from her first marriage to James Bryan and that James Perry's portion was to be set aside for his children with Emily.

Austin described the land in a letter: "Any place which I have you may have for a residence or farm or what you please—The place where I originally intended to settle all my family is at peach point below Brasoria [sic], on the Sea Shore prairie at the edge of the timber 6 miles from the sea beach—Every body says it is the best land and the best situation in the colony—It is my first choice for a residence, and on Chocolate Bayou is my second choice . . ."[58]

Moses Austin Bryan, Emily's son from her first marriage, was the first of the Austin-Perry clan to come to Texas. He arrived with his friend and business partner William W. Hunter, and together the two young men sought to establish a mercantile store. On June 17, 1880, James Perry sold his family residence in Potosi, Missouri, and had the remains of his in-laws—Moses and Maria Austin—removed from his property and interred in St. Genevieve Catholic Cemetery.

Before he left, Stephen Austin drew up numerous long and meticulous instructions for the journey, including multiple lists of every item his sister and her family were to bring. In one letter he wrote: "Bring all manner, and great quantities of fruit seeds with you and some Gooseberry and raspberry roots, in particular. Furniture is scare here

and high, but as we are all poor backwoodsmen, costly furniture is unknown and unnecessary, but you ought to have enough to be comfortable . . . Try and bring some of the breed of English cattle, nature never made a better place for stock than the land I have asked for . . . Bring all your capital it can be well employed here."[59]

James and Emily arrived in San Felipe on August 14, 1831, with their children, James's niece Lavinia, and their indentured servants. Austin had made sure that the Perrys had indentured their slaves prior to their departure, as slavery was technically illegal in the Mexican state.

Originally, James settled at an idyllic spot between Pleasant and Chocolate bayous, while the Peach Point lands were being developed. This original Perry plantation is today occupied by a petrochemical plant. When the Peach Point property was ready for occupation, Austin wrote to his brother-in-law: "Remove all your stock to peach point, make corn there in the cane brake—let the work at Chocolate go and begin down here at once—and from this time forward make up your mind finally and definitively on the subject—and also keep up your sperits [sic]—no low sperits [sic] will do in any one as nearly connected to me as you are—it is noticed by others and attributed to the wrong cause."[60]

It is interesting to note Austin's rebuke of his brother-in-law's mood. No historical evidence exists to suggest why James Perry was disillusioned, but certainly having someone as overbearing and particular as Austin attempting to control one's life could not have been trouble-free.

By November 1831, Austin had drawn meticulous plans for the Perry home at Peach Point. The original plan called for a central hall with a staircase flanked by a twenty-four-by-twenty-four-foot room to the east and parallel twelve-by-twenty-four-foot rooms to the west. Small east and west wings, each with small back galleries, further flanked these central rooms. In the front of the house, to the south, twelve-by-ten-foot rooms enclosed each end of the thirty-four-foot-long front gallery. In the rear of the house to the north, two rooms enclosed each end of the smaller rear gallery, for a total of four rooms in the rear of the house. In total, Austin's original plan called for fourteen rooms. Two of these were to be set aside for his personal use, one as an office and the other as a bedroom.

Austin even advised the Perrys about the bricks they should use to construct the master house: "The place where you ought to make the brick is up the Chocolate bayou at Brays old Cabbin [sic] where there is Clay and Timber, and take the brick down by water[.] By beginning on this plan and finishing it by degrees you can do it all in a year or 18 months and not feel it materially—and when it is done you will have a valuable place and a convenient one."[61]

In addition to his design for the plantation house, Austin plotted the entire Peach Point Plantation for the Perrys meticulously devising where outbuildings—from outhouses and stables to gin houses and kitchens—were to be placed. He also laid out the fields and provided direction for what was to be planted in each. Austin described the Peach Point tracts to the Perrys in a letter: "The tracts you now live on will make as good a farm or plantation as any in Texas. It has a good situation on the river also—is in a good neighborhood—convenient to the sea, to the river, to market will do for stock and planting—takes in part of jones Creek—has plenty of timber and prairie[.]"[62]

Sadly, only a short time after the Perrys moved to Peach Point, the plantation was besieged by an outbreak of malaria. The disease threatened the entire colony, and families began leaving in great numbers in a massive exodus to escape the feared killer. Nearly everyone at Peach Point grew ill; there was hardly anyone well to care for the sick. Most recovered eventually, but Emily's eleven-year-old daughter, Mary Elizabeth Bryan, succumbed to the disease. To make matters even worse, a large flood destroyed the annual crops at Peach Point and at neighboring plantations.

With devastation from disease and flood, developments at Peach Point and other estates lagged, but eventually cotton became a major cash crop of the area. By 1835, the Perrys had sixty-five to seventy acres of cotton planted, and by 1838, they made 127 bales. A cotton gin was eventually constructed on the plantation grounds, which served as an industrialized center of production for the estate.

In 1835, Peach Point, along with all of Texas, experienced sweeping changes as tensions rose between the region and its government in Mexico. Santa Anna had assumed dictatorship of the country and his policies angered many. In east Texas Sam Houston was named commander of armed forces, and Stephen F. Austin took the position of commander in chief of the volunteers at Gonzales. Austin also joined his former political nemeses, William H. Wharton and Dr. Branch T. Archer, on a political mission to Washington, D.C., where they petitioned for funds from the U.S. government to further their cause.

With the Texas Revolution in full force, many settlers including the Perrys fled Austin's colony and other areas of Texas in a large exodus to the northeast. After Santa Anna's capture, the Perrys, along with their neighbors, retuned home. It is said that Peach Point was found in much disarray, with chickens nesting in the manor house and numerous other damages incurred.

After the revolution, Texas became an independent republic, and Sam Houston took the office of president. He named Stephen Austin as secretary of state, a position he held only a short time before he died in 1836. Austin's body was transported down the Brazos River to Peach Point, where it was interred. Houston and many other officials attended the burial. Austin's body was later moved to the Texas State Cemetery at Austin in 1910.

The Perry family continued to live at Peach Point, planting and partaking in the social functions of the community. They regularly entertained guests, and Emily's son, Guy Bryan, enjoyed having friends stay with him at the estate. One such visitor was Guy's school friend Rud, who stayed at Peach Point with his uncle, Sardis Birchard. Rud, known formally as Rutherford B. Hayes, later served as the nineteenth president of the United States. It was at

Peach Point, many argue, that Hayes was first immersed in southern plantation culture and developed sympathies towards white plantation masters. Such ideas would later have major political impact on his administration.

In a letter to his mother written from Peach Point, Hayes noted: "Mrs. Perry, for example, instead of having the care of one family, is the nurse, physician, and spiritual adviser of a whole settlement of careless slaves. She feels it is her duty to see to their comfort when sick or hurt, and among so many there is always some little brat with a scalded foot or a hand half cut off, and 'Missus' must always see to it or there is sure to be a whining time of it in the whole camp."[63]

As plantation life went on at Peach Point, politics outside made dramatic changes in the history of Texas and on the plantation. In 1845, Texas was annexed as a constituent state of the United States. The Perrys supported annexation and reaped financial rewards that American citizenship wrought.

By the 1850s, the Perrys had turned their sights from cotton to sugar, constructing a large sugar mill at Peach Point. The census of the year noted that the family owned forty-three slaves, and it is clear that most of these men and women were now engaged in the business of making sugar. The Perrys' cotton crop, which had fairly regularly exceeded one hundred bales per annum previously, had steadily dropped to only thirty-nine bales in 1849, likely further indicating an agricultural shift from cotton to cane.

With the sweet business of sugar booming, Emily Perry died in 1851. She was followed in death by her husband two years later. After James Perry's death, Emily's son, William Joel Bryan, set aside two hundred acres of the Peach Point Plantation and developed it into a thriving cotton and cattle estate called Durazno Plantation. The main Peach Point tract was managed by James and Emily's oldest son, Stephen Perry, who later served as a major in the Fourth Regiment, Texas Volunteers, in the War Between the States.

During the war, Stephen Perry's wife, Sarah McLean Brown, fled the plantation with her children and slaves. They faced trying times, finding it nearly impossible to get enough food to eat in the war-ravaged South. While the family was away, federal soldiers set up camp at Peach Point, wreaking havoc upon the estate.

When the Perrys returned, the plantation was in shambles, but Stephen and his family worked diligently to restore their estate and their lives. Stephen Perry died in 1874, and his son, James "Jimmie" Perry II, took over plantation operations. Only a year after his father's death, Jimmie had to contend with a fierce hurricane that destroyed a number of buildings on the plantation, including the plantation church.

A quarter century later, the infamous Galveston hurricane of 1900 destroyed all of the slave cabins at Peach Point and ruined the sugar mill. It also devastated the year's crops. Then, less than a decade later, the 1909 Galveston storm further destroyed the plantation, demolishing the master house—all except Stephen Austin's two personal rooms—and tearing down the plantation office building.

During these trying years and beyond, the Perrys faced near ruin not only from hurricanes, but also from other floods, storms, and freezes that seemed to continually destroy their crops. In 1935, most of the plantation was leased for oil. The little remaining antebellum architectural legacy fell into even greater ruin as the elements encroached.

In 1948, Jimmie Perry's son, Stephen Perry, Sr., and Stephen's daughter, May Perry Hamill, took it upon themselves to restore the plantation's remaining architectural elements—the ruins of Stephen Austin's two rooms. They meticulously labored over years to re-create the rooms, using bricks salvaged from the crumbled sugar mill to construct a fireplace. They filled the rooms with family heirlooms and plantation artifacts, including a dress dagger belonging to Stephen Austin.

In 1949, Stephen Perry, Sr., and his wife, Corrilla Hawes, built a new, modern home on the plantation site. Later it was home to Stephen Perry, Jr., and his family. His grandchildren were the seventh generation to make Peach Point their home. In 1982, upon the 150th anniversary of the plantation, a book detailing the history of Peach Point was written by local journalist Mary Beth Jones. It was published by Texian Press in Waco.

In the mid-to-late 1980s, much of the Peach Point property was purchased and consolidated into the Peach Point Wildlife Management Agency, a branch of the Central Coast Wetlands Ecosystem Project. Today, portions of the historic property are open to the public for hunting, biking, hiking, and fishing. And, while much of the architectural and built past of Peach Point is gone, the little remaining portions of this once-noble plantation speak volumes to all those who visit.

# Conclusions

To build may have to be the slow and laborious task of years. To destroy can be the thoughtless act of a single day.

—*Sir Winston Churchill*

The heritage of the past is the seed that brings forth the harvest of the future.

—Inscription at the base of a statue near the entrance
of the National Archives Building in Washington, D.C.

Over the years, the agricultural enterprises that dominated the southern antebellum landscape, culture, and economy have largely dissipated. Most of the iconic columns and abodes that defined these built spaces and represented the eras in which they were created are likewise gone. The stories of the physical decline of the plantation form an intriguing tale. It leads to the many causes of architectural decay and demolition, and, further, to lessons of how and why we must preserve those few remaining architectural gems of the Old South.

## Plantations after the Civil War

There are no accurate numbers to suggest exactly how many plantations were destroyed during the Civil War. Certainly, though, it is clear that hundreds were completely destroyed, and thousands were physically damaged. Most, however, survived the war. And a great number of these estates were utilized again as agricultural enterprises, even if only temporarily. As described in the previous chapters, life after the war was dramatically different from life before it.

The greatest change was the emancipation of the slave labor force. A variety of schemes to incorporate former slaves as workers on plantation lands were undertaken, most popularly sharecropping—a system in which landowners allow workers to farm their lands in return for a share of the crops. By the turn of the century, many poor whites had joined former slaves as sharecroppers.

Former slaves weren't the only workers sought to farm cane and cotton fields. Experiments using Italian immigrants as exemplified on Arkansas's Sunnyside Plantation and Chinese laborers as exemplified on Louisiana's Millaudon Plantation[1] were implemented, although not in a particularly successful manner.

Economic factors since the Civil War had, over the years, deemphasized agriculture in favor of industry, but the Agricultural Adjustment Act of 1933 dealt the final death blow to sharecropping. It restricted agricultural production during the New Deal by subsidizing farmers to leave portions of their fields unused, ultimately reducing crop supply in an effort to stabilize their value.

As agriculture declined after the Civil War and through the twentieth century, plantations took a variety of interesting paths. Multiple volumes have been written on plantation agriculture and labor during and beyond Reconstruction, so to do more than mention that obvious use of plantations briefly here would be redundant. It is the other uses, often nonagricultural in nature, of plantations and their mansions after the war that is most telling both socially and culturally.

For example, in Texas, Lake Jackson Plantation was used as a prison, where mostly black convicts were severely treated and forced to work as virtual slaves in the fields of this state farm. About 250 miles to the north in Marshall, Texas, Wyalucing Plantation became a college, where the descendants of slaves elevated their stations through higher education. The stark contrast between the functions of these two plantations alone provides a brief reflection of the complicated and paradoxical world of race, culture, and southern society at the turn of the century and how the physical vestiges of antebellum plantations played a part.

Likewise mirroring post–Civil War shifts was Brierfield Plantation in Mississippi. The former plantation of Confederate president Jefferson Davis was sold to his former slaves after the war, although it later reverted back to him. Brierfield was not alone, however; plantations being owned by former slaves were not entirely uncommon.

But, as culture and economics changed, the question of what to do with these great complexes arose. Mostly, outbuildings such as cabins and kitchens were moved and utilized as small houses or storage places or were simply allowed to decay and then taken down. Plantation master houses usually outlasted most of their ancillary structures. But the question remained of what to do with these houses.

Most served their original purpose as private homes, as location played a major role in the changing functions of these structures. Louisiana's Seven

Oaks is an example; its location next to a railroad ensured its use as a military barracks (as soldiers guarded these railways during World War I) and later as a home, when a railroad official was moved there in the twentieth century. Likewise, its location across the river from New Orleans also influenced its earlier role as a resort attraction. Visitors enjoyed the quick steamboat ride from the foot of the Crescent City's famed Canal Street across the Mississippi River to the plantation.

Maryland's Marshall Hall Plantation served a similar function, and its location directly across the Potomac River from Mount Vernon and a few miles away from the nation's capital also heavily influenced its development as an early resort attraction and later as a modern theme park.

Many plantations were constructed with easy access to waterways that often served as transportation routes during antebellum times. These waterways were also utilized by industry in more modern times. For most plantations this meant devastation. For example, the American Sugar Company (later Domino Sugar) built their plant on Three Oaks Plantation downriver from New Orleans. The columned mansion at Three Oaks was renowned for its history and beauty, but was only a hindrance to company officials, who tore the structure down under the cloak of night.

For some few plantations, however, industry has been a savior. San Francisco Plantation, also in Louisiana, was purchased by ECOL (later Marathon Oil) which used the vast fields to build a major oil refinery. But, unlike the American Sugar Company and countless other companies, Marathon Oil restored San Francisco to its original splendor, sectioning off a large portion from its refinery to maintain a tranquil atmosphere. Because the beautifully landscaped grounds are filled with strategically planted trees and shrubs, one cannot even see that the house is virtually surrounded by the mammoth oil refinery, and instead feels that he or she is in the middle of a vast agricultural estate. Today, San Francisco is opened to visitors, who marvel at the exquisite paintings that decorate the ceilings of the mansion.

Most remaining plantation homes today serve far different functions than they did during antebellum times, although it is important to note that many plantations are still used as large farms. Remaining plantation mansions serve as private homes, museums, and organizational, government, or corporate offices. Other southern plantations have been transformed over the years to serve yet other purposes. Many serve as hunting venues, country clubs, and golf courses. But, for each plantation that remains today, hundreds more have been lost to the destructive forces of time.

## Destructive Forces: Causes of Plantation Loss

Just as each of the plantations presented had an intriguing history, each also had an intriguing death. Broadly, these losses can be divided into two categories: preventable losses vs. nonpreventable losses. These categories are not entirely mutually exclusive, as prevention is somewhat relative in many cases. For example, the loss of Orozimbo via the great Galveston hurricane of 1900 was certainly an unpreventable loss. There is little, if anything, anyone at the time could have done to stave off a hurricane or lessen its toll on the built environment of the historic plantation.

In contrast, the loss of Louisiana's Seven Oaks was absolutely preventable. Although there were political barriers to overcome, local city and parish officials could have easily saved the monumental estate had they truly desired to. They fully understood that their actions (or lack thereof) would ultimately lead to the home's destruction at the malevolent edge of a bulldozer. Likewise, the destruction of Kentucky's Mount Brilliant could have also easily been prevented. Had its unappreciative owner not sent a bulldozer through it, the house would obviously still stand. However, saving both of the houses simply represented an inconvenience for their owners, and historic preservation was plainly not a priority. This argument opens a Pandora's box of questions surrounding what motivates historic preservation and what factors prevent it. Although it is clear that such motivations are multifactorial and rooted in financial and emotional issues.

In the story of the destruction of Louisiana's Woodlawn, the case is even more complicated. The master house was abandoned, as were many, and it was later inhabited by a lone sharecropper, who used the plantation mansion's massive rooms as a barn. Although arguably some group or government could have technically restored the house, rescuing it from neglect, in reality little could ultimately be done because the nation was in the grip of World War II. Men were far away on the European front or serving in the Pacific, and most women were busy supporting the war efforts at home while single-handedly raising families. The preservation of plantation architecture was obviously, for understandable reasons, not a main concern. So, although Woodlawn's destruction was in theory preventable, it was certainly not feasible. Therefore, for some purposes it's useful to place the histories of these estates in boxes marked "preventable" vs. "nonpreventable," but there are some that cannot easily fit into one category or the other.

The destruction of these estates can similarly be divided between those that were caused by natural disasters such as flood, natural fires, and hurricanes, and those caused by the hand of man, namely neglect, outright demolition, arson, and the like. These two categories provide a more robust framework, allowing for less ambiguity overall.

Alabama's prized Forks of Cypress plantation mansion, for example, could certainly fit cleanly in the "natural disaster" category. It was struck by lightning and burned to the ground. One could argue that this could have been prevented by equipping the historic structure with modern fire protection devices such as sprinklers (although this would also arguably alter the untouched historic nature of the structure), but our current framework does not consider prevention as a category element.

Likewise Georgia's Casulon plantation mansion was destroyed by fire. However, it would fit cleanly into the "destroyed-by-man" category, as the mysterious fire was maliciously set by an arsonist. Fire, it seems, is perhaps the most common cause of loss

in regards to plantation architecture over the years. Mississippi's Malmaison, Louisiana's Belle Grove, Arkansas's Sylvan Home, and many thousands of others have met their fates in the flames.

"Progress" has destroyed many plantations, and the most poignant examples can be found in South Carolina, where the Santee Cooper Hydroelectric and Navigation Project created two beautiful lakes, a waterway transportation route that spurred much commerce and development, and electricity to power great cities, but it also led to the destruction of two dozen historic plantations. No one can doubt the benefits of the project, but we must also remember what was sacrificed for this gain.

While demolition may be arguably justified in some instances, most cases represent the culmination of years of neglect and failed stewardship on the parts of owners and communities. A prevailing theme is that many lost plantation estates (those that survived the Civil War and natural disasters) were not truly victims of progress, as is often purported. Some were surely destroyed to make way for new and improved structures, as above. And it is obvious that the sites of some former plantations are now occupied by modern buildings. But many plantations were destroyed prior to new construction. After the physical demise of the estates (often years or decades later), the property was empty and available for development.

A predominate story repeated over and over again is one which parallels that of the South itself. The Civil War brought economic devastation. Try as they might, planters could not overcome this ruin, and eventually lost their plantations. Plantations usually passed through various hands and were used for a multitude of functions, as discussed above. Eventually, most then fell into ruin and decay, a state perpetuated and exacerbated by abandonment. And it is here that the real story of the lost plantations is found. As there was no economic role for the built environment of the plantation and as many did not recognize the significance of the structures (especially in years past when there were many remaining plantations), they were often neglected and abandoned.

During the first half of the twentieth century,

few saw the cultural value and even economic potential of the South's many decaying antebellum estates. Certainly the huge profits that had been reaped in antebellum times were long gone, and plantations existed as icons of a bygone, idealized past.

Sentimental locals usually appreciated romantic notions of the old plantations, but often expressed these inclinations through what was essentially vandalism and theft (i.e., removing "souvenirs" from the estates, or "treasure hunting" within the walls or floorboards). Some local and state governments, civic organizations, and other community leadership groups took little notice of these massive heaps of history. Few realized the immeasurably important historical information these disappearing properties held within their built environments, most especially in the architecture outside and around the big house—slave cabins, kitchens, barns, production structures, etc.

Eventually, owners of many properties wanted the estates destroyed, especially in those cases as already discussed, when plantations took on roles different from those they were originally constructed for. Sometimes, this upset locals, politicians, and/or civic or preservation organizations, and sometimes not. Little was done to preserve many of the mansions before these threats, but after such demolition risks were realized there were sometimes outcries ranging from mild community displeasure to outright preservation wars. A few of these efforts were successful, but often they were not.

Of course, this generalization certainly can not fit the histories of most plantations, but it is a story that seems to be repeated over and over again. Kentucky's Mount Brilliant provides the perfect example. The estate was transformed from an antebellum farm to a modern weekend retreat, and its owners wanted the built environment of the property to change with it. Hearing the threats to the historic house, community members cried out, but, in the end, their efforts were useless and the structure was destroyed.

What happened to these estates after their destruction and how communities dealt with the memories of them is yet another tale that illuminates the changing culture of the time.

## Life after Loss

What happened to the plantations of the South after their deaths is in some cases perhaps nearly as intriguing a tale as those of their lives and their declines. It certainly reflects on our own changing culture and in some cases the ways we as a society deal with our past.

Many sites of lost plantations are still historically and culturally valuable to both their local communities and the nation as a whole, while others have faded away to be replaced by various other developments and industries.

Throughout the South, one can easily find neighborhoods that rest upon the former sites of plantations, and a few even bear testimony to this fact, in the neighborhood names, street names, or in informational signage. The residents of Georgia's Retreat Plantation are remembered in the street names of the local area. In other instances, towns, such as Lake Jackson, Texas, have been named in honor of lost plantations.

Many lost plantations are remembered through historical markers, ranging from small informational signs to large monuments. These markers speak to our need as a community to memorialize and remember what came before and how particular locales evolved over time. The markers also represent our own need to remember that which we have lost, and it is to be hoped that they provide a reminder that much is still at risk.

From the Upper South to the Gulf Coast, there are examples of other lost plantation sites that sit vacant, reverting to their natural states. In some cases, "lost" plantations exist in decayed form, ranging from delapidated complexes to overgrown foundations. Arguably, the most picturesque and romantic remains are those of the grand Greek Revival columns standing steadfastly against the winds of time as the structures around them crumbled. The famed columns of Windsor represent such a site. The columns are set in their original location, now a wooded retreat. They give a glimpse of what the main house once was, and provide Americans with something very rare in our country—stone and mortar ruins.

The ruins of Europe and other continents and nations attract great attention and a large number of admirers, but our young country is virtually barren of these noble testaments to time past. The few remaining ruins of plantations are often long forgotten in remote, overgrown locales. But some have been stabilized, preserved, and incorporated into interpretive sites. The ruins at Bulowville in Florida represent such a site, which attracts numerous visitors each year. Other plantation ruins have been incorporated into new developments, such as neighborhoods and golf courses, as small local parks, and as roadside attractions.

Lost plantations have been the site of much archeology, and almost invariably net a prolific amount of artifacts and a greater knowledge of our history. Likewise, although scholarship on these forgotten estates is limited, some plantations have inspired academic dissertations, books, and even exhibits, as is the case with Georgia's Retreat Plantation.

A small number of lost plantations exist as a strong memory among the residents of their former communities. In Louisiana, for example, Belle Grove fans have created everything from prints and needlepoint kits to an Internet discussion group devoted to the memory of the lost plantation. Also in Louisiana, the memory of Seven Oaks and its malicious destruction rests firmly in the minds of local citizens. Artifacts and photographs of the plantation are among the most popular exhibits at the Westwego Historical Museum, and a small roadside park memorializes the plantation site.

A handful of lost plantations have been reconstructed. Greenwood Plantation in St. Francisville, Louisiana (not to be confused with Butler-Greenwood Plantation, also in St. Francisville), is among the most accurate reconstructions in the South. Originally built in 1830 by William Ruffin Barrow, Greenwood Plantation mansion was an imposing columned structure with an unusually heavy cornice and crowning cupola. The house was struck by lightning on August 1, 1960, and it burned to the ground. Eight years later the three-thousand-acre site and remaining charred ruins were purchased by Walton Barnes, who, along with his son Richard, painstakingly rebuilt the mansion using period photographs and images of the structure as guides. Construction was finally completed in November 1984, but it wasn't until the house served as the film location for several movies that furnishings were fully restored.

Although not a complete reconstruction, the exterior of the mansion at Forks of Cypress Plantation inspired the design of the AmSouth (now Regions) Bank in downtown Florence, Alabama. The original columns at Forks of Cypress still stand, and, like those of Mississippi's Windsor, provide a stunning, romantic ruin for local citizens.

Likewise in recent years, there has been a resurgence of immediate reconstruction following grave damage. The mansion at Beauvoir, Confederate president Jefferson Davis's beachfront estate at Biloxi, was badly damaged by Hurricane Katrina. Work began without delay on its total restoration. Laura Plantation in Vacherie, Louisiana, was one of the state's most frequented tourist destinations, with annual attendance of over a hundred thousand visitors. Its innovative tours that meshed local history with the cherished memories from the diary of its inhabitants earned the plantation great acclaim. It was one of the top twenty-five most popular historic house museums in the United States and won the designation of "best history tour in the U. S." by Lonely Planet Travel Network. An August 9, 2004, fire nearly destroyed the house completely. All that remained were charred remnants, but the herculean effort of restoring the mansion inch for inch commenced immediately and continued unceasingly until the plantation was restituted in perfect form.

Lost plantations still hold great cultural significance for Americans. These estates and their inhabitants were once the principal cultural, economic, and political institutions of the South. And, as much as they represent the glory of antebellum times and great achievements in art and architecture, these long-gone plantations also represent man's inhumanity to man—vanished physical evidence of American slavery. But, just as the memories and histories of lost southern plantations should be preserved, the relative few remaining estates must be closely and aggressively protected from both natural threats and individuals and groups that would do them harm.

## Preserving What's Left

There are hundreds of endangered plantation mansions and many plantation complexes that are at risk across the South. If nothing else, this study should provide a cautionary tale for local preservationists and public leaders regarding what can happen and has happened when indifference outweighs active involvement. It should also provide a framework for an understanding of why so many previous efforts have failed, therefore better equipping future preservation projects.

Likewise, by examining what has worked and why it was successful in the past, local governments and citizens can be inspired to fight for future preservation with greater knowledge and information. Although it would certainly take at least another book to truly study the broad successes in plantation preservation, an attempt will be made to briefly mention some of the more obvious traits of effective efforts.

Among the more successful preservation efforts are those undertaken by individuals with a great deal of money, time, and often political influence. Louisiana's Whitney Plantation provides a prime example. Once crumbling, the plantation mansion is currently undergoing a massive renovation to its original state, while structures of the wider complex are being renovated and buildings from other plantation sites are being integrated. Wealthy attorney John Cummings is to be applauded for his efforts in this undertaking. He is spending massive amounts of his own money and time to preserve the historic estate as a memorial to southern slaves. He has also enlisted the help of powerful elected officials including Lieutenant Governor Mitch

Landrieu, who envisions Whitney as an economic and cultural engine for its surrounding region.

For most individuals and communities, the millions of dollars, thousands of hours, and political savvy needed to fuel such an undertaking are not as readily available. But many plantations have been successfully preserved without these resources being present initially. Often, this requires the collective efforts of an organization of concerned members.

The most successful plantation preservation effort by a committee or organization is unquestionably Mount Vernon, the historic home of George Washington. It had fallen into disrepair over the years, and was finally offered for sale by Washington's heirs in 1848, but both the U. S. federal government and the Commonwealth of Virginia declined to purchase it. About ten years later, the Mount Vernon's Ladies Association, led by Ann Pamela Cunningham, bought the plantation for two hundred thousand dollars. Today, the association is the oldest national historic preservation organization in the county, and annually welcomes one million visitors to the plantation. About 450 paid employees and 400 volunteers operate the attraction, which has become the most popular historic estate in America.

While the vast success of Mount Vernon can not be expected of other plantation museums, many similar estates and historic houses have been preserved by organizations of concerned community members and preservationists, and have been quite successful. Many operate as house museums, are self-supportive, and some even turn a respectable profit. The most successful create huge economic impacts for the surrounding communities.

In order for one to begin the process of preserving such an estate, it would be advisable to enlist the help of other concerned people, and incorporation into a nonprofit organization is most helpful. The fact that such a group is actively working ensures that the greatest threat to plantation loss—neglect—is being addressed.

The organization can begin by exploring options, contacting concerned parties, involving the media, bolstering community support, lobbying public officials, and raising funds. And the support of local colleges and universities and similar academic organizations should be actively sought in all of these efforts. A combined effort or at least mutual support from existing local historical societies, preservation organizations, and other similar groups is often beneficial.

The National Trust for Historic Preservation's materials and resources should certainly be consulted early. Also, the National Park Service's Heritage Preservation arm provides grants, guidelines, technical support, and helpful publications for those laboring to preserve historic American buildings.

The creation of a historic district around a threatened estate, its registration with the state historic preservation office and archeological department, and listing on the National Register of Historic Places are all accomplishments that aid the preservation undertaking. Another aid to preservation is the careful documentation of structures in photographs and measured drawings. Such images can and should be submitted to the Historic American Buildings Survey (HABS) to further emphasize and communicate an estate's historic importance. Such organizations face numerous hurdles, but success is achievable. Louisiana's St. Joseph Plantation provides a good example.

Like many Louisiana sugar plantations, St. Joseph has been passed down through a single family for generations, but as families expand, a few generations can net hundreds of heirs. Family sugar corporations, in which family members own stock and vote to install a governing board of cousins, are not at all uncommon in the state even today. The board of St. Joseph Plantation had long pondered over what to do with their decaying mansion, as, long after the death of the grandmother matriarch, the house sat empty and abandoned. In recent years, the distant relatives in the corporation decided to restore the grand columned mansion and open it for tours. The organization enlisted the help of hundreds of family members, sought donations,

and began communicating their efforts to the media and larger community. They also successfully listed the house on the National Register. Today, the renovation of the house is almost completely finished, and outbuildings are being restored as well. The complex is open for tours, and the family corporation and cousins couldn't be happier.

While the St. Joseph project had obvious advantages (i.e., an already established organization that held ownership of the estate, familial ties to the plantation, and some money to begin restoration), community groups and small nonprofits have been similarly successful in saving plantations from demolition. These efforts are, of course, easier if the organization has ownership of the plantation, but if not, a dialogue should be undertaken with whoever does hold it. Donation of plantations to concerned citizens' groups has been accomplished in the past, as in the case of American Oil Company's outright donation of Destrehan Plantation to the River Road Historical Society.

If donation cannot be accomplished, certainly agreements should be drawn up as to the future preservation efforts and role that a community group might play. The group may also play a role in ensuring that owners who are preservation minded are sought for endangered estates. And, if all else fails, groups can lobby for the removal and restitution of plantation structures to safer locations, although this would arguably be at the cost of some of the inherent historical value of the estate. Certainly, legal counsel is advised at this juncture, and the help of both state and national preservation bodies should also be sought. Likewise, there are numerous private preservation and historical organizations that may be willing to aid a like-minded group.

Once ownership or at least control of an estate is gained, there are certainly steps that can and should be taken to preserve these structures, and organizations can begin by focusing on the greatest threats to preservation. In the beginning of this section we discussed categorizing destructive forces into preventable vs. nonpreventable causes. With this framework in mind, one can begin to envision ways to modify preventable causes of loss that may ultimately preserve historic plantation structures.

First, if control of the plantation property is gained by a preservation group, one of the biggest threats—outright demolition—is negated. Next, the threat of fire is one of the principal forces of plantation destruction in the past. Securing plantations from potential arsonists and other vandals by locking gates and doors and installing fences and other security measures should be undertaken. The installation of sprinklers arguably distracts from the historic nature of a structure, but may save it from a future fire. Also, such alterations can be done in a careful and sensitive manner that minimizes the impact. At the very least fire extinguishers should be available.

The stabilization of plantation structures—even ruins—should be of utmost concern. And roofs should be carefully inspected and repaired to prevent damage from rain and other hazardous weather. Historic restoration should be undertaken under the strictest conditions, following local codes while remaining accurate with regards to period architecture. A great wealth of literature has been written pertaining to accurate historical restoration, and most good public libraries should contain at least a few choice references on the topic. Of course, the Internet offers much information as well.

Finally, the function of the building should be addressed. Actually, this is something that should be addressed throughout the project, as the function of a plantation house or complex can guide the evolution of preservation efforts. Developing alternative uses for plantation houses can be most helpful. In some cases, nonprofits have successfully lobbied state or local governments, colleges or universities, or other organizations to purchase plantations for use as parks, museums, libraries, or offices. Other groups have used plantations as their own private headquarters. Several local historical societies, for example, call plantation mansions their home. Yet others have involved business partners to occupy plantation houses as corporate offices or retreats, while maintaining the structures and grounds.

Regardless of the use of a building, the best preservation plans invariably include the preparation of a detailed Historic Structure Report (HSR) and the creation of a long-term management plan. Having a vision and established written goals for a project not only lends an air of professionalism, but also guides and focuses efforts.

If a traditional museum/tour is developed around the plantation, the utmost attention should be paid to robust and well-rounded depictions of the past. In-depth scholarship should be undertaken and a concerted effort to present a full picture of plantation life should be paramount. Such museums can be financially sustaining, and the incorporation of bed and breakfast facilities, gift shops, restaurants, and wedding and event services can certainly bolster funding for upkeep.

The creation of a plantation museum is a tremendous undertaking and most often requires large sums of money, years of dedication, and great endurance by an active organization. Even then, the strongest efforts can sometimes fail. If you don't have the opportunity to spearhead such an undertaking yourself, there are many ways to get involved in local preservation efforts. For example, readers can make a difference by supporting and volunteering with organizations that are involved in similar preservation pursuits and by keeping informed of preservation crises, especially as they are related to threats to southern plantations. Simply reading these lines and educating yourself about what treasures we have lost and are currently losing is a great start!

## Final Thoughts

The South is a unique and marvelous invention of America—a turbulent adolescent of a nation that, like a rising phoenix, tends to reinvent itself periodically. Proud and honorable, the United States has achieved more in our short history than any other country, but it is those traits that define and engender our success—present-minded progress, innovation, and independence—that have also led some to disregard historic architecture, often abandoning it completely. In Europe, our older, steadier predecessor, architecture routinely survives for centuries. Much of the built environment of the continent was constructed long before the idea of the United States was even conceived in the minds of our founding fathers. The ideas of civic duty, stewardship, and accountability to future generations that pervade more ancient nations did not deeply permeate the American psyche. But, as America matures, interest in our past and concern for the preservation of our historic architecture is ever more present, and Americans are participating and actively getting involved in preservation projects. Still, more must be done.

Those relatively few remaining plantations that dot the modern American landscape must be preserved. The reality that not many truly grasp is that once one of these magnificent estates is lost, it can never be fully regained, even with a complete reconstruction (which is an incredibly rare feat in and of itself). Sadly, plantation houses and complexes represent much of the South's only physical connection to its antebellum era—a time when humans were held as property. If nothing else, the plantations of the South, our quickly dissolving architectural links to the past, should be preserved to memorialize those whose forced labor and ingenuity built them.

Certainly future generations of Americans will look favorably upon those heroes who fight to save history, and likewise they will frown upon those who destroy it, just as we feel incredible disappointment towards those men and women who played a role in the deliberate, often malicious destruction of many of the structures showcased in this volume. Perhaps the stewardship of future societies will differ from our own, but we should at least allow future peoples the option of exercising such stewardship—it is impossible for forthcoming preservationists to save that which a previous generation has already destroyed.

Furthermore, Americans must fight diligently to preserve the rapidly fading memories of those plantations already lost. The documents, images, records, and stories of these historic estates can be and often are easily lost, unless active efforts are undertaken to share and protect them. More scholarship is needed with regards to these estates that make up the great bulk of the plantation past.

The memories of the South are the memories of America, defining our past and shaping our future. Our dynamically emerging preservation efforts also define who we are, as we sustain and defend the fragile yet paramount pieces of our past for their value now and in the future.

"It has been most truly said . . . that these old buildings do not belong to us only; that they have belonged to our forefathers, and they will belong to our descendants unless we play them false. They are not in any sense our property, to do as we like with. We are only trustees for those that come after us. So I say nothing but absolute necessity can excuse the destruction of these buildings; and I say, further, that such a necessity has never yet existed in our time."
—William Morris

# Notes

## Introduction

1. In *Delta Sugar: Louisiana's Vanishing Plantation Landscape* (53), John B. Rehder estimates that in 1860, in the U.S. South there were 46,274 agricultural estates with twenty or more slaves.

2. Scholarship in general is greatly lacking with regard to the built environments where slaves actually lived and worked, but one notable exception is John Michael Vlach's *Back of the Big House: The Architecture of Slavery*, which broke new ground in its analysis and portrayal of the physical realm of slaves on southern plantations.

## Chapter 1. The Upper South, East: Virginia, West Virginia, and Maryland

1. Historical information on Rosewell was collected from several reliable sources: Rosewell, Historic American Buildings Survey, Library of Congress, Washington, D.C.; Bryan Clark Green, Calder Loth, and William M. S. Rasmussen, *Lost Virginia: Vanished Architecture of the Old Dominion* (Charlottesville: Howell Press, 2001), 11–12; "Rosewell Ruins," http://www.rosewell.org/history.shtml; "Timeline," http://www.rosewell.org/timeline.shtml (accessed 2 December 2007).

2. Mabel Moses, "Oak Hill," Works Progress Administration of Virginia, 1937.

3. Samuel Hairston, the builder of Oak Hill, was the great-grandson of Peter Hairston, the progenitor of the family. Samuel married his cousin, Agnes J. P. Wilson, who was the great-great-granddaughter of Peter Hairston. Such consanguinity was common, and it served to consolidate family wealth and power, among other purposes. See lineage charts in Henry Wiencek, *The Hairstons: An American Family in Black and White* (New York: St. Martin's, 2000).

4. Moses, "Oak Hill."

5. Ibid.

6. Edith Tunis Sale, ed., *Historic Gardens of Virginia* (Richmond: James River Garden Club, 1923), 320–323.

7. Biographical Note, George Hairston Papers, University of North Carolina at Chapel Hill; Moses, "Oak Hill."

8. Ibid; Sale, *Historic Gardens*, 320–323.

9. See the similar story involving the slaves of Mississippi's Homewood Plantation in chapter six.

10. Wiencek, *The Hairstons*, 36.

11. George Hairston was the second of seven children of Samuel Hairston and Agnes John Peter Wilson. He was born in 1822, and died in 1925.

12. Anne Elizabeth Lash was the daughter of William Lash and Anne Powell Hughes. She was born in 1834, and died in 1925.

13. George Hairston Papers.

14. Wiencek, *The Hairstons*, 40–43.

15. Information on Ossian Hall comes from several definitive sources, among them: Ossian Hall, Historic American Buildings Survey, Library of Congress, Washington, D. C.; Bryan Clark Green, Calder Loth, and William M. S. Rasmussen, *Lost Virginia: Vanished Architecture of the Old Dominion* (Charlottesville: Howell Press, 2001), 34; Donna Chasen, "Ossian Hall Destroyed Mansion Had Ties to Lee-Custis family," *The Free Lance-Star*, 14 January 2006.

16. Today, there is debate over the authenticity of Macpherson's work. Some doubt that Macpherson's works were based on translations of ancient texts, while others argue that Macpherson used ancient texts, but added significantly to them and changed them dramatically. Still others quarrel regarding the origins of the material, suggesting that the texts were in fact Irish rather than Scottish. The debates rage on.

17. Eleanor Custis was the widow of John Parke Custis, Martha Washington's son. Dr. Stuart is mentioned extensively in the diaries of George Washington.

18. For more information on Joseph L. Bristow, see Adelbert Bower Sageser, *Joseph L. Bristow: Kansas Progressive* (Lawrence: University Press of Kansas, 1968); William H. Mitchell, "Joseph L. Bristow, Kansas Insurgent in the U. S. Senate, 1909–1915," master's thesis, University of Kansas, 1952; and Joseph W. Snell, ed., *Joseph Little Bristow Papers, 1894–1925, in the Kansas State Historical Society* (Topeka: Kansas State Historical Society, 1967), microfilm, 119 reels with guide.

19. Although both Matthews and Fitzhugh believed the acreage to be accurate, the original tract sold to Fitzhugh was actually closer to twenty-four thousand acres.

20. A number of important documents, along with reliable secondary sources, piece together the history of Ravensworth. Among them are Ravensworth, Historic American Buildings Survey, Library of Congress, Washington, D.C.; Green, Loth, and Rasmussen, *Lost Virginia*, 39; William Fitzhugh, *William

tions by Assistant U.S. Attorney Mary Grace Quackenbos, including her final report on Sunnyside, are held in the National Archives in Washington, D.C.

21. As quoted in Willard B. Gatewood, "Sunnyside: The Evolution of an Arkansas Plantation, 1840–1945," in *Shadows over Sunnyside*, ed. Jeannie M. Whayne, 14.

22. Elisabeth Garr Lawrence, "Preserve Farm's Brilliant History," *Lexington Herald-Leader,* 18 November 2002; John Stamper, "Mount Brilliant to Be Razed," *Lexington Herald-Leader,* 19 October 2002.

23. Ibid.

24. Associated Press, "Historic Mansion Faces Wrecking Ball," *The Enquirer,* 11 August 2002.

25. Lawrence, "Preserve Farm's Brilliant History."

26. Ibid.; Nell Blair Vaughn, "Polio Fight Part of Mt. Brilliant's History," *Lexington Herald-Leader,* 21 October 2002.

27. Beverly Fortune, "Brilliant Moves," *Lexington Herald-Leader,* 8 November 2002.

28. Ibid.

29. Ibid.

30. Stamper, "Mount Brilliant to Be Razed."

31. Ibid.

32. Associated Press, "Historic Mansion Faces Wrecking Ball."

33. "The Loss of Mount Brilliant," Joint Statement of Blue Grass Trust and Greg Goodman, http://www.bluegrasstrust .org/news/stories/BRILLIANt-2.htm (accessed 30 March 2005).

34. Stamper, "Mount Brilliant to Be Razed"; Associated Press, "Mansion Razed after Attempts to Preserve It Come Up Short," *Courier-Journal,* 24 November 2002.

35. The greatest sources of information on the history of Reverie are John and Betty Walley, who graciously shared information with the author. An interview conducted with the last owner of the house, John Walley, by Dr. John H. DeBerry for the Memphis State University Oral History Research Office Project on June 8, 1970, also contains much information about the estate. A transcript of this interview is held in the Special Collections of the Ned R. McWherter Library at the University of Memphis. Published materials on the early history of the plantation include John H. DeBerry, "La Grange–La Belle Village" *Tennessee Historical Quarterly* (Summer 1971): 133–153, and Dorothy Rich Morton, *Nineteenth Century Homes of Fayette County,* published by the author, 1974. History on the Walleys' restoration of the plantation is chronicled in Mary

Alice Quinn, "The Homes of La Belle Village," *Commercial Appeal,* 22 January 1967. The tragic story of the loss of the mansion was recounted after it occurred in Lawrence Buser, "Blaze Consumes Home, History," *Commercial Appeal,* 12 November 1987.

36. Mary Alice Quinn, "The Homes of La Belle Village," *Commercial Appeal*, 22 January 1967.

37. Ibid.

38. Ibid.

39. Buser, "Blaze Consumes Home, History."

## Chapter 3. The Carolinas

1. Anne Sinkler Whaley LeClercq, ed., *Between North and South: The Letters of Emily Wharton Sinkler, 1842–1865* (Columbia: University of South Carolina Press, 2001), 200. See also Douglas W. Bostick. *Sunken Plantations: The Santee Cooper Project* (Charleston, South Carolina: The History Press, 2008).

2. It is interesting to note that today the impact to historic and culturally significant properties and resources would have to be studied before a federally funded project such as the Santee Cooper project could move forward. The National Historic Preservation Act of 1966 as amended provides certain protections and mandates a so-called Section 106 Review of federal actions in order to guage impact. It also provides the Advisory Council on Historic Preservation the opportunity to comment on such projects. A prime example of this process in action can be seen through the development of the Tennessee-Tombigbee Waterway, which connects the Tennessee and Tombigbee rivers. For example, in 1987, the impact that the construction and expansion of a barge-loading facility in Columbus, Mississippi, would have on Waverly Plantation, a National Historic Landmark, was taken into consideration. A resulting agreement protected Waverly and its surrounding environment while allowing for the necessary industrial constructions in a way that limited its impact and maximized its economic impact. For more information, see Jeffrey K. Stine, "The Tennessee-Tombigbee Waterway and the Evolution of Cultural Resources Management," *The Public Historian*, vol. 14, no. 2 (Spring 1992): 7–30.

3. J. Russell Cross, *Historic Ramblin's through Berkeley* (Columbia, South Carolina: R. L. Bryan, Co., 1985), 287–288.

4. Pooshee, Historic American Buildings Survey (HABS); Samuel Wilson Ravenel, "Christmas at Pooshee," unpublished

manuscript, 1903, Charles Stevens Dwight Papers, University of South Carolina, South Caroliniana Library.

5. Ravenel, "Christmas at Pooshee," 4.

6. Ibid., 6.

7. Cross, *Historic Ramblin's*, 287–289.

8. Ravenel, "Christmas at Pooshee," 1.

9. Ibid., 7–8.

10. Ibid., 4–5.

11. Ibid., 8–9.

12. Ibid., 10.

13. Ibid., 10–11.

14. Ibid., 11–14.

15. Ibid., 17–19.

16. Ibid., 15–19.

17. Buzz Williams, "General Wade Hampton III: Noble Summer Resident," *The Chattooga Quarterly* (Spring 1999).

18. Millwood (Wade Hampton Mansion) Ruins, Historic American Buildings Survey (HABS), Library of Congress.

19. Ibid.; Millwood—National Register of Historic Places Nomination Folder, South Carolina Department of Archives and History.

20. Ibid.

21. Ibid.; Virginia Meynard, *The Venturers: The Hampton, Harrison, Earle Families of Virginia, South Carolina, and Texas* (Greenville, South Carolina: Southern Historical Press, 1981), 173.

22. Houmas, a famed plantation with a mansion significant for its incredible architecture, is currently open for tours to the public.

23. Meynard, *The Venturers*, 976–981.

24. Millwood—National Register of Historic Places Nomination Folder, South Carolina Department of Archives and History; Buzz Williams, "General Wade Hampton III."

25. Ibid.; Millwood, HABS.

26. "Possessions Saved, Pillars Remain, the Past Remembered," *Historically Speaking, A Quarterly Newsletter of Historic Columbia*, vol. 43, issue 3 (Winter 2005).

27. Prospect Hill references include "Prospect Hill," Historic American Buildings Survey, Library of Congress; Frances Benjamin Johnston and Thomas Tileston Waterman, *The Early Architecture of North Carolina* (Chapel Hill: University of North Carolina Press, 1941), 112–120, 40–41; Constance M. Greiff, ed., *Lost America: From the Atlantic to the Mississippi* (Princeton, New Jersey: Pyne Press, 1971), 86–87; Sarah E. Mitchell, "Similar Federal Homes in Southside Virginia and Northern North Carolina," http://www.vintagedesigns.com/architectuer/fed/vanchome/ (accessed 15 December 2005).

28. Samuel Gaillard Stoney, *Plantations of the Carolina Low Country* (repr.; New York: Dover Publications, 1989), 77.

29. As quoted in LeClercq, ed., *Between North and South*, 11.

30. As quoted in LeClercq, ed., *Between North and South*, 13–14.

31. Stoney, *Plantations*, 77.

32. LeClercq, ed., *Between North and South*, 18–19.

33. Information on the history of Springfield was abstracted from several sources: Springfield and Springfield, Kitchen Oven, Historic American Buildings Survey, Library of Congress, Washington, D.C.; Thomas T. Waterman, *A Survey of the Early Buildings in the Region of the Proposed Santee and Pinopolis Reservoirs in South Carolina* (National Park Service, 1939); Stoney, *Plantations*; F. M. Kirk, "Springfield Plantation," http://www.rootsweb.com/scbchs/spring.html (accessed 5 November 2007).

34. Information on Stoney-Baynard Plantation can be found documented in Stoney-Baynard House, SC-863, Historic American Buildings Survey, Library of Congress. Furthermore, two publications of the Chicora Foundation provide additional insight: Natalie Adams and Michael Trinkley, *Archaeological Testing of the Stoney/Baynard Plantation, Hilton Head Island, Beaufort County, South Carolina,* Research Series 28 (Columbia: Chicora Foundation, 1991); and Michael Trinkley, *Further Investigation of the Stoney/Baynard Main House, Hilton Head Island, Beaufort County, South Carolina,* Research Series 47 (Columbia: Chicora Foundation, 1996).

35. See the U.S. Coastal and Geodesic Survey Chart: *Sea coast of South Carolina from the mouth of the Savannah River to the May River, 1859–60*.

36. The Inflation Calculator http://www.westegg.com/inflation/infl.cgi (accessed 10 February 2008).

37. The history of White Hall Plantation is abstracted from several definite sources, among them Waterman, *A Survey of the Early Buildings*; Stoney, *Plantations*; F. M. Kirk, "White Hall Plantation, White and Porcher Families," http://www.rootsweb.ancestry.com/~scbchs/whitehall.html (accessed 23 February 2008).

38. Susan R. Jervey and Charlotte St. J. Ravenel, *Two Diaries from Middle St. John's, Berkeley, South Carolina* (Pinopolis, South Carolina: St. John's Hunting Club, 1921), 37.

39. J. H. Easterby, "Memoirs of Frederick Augustus

Porcher," *South Carolina Historical and Genealogical Magazine,* vol. 45 (1944): 39.

40. Mrs. A. P. Leise Palmer Gaillard, "The Rocks: A Sketch," August 11, 1942, http://www.rootsweb.ancestry.com/~scbchs/r5.html (accessed 14 April 2008).

41. Ibid.

42. Jonathan Edwards (1703–1758) was said to have been America's "most important and original philosophical theologian." Jonathan Edwards College, the oldest residential college of Yale University, was named for him. Numerous books and articles have been written about his life, his beliefs, and his work.

43. Margaret Devereux, *Plantation Sketches* (Cambridge: Riverside Press, 1906), ix.

44. Ibid., 3.

45. Ibid., 4.

46. Ibid., 23.

47. Ibid., 31.

48. Ibid., 25.

49. Ibid., 18.

## Chapter 4. Georgia

1. James W. Harris was born in 1794. He was the son of Revolutionary War hero John Harris, who had fought in the Battle of Kettle Creek.

2. Much of the early history of Casulon was abstracted from an article by Kathryn Gray-White, "Casulon Plantation Lives On," *North Georgia Journal* (Summer 1998). Primary sources were consulted and are cited in subsequent notes. Much of the contemporary history has been documented in various newspaper articles also cited in later notes.

3. Harold Bush-Brown, "Casulon Plantation," Historic American Buildings Survey, Library of Congress.

4. Gray-White, "Casulon Plantation Lives On."

5. James S. Boynton was a lawyer by profession. He fought bravely during the Civil War and was elevated to the rank of colonel.

6. "Governor Boynton's Marriage," *Atlanta Constitution,* 1 May 1883.

7. Gray-White, "Casulon Plantation Lives On."

8. Kimball House has the distinction of being Atlanta's first hotel. It burned to the ground only months after the governor and Susie Harris had honeymooned there. A new Kimball House was built and the hotel reopened in 1885.

9. Gray-White, "Casulon Plantation Lives On"; "Governor Boynton's Marriage."

10. Wayne Ford, "Casulon Remembered, Oconee Residents Have Fond Memories of Antebellum Mansion," *Athens Banner-Herald,* 29 May 2002.

11. Ibid.; Gray-White, "Casulon Plantation Lives On."

12. Ibid.

13. "Georgia Plantation House Survives War and Time Only to Succumb to Fire," *Civil War Interactive,* 29 March 2002, http://www.civilwarinteractive.com/casulonfire.htm (accessed 11 July 2002).

14. Ibid.; Wayne Ford, "Fire Destroys Historic Walton Plantation," *Athens Banner-Herald,* 27 March 2002; Wayne Ford, "Sheriff: Plantation Fire Cause May Never Be Known," *Athens Banner-Herald,* 16 February 2003.

15. Kevin Conner, "Quarry Still Has Stone Cold Opposition," *Athens Banner-Herald*, 28 April 2002; Julie Phillips Jordan, "Rockin' the Quarry, Benefit Concert Is Part of Residents' 12-year Battle to Fight Proposed Rock Quarry," *Athens Banner-Herald,* 4 April 2002.

16. The history of Mulberry Grove has been meticulously documented by Works Progress Administration's Savannah Writers' Project. Originally published in the *Georgia Historical Quarterly,* a set of articles on Mulberry Grove was later compiled, together with other similar plantation histories from the Savannah Writers' Project, into a volume called *Savannah River Plantations,* which itself was originally published in 1947 by the Georgia Historical Society. It was reprinted in 1997 by Oglethorpe Press of Savannah. The articles on Mulberry Grove appear on pages 55–92 of the reprinted book.

17. Mary Granger, ed., *Savannah River Plantations* (Savannah: Oglethorpe Press, 1997), 60.

18. Ibid., 68.

19. Ibid., 72.

20. Ibid., 73.

21. The history of Hampton Plantation has been meticulously documented in R. Edwin Green and Mary A. Green, *St. Simons: A Summary of Its History* (St. Simons Island, Georgia: published by the authors, 1982).

22. For more information about the interesting public life of Major Pierce Butler, see Francis Coglan, "Pierce Butler, 1744–1822, First Senator from South Carolina," *South Carolina Historical Magazine* 78 (April 1977): 104–119; Lewright B. Sikes, *The Public Life of Pierce Butler, South Carolina Statesman* (Washington: University Press of America, 1979).

23. John and Pierce were the sons of Major Pierce Butler's daughter Sarah and Dr. John Mease of Philadelphia.

24. Fanny Kemble was born on November 27, 1809, in London, England. She came from a prominent family of actors. She was a very popular actress, having begun in the profession in an effort to support her family financially. Although she found much success in the theater, her true love was literature and writing.

25. Frances Anne Kemble, *Journal of a Residence on a Georgia Plantation,* Project Gutenberg EBook, http://www.gutenberg.org/files/12422/12422-h/12422-h.htm (accessed 5 May 2005).

26. Ibid.

27. Ibid.

28. The Inflation Calculator, http://www.westegg.com/inflation/infl.cgi (accessed 8 February 2008).

29. A definitive history of the Hermitage appears in Granger, ed., *Savannah River Plantations,* 418–450. The Historic American Buildings Survey contains important architectural drawings, photographs, and written text regarding this estate.

30. As quoted in Granger, ed., *Savannah River Plantations,* 423–424.

31. *Georgia Gazette,* 22 September 1763; Granger, ed., *Savannah River Plantations,* 424.

32. *Georgia Gazette,* 10 January 1776.

33. *The Georgian,* 11 June 1821.

34. These six McAlpin children were the offspring of Henry's second wife, who died at the age of thirty-two. The boys were raised at the Hermitage by their father's mother-in-law from his first marriage, Mrs. Melrose, while the girls were sent to a relative in Charleston. The children were Angus McAlpin, Henry McAlpin, James Wallace McAlpin, Donald McAlpin, Ellen McAlpin, who later married John Schley, and Isabel McAlpin, who later married William Schley.

35. As quoted in Granger, ed., *Savannah River Plantations,* 449.

36. Several important sources regarding the history of Retreat Plantation are available. R. Edwin Green and Mary A. Green's *St. Simons: A Summary of Its History* (published by the authors, 1982) meticulously documents the history of this and several other lost plantations. Florence Marye's *The Story of the Page-King Family of Retreat Plantation, St. Simons Island and of the Golden Islands of Georgia* (published by the author, 2000) provides much useful information, as does Mildred Nix Huie and Bessie Lewis's *King's Retreat Plantation, St. Simons*

*Island, Georgia Today and Yesterday* (published by the authors, 1980). Retreat Plantation and its associated slave hospital have also both been separately documented in Historic American Buildings Survey. Several publications focus on Thomas Butler King and his family; among them are Stephen Berry, "More Alluring at a Distance: Absentee Patriarchy and the Thomas Butler King Family," *Georgia Historical Quarterly,* vol. 81, no. 4 (Winter 1997): 863–896; Malcolm Bell, Jr., *Major Butler's Legacy: Five Generations of a Slaveholding Family* (Athens: University of Georgia Press, 1987) and *T. Butler King of Georgia* (Athens: University of Georgia Press, 1964). A variety of original documents from the plantation have been preserved by the University of North Carolina at Chapel Hill and are in the William Page Papers, the Thomas Butler King Papers, and also in the associated William Audley Couper Papers. The Georgia Department of Archives and History holds an original record book from Retreat Plantation. As noted in the text, the plantation and its slave community have been the subject of much recent scholarship and celebration. Historian Melanie Pavich-Lindsay and artist Lisa Tuttle produced a successful exhibit, "Retreat: Palimpsest of a Georgia Sea Island Plantation," and a companion installation called "A Slave Speaks of Silence." Both were very well received. In addition, Pavich-Lindsay has edited a book entitled *Anna: The Letters of a St. Simons Island Plantation Mistress, 1817–1859* (Athens: University of Georgia Press, 2002), which further illuminates Anna Matilda Page King's unusual role on this intriguing lost plantation.

37. Pavich-Lindsay, ed., *Anna,* xx–xxi.

38. Ibid., 66, 129.

39. Ibid., 128.

40. Neptune Small was born in 1831. His primary role at Retreat was serving the King children and particularly being a close companion to Lord King, who was nearly the same age. After being freed and returning from the war he retired to Retreat, where he was given a tract of land from the Kings' property in reward for his faithful service. He died in 1907, and he was buried on Retreat Plantation. Today, his property has been turned into Neptune Park, a recreational area named in honor of this remarkable man. Neptune Small's intriguing story has been memorialized in a children's book by Pamela Bauer Mueller, *Neptune's Honor: A Story of Loyalty and Love* (St. Simons Island, Georgia: Pinata Publishing, 2005).

41. The transcript of Neptune Small's statement was recorded in an article, "Faithful Neptune Small," by J. E. Dart that was published in an unknown local newspaper. It was found

in a collection of clippings compiled by Abbie Fuller Graham called "Old Mill Days 1874–1908" at St. Simons Island Public Library. This article was graciously submitted to the author by Ms. Amy Hedrick of Waynesville, Georgia. It is also published online at: http://www.rootsweb.com/~gaglynn/history/people/neptune/article1.htm (accessed July 2006).

42. There are numerous published articles and documents about Jekyll Island and Horton House Plantation; however, the definitive history of the estate is an unpublished report by Colin Brooker entitled "The Major William Horton House, Jekyll Island, Georgia. Analysis, Care and Display." It was written for Brooker Preservation Design Consultants in 2001. The Historic American Buildings Survey documents regarding Horton House (including reports, photographs, and measured drawings) also provide much insight into this important estate. The Jekyll Island Museum holds an archive of important documents relating to the history of the island and of the plantation and families who lived there. Martha L. Keber has written a fascinating biography of Christophe du Bignon entitled *Seas of Gold, Seas of Cotton: Christophe Poulain DuBignon of Jekyll Island* (Athens: University of Georgia Press, 2002). A handful of books have been written about various aspects of Jekyll Island; among the most notable are William B. McCash, *The Jekyll Island Club: Southern Haven for America's Millionaires.* (Athens: University of Georgia Press, 1989); June Hall McCash, *The Jekyll Island Cottage Colony* (Athens: University of Georgia Press, 1998); and June Hall McCash, *Jekyll Island's Early Years: From Prehistory Through Reconstruction* (Athens: University of Georgia Press, 1998).

43. Francis Moore, *A Voyage to Georgia Begun in the Year 1735* (London: Jacob Robinson, 1744).

44. As quoted in "Horton House (Remains)," addendum, Historic American Buildings Survey.

45. Ibid.

46. Ibid.

47. As quoted in Colin Brooker, "The Major William Horton House, Jekyll Island, Georgia. Analysis, Care and Display," Brooker Preservation Design Consultants, 2001, 30.

48. Ibid.

49. One week prior to the *Wanderer's* arrival, the du Bignons had published an advertisement in the *Savannah Daily Morning News* warning that no one was allowed to trespass on Jekyll Island, lending some evidence to the theory that the ship's arrival at their plantation had been preplanned.

50. For more information about the interesting incident of the illegal slave ship landing at Jekyll Island, see Erik Calonius, *The Wanderer: The Last American Slave Ship and the Conspiracy That Set Its Sails* (New York: St. Martin's Press, 2006).

**Chapter 5. Alabama and Florida**

1. Lewis N. Wynne and John T. Parks, *Florida's Antebellum Homes* (Charleston, South Carolina: Arcadia Publishing, 2004), 22.

2. Information on the history of Rocky Hill was compiled from several authoritative sources, among them "Rocky Hill Mansion," Historic American Buildings Survey, Library of Congress, Washington, D.C.; Dorothy Gentry, *Life and Legend of Lawrence County, Alabama* (Tuscaloosa: Nottingham, 1962); Evelyn Wood Owen, "Rocky Hill Castle," in *Historic Homes of Alabama and Their Traditions*, Alabama Members of the National League of American Pen Women, eds. (Birmingham: Birmingham Pub. Co., 1969); and Lawrence County Heritage Book Committee, *The Heritage of Lawrence County, Alabama* (Clanton, Alabama: Heritage Pub. Consultants, 1998).

3. It is interesting to note that once the construction of the tower was complete, carpenter Hugh Jones went to work at Oak Grove, a neighboring plantation. Here he devised and operated an unusual experimental mill for Mrs. George Washington Foster. Together the duo attempted to granulate sugar by crushing ripe watermelons. Apparently the trials failed.

4. Lawrence County Heritage Book Committee, *Heritage of Lawrence County*, 45.

5. As quoted in Owen, "Rocky Hill Castle."

6. James Jackson was the eleventh child of James and Mary Steel Jackson. The family owned a linen bleachery in Ireland.

7. Sarah Moore grew up in Halifax, North Carolina. In her family were three colonial governors of Carolina, including Sir John Yeamans, who was one of the founders of Charleston, and Colonel James Moore. At the age of seventeen, she married her cousin Samuel McCullough, but he tragically drowned soon after the wedding.

8. Sally Moore Brace, "James Jackson," *Lauderdale County Pictures of the Past,* 1 September 1999, http://www.rootsweb.com/~allauder/pic-jamesjackson.htm (accessed 28 March 2006); William Lindsey McDonald, *A Walk Though the Past: People and Places of Florence and Lauderdale County, Alabama* (Florence: Country Lane Printing, 1997), 9; J. Frazer Smith, *Plantation Houses and Mansions of the Old South* (New York: Dover Publications, 1993), 78; Elizabeth Kirkman O'Neal, "The

Forks of Cypress: The Home of James Jackson," unpublished academic paper, n.d. (from the Local History/Genealogy Department, Florence-Lauderdale Public Library, Florence, Alabama).

9. O'Neal, "Forks of Cypress"; Cherovise Hamilton, "The Forks of Cypress," unpublished academic paper, 1978 (from the Local History/Genealogy Department, Florence-Lauderdale Public Library, Florence, Alabama).

10. Smith, *Plantation Houses*, 77–78.; Forks of Cypress, HABS.

11. Ibid.

12. Ibid.; O'Neal, "Forks of Cypress"; Hamilton, "Forks of Cypress."

13. Ibid.; http://www.legislature.state.al.us/misc/history/past_senate_ldrs.html (accessed 29 March 2006).

14. Smith, *Plantation Houses*, 77–78; Forks of Cypress, HABS; Bill Warren, personal correspondence with the author, 22 February 2006.

15. "Imported Stallion, for 1838" (advertisement), *North Alabamian* (Tuscumbia, Alabama), 6 April 1838; "The Thorough Bred Stallion" (advertisement), *North Alabamian* (Tuscumbia, Alabama), 6 April 1838.

16. "A beloved Friend has fallen! and the People mourn!," *The Enquirer* (Florence, Alabama), 22 August 1840.

17. Obituary of Sarah M. Jackson, *Florence Gazette,* 27 December 1979, 3.

18. Ibid.; http://www.nostalgiaville.com/travel/Alabama/florence/florence%20al.htm (accessed 11 February 2006); "Historic Forks Burns to Ground Monday," *Florence Herald,* 9 June 1966, p. 1.

19. Hamilton, "Forks of Cypress," 12.

20. Smith, *Plantation Houses*, 77–78; Bob Martin, "Historic Forks Burns," *Tri-Cities Daily,* 6 June 1966, p. 1; Forks of Cypress, HABS; Bill Warren, personal correspondence with the author, 22 February 2006.

21. Hamilton, "Forks of Cypress," 11.

22. Ibid.

23. Bill Warren, personal correspondence with the author, 22 February 2006.

24. See Jeff McGee, "Jackson Cemetery," unpublished academic paper, University of North Alabama, 1976; and Loftin Flowers and Thompson Mefford, "The Forks of Cypress Black Cemetery" [s.l.: s.n., n.d.] (both from the Local History/Genealogy Department, Florence-Lauderdale Public Library, Florence, Alabama).

25. Ibid.

26. A few sources provide scant histories of Samuel Pickens's Umbria Plantation. The most notable is a government report: Jeff Mansell, *A Report Compiled for the Cahaba Trace Commission,* Cahaba Trace Commission with support from the Alabama Legislature, July 1992. Primary source material including the extensive diaries of two of Samuel Pickens's sons—James "Jamie" Pickens and Samuel Pickens—has been published in G. Ward Hubbs, ed., *Voices from Company D: Diaries by the Greensboro Guards, Fifth Alabama Infantry Regiment, Army of Northern Virginia* (Athens: University of Georgia Press, 2003).

27. The Inflation Calculator, http://www.westegg.com/inflation/infl.cgi (accessed 9 February 2008).

28. Hubbs, ed., *Voices from Company D*, 99–100.

29. Ibid., 108.

30. Ibid., 260-261.

31. The history of New Smyrna Plantation has been extensively explored in several definitive works. This study relied primarily on three well-documented sources: Patricia C. Griffin, "Blue Gold: Andrew Turnbull's New Smyrna Plantation," in *Colonial Plantations and Economy in Florida*, ed. Jane G. Landers (Gainesville: University Press of Florida, 2000), 39–68; Alice Strickland, *Ashes on the Wind: The Story of the Lost Plantations* (Volusia County, Florida: Volusia County Historical Commission, 1985); and Carita Doggett Corse, *Dr. Andrew Turnbull and the New Smyrna Colony of Florida* (Chapel Hill: University of North Carolina Press, 1919).

32. Griffin, "Blue Gold," 58.

33. The history of Bulowville was abstracted from E. H. Butts, "Bulowville," in *Ashes on the Wind: The Story of the Lost Plantations,* ed. Alice Strickland (Volusia County, Florida: Volusia County Historical Commission, 1985), 51–53.

34. Transcribed letter from John James Audubon, 31 December 1831, in Strickland, *Ashes on the Wind*, 55-58.

35. Ibid.

36. There are several important resources regarding the history of David Levy Yulee and his plantations, Margarita at Homosassa and Cottonwood near Archer. The University of Florida holds forty-two boxes of Yulee's personal, political, and business papers, including letters, legal papers, newspaper clippings, and much other ephemera that has been meticulously preserved and microfilmed. In addition, other sources include Robin L. Denson, *Yulee Sugar Mill Ruins: The Archaeological and Historical Study of the State Historic Site, Citrus County*

(Crystal River, Florida: Gulf Archaeology Research Institute, 1977); Leon Hühner, "David L. Yulee, Florida's First State Senator," in *Jews in the South,* ed. Leonard Dinnerstein and Mary Dale Palsson (Baton Rouge: Louisiana State University Press, 1973); Celeste H. Kavanaugh, *David Levy Yulee: A Man and His Vision* (Fernandina Beach, Florida: Amelia Island Museum of History, 1995); Joseph Cary Adler, "The Public Career of Senator David Levy Yulee," Ph.D. dissertation, Case Western Reserve University, 1973; Mills M. Lord, Jr., "David Levy Yulee, Statesmen and Railroad Builder," master's thesis, University of Florida, 1940; Arthur W. Thompson, "David Yulee: A Study of Nineteenth Century Thought and Enterprise," Ph.D. dissertation, Columbia University, 1954.

37. Ada Sterling, *A Belle of the Fifties: Memoirs of Mrs. Clay, of Alabama* (New York: Doubleday, 1905), 54.

38. As quoted in Hühner, "David L. Yulee," 70.

39. Sterling, *Belle of the Fifties,* 147–148.

40. The history of Richard Oswald's Mount Oswald Plantation is well documented. A well-researched and written account of the estate's history can be found in Daniel L. Schafer, "'A Swamp of an Investment'?: Richard Oswald's British East Florida Plantation Experiment," in Landers, ed., *Colonial Plantation and Economy in Florida,* 11–38. Also, the plantation is documented in Strickland, *Ashes on the Wind,* 13–15. A variety of primary source material can be found in George E. Rogers with David R. Chestnut, eds., *The Papers of Henry Laurens* (Columbia: University of South Carolina Press, 1974).

41. Henry Laurens (March 6, 1724–December 8, 1792) was born in Charleston, South Carolina, and became a prominent rice planter. He later served in numerous leadership positions during the American Revolution, including being a delegate to the Continental Congress, third president of the Second Continental Congress, vice president of South Carolina, and minister to Holland, among others.

42. Rogers with Chestnut, eds., *Papers of Henry Laurens,* vol. 4, 585.

43. As quoted in Schafer, "'A Swamp of an Investment'?," 21.

44. Ibid., 24.

45. Verdura Plantation's past is documented in the following works: Clifton Paisley, *From Cotton to Quail: An Agricultural Chronicle of Leon County, Florida, 1860–1967* (Gainesville: University of Florida Press, 1968); Clifton Paisley, *The Red Hills of Florida, 1528–1865* (Tuscaloosa: University of Alabama Press, 1989), 89–90; Julia Floyd Smith, *Slavery and Plantation Growth in Antebellum Florida, 1821–1860* (Gainesville: University of

Florida Press, 1973); Wynne and Parks, *Florida's Antebellum Homes,* 44–45; Sharon Heiland, "The Verdura Place: A Historical Overview and Preliminary Archaeological Survey," master's thesis, Florida State University, 2000.

46. The Inflation Calculator, http://www.westegg.com/inflation/infl.cgi (accessed 9 February 2008).

**Chapter 6. Mississippi**

1. United States census records; Eugene R. Dattel, "Cotton in a Global Economy: Mississippi (1800–1860)," *Mississippi History Now,* http://mshistory.k12.ms.us/index.php?s=articles (accessed 17 November 2007).

2. Mary Carol Miller, *Lost Mansions of Mississippi* (Jackson: University Press of Mississippi, 1996), xi.

3. Fred Daspit, *Louisiana Architecture 1820–1840* (Lafayette, Louisiana: The Center for Louisiana Studies, 2005), 242.

4. The history of Goat Castle, also known as Glenwood, was abstracted from several authoritative sources, including Sim C. Callon and Carolyn Vance Smith, *The Goat Castle Murder* (Natchez, Mississippi: Plantation Publishing Company, 1985); Carolyn Vance Smith, "Dana and Dockery Charged with Murder," *Natchez Democrat,* 19 August 1984; Carolyn Vance Smith, "Goat Castle: 52 Years Ago, a Calamity Shocked the World," *Clarion-Ledger,* 26 August 1984; Carolyn Vance Smith, "In 1933, Goat Castle Opened for Tours," *Natchez Democrat,* 26 August 1984.

5. Much of the early history of Brierfield came from two well-researched sources: Frank E. Everett, Jr., *Brierfield: Plantation Home of Jefferson Davis* (Hattiesburg, Mississippi: University and College Press of Mississippi, 1971); and Miller, *Lost Mansions,* 40–43.

6. As quoted in Everett, *Brierfield,* 29.

7. Ibid., 54.

8. Ibid., 27.

9. Ibid., 69.

10. Much of the early history of Hurricane also came from these two well-researched sources: Everett, *Brierfield,* and Miller, *Lost Mansions,* 40–43.

11. Benjamin Thornton Montgomery had been purchased by the Davis family at the Natchez slave market. He had previously been enslaved in Louden County, Virginia. It was here that his previous master had taught him to read and write. Mound Bayou, http://www.moundbayou.org/ (accessed 31 March 2006); "Hurricane Plantation," *Sankofa's Slavery Data*

*Collection*, http://www.rootsweb.com/~afamerpl/plantations_usa/MS/hurricane.html (accessed 31 March 2006); Slavery in America—Encyclopedia (accessed 31 March 2006).

12. Warren County Slave Schedules,1860, U.S. census.

13. Mound Bayou, http://www.moundbayou.org/ (accessed 31 March 2006); "Hurricane Plantation," *Sankofa's Slavery Data Collection*, http://www.rootsweb.com/~afamerpl/plantations_usa/MS/hurricane.html (accessed 31 March 2006); Slavery in America—Encyclopedia (accessed 31 March 2006).

14. As quoted in Everett, *Brierfield*, 19 fn.

15. Mound Bayou, http://www.moundbayou.org/ (accessed 31 March 2006).

16. Everett, *Brierfield*, 19.

17. For more information about Windsor Plantation, see Miller, *Lost Mansions*, 27–30, and Stella Pitts, "Magnificent Windsor Ruins Due Historical Restoration," *Times-Picayune*, 17 April 1977.

18. The Inflation Calculator, http://www.westegg.com/inflation/infl.cgi (accessed 9 February 2008).

19. Quoted in Rebecca B. Drake, "Windsor: Yankees Crash the Party," http://battleofraymond.org/history/windsor.htm (accessed 14 April 2006).

20. Information about the history of Prairie Mont can be found in multiple sources, among them George M. Moreland, "Vaiden: City of Fine Traditions," *Commercial Appeal*, 1 December 1929, sec. 1, p. 12.; Miller, *Lost Mansions,* 62–64; "Death of Dr. C. M. Vaiden," *Daily Clarion*, 7 February 1880, p. 2.; "In Memoriam: The Late Dr. Cowles Mead Vaiden," *Daily Clarion*, 18 February 1880, p. 2; Lucie Magee, "Vaiden . . . a Romantic Past and a Promising Spot for Industry," *Jackson Daily News*, 30 April 1950.

21. "In Memoriam: The Late Dr. Cowles Mead Vaiden."

22. Moreland, "Vaiden: City of Fine Traditions."

23. As quoted in Miller, *Lost Mansions*, 63.

24. Numerous resources piece together the history of Malmaison Plantation. The estate is featured in the Historic American Buildings Survey and in several chapters and articles, among them Mrs. Lee J. Langley, "Malmaison, Palace in a Wilderness, Home of General LeFlore," *Chronicles of Oklahoma*. vol. 5, no. 4, 371–380; Miller, *Lost Mansions*, 64–66; J. Frazer Smith, *Plantation Houses and Mansions of the Old South* (New York: Dover Publications, 1993), 98–101. The mansion's demise was documented in several period journalistic accounts: "Malmaison Destroyed by Fire Last Tuesday Night," *The Conservative*, 3 April 1942, p. 1; "Historic Carriage Saved,"

*Greenwood Commonwealth*, 1 April 1942, p. 6; "Historic Landmark Burns," *Jackson Daily News*, 2 April 1942, sec. 2, p. 8; "Malmaison," *The Conservative*, 10 April 1942, p. 1. The controversial purchase and contemporary development plans are detailed in modern news accounts: Reed Branson, "LeFlore Property Wrapped Again in Intrigue," *Commercial Appeal*, 2 June 2002, p. E1+; Susan Montgomery, "Malmaison Purchase Completed," *The Conservative*, 8 November 2001, p. 1; Allen Roark, "Choctaws Purchase Carroll County Land of Former Chief Leflore," *Delta Business Journal*, August 2002. Other published accounts include Susie James, "Cemetery All That Remains of Fabled Malmaison," *Greenwood Commonwealth*, 23 March 1995; George Zepp, "Choctaw Leader Educated in Nashville by Local Family," *Tennessean*, 27 August 2003; George Zepp, "Tribal Chief Revered by Whites, Scorned by Choctaw Nation," *Tennessean*, 3 September 2003.

25. Branson, "LeFlore Property."

26. Sources disagree on Leflore's precise age at his election as chief. Some note that he was twenty-two when he assumed leadership of the Choctaws, while others place his age at twenty-four.

27. Montgomery "Malmaison Purchase Completed."

28. Branson, "LeFlore Property."

29. Ibid.

30. A wealth of information about Homewood Plantation and the Hunt family can be found in the David Hunt Letters at the Special Collections of LSU Libraries in Baton Rouge. Brief published accounts of Homewood can be found in Catharine Van Court, *In Old Natchez* (New York: Doubleday, 1937), 92–93; and Miller, *Lost Mansions,* 15–16.

31. *Slave Narratives: A Folk History of Slavery in the United States from Interviews with Former Slaves, Arkansas Narratives, Part 1*, Work Projects Administration, 1941.

32. Ibid.

33. See the similar story involving the slaves of Virginia's Oak Hill Plantation in chapter one.

34. Van Court, *In Old Natchez*.

35. Ibid.

36. The history of Windy Hill Manor is documented in Miller, *Lost Mansions*, 5–8; Windy Hill Manor, Historic American Buildings Survey, Library of Congress; "Burr's Mississippi Sweetheart, Madeline," *New York Times*, 10 July 1904; Van Court, *In Old Natchez*, 33–35.

37. Harnett T. Kane, *Natchez on the Mississippi* (New York: William Morrow & Co., 1947), 41.

Chapter 7. Louisiana

1. Roulhac B. Toledano, "Louisiana's Golden Age: Valcour Aime in St. James Parish," *Louisiana History* 10, 3 (1969): 212.

2. Josephine Roman was the daughter of Louise Patin Roman and Jacques Etiènne Roman. Her brother was Louisiana governor Andre Bienvenu Roman of Cabahanoce Plantation.

3. Toledano, "Louisiana's Golden Age," 213.

4. Ibid.; Fred Daspit, *Louisiana Architecture, 1820–1840* (Lafayette, Louisiana: Center for Louisiana Studies, 2005), 150–151.

5. Ibid.

6. Toledano, "Louisiana's Golden Age," 215–216; Daspit, *Louisiana Architecture, 1820–1840*, 150–151; Mary Ann Sternberg, *Along the River Road: Past and Present on Louisiana's Historic Byway* (Baton Rouge: Louisiana State University Press, 2001), 291–292; Doris Kent, "'Petit Versailles' a Memory: Only Charred Wall Remains," *Times-Picayune*, 25 April 1920.

7. Toledano, "Louisiana's Golden Age," 215–216.

8. Eliza Ripley, *Social Life in Old New Orleans* (New York: D. Appleton and Co., 1912), 188–189.

9. Valcour Aime, *Plantation Diary* (New Orleans: Clark & Hofeline, 1878).

10. Aime's plantation was so aligned with the St. James Sugar Refinery that the estate was actually known to many as "the Refinery," and is noted in several published sources as such.

11. Jefferson College was closed by the Marist Fathers in 1927. The celebrated columned Greek Revival campus was purchased by the Jesuits in 1931. Today, the Jesuits use it as a private retreat for laymen called Manresa House. For additional information on the history and architecture of Jefferson College, see J. Frazer Smith, *Plantation Houses and Mansions of the Old South* (New York: Dover Publications, 1993), 196–199.

12. Ripley, *Social Life*, 186–187.

13. Felicity Plantation is most well known in today's popular culture for its pivotal role in the popular film *The Skeleton Key*. For more information on this interesting estate, see Stephanie Bruno, "High Life on the Acadian Coast," *Times-Picayune*, 6 August 2005.

14. Toledano, "Louisiana's Golden Age," 220–221.

15. Daspit, *Louisiana Architecture, 1820–1840*, 150–151; Arthur W. Bergeron, *Guide to Louisiana Confederate Military Units, 1861–1865.* (Baton Rouge: Louisiana State University Press, 1989), 141.

16. As quoted in Toledano, "Louisiana's Golden Age," 224.

17. The death of his only son was quite a blow for Valcour. He wrote in his diary, "Let him who wishes continue. My time is finished." See *Daily Picayune*, obituary of Gabriel Aime, 24 September 1854.

18. *Evening Picayune*, obituary of Valcour Aime, 3 January 1867.

19. Toledano, "Louisiana's Golden Age," 224; Sternberg, *Along the River Road*, 292.

20. Ibid.; John B. Rehder, *Delta Sugar: Louisiana's Vanishing Plantation Landscape* (Baltimore: Johns Hopkins University Press, 1999), 67; Daspit, *Louisiana Architecture, 1820–1840*, 150–151.

21. Any study of Belle Grove Plantation must begin with the definitive work "Apocryphal Grandeur: Belle Grove Plantation in Iberville Parish, Louisiana," a master's thesis by Robert Mark Rudd (University of Delaware, 2002). This thesis proved invaluable to the author of this volume, but unfortunately it has not been published to date, making its distribution and access somewhat limited. Additionally, a number of articles and accounts have been written of Belle Grove over the years. Some of these works, such as those subsequently noted, provide important information, but many others are fraught with romanticized depictions and factual errors. So popular is the memory of this lost plantation that an Internet discussion group devoted exclusively to Belle Grove has been founded (http://groups.yahoo.com/group/bellegrove/) and an associated digital library of reference material has even been published online by fans of this historic estate. These electronic sources are invaluable compilations of information on the history of Iberville Parish's most famed lost plantation.

22. For more information on Henry Howard, see Charles DuFour, "Henry Howard, Forgotten Architect," *Journal of Architectural Historians*, vol. XI, no. 4 (December 1952); and Victor McGee and Robert Brantly, "Greek Revival to Greek Tragedy, Henry Howard, Architect (1818–1884)," master's thesis, Louisiana State University, 1983.

23. William Edwards Clement, *Plantation Life on the Mississippi* (New Orleans: Pelican Publishing Company, 1952).

24. For more information on Henry Ware, see Mary Ware Anderson, "The Life & Times of Henry Ware," *Louisiana Genealogical Review* (June 1989).

25. Harnett T. Kane, *Plantation Parade: The Grand Manner in Louisiana* (New York: Bonanza Books, 1945).

26. Ibid.

27. Sam Mims, "Our Dream House: Beautiful Belle Grove," *Louisiana Conservation Review* (Winter 1940/1941).

28. Ibid.

29. "Woodlawn Plantation," Historic American Buildings Survey (HABS), Library of Congress.

30. Ibid.

31. The Inflation Calculator, http://www.westegg.com/inflation/infl.cgi (accessed 6 February 2008).

32. "Woodlawn Plantation," HABS; Daspit, *Louisiana Architecture, 1820–1840*, 158–159.

33. Ibid.; Smith, *Plantation Houses and Mansions*, 174–175.

34. Ibid.

35. Daspit, *Louisiana Architecture, 1820–1840*, 158–159.

36. Ibid.; Clarence John Laughlin, *Ghosts Along the Mississippi* (New York: C. Scribner's Sons, 1948).

37. H. B. Price, "Terrebonne Parish, Louisiana" *Debow's review, Agricultural, commercial, industrial progress and resources*, vol. 8, issue 2 (February 1850): 146–147.

38. Darrell Overdyke, *Louisiana Plantation Homes, Colonial and Antebellum* (New York: American Legacy Press, 1981), 205–207; Claire Puneky, "Bayou Landmarks," *Times-Picayune*, 26 February 1978.

39. Barnes F. Lathrop, "The Lafourche District in 1862: Confederate Revival," *Louisiana History*, vol. 1, no. 4 (Fall 1960): 300–319. See also W. W. (William Whitmell) Pugh Papers at Louisiana State University Libraries, Special Collections, in Baton Rouge and Pugh Family Papers at the University of Texas at Austin, Center for American History.

40. As quoted in Lathrop, "Lafourche District," 304.

41. Ibid.

42. Ibid., 310.

43. Laughlin, *Ghosts*.

44. Ibid.

45. Daspit, *Louisiana Architecture, 1820–1840*, 158.

46. Prior to its destruction by fire in 1963, the Barrow family's Afton Villa Plantation mansion in West Feliciana Parish near St. Francisville joined Orange Grove as one of the few Gothic Revival plantation mansions in Louisiana. Today, all that remains of Afton Villa are its terraced gardens, which are maintained as a tourist attraction, open to the public for a fee.

47. There are a number of important references and sources related to Orange Grove Plantation. Original plans as well as a plantation ledger are held at the Louisiana State Museum's Historical Center in New Orleans. Tulane University's Special Collections holds the important thesis by Tulane archivist and architect William Rex Cullison entitled "Orange Grove: the design and construction of an ante-bellum neo-Gothic plantation house on the Mississippi River, with remarks on the career of its architect, William L. Johnston, and notes concerning the mid-nineteenth-century romantic picturesque aesthetic," which he submitted as part of the requirements towards his master's degree. In addition, several contemporaneous newspaper accounts provide a glimpse into the battle to save Orange Grove and the many hurdles preservationists faced. Among these articles are Bert Hyde, "Plaquemines Mansion Rich in History: Showplace of Another Era," *States-Item*, n.d.; Stella Pitts, "Orange Grove Only Ghost of Former Self," *Times-Picayune*, 14 January 1979; Stella Pitts, "Plantation Post-Mortem: Grand Home of Another Era Is Dead; Indifference Killed It," *Times-Picayune*, 16 June 1974; John Ferguson, "Decay, Vandals Seal Plantation's Fate," *Times-Picayune/States-Item*, 6 February 1982. Brief mention is made of the plantation in Laughlin, *Ghosts*, plate 77.

48. William L. Johnston was born in 1811. He taught "Shadeing [sic], Perspective and Ornamental Drawing," at Philadelphia's Carpenter's Company architectural school. He designed numerous buildings and structures during his career, but found fame for an eight-story granite protoskyscraper called the Jayne Building in Philadelphia that was demolished by the National Park Service in 1957. Roger W. Moss of Philadelphia Architects and Buildings described this loss as "one of the most culpable acts of architectural vandalism in a good cause on record." Johnston died of tuberculosis in 1849. For more information, see Roger W. Moss's article at http://www.philadelphiabuildings.org/pab/app/ar_display.cfm/66310.

49. The Gothic Revival style was popular at the time, but did not have a great influence on the plantation South, especially in the Deep South, where massively columned Greek Revival mansions were the stylistic ideal. The Gothic style was widely popularized elsewhere by the novels of Sir Walter Scott, which included romanticized depictions of medieval castles and English manor houses. Andrew Jackson Downing, an American landscape architect, furthered the ideal with his publications of Gothic Revival designs for villas and other structures.

50. Morgan thought that bricks made in Philadelphia were much stronger and more solid than the soft bricks produced in Louisiana by slaves. Shipping enough bricks to construct an entire plantation mansion would have been quite an expensive endeavor, even for someone in the shipping industry. This act

Ross-Stockhouse Papers (Belle Grove Plantation)

Valcour Aime Ledgers

Louisiana State University Libraries, Special Collections — Baton Rouge

David Hunt Letters

Family Plantation Records

John Hampden Randolph Family Letters

John Hampden Randolph Family Papers

Uncle Sam Plantation Papers

W. W. (William Whitmell) Pugh Papers

Mississippi Department of Archives and History — Jackson

Brandon (Gerard C.) Papers

Daniell (Smith Coffee, IV) Collection, 1798–1970

Leflore (Greenwood) Files

Leflore (Greenwood) Promissory Note

Malmaison File

Percy Family Papers

Stanton (Elizabeth Brandon) Papers

Windy Hill File

New Orleans Notarial Archives — Louisiana

Antebellum Notarial Acts

Plan Book Collection

North Carolina State Archives

John Devereux Papers

Pollock-Devereux Papers

Thomas Pollock Papers

Sherman Public Library—Texas

Butts Papers

Coffee Papers

Grayson County Historical Commission Papers

Sophia Porter Papers

Society of the Sacred Heart, National Archives, U.S. Province — St. Louis, Missouri

Lettres Annuelles

South Carolina Department of Archives and History — Columbia

Millwood — National Register of Historic Places Nomination Folder

St. James Parish Courthouse — Convent, Louisiana

Conveyance Records

State Library of Louisiana, Louisiana Collection — Plantation Files — Baton Rouge

Texas Brigade — http://texas-brigade.com (accessed 22 July 2005)

War Letters of Captain Tacitus T. Clay, C.S.A.

Tulane University, Special Collections — New Orleans, Louisiana

Richard Koch Collection

Southeastern Architectural Archives Files

Vertical Files Collection

University of Florida, Smathers Library — Gainesville

David Levy Yulee Papers

University of South Carolina, South Caroliniana Library — Columbia

Charles Stevens Dwight Papers

Henry William Ravenel Papers

University of North Carolina at Chapel Hill, Southern Historical Collection

George Hairston Papers

George Mordecai Papers

Margaret Mordecai Devereux Papers

Mordecai Family Papers

Peter Gaillard Plantation Records

Samuel Hairston Papers

Thomas Butler King Papers

William Audley Couper Papers

William Page Papers

University of Texas at Austin, Center for American History

Barnes F. Lathrop Papers

James F. and Stephen S. Perry Papers

**Theses, Dissertations, Academic Papers, and Unpublished Manuscripts**

Adler, Joseph Cary. "The Public Career of Senator David Levy Yulee." Ph.D. dissertation, Case Western Reserve University, 1973.

Appleyard, Lula D. "Plantation Life in Middle Florida, 1821–1845." Master's thesis, Florida State College for Women, 1940.

Boucher, Ann. "Wealthy Planter Families in Nineteenth-Century Alabama." Ph.D. dissertation, University of Connecticut, 1978.

Bowman, Mary D. Leavell. "This Unnatural War, 1861–1865: The Diary of John Brown of Camden, Arkansas." Master's thesis, Northwestern State College of Louisiana, 1965.

Bradley, Denise Anne. "The Evolution of a Sugar Cane Plantation Landscape." Master's thesis, Louisiana State University, 1986.

Brooker, Colin. "The Major William Horton House, Jekyll Island, Georgia. Analysis, Care and Display." Brooker Preservation Design Consultants, 2001.

Bruce, Edwin Ney. "Westwego, Louisiana: A Community Study." Master's thesis, Tulane University, 1947.

Carmichael, Maude. "The Plantation System in Arkansas, 1850–1876." Ph.D. dissertation, Radcliff College, 1935.

Cheatham, Edgar J., Jr. "Washington County, Mississippi: Its Antebellum Generation." Master's thesis, Tulane University, 1950.

Close, Stacey K. "Elderly Slaves of the Plantation South: Somewhere Between Heaven and Earth." Ph.D. dissertation, Ohio State University, 1992.

Conner, Virgil Henry. "Odyssey of a Southern Family in the Nineteenth Century." Ph.D. dissertation, Florida State University, 1980.

Cowden, G. S. "The Randolphs of Turkey Island: A Prosopography of the First Three Generations, 1650–1806." Ph.D. dissertation, William and Mary College, 1977.

Craig, Shannon. "Arkansas and Foreign Immigration, 1890–1915." Master's thesis, University of Arkansas, 1979.

Cullison, William Rex. "Orange Grove: the design and construction of an ante-bellum neo-Gothic plantation house on the Mississippi River, with remarks on the career of its architect, William L. Johnston, and notes concerning the mid-nineteenth-century romantic picturesque aesthetic." Master's thesis, Tulane University, 1969.

Cumberland, Sharon. "The Two-Ply Yarn: Slave Narratives and Slave Owner Narratives in the Antebellum South." Ph.D. dissertation, University of New York, 1994.

Curlee, Abigail. "A Study of Texas Slave Plantations, 1822–1865." Ph.D. dissertation, University of Texas, 1932.

Dennard, David C. "Religion in the Quarters: A Study of Slave Preachers in the Antebellum South, 1800–1860." Ph.D. dissertation, Northwestern University, 1983.

Ellenberg, George Bolton. "Mule South to Tractor South: Mules, Machines, Agriculture, and Culture in the Cotton South, 1850–1950." Ph.D. dissertation, University of Kentucky, 1994.

Follett, Richard J. "The Sugar Masters: Slavery, Economic Development, and Modernization on Louisiana Sugar Plantations, 1820–1860." Ph.D. dissertation, Louisiana State University, 1997.

Ford, Hiram W. "A History of the Arkansas Penitentiary to 1900." Master's thesis, University of Arkansas, 1936.

Foster, Shirley Pribbenow. "Women and Refinement in Antebellum Alabama: Privacy, Comfort, and Luxury, 1830–1860." Ph.D. dissertation, University of Alabama, 1998.

Fotenot, Carl L. "Nottoway Plantation: The Restoration and Revitalization of the Estate." Final project, Louisiana State University, 1989.

Frankel, Noralee. "The Slaves' Christmas in the South, 1800–1860." Master's thesis, George Washington University, 1977.

Greenberg, Michael. "Gentleman Slaveholders: The Social Outlook of the Virginia Planter Class." Ph.D. dissertation, Rutgers University, 1971.

Hale, Laura. "The Groces and Whartons in the Early History of Texas." Master's thesis, University of Texas, 1942.

Hamilton, Cherovise. "The Forks of Cypress." Unpublished academic paper, 1978 (from the Local History/Genealogy Department, Florence-Lauderdale Public Library, Florence, Alabama).

Heiland Sharon, "The Verdura Place: A Historical Overview and Preliminary Archaeological Survey." Master's thesis, Florida State University, 2000.

Johnston-Miller, Mary Margaret. "Heirs to Paternalism: Elite Women and Their Servants in Alabama and Georgia, 1861–1874." Ph.D. dissertation, Emory University, 1994.

Jung, Moon-Ho. "'Coolies' and Cane: Race, Labor and Sugar Production in Louisiana, 1852–1877." Ph.D. dissertation, Cornell University, 2000.

Kelley, Sean Michael. "Plantation Frontiers: Race, Ethnicity, and Family along the Brazos River of Texas, 1821–1886." Ph.D dissertation, University of Texas at Austin, 2000.

Lamp, Kimberly Ann. "Empire for Slavery: Economic and Territorial Expansion in the American Gulf South, 1835–1860." Ph.D. dissertation, Harvard University, 1991.

Lord, Mills M., Jr. "David Levy Yulee, Statesmen and Railroad Builder." Master's thesis, University of Florida, 1940.

Madere, Beverly Anne. "Three Centuries on Nine Mile Point: Patterns of Ownership and Land Utilization." Academic thesis, University of New Orleans, 1998.

McDonald, Roderick A. "Goods and Chattels: The Economy of Slavery on Sugar Plantations in Jamaica and Louisiana." Ph.D. dissertation, University of Kansas, 1981.

McGee, Jeff. "Jackson Cemetery." Unpublished academic paper, University of North Alabama, 1976 (from the Local History/Genealogy Department, Florence-Lauderdale Public Library, Florence, Alabama).

McGee, Victor, and Robert Brantly. "Greek Revival to Greek Tragedy, Henry Howard, Architect (1818–1884)." Master's thesis, Louisiana State University, 1983.

Mehlman, Michael H. "The Resettlement Administration and the Problems of Tenant Farmers in Arkansas, 1935–1936." Ph.D. dissertation, New York University, 1970.

Millender, Michael J. "Crossed Ambitions: Planters, Slaves, and Small Farmers in Greene County, Alabama, 1830–1865." Honors paper, Duke University, 1988.

Mitchell, William H. "Joseph L. Bristow, Kansas Insurgent in the U.S. Senate, 1909–1915." Master's thesis, University of Kansas, 1952.

Morgan, Sam. "Blue Delta: The Union Occupation of Helena, Arkansas, During the Civil War." Master's thesis, Arkansas State University, 1993.

Mummert, John William. "Food, Clothing, and Shelter of American Plantation Negro Slaves, 1830–1860." Master's thesis, University of Alabama, 1952.

O'Neal, Elizabeth Kirkman. "The Forks of Cypress: The Home of James Jackson." Unpublished academic paper, n.d. (from the Local History/Genealogy Department, Florence-Lauderdale Public Library, Florence, Alabama).

Parker, Sheryl H. "Seven Oaks Plantation." Unpublished academic paper, Special Collections of Tulane University, n.d.

Shurden, Irene. "A History of Washington County, Mississippi, to 1900." Master's thesis, Mississippi College, 1963.

Smith, D. T. "Tobacco and Its Role in the Life of the Confederacy." Master's thesis, Old Dominion University, 1993.

Stone, James Herbert. "Black Leadership in the Old South: The Slave Drivers of the Rice Kingdom." Ph.D. dissertation, Florida State University, 1976.

Swan, Dale Evans. "The Structure and Profitability of the Antebellum Rice Industry, 1859." Ph.D. dissertation, University of North Carolina at Chapel Hill, 1972.

Rahe, Lee Wayne. "Residential Furnishings of Deceased Greene County, Alabama Slave Owners, 1845–1860." Ph.D. dissertation, University of Tennessee, 1992.

Rehder, John B. "Sugar Plantation Settlement of Southern Louisiana: A Cultural Geography." Ph.D. dissertation, Louisiana State University, 1971.

Richardson, Jeffrey Doyle. "Nothing More Fruitful: Debt and Cash Flow on the Antebellum Rice Plantation." Master's thesis, University of North Carolina at Chapel Hill, 1996.

Rudd, Robert Mark. "Apocryphal Grandeur: Belle Grove Plantation in Iberville Parish, Louisiana." Master's thesis, University of Delaware, 2002.

Thompson, Alan Smith. "Mobile, Alabama, 1850–1861: Economic, Political, Physical, and Population Characteristics." Ph.D. dissertation, University of Alabama, 1979.

Thompson, Arthur W. "David Yulee: A Study of Nineteenth Century Thought and Enterprise." Ph.D. dissertation, Columbia University, 1954.

Touchstone, Donald Blake. "Planters and Slave Religion in the Deep South." Ph.D. dissertation, Tulane University, 1973.

Walz, Robert B. "Migration Into Arkansas, 1834–1880." Ph.D. dissertation, University of Texas, 1958.

Wright, Gavin. "The Economics of Cotton in the Antebellum South." Ph.D. dissertation, Yale University, 1969.

Yeates, Marian. "Domesticating Slavery: Patterns of Cultural Rationalization in the Antebellum South, 1820–1860." Ph.D. dissertation, Indiana University, 1996.

Zapletal, Mirka. "The Slave Quarters of Orange Grove Plantation: A Material Analysis." Master's thesis, Tulane University, 1999.

## Government Reports and Documents

Bailey, Robert J., and Priscilla M. Lowrey, eds. *Historic Preservation in Mississippi: A Comprehensive Plan.* Jackson: Mississippi Department of Archives and History, 1975.

Douglas, Ed Polk. *Architecture in Claiborne County, Mississippi.* Jackson: Mississippi Department of Archives and History, 1974.

Hughes, Brady A., and Sarah S. Hughes. *A Historical Study of the Marshall Hall Site, 1634 to 1984.* National Park Service, n.d.

Long, Susan. *Historic Structure Report, Architectural Data Section for Marshall Hall, Piscataway Park.* Denver Service Center, National Park Service, January 1983.

Mansell, Jeff. *Hale County, Alabama: An Inventory of Significant and Historic Resources.* Cahaba Trace Commission with support from the Alabama Legislature, July 1992.

*Mississippi: A Guide to the Magnolia State.* Federal Writers' Project, April 1938.

Quackenbos, Mary Grace. *Report on general conditions of Delta cotton plantations.* Department of Justice Records, Record Group 59, 866.55/8–9, National Archives, 10 January 1908.

———. *Report on Sunnyside Plantation.* Department of Justice Records, Record Group 60, 100937, National Archives, 28 September 1907.

*Slave Narratives: A Folk History of Slavery in the United States from Interviews with Former Slaves, Arkansas Narratives, Part 1.* Work Projects Administration, 1941.

Snell, Charles W. *A Short History of Marshall Hall, Charles County, Maryland.* Denver Service Center, National Park Service, January 1980.

Toogood, Anna Coxe. *Piscataway Park, Maryland — General Historical Background Study.* Office of Archeology and Historic Preservation, National Park Service, 1969.

Waterman, Thomas T. *A Survey of the Early Buildings in the Region of the Proposed Santee and Pinopolis Reservoirs in South Carolina.* National Park Service, 1939.

## Books and Chapters (Including Published Primary Sources)

Adams, Natalie, and Michael Trinkley. *Archaeological Testing of the Stoney/Baynard Plantation, Hilton Head Island, Beaufort County, South Carolina.* Research Series 28. Columbia: Chicora Foundation, 1991.

Aime, Valcour. *Plantation Diary.* New Orleans: Clark & Hofeline, 1878.

Anderson, J. Sherburne. "Andrew, John." In *Iberville Parish History, Vol. I,* edited by Judy Riffel et al. Baton Rouge: Le Comité des Archives de la Louisiane, 1985.

Andrews, Eliza Frances. *The War-Time Journal of a Georgia Girl, 1864–1865.* New York: D. Appleton and Company, 1908.

Andrews, Wayne. *Pride of the South: A Social History of Southern Architecture.* New York: Athenaeum Press, 1979.

Arthur, Stanley Clisby. *Old New Orleans.* Gretna, Louisiana: Pelican Publishing Company, 1990.

Baldwin, William, and V. Elizabeth Turk. *Mantelpieces of the Old South: Lost Architecture and Southern Culture.* Charleston: History Press, 2005.

Ball, Edward. *Slaves in the Family.* New York: Farrar, Straus, and Giroux, 1998.

Baptist, Edward E. *Creating an Old South: Middle Florida's Plantation Frontier before the Civil War.* Chapel Hill: University of North Carolina Press, 2002.

Bardaglio, Peter W. *Reconstructing the Household, Families, Sex, and the Law in the Nineteenth Century South.* Chapel Hill: University of North Carolina Press, 1995.

Baudier, Roger. *The Catholic Church in Louisiana.* New Orleans, 1939. Reprinted by the Louisiana Library Association, Public Library Section, 1972.

Baum, Dale. *The Shattering of Texas Unionism: Politics in the Lone Star State during the Civil War Era.* Baton Rouge: Louisiana State University Press, 1998.

Becnel, Thomas A. *The Barrow Family and the Barataria and Lafourche Canal: The Transportation Revolution in Louisiana, 1829–1925.* Baton Rouge: Louisiana State University Press, 1989.

Begnaud, Allen. "The Louisiana Sugar Cane Industry." In *Green Fields, Two Hundred Years of Louisiana Sugar.* Lafayette, Louisiana: The Center for Louisiana Studies, University of Southwestern Louisiana, 1980.

Bell, Malcolm, Jr. *Major Butler's Legacy: Five Generations of a Slaveholding Family.* Athens: University of Georgia Press, 1987.

Bergeron, Arthur W. *Guide to Louisiana Confederate Military Units, 1861–1865.* Baton Rouge: Louisiana State University Press, 1989.

Bibb, Henry. *Narrative of the Life and Adventures of Henry Bibb, An American Slave.* New York: Published by Henry Bibb, 1849.

Billings, Dwight B., Jr. *Planters and the Making of a 'New South': Class, Politics, and Development in North Carolina, 1865–1900.* Chapel Hill: University of North Carolina Press, 1979.

Bishir, Catherine W. *North Carolina Architecture.* Chapel Hill: University of North Carolina Press, 2005.

Blessingame, John. *The Slave Community: Plantation Life in the Antebellum South.* New York: Oxford University Press, 1972.

Boehm, Randolph H. "Mary Grace Quackenbos and the Federal Campaign against Peonage." In *Shadows Over Sunnyside: An Arkansas Plantation in Transition, 1830–1945,* edited by Jeannie M. Whayne. Fayetteville: University of Arkansas Press, 1993.

*The Book of a Hundred Houses: A Collection of Pictures, Plans and Suggestions for Householders.* Chicago: Herbert S. Stone & Company, 1902.

Bostick, Douglas W. *Sunken Plantations: The Santee Cooper Project.* Charleston, South Carolina: The History Press, 2008.

Bouchereau, A. *Statement of the Sugar and Rice Crops Made in Louisiana in 1881–82.* New Orleans: L. Graham and Sons, Printers, 1882.

Bouchereau, L. *Statement of the Sugar and Rice Crops Made in Louisiana in 1872–73.* New Orleans: Pelican Book and Job Printing Office, 1873.

Bourgeois, Lillian C. *Cabanocey: The History, Customs, and Folklore of St. James Parish.* Gretna, Louisiana: Pelican Publishing, 1976.

Breen, T. H. *Tobacco Culture.* Princeton, New Jersey: Princeton University Press, 1988.

Brewster, Lawrence Fay. *Summer Migrations and Resorts of South Carolina Lowcountry Planters.* Durham, North Carolina: Duke University Press, 1947.

Brooks, Victor. *African Americans in the Civil War.* Philadelphia: Chelsea House Publishers, 1999.

Brown, Lynda W. *Alabama History: An Annotated Bibliography.* Westport, Connecticut: Greenwood Press, 1998.

Brown, William W. *Narrative of William W. Brown, An American Slave.* London: Charles Gilpin, Bishopgate-St.Without, 1849.

Bruce, Dickson. *Violence and Culture in the Antebellum South.* Austin: University of Texas Press, 1979.

Brueckheimer, William R. *Leon County Hunting Plantations: An Historical and Architectural Survey.* Tallahassee: Historic Tallahassee Preservation Board of Trustees, 1988.

Buenger, Walter L. *Secession and the Union in Texas.* Austin: University of Texas Press, 1984.

Burke, Marilyn W. *312 Queen Street: A History of an 18th Century Alexandria House.* S.n., 1987.

Butler, W. E. *Down Among the Sugarcane.* Baton Rouge: Moran Publishing Corporation, 1990.

Butts, E. H. "Bulowville." In *Ashes on The Wind: The Story of the Lost Plantations,* edited by Alice Strickland, 51–53. Volusia County: Volusia County Historical Commission, 1985.

Callon, Sim C., and Carolyn Vance Smith. *The Goat Castle Murder.* Natchez, Mississippi: Plantation Publishing Company, 1985.

Calonius, Erik. *The Wanderer: The Last American Slave Ship and the Conspiracy That Set Its Sails.* New York: St. Martin's Press, 2006.

Campbell, Randolph B. *An Empire for Slavery: The Peculiar Institution in Texas, 1821–1865.* Baton Rouge: Louisiana State University Press, 1989.

Campbell, Randolph B., and Richard G. Lowe. *Wealth and Power in Antebellum Texas.* College Station: Texas A&M University Press, 1977.

Cauthen, Charles E. *Family Letters of Three Wade Hamptons, 1782–1901.* Columbia: University of South Carolina Press, 1953.

Chambers, S. Allen. *Buildings of West Virginia.* Oxford: Oxford University Press, 2004.

Champomier, P. A. *Statement of the Sugar Crop Made in Louisiana in 1849–50.* New Orleans: Cook, Young and Company, 1850.

———.*Statement of the Sugar Crop Made in Louisiana in 1853–54.* New Orleans: Cook, Young and Company, 1854.

Chastellux, Marquis de. *Travels in America in the Years 1780, 1781 and 1782.* Vol. 2. Translated by Howard C. Rice, Jr. Chapel Hill: University of North Carolina Press, 1963.

Chestnut, Mary. *A Diary from Dixie.* New York: Gramercy Books, 1997.

Clark, Bernal Emerson, and Carita Doggett Corse. *Dr. Andrew Turnbull and the New Smyrna Colony of Florida.* Chapel Hill: University of North Carolina Press, 1919.

Clement, William Edwards. *Plantation Life on the Mississippi.* New Orleans: Pelican Publishing Company, 1952.

Clinton, Catherine. *The Plantation Mistress.* New York: Pantheon Books, 1982.

Clinton, Catherine, and Michele Gillespie, eds. *The Devil's Lane: Sex and Race in the Early South.* New York: Oxford University Press, 1997.

Cohen, Lucy M. *Chinese in the Post–Civil War South: A People Without a History.* Baton Rouge: Louisiana State University Press, 1984.

Conrad, Glenn R., and Ray F. Lucas. *White Gold: A Brief History of the Louisiana Sugar Industry 1795–1995.* Lafayette, Louisiana: The Center for Louisiana Studies, University of Southwestern Louisiana, 1995.

Cooper, Chip. *Silent in the Land.* Tuscaloosa, Alabama: CKM Press, 1993.

Cooper, J. Wesley. *Antebellum Houses of Natchez.* Natchez: Southern Historical Publications, 1970.

Cooper, William J., Jr. *Liberty and Slavery: Southern Politics to 1860.* New York: McGraw-Hill Publishing Company, 1983.

Coleman, Kenneth. *Colonial Georgia: A History.* New York: Charles Scribner's Sons, 1976.

Coulter, E. Merton. *Wormsloe: Two Centuries of a Georgia Family.* Athens: University of Georgia Press, 1955.

Crété, Liliane. *Daily Life in Louisiana 1815–1830.* Translated by Patrick Gregory. Baton Rouge: Louisiana State University Press, 1981.

Crocker, Mary Wallace. *Historic Architecture in Mississippi.* Jackson: University Press of Mississippi, 1973.

Crook, J. Mordaunt. *The Greek Revival.* London: Murray Company, 1972.

Cross, J. Russell. *Historic Ramblin's through Berkeley.* Columbia, South Carolina: R. L. Bryan, Co., 1985.

Daniel, Harriet Bailey Bullock. *A Remembrance of Eden: Harriet Bailey Bullock Daniel's Memories of a Frontier Plantation in Arkansas, 1849–1872.* Edited with an introduction by Margaret Jones Bolsterli. Fayetteville: University of Arkansas Press, 1993.

Daniel, Pete. *The Shadow of Slavery: Peonage in the South, 1901–1969.* Urbana: University of Illinois Press, 1982.

Daspit, Fred. *Louisiana Architecture, 1714–1820.* Lafayette, Louisiana: The Center for Louisiana Studies, 2004.

———. *Louisiana Architecture, 1820–1840.* Lafayette, Louisiana: The Center for Louisiana Studies, 2005.

———. *Louisiana Architecture, 1840–1860.* Lafayette, Louisiana: The Center for Louisiana Studies, 2006.

Davis, Harold E. *The Fledgling Province: Social and Cultural Life in Colonial Georgia, 1733–1776.* Chapel Hill: University of North Carolina Press, 1976.

DeCanio, Stephen J. *Agriculture in the Postbellum South: The Economics of Production and Supply.* Cambridge: MIT Press, 1974.

Deiler, John Hanno. *The Settlement of the German Coast of Louisiana and the Creoles of German Descent.* Updated by Jack Belson. Baltimore: Genealogical Publishing Company, 1969.

Denson, Robin L. *Yulee Sugar Mill Ruins: The Archaeological and Historical Study of the State Historic Site, Citrus County.* Crystal River, Florida: Gulf Archaeology Research Institute, 1977.

Devereux, Margaret. *Plantation Sketches.* Cambridge, Massachusetts: Riverside Press, Cambridge, 1906.

Dinnerstein, Leonard, and Mary Dale Palsson. *Jews in the South.* Baton Rouge: Louisiana State University Press, 1973.

Dougan, Michael B. *Confederate Arkansas: The People and Policies of a Frontier State in Wartime.* University, Alabama: University of Alabama Press, 1976.

Dusinberre, William. *Them Dark Days: Slavery in the American Rice Swamps.* Athens, Georgia: University of Georgia Press, 2000.

Eaton, Clement. *The Growth of Southern Civilization, 1790–1860.* New York: Harper & Row, 1961.

Eichstedt, Jennifer L., and Stephen Small. *Representations of Slavery, Race and Ideology in Southern Plantation Museums.* Washington, D.C.: Smithsonian Institution Press, 2002.

Equiano, Olaudah. *The Interesting Narrative of the Life of Olaudah Equiano, or Gustavus Vassa, the African. Written by Himself.* 2 vols. London: Published by the author, 1789.

Escott, Paul D. *Slavery Remembered: A Record of Twentieth-Century Slave Narratives.* Chapel Hill: University of North Carolina Press, 1979.

Estaville, Lawrence E., Jr. *Confederate Neckties: Louisiana Railroads in the Civil War.* Ruston, Louisiana: McGinty Publications, 1989.

Everett, Frank E., Jr. *Brierfield: Plantation Home of Jefferson Davis.* Hattiesburg, Mississippi: University and College Press of Mississippi, 1971.

Fairbairn, Charlotte Judd. *George Washington's Lost Plantation in Jefferson County, West Virginia.* Berryville, Virginia: The Blue Ridge Press, 1954.

Faust, Drew Gilpin. *The Ideology of Slavery: Proslavery Thought in the Antebellum South.* Baton Rouge: Louisiana State University Press, 1981.

Ferguson, T. Reed. *The John Couper Family at Cannon's Point.* Macon, Georgia: Mercer University Press, 1994.

Fields, Barbara J. *Slavery and Freedom on the Middle Ground: Maryland during the Nineteenth Century.* New Haven: Yale University Press, 1985.

Finkelman, Paul, ed. *Rebellions, Resistance and Runaways Within the Slave South.* New York: Garland Pub., 1989.

Fitzhugh, William. *William Fitzhugh and His Chesapeake World, 1676–1701.* Charlottesville: University Press of Virginia, 1963.

Fleming, Walter Lynwood. *Civil War and Reconstruction in Alabama.* New York: Columbia University Press, 1905.

Forbes, Ella. *African American Women During the Civil War.* New York: Garland, 1998.

Foreman, Agnes Rita Zeringue. *Zerangue, Zeringue, Zyrangue and Allied Families.* Baltimore: Gateway Press, Inc., 1979.

Forman, Henry Chandlee. *Early Manor and Plantation Houses of Maryland.* McLean, Virginia: EPM Publications, 1989.

———. *Maryland Architecture: A Short History from 1634 through the Civil War.* Centreville, Maryland: Tidewater Publishers, 1968.

———. *Tidewater Maryland Architecture and Gardens.* New York: Architectural Book Publishers, 1956.

Fortier, Alcée. *A History of Louisiana*. Multivolume set. Second edition by Mark T. Carleton. Baton Rouge: Claitor's Publishing Division, 1985.

Fox-Genovese, Elizabeth. *Within the Plantation Household*. Chapel Hill: University of North Carolina Press, 1988.

Franklin, John Hope, and Loren Schweninger. *Runaway Slaves: Rebels on the Plantation*. Oxford: Oxford University Press, 1999.

Gaines, Francis Pendleton. *The Southern Plantation: A Study in the Development and Accuracy of a Tradition*. New York: Columbia University Press, 1925.

Gamble, Robert. *Historic Architecture in Alabama: A Guide to Styles and Types, 1810– 1930*. Tuscaloosa: University of Alabama Press, 1990.

Gatewood, Willard B. "Sunnyside: The Evolution of an Arkansas Plantation, 1840– 1945." In *Shadows Over Sunnyside: An Arkansas Plantation in Transition, 1830–1945*, edited by Jeannie M. Whayne. Fayetteville: University of Arkansas Press, 1993.

Gayarré, Charles. *History of Louisiana*. Republished. New Orleans: Pelican Publishing Company, 1965.

Genovese, Eugene D. *Roll, Jordan, Roll: The World the Slaves Made*. New York: Pantheon Books, 1974.

Gentry, Dorothy. *Life and Legend of Lawrence County Alabama*. Tuscaloosa: Nottingham, 1962.

Gleason, David King. *Plantation Homes of Louisiana and the Natchez Area*. Baton Rouge: Louisiana State University Press, 1982.

Glenn, Thomas Allen. *Some Colonial Mansions and Those Who Lived in Them*. Philadelphia: Henry T. Coates, 1899.

Goodwin, Christopher R., Jill-Karen Yakubik, and Cyd Heymann Goodwin. *Elmwood: The Historic Archeology of a Southeastern Louisiana Plantation*. Metairie, Louisiana: Jefferson Parish Historical Commission, 1984.

Granger, Mary, ed. *Savannah River Plantations*. Savannah: Oglethorpe Press, 1997.

Gray, Lewis Cecil. *History of Agriculture in the Southern United States to 1860*. Washington: Carnegie Institution, 1933.

Green, Bryan Clark, Calder Loth, and William M. S. Rasmussen. *Lost Virginia: Vanished Architecture of the Old Dominion*. Charlottesville, Virginia: Howell Press, 2001.

*Green Fields, Two Hundred Years of Louisiana Sugar*. Lafayette, Louisiana: The Center for Louisiana Studies, University of Southwestern Louisiana, 1980.

Green, R. Edwin, and Mary A. Green. *St. Simons: A Summary of Its History*. St. Simons Island, Georgia: Published by the authors, 1982.

Greer, Jack Thorndyke. *Leaves from a Family Album*. Waco, Texas: Texian Press, 1975.

Greiff, Constance M., ed. *Lost America: From the Atlantic to the Mississippi*. Princeton, New Jersey: Pyne Press, 1971.

Griffen, Patricia C. "Blue Gold: Andrew Turnbull's New Smyrna Plantation." In *Colonial Plantations and Economy in Florida*, edited by Jane G. Landers, 39–68. Gainesville: University Press of Florida, 2000.

Groene, Bertram H. *Antebellum Tallahassee*. Tallahassee: Florida Heritage Foundation, 1971.

Gutman, Herbert. *The Black Family in Slavery and Freedom, 1750–1925*. New York: Pantheon Books, 1976.

Haggard, M.C., and L. C. Montgomery. *A Pictorial History of Preston Bend on the Red River*. Denison, Texas: Grayson County Frontier Village, n.d.

Hague, Parthenia. *A Blockaded Family: Life in Southern Alabama During the Civil War*. Boston: Riverside Press, 1888.

Hall, Gwendolyn Midlo. *Africans in Colonial Louisiana*. Baton Rouge: Louisiana State University Press, 1992.

———. *Afro-Louisiana History and Genealogy 1718–1820*. Database. www.ibiblio.org/laslave/.

Hamlin, Talbot. *Greek Revival Architecture in America*. Cambridge: Oxford University Press, 1944.

Hammond, Ralph. *Ante-Bellum Mansions of Alabama*. New York: Bonanza Books, 1951.

Hanighen, Frank C. *Santa Anna, the Napoleon of the West*. New York: Coward McCann, Inc., 1934.

Harrold, Stanley. *The Abolitionists and the South, 1831–1861*. Lexington: University Press of Kentucky, 1995.

Hawks, Joanne V., and Shelia L. Skemp, eds. *Sex, Race, and the Role of Women in the South*. Jackson, Mississippi: University Press of Mississippi: 1983.

Hermann, Janet Sharp. *Joseph E. Davis: Pioneer Patriarch*. Jackson: University Press of Mississippi, 1991.

———. *The Pursuit of a Dream*. Jackson: University Press of Mississippi, 1999.

Howells, John Meade. *Lost Examples of Colonial Architecture*. New York: William Helburn, Inc., 1931.

Hubbs, G. Ward, ed. *Voices from Company D: Diaries by the Greensboro Guards, Fifth Alabama Infantry Regiment, Army of Northern Virginia*. Athens: University of Georgia Press, 2003.

Hühner, Leon. "David L. Yulee, Florida's First State Senator." In *Jews in the South,* edited by Leonard Dinnerstein and Mary Dale Palsson. Baton Rouge: Louisiana State University Press, 1973.

Huie, Mildred Nix, and Bessie Lewis. *King's Retreat Plantation, St. Simons Island, Georgia Today and Yesterday.* St. Simons Island, Georgia: Published by the authors, 1980.

Hull, Barbara. *St. Simons, Enchanted Island: A History of the Most Historic of Georgia's Fabled Golden Isles.* Atlanta: Cherokee Publishing Company, 1980.

Jackson, C. B. *Biographical Sketches of the Jackson Families of Alabama and Their Ancestors.* Jasper, Alabama: Eagle Print, 1930.

Jacobs, Harriet A. *Incidents in the Life of a Slave Girl, Written by Herself.* Boston: H. Jacobs, 1861.

James, Doug. *Lord of the Hill: James Jackson and the Forks of Cypress.* S.l.: s.n., 2002.

Jervey, Susan R., and Charlotte St. J. Ravenel. *Two Diaries from Middle St. John's Berkeley, South Carolina.* Pinopolis, South Carolina: St. John's Hunting Club, 1921.

Johnson, Guion Griddis. *Ante-Bellum North Carolina: A Social History.* Chapel Hill: University of North Carolina Press, 1937.

Johnson, William Russell. *A Short History of the Sugar Industry in Texas.* Houston: Texas Gulf Coast Historical Association, 1961.

Johnston, Frances Benjamin, and Thomas Tileston Waterman. *The Early Architecture of North Carolina.* Chapel Hill: University of North Carolina Press, 1941.

Jones, C. Allen. *Texas Roots: Agriculture and Rural Life Before the Civil War.* College Station: Texas A&M Press, 2005.

Jones, Katharine M. *The Plantation South.* Indianapolis: The Bobbs-Merrill Company, Inc., 1957.

Jones, Marie Beth. *Peach Point Plantation: The First 150 Years.* Waco: Texian Press, 1982.

Kane, Harnett T. *Natchez on the Mississippi.* New York: William Morrow & Co., 1947.

———. *Plantation Parade: The Grand Manner in Louisiana.* New York: Bonanza Books, 1945.

Kavanaugh, Celeste H. *David Levy Yulee: A Man and His Vision.* 2nd ed. Fernandina Beach, Florida: Amelia Island Museum of History, 1995.

Keber, Martha L. *Seas of Gold, Seas of Cotton: Christophe Poulain DuBignon of Jekyll Island.* Athens: University of Georgia Press, 2002.

Kelso, William M. *Captain Jones's Wormsloe: A Historical, Archeological, and Architectural Study of an Eighteenth-Century Plantation Site Near Savannah, Georgia.* Athens: University of Georgia Press, 1979.

Kemble, Frances Anne. *Journal of a Residence on a Georgian Plantation.* Project Gutenberg E-Book, http://www.gutenberg.org/files/12422/12422-h/12422-h.htm (accessed 5 May 2005).

Kolchin, Peter. *American Slavery 1619–1877.* New York: Hill and Wang, 1993.

Kukla, Jon. *A Wilderness So Immense: The Louisiana Purchase and the Destiny of America.* New York: Alfred A. Knopf, 2003.

Kulikoff, Allan. *Tobacco and Slaves.* Chapel Hill: University of North Carolina Press, 1986.

Lancaster, Clay. *Antebellum Architecture of Kentucky.* Lexington: University Press of Kentucky, 1991.

———. *Greek Revival Architecture in Alabama.* Booklet. S.l.: Alabama Historical Commission, 1977.

Lancaster, Robert A., Jr. *Historic Virginia Homes and Churches.* Philadelphia: J. B. Lippincott, 1915.

Landers, Jane G. *Colonial Plantations and Economy in Florida.* Gainesville: University Press of Florida, 2000.

Lane, Mills. *Architecture of the Old South: Colonial & Federal.* Savannah, Georgia: Beehive Foundation, 1996.

———. *Architecture of the Old South: Kentucky and Tennessee.* Savannah, Georgia: Beehive Press, 1993.

———. *Architecture of the Old South: North Carolina.* New York: Abbeville Press, 1990.

———. *Architecture of the Old South: Mississippi and Alabama.* New York: Abbeville Press, 1989.

———. *Architecture of the Old South: Georgia.* New York: Abbeville Press, 1986.

———. *Architecture of the Old South: South Carolina.* Savannah, Georgia: Beehive Press, 1984.

———. *Architecture of the Old South: Virginia.* New York: Abbeville Press, 1984.

Laughlin, Clarence John. *Ghosts Along the Mississippi.* New York: C. Scribner's Sons, 1948.

Lawrence County Heritage Book Committee. *The Heritage of Lawrence County, Alabama.* Clanton, Alabama: Heritage Pub. Consultants, 1998.

Lee, Susan. *The Westward Movement of the Cotton Economy, 1840–1860: Perceived Interests and Economic Realities.* New York: Arno Press, 1977.

Linley, John. *The Georgia Catalog, Historic American Buildings Survey: A Guide to the Architecture of the State.* Athens: University of Georgia Press, 1982.

Lovell, Caroline Couper. *The Golden Isles of Georgia.* Boston: Little, Brown, 1933.

Lowe, Richard G., and Randolph B. Campbell. *Planters and Plain Folk: Agriculture in Antebellum Texas.* Dallas: Southern Methodist University Press, 1987.

Maguire, Jack. "Sophia Porter: Texas' Own Scarlett O'Hara." In *Legendary Ladies of Texas*, edited by Francis Edward Abernethy. Nacogdoches, Texas: Texas Folk Society, 1981.

Main, Gloria L. *Tobacco Colony: Life in Early Maryland, 1650–1720.* Princeton, New Jersey: Princeton University Press, 1983.

Malone, Ann Patton. *Sweet Chariot: Slave Family and Household Structure in Nineteenth-Century Louisiana.* Chapel Hill: University of North Carolina Press, 1992.

Margavio, A. V., and Jerome J. Salomone. *Bread and Respect: The Italians of Louisiana.* Gretna, Louisiana: Pelican Publishing, 2002.

Marye, Florence. *The Story of the Page-King Family of Retreat Plantation, St. Simons Island and of the Golden Isles of Georgia.* Darien, Georgia: Published by the author, 2000.

Mathews, Donald G. *Religion in the Old South.* Chicago: University of Chicago Press, 1977.

Matrana, Marc R. *Lost Plantation: The Rise and Fall of Seven Oaks.* Jackson: University Press of Mississippi, 2005.

McCash, June Hall. *The Jekyll Island Cottage Colony.* Athens: University of Georgia Press, 1998.

———. *Jekyll Island's Early Years: From Prehistory Through Reconstruction.* Athens: University of Georgia Press, 1998.

McCash, William B. *The Jekyll Island Club: Southern Haven for America's Millionaires.* Athens: University of Georgia Press, 1989.

McDonald, William Lindsey. *A Walk Though the Past: People and Places of Florence and Lauderdale County, Alabama.* Florence: Country Lane Printing, 1997.

McLeRoy, Sherrie S. *Black Land, Red River: A Pictorial History of Grayson County, Texas.* Virginia Beach, Virginia: The Donning Company Publishers, 1993.

———. *Red River Women.* Plano: Republic of Texas Press, 1996.

McNeilly, Donald P. *Old South Frontier: Cotton Plantations and the Formation of Arkansas Society, 1819–1861.* Fayetteville: University of Arkansas Press, 2000.

Menn, Joseph Karl. *The Large Slaveholders of Louisiana—1860.* New Orleans: Pelican Publishing Company, 1964.

Meynard, Virginia. *The Venturers: The Hampton, Harrison, Earle Families of Virginia, South Carolina, and Texas.* Greenville, South Carolina: Southern Historical Press, 1981.

Milani, Ernesto R. "Marchigiani and Veneti on Sunnyside Plantation." In *Italian Immigrants in Rural and Small Town America*, edited by Rudolph J. Vecoli. New York: American Italian Historical Association, 1987.

———. "Peonage at Sunnyside and the Reaction of the Italian Government." In *Shadows Over Sunnyside: An Arkansas Plantation in Transition, 1830–1945*, edited by Jeannie M. Whayne. Fayetteville: University of Arkansas Press, 1993.

Miller, Mary Carol. *Lost Mansions of Mississippi.* Jackson: University Press of Mississippi, 1996.

Miller, Mary Warren, Ronald W. Miller, and David King Gleason. *The Great Houses of Natchez.* Jackson: University Press of Mississippi, 1986.

Moneyhon, Carl H. *The Impact of the Civil War and Reconstruction on Arkansas: Persistence in the Midst of Ruin.* Baton Rouge: Louisiana State University, 1994.

Moody, V. Alton. *Slavery on Louisiana Sugar Plantations.* New York: AMS Press, 1976.

Moore, Francis. *A Voyage to Georgia Begun in the Year 1735.* London: Jacob Robinson, 1744.

Morris, Thomas D. *Southern Slavery and the Law, 1619–1860.* Chapel Hill: University of North Carolina Press, 1996.

Morton, Dorothy Rich. *Nineteenth Century Homes of Fayette County.* Published by the author, 1974.

Mueller, Pamela Bauer. *Neptune's Honor: A Story of Loyalty and Love.* St. Simons Island: Pinata Publishing, 2005.

Mullin, Gerald W. *Flight and Rebellion, Slave Resistance in Eighteenth-Century Virginia.* London: Oxford University Press, 1975.

Mullins, Lisa C., ed. *Early Architecture of the South.* Washington: National Historical Society, 1987.

Mumford, Lewis. *The South in Architecture.* New York: Da Capo Press, 1967.

Murtagh, William J. *Keeping Time: The History and Theory of Preservation in America.* New York: John Wiley & Sons, 1997.

National Society of the Colonial Dames of America in the State of Alabama—Historical Activities Committee. *Alabama Portraits Prior to 1870.* Mobile : Gill Printing and Stationery Company, 1969.

Nichols, Frederick Doveton. *The Early Architecture of Georgia*. Chapel Hill: University of North Carolina Press, 1957.

Northup, Solomon. *Twelve Years a Slave*. Edited by Sue Eakin and Joseph Logsdon. Baton Rouge: Louisiana State University Press, 1968.

Oakes, James. *The Ruling Race: A History of American Slaveholders*. New York: Alfred A. Knopf, 1982.

Otto, John Solomon. *Southern Agriculture During the Civil War Era, 1860–1880*. Westport, Connecticut: Greenwood Press, 1994.

Overdyke, Darrell. *Louisiana Plantation Homes, Colonial and Antebellum*. New York: American Legacy Press, 1981.

Owen, Evelyn Wood. "Rocky Hill Castle." In *Historic Homes of Alabama and Their Traditions*, edited by Alabama Members of the National League of American Pen Women. Birmingham: Birmingham Pub. Co., 1969.

Paisley, Clifton. *From Cotton to Quail: An Agricultural Chronicle of Leon County, Florida, 1860–1967*. Gainesville: University of Florida Press, 1968.

———. *The Red Hills of Florida, 1528–1865*. Tuscaloosa: University of Alabama Press, 1989.

Patrick, James. *Architecture in Tennessee, 1768–1897*. Knoxville: University of Tennessee Press, 1990.

Percy, William Alexander. *Lanterns on the Levee: Recollections of a Planter's Son*. Baton Rouge: Louisiana State University Press, 1973.

Perrin, W. H., J. H. Battle, and G. C. Kniffer. *Kentucky: A History of the State*. Louisville: F. A. Batley Co., 1886.

Phillips, Ulrich B. *Life and Labor in the Old South*. Boston: Little, Brown and Company, 1963.

Plummer, Betty. *Historic Homes of Washington County, 1821–1860*. San Marcos, Texas: Rio Fresco, 1971.

Poesch, Jessie, and Barbara Bacot. *Louisiana Buildings 1720–1940*. Baton Rouge: Louisiana State University Press, 1997.

Postell, William Dosite. *The Health of Slaves on Southern Plantations*. Baton Rouge: Louisiana State University Press, 1951.

Pugh, Alexander Franklin. *Memorandum Book, 1850–1852*. Bethesda: University Publications of America, 1989.

Raboteau, Albert J. *Slave Religion: The "Invisible Institution" in the Antebellum South*. New York: Oxford University Press, 1978.

Ramsdell, Charles. *Reconstruction in Texas*. New York: Columbia University Press, 1910.

Ray, Bright. *Legends of the Red River Valley*. San Antonio, Texas: The Naylor Company, 1941.

Reeves, William D., with Daniel Alario, Sr. *Westwego, from Cheniere to Canal*. Westwego, Louisiana: Published privately by Mr. and Mrs. Daniel Alario, Sr., 1996.

Rehder, John B. *Delta Sugar: Louisiana's Vanishing Plantation Landscape*. Baltimore: Johns Hopkins University Press, 1999.

Riffel, Judy, ed. *Iberville Parish History*. Baton Rouge: Comité des Archives de la Louisiane, 1985.

Rifkind, Carole. *A Field Guide to American Architecture*. New York: New American Library, 1980.

Ripley, Eliza. *Social Life in Old New Orleans*. New York: D. Appleton and Co., 1912.

Roark, James L. *Masters Without Slaves: Southern Planters in the Civil War and Reconstruction*. New York: W.W. Norton & Company, 1977.

Robertson, James I., Jr. *The History of the Civil War*. New York: Eastern Acorn Press, 1979.

Robichaux, Albert J., Jr. *German Coast Families: European Origins and Settlement in Colonial Louisiana*. Rayne, Louisiana: Hebert Publications, 1997.

Robinson, Willard B. *Gone from Texas: Our Lost Architectural Heritage*. College Station: Texas A&M University Press, 1981.

Rodrigue, John C. *Reconstruction in the Cane Fields: From Slavery to Free Labor in Louisiana's Sugar Parishes 1862–1880*. Baton Rouge: Louisiana State University Press, 2001.

Rogers, George E., with David R. Chestnut, eds. *The Papers of Henry Laurens*. Columbia: University of South Carolina Press, 1974.

Rogers, Mary Nixon. "A History of Brazoria County, Texas." In *A History of Brazoria County, Texas*, edited by T. L. Smith, Jr. Privately published by the author, 1958.

Rogers, William Warren, Robert David Ward, et al. *Alabama: The History of a Deep South State*. Tuscaloosa: University of Alabama Press, 1994.

Roos, Netherton. *The Preservation of History in Fairfax County, Virginia: A Report Prepared for the Fairfax County History Commission, Fairfax County, Virginia, 2001*. Lanham, Maryland: University Press of America, 2002.

Sageser, Adelbert Bower. *Joseph L. Bristow: Kansas Progressive*. Lawrence: University Press of Kansas, 1968.

Sale, Edith Tunis, ed. *Historic Gardens of Virginia*. Richmond: James River Garden Club, 1923.

Schafer, Daniel L. "'A Swamp of an Investment'?: Richard Oswald's British East Florida Plantation Experiment." In *Colonial Plantations and Economy in Florida,* edited by Jane G. Landers, 11–38. Gainesville: University Press of Florida, 2000.

Schweninger, Loren. *Black Property Owners in the South, 1790–1915.* Champaign: University of Illinois Press, 1990.

Sellers, James Benson. *Slavery in Alabama.* Tuscaloosa: University of Alabama Press, 1994.

Severens, Kenneth. *Southern Architecture: 350 Years of Distinctive American Buildings.* New York: E. P. Dutton, 1981.

Sexton, Richard. *Vestiges of Grandeur: The Plantations of Louisiana's River Road.* San Francisco: Chronicle Books, 1999.

Sherwood, Waring. *The Story of James Jackson of "The Forks": An Historical Narrative.* S.l.: Graphic Arts, c. 1978.

Sikes, Lewright B. *The Public Life of Pierce Butler, South Carolina Statesman.* Washington: University Press of America, 1979.

Silverthorne, Elizabeth. *Plantation Life in Texas.* College Station, Texas: Texas A&M University Press, 1986.

Sizemore, Jean. *Ozark Vernacular Houses: A Study of Rural Homeplaces in the Arkansas Ozarks, 1830–1930.* Fayetteville: University of Arkansas Press, 1994.

Smedes, Susan Dabney. *Memorials of a Southern Planter.* Baltimore: Cushings & Bailey, 1887.

Smith, Allene De Shazo. *Greenwood Leflore and the Choctaw Indians of the Mississippi Valley.* Memphis: C. A. Davis Print. Co., 1951.

Smith, J. Frazer. *Plantation Houses and Mansions of the Old South.* New York: Dover Publications, 1993. Originally published as *White Pillars,* 1941.

Smith, Julia Floyd. *Slavery and Plantation Growth in Antebellum Florida, 1821–1860.* Gainesville: University of Florida Press, 1973.

———. *Slavery and Rice Culture in Low Country Georgia, 1750–1860.* Knoxville: University of Tennessee Press, 1985.

Smith, Reid. *Majestic Middle Tennessee.* Gretna, Louisiana: Pelican Publishing, 1976.

Smith, T. L., Jr., ed. *A History of Brazoria County, Texas.* Privately published by the author, 1958.

Starobin, Robert S., ed. *Blacks in Bondage: Letters of American Slaves.* New York: Barnes and Nobles Books, 1998.

Steel, Edward M., Jr. *T. Butler King of Georgia.* Athens: University of Georgia Press, 1964.

Sterkx, H. E. *Partners in Rebellion: Alabama Women During the Civil War.* Rutherford, NJ: Fairleigh Dickinson University Press, 1970.

Sterling, Ada. *A Belle of the Fifties: Memoirs of Mrs. Clay, of Alabama.* New York: Doubleday, 1905.

Sternberg, Mary Ann. *Along the River Road: Past and Present on Louisiana's Historic Byway.* Baton Rouge: Louisiana State University Press, 2001.

Stetson, Charles W. *Washington and His Neighbors.* Richmond, Virginia: Garrett and Massie, 1956.

Stoney, Samuel Gaillard. *Plantations of the Carolina Low Country.* New York: Dover, 1989.

Strickland, Alice. *Ashes on the Wind: The Story of the Lost Plantations.* Volusia County, Florida: Volusia County Historical Commission, 1985.

Strobel, Abner J. "The Old Plantations and Their Owners of Brazoria County, Texas." In *A History of Brazoria County, Texas,* edited by T. L. Smith, Jr. Privately published by the author, 1958.

Styron, William. *The Confessions of Nat Turner.* New York: Vintage International, 1993.

Swanson, Betsy. *Historic Jefferson Parish, From Shore to Shore.* Gretna, Louisiana: Pelican Publishing, 1975.

Takaki, Ronald T. *The Pro-Slavery Crusade: The Agitation to Reopen the African Slave Trade.* New York: Free Press, 1971.

Taylor, Helen. *Circling Dixie: Contemporary Southern Culture through a Transatlantic Lens.* New Brunswick, New Jersey: Rutgers University Press, 2001.

Trinkley Michael. *Further Investigation of the Stoney/Baynard Main House, Hilton Head Island, Beaufort County, South Carolina.* Research Series 47. Columbia: Chicora Foundation, 1996.

United Confederate Veterans, Arkansas Division. *Confederate Women of Arkansas in the Civil War, 1861–'65.* Little Rock: Confederate Veterans, 1907.

Usner, Daniel H., Jr. *Indians, Settlers, and Slaves in a Frontier Exchange Economy: The Lower Mississippi Before 1783.* Chapel Hill: University of North Carolina Press, 1992.

Van Court, Catharine. *In Old Natchez.* New York: Doubleday, 1937.

Van Deburg, William L. *The Slave Drivers: Black Agricultural Labor Supervisors in the Antebellum South.* Westport, Connecticut: Greenwood Press, 1979.

Vanstory, Burnette. *Georgia's Land of the Golden Isles.* Athens: University of Georgia Press, 1970.

Vecoli, Rudolph J., ed. *Italian Immigrants in Rural and Small Town America*. New York: American Italian Historical Association, 1987.

Vlach, John Michael. *Back of the Big House: The Architecture of Plantation Slavery*. Chapel Hill: University of North Carolina Press, 1993.

Waterman, Thomas Tileston. *Mansions of Virginia, 1706–1776*. New York: Bonanza Books, 1945.

Webber, Thomas L. *Deep Like the Rivers: Education in the Slave Quarter Community, 1831–1865*. New York: Norton, 1978.

Whayne, Jeannie M., ed. *Shadows over Sunnyside: An Arkansas Plantation in Transition, 1830–1945*. Fayetteville: University of Arkansas Press, 1993.

White, Deborah Gray. *Ar'n't I a Woman? Female Slaves in the Plantation South*. Rev. ed. New York: W. W. Norton and Company, 1999.

Whittington, Hiram Abiff. *Observations of Arkansas: The 1824–1863 Letters of Hiram Abiff Whittington*. Hot Springs, Arkansas: Garland County Historical Society, 1997.

Wiencek, Henry. *The Hairstons: An American Family in Black and White*. New York: St. Martin's Griffin, 2000.

Williams, James. *James Williams, an American Slave, Who Was for Several Years a Driver on a Cotton Plantation in Alabama*. New York: The American Anti-Slavery Society, 1838.

Wish, Harvey, ed. *Slavery in the South: First-Hand Accounts of the Ante-Bellum Southland From Northern and Southern Whites, Negroes & Foreign Observers*. New York: Farrar, Straus & Giroux, 1964.

Wood, Betty. *The Origins of American Slavery*. New York: Hill and Wang, 1997.

Woodward, C. Vann. *The Burden of Southern History*. New York: Vintage Books, 1960.

Worley, Ted R., ed. *At Home in Confederate Arkansas: Letters to and from Pulaski Countians*. Little Rock, Arkansas: Pulaski County Historical Society, 1955.

Wyatt-Brown, Bertram. *Honor and Violence in the Old South*. Oxford: Oxford University Press, 1986.

———. "Leroy Percy and Sunnyside: Planter Mentality and Italian Peonage in the Mississippi Delta." In *Shadows Over Sunnyside: An Arkansas Plantation in Transition, 1830–1945*, edited by Jeannie M. Whayne. Fayetteville: University of Arkansas Press, 1993.

Wynne, Lewis N., and John T. Parks. *Florida's Antebellum Homes*. Charleston, South Carolina: Arcadia Publishing, 2004.

Yetman, Norman R. *Voices From Slavery*. Mineola, New York: Dover Publications, 2000.

**Articles in Journals and Periodicals (Including Published Primary Sources)**

Anderson, Mary Ware. "The Life & Times of Henry Ware." *Louisiana Genealogical Review* (June 1989).

Andreassen, John C. "Frances Benjamin Johnston and Her Views of Uncle Sam." *Louisiana History*, vol. 1, no. 2 (Spring 1960): 130–136.

"Another Deadline for Seven Oaks." *New Orleans States-Item*, 10 May 1977.

Ash, Stephen V. "Poor Whites in the Occupied South, 1861–1865." *Journal of Southern History*, vol. 57, issue 1 (February 1991): 39–62.

Associated Press. "Historic Mansion Faces Wrecking Ball." *The Enquirer*, 11 August 2002.

Associated Press. "Mansion Razed after Attempts to Preserve It Come Up Short." *The Courier-Journal*, 24 November 2002.

Avans, D'Anne, and Elizabeth David. "Franconia Saves a Church." *Fairfax Chronicles*, vol. 8, no. 4 (November 1984).

Barker, Eugene C. "The African Slave Trade in Texas." *Quarterly of the Texas State Historical Association*, vol. 6 (October 1902): 145–158.

Barry, Fred. "7 Oaks Grant Request Okayed by Jeff Council." *Times-Picayune*, 9 April 1976.

———. "Bid to Save Mansion Accelerates." *Times-Picayune*, 20 March 1976.

———. "Demolition of Ruins Extended 6 Months." *Times-Picayune*, 9 November 1976.

———. "Fate of Seven Oaks." *Times-Picayune*, 14 March 1976.

———. "Once Splendid Orleans Mansion Now Crumbling Towards Death." *Times-Picayune*, 26 July 1970.

———. "Seven Oaks." *Times-Picayune*, 29 February 1976.

———. "Seven Oaks Finale." *Times-Picayune*, 24 October 1976.

———. "State Funds Available to Restore Seven Oaks." *Times-Picayune*, 6 April 1976.

Behre, Patricia. "Update: Elmwood to Be Restored." *Times-Picayune*, 11 August 1985, F–1.

Behre, Robert. "Plantation House Ruins Vulnerable." *Post and Courier* (Charleston), 2 August 2004.

Bell, Alexander H. "Marshall-Dent Family Notes." *National Genealogical Society Quarterly* 19 (1931): 1–4.

———. "Some Maryland and Virginia Ancestors: Dent, Wilkinson, Marshall, Brooke, Fowke, Harrison, Etc." *National Genealogical Society Quarterly* 20 (1932): 86–96.

"Belle Grove, Called Finest of Homes, Doomed by Desertion." *Morning Advocate* (Baton Rouge), 20 September 1936.

"A Beloved Friend Has Fallen! and the People Mourn!" *The Enquirer* (Florence, Alabama), 22 August 1840.

Berkley, Henry J. "Maryland Physicians at the Period of the Revolutionary War." *Maryland Historical Magazine* 24 (1929): 1–10.

Berlin, Ira et al. "Family and Freedom: Black Families in the American Civil War." *History Today* 37 (January 1987): 8–15.

Berry, Stephen. "More Alluring at a Distance: Absentee Patriarchy and the Thomas Butler King Family." *Georgia Historical Quarterly*, vol. 81, no. 4 (Winter 1997): 863–896.

"Bishop Deal Near Final." *Marshall News Messenger*, 20 November 1962.

"Bishop Purchase Ends 81 Years of Ownership." *Marshall News Messenger*, 16 March 1961.

"Bishop Purchase Rescinded by City." *Marshall News Messenger*, 26 March 1961.

Bonner, James C. "Plantation Architecture of the Lower South on the Eve of the Civil War." *Journal of Southern History*, vol. 11 (1965).

Borne, Frank J., Jr. "Avondale—Waggaman: The Legacy of a Family and Their Land." *Jefferson History Notebook*, vol. 10, no. 1 (August 2006).

Brace, Sally Moore. "James Jackson." *Lauderdale County Pictures of the Past*, 1 September 1999, http://www.rootsweb.com/~allauder/pic–jamesjackson.htm (accessed 28 March 2006).

Branson, Reed. "LeFlore Property Wrapped Again in Intrigue." *Commercial Appeal*, 2 June 2002, p. E1+

Britton, Morris L. "Coffee, Holland." *Handbook of Texas Online*, http://www.tsha.utexas.edu/handbook/online/articles/CC/fco12.html (accessed 23 July 2006).

———. "Glen Eden Plantation." *Handbook of Texas Online*, http://www.tsha.utexas.edu/handbook/online/articles/GG/ccg2.html (accessed 23 July 2006).

———. "Porter, Sophia Suttonfield." *Handbook of Texas Online*, http://www.tsha.utexas.edu/handbook/online/articles/PP/fpo18.html (accessed 23 July 2006).

Broadbent, Stephanie. "Long-gone Plantations Left Legacy— Homes May Be Ruins, but Their Names Live On." *Carolina Morning News*, 13 July 1999.

Bruno, Stephanie. "High Life on the Acadian Coast." *Times-Picayune*, 6 August 2005.

Bugbee, Lester G. "Slavery in Early Texas." *Political Science Quarterly*, vol. 13 (September 1898): 389–412.

Burke, John. "Requiem for Belle Grove: How a Famous Showplace Became a Famous Ruin." *Times-Picayune*, 23 October 1988.

"Burr's Mississippi Sweetheart, Madeline." *New York Times*, 10 July 1904.

Busby, Charles. "History Is Business, Natchezians Produce Book on '32 Murder." *Natchez Democrat*, 13 October 1985.

Buser, Lawrence. "Blaze Consumes Home, History." *Commercial Appeal*, 12 November 1987.

Canova, Johnnie. "Belle Grove: How One of the Grandest Plantation Homes in the South Was Lost." *Post South* (Plaquemine, Louisiana), 8 August 1996.

Capone, Audrey B. "Ravensworth: A Short History of Annandale, Virginia." *Annandale Flag*, http://www.annandaleflag.com/histroy.htm (accessed 3 November 2007).

Carpenter, Alma. "A Note on the History of the Forest Plantation, Natchez." *Journal of Mississippi History*, vol. 46 (1984): 130–37.

Cashin, Joan. "The Structure of Antebellum Planter Families: 'The Ties that Bound Us Was Strong.'" *Journal of Southern History*, vol. 56 (February 1990): 55–70.

Chasen, Donna. "Ossian Hall Destroyed Mansion Had Ties to Lee-Custis Family." *Free Lance-Star*, 14 January 2006.

Coglan, Francis. "Pierce Butler, 1744–1822, First Senator from South Carolina." *South Carolina Historical Magazine* 78 (April 1977): 104–119.

"Col. Charles L. Bullock, His Family and Home." *Clark County Historical Journal* (Winter 1979–80): 205–17.

"Commitment Is Delivered." *Marshall News Messenger*, 16 March 1961.

Conner, Kevin. "Quarry Still Has Stone Cold Opposition." *Athens Banner-Herald*, 28 April 2002.

Corley, Dawson. "137 Years of History." *State Times*, 13 October 1978.

Coulter, E. Merton. "A Century of a Georgia Plantation." *Mississippi Valley Historical Review*, vol. 16, no. 3 (December 1929): 334–346.

Criss, Leslie. "1863 Drawing Shows Windsor Before Fire." *Vicksburg Evening Post*, 7 August 1992.

Curlee, Abigail. "The History of a Texas Slave Plantation, 1831–63." *Southwestern Historical Quarterly,* vol. 26 (October 1922): 79–127.

*Daily Picayune.* Obituary of Gabriel Aime, 24 September 1854.

D'Amato, Ray. "History of Ravensworth." *Ravensworth Farm Online,* http://www.ravensworthfarm.org/history.htm (accessed 3 November 2007).

Dattel, Eugene R. "Cotton in a Global Economy: Mississippi (1800–1860)." *Mississippi History Now,* http://mshistory.k12.ms.us/index.php?s=articles (accessed 17 November 2007).

"Davidson Urges Steps to Purchase Wyalucing." *Marshall News Messenger,* 15 November 1962.

"Deal Pending on Wyalucing." *Marshall News Messenger,* 18 November 1962.

"Death of Dr. C. M. Vaiden." *Daily Clarion,* 7 February 1880, p. 2.

DeBerry, John H. "La Grange–La Belle Village." *Tennessee Historical Quarterly* (Summer 1971): 133–153.

de Golyer, Homer. "Sophia Porter's Texas Adventures Read Like Arabian Nights Chapters." *Dallas Morning News,* 11 April 1942.

"Demolition Delay OK'd." *Times-Picayune,* 6 July 1977.

"Demolition of Wyalucing Near." *Marshall News Messenger,* 16 December 1962.

Donze, Frank. "Fire Destroys Plantation, Ends Restoration Dreams." *Times-Picayune/States-Item,* 30 January 1982, sec. 1, p. 17.

Drake, Rebecca B. "Windsor: Yankees Crash the Party." http://battleofraymond.org/history/windsor.htm (accessed 14 April 2006).

DuFour, Charles. "Henry Howard, Forgotten Architect." *Journal of Architectural Historians,* vol. XI, no. 4 (December 1952).

Dufour, Pie. "Preview of Seven Oaks." *Times-Picayune,* 5 May 1957.

Easterby, J. H. "Memoirs of Frederick Augustus Porcher." *South Carolina Historical and Genealogical Magazine,* vol. 45 (1944): 39.

"Elmwood Deadline Passes; Preservationists Still Hope." *Times-Picayune/States-Item,* 21 July 1982. sec. 1, p. 16.

"Elmwood Group Pessimistic as Deadline Nears." *Times-Picayune/States-Item,* 17 April 1982, sec. 1, p. 19.

"Elmwood Plantation Gets Marker." *Times-Picayune,* 2 May 1977.

Emery, Theo. "More Family Cemeteries Dying Away in the South as Rural Land Is Developed, Ancestral Graves Are Relocated, Bulldozed or Encircled by Construction." *Washington Post,* 27 March 2006, A3.

"End to Wyalucing Appears Near—Unless Steps Taken." *Marshall News Messenger,* 9 September 1962.

*Evening Picayune.* Obituary of Valcour Aime, January 3, 1867.

"Expect Old Home Will Be Preserved." *Sherman Daily Democrat,* 13 August 1939, p. 6.

"Famed Mansion Appears Doomed." *Marshall News Messenger,* 19 August 1962.

Faust, Drew Gilpin. "Culture, Conflict, and Community: The Meaning of Power on an Ante-bellum Plantation." *Journal of Southern History,* vol. 14, no. 1 (1980).

Feare, Varian. "Rocky Hill Mansion in Highlands." *Birmingham News,* 15 November 1936.

Ferguson, John. "Decay, Vandals Seal Plantation's Fate." *Times-Picayune/States-Item,* February 1982.

———. "Elmwood Resurrection May Be Folly." *Times-Picayune/States-Item,* 13 February 1982, sec. 3, p. 1.

Ferleger, Louis. "Farm Mechanization in the Southern Sugar Section After the Civil War." *Louisiana History,* vol. 23 (Winter 1982): 21–34.

Ford, Wayne. "Casulon Remembered, Oconee Residents Have Fond Memories of Antebellum Mansion." *Athens Banner-Herald,* 29 May 2002.

———. "Fire Destroys Historic Walton Plantation." *Athens Banner-Herald,* 27 March 2002.

———. "Sheriff: Plantation Fire Cause May Never Be Known." *Athens Banner-Herald,* 16 February 2003.

Fortune, Beverly. "Brilliant Moves." *Lexington Herald-Leader,* 8 November 2002.

"Franconia Mansion Dates From 1763." *Springfield Independent,* 10 November 1954.

Frazer, Tom. "Seven Oaks Plantation Torn Down, Carted Off." *New Orleans States-Item,* 30 August 1977.

Fuchs, Nancy. "One–time Owner of Bush Hill Buried Near Centreville." *Centre View,* 21 June 1986.

Gaillard, Mrs. A. P. Leise Palmer. "The Rocks: A Sketch." August 11, 1942, http://www.rootsweb.ancestry.com/~scbchs/r5.html (accessed 14 April 2008).

Gamble, Robert. "The White Columns Tradition: Classical Architecture and the Southern Mystique." *Southern Humanities Review,* vol. 11 (1997.)

"Georgia Plantation House Survives War and Time Only to Succumb to Fire." *Civil War Interactive,* 29 March 2002, http://www.civilwarinteractive.com/casulonfire.htm (accessed 11 July 2002).

Gerald, Herbert P. "Marshall Bible Records." *National Genealogical Society Quarterly* 15 (1927): 36–41.

———."Marshall Hall Burying Ground at Marshall Hall, Md." *Maryland Historical Magazine* 24 (1929): 172–176.

Gill, James. "Jeff Plantation Can Rise Again, 2 Groups Claim." *Times-Picayune/States-Item,* 16 January 1982, sec. 1, p. 15.

"Glen Eden Plantation." *Sherman Democrat,* 28 January 1951, sec. 2, p. 8.

"Governor Boynton's Marriage." *Atlanta Constitution,* 1 May 1883.

"The Governor's Nuptials to Take Place on Monday Evening." *Atlanta Constitution,* 29 April 1883.

Gray-White, Kathryn. "Casulon Plantation Lives On." *North Georgia Journal* (Summer 1998).

Grootkerk, Paul. "Artistic Images of Mythological Reality: The Antebellum Plantation." *Southern Quarterly,* vol. 32 (Summer 1994).

Gunnell, Virginia Burt. "A Gentleman Gardener of Virginia." *Garden Club of Virginia Journal,* vol. 1, no. 6 (July–August 1956).

Hailey, James L. "Clay Castle." *Handbook of Texas Online,* http://www.tsha.utexas.edu/handbook/online/articles/CC/ccc3.html (accessed 13 November 2004).

Harper, C. W. "House Servants and Field Hands: Fragmentation in the Antebellum Slave Community." *North Carolina Historical Review,* vol. 55 (1978).

Harris, René. "Ellersly Plantation." *Handbook of Texas Online,* http://www.tsha.utexas.edu/handbook/online/articles/EE/ace2.html (accessed 10 April 2006).

"Historic Carriage Saved." *Greenwood Commonwealth,* 1 April 1942, p. 6.

"Historic Forks Burns to Ground Monday." *Florence Herald,* 9 June 1966, p. 1.

"Historic Landmark Burns." *Jackson Daily News,* 2 April 1942, sec. 2, p. 8.

"History of Lake Jackson Plantation." *Texas Beyond History,* http://www.texasbeyondhistory.net/jackson/history.html (accessed 1 August 2004).

Hodge, Paul. "Fire Destroys Historic Md. Mansion." *Washington Post,* 17 October 1981, B1.

Holbrook, Abigail Curlee. "Cotton Marketing in Antebellum Texas." *Southwestern Historical Quarterly,* vol. 73 (April 1970): 431–455.

Holcombe, Franklin. "Lucy Holcombe Pickens." *Harrison County Historical Herald,* vol. III, no. 1 (September 1966).

Hosch, Robert, Jr. "Plantation Restoration Is Key." Letter to the editor, *Times-Picayune,* 2 August 2003, B–6.

"Houma Fire Destroys Plantation." *The Advocate* (Baton Rouge), 10 December 1987, 5–B.

House, Albert V., Jr. "The Management of a Rice Plantation in Georgia, 1834–1861, as Revealed in the Journal of Hugh Fraser Grant." *Agricultural History,* vol. 13 (October1939): 208–217.

Howie, Bob. "Ruins of Windsor Given to State." *Clarion-Ledger,* 12 May 1974.

Hunt, Donna. "Memories of Sophia Porter Alive, Well." *Denison Herald,* 12 August 1979.

Hyde, Bert. "Plaquemines Mansion Rich in History: Showplace of Another Era." *States-Item,* n.d.

"Imported Stallion, for 1838" (advertisement). *North Alabamian* (Tuscumbia, Alabama), 6 April 1838.

"In Memoriam: The Late Dr. Cowles Mead Vaiden." *Daily Clarion,* 18 February 1880, p. 2.

Jackson, Lily. "Old South, New Address." *Times-Picayune,* 17 December 1993.

James, Susie. "Cemetery All That Remains of Fabled Malmaison." *Greenwood Commonwealth,* 23 March 1995.

"Jeff Council Hit by Alario." *Times-Picayune,* 13 April 1976.

"Jeff Council Turns Back on Seven Oaks Home." *Times-Picayune,* 10 September 1976.

"Jeff Plans to Preserve Seven Oaks." *Times-Picayune,* 26 March 1976.

"Jesse James Deleted in Mansion Resolution." *Times-Picayune,* 21 August 1976.

Jordan, Julie Phillips. "Rockin' the Quarry, Benefit Concert Is Part of Residents' 12-year Battle to Fight Proposed Rock Quarry." *Athens Banner-Herald,* 4 April, 2002.

Kaiser, Keith. "Effort Will Be Made to Restore Ancient Mansion." *West Bank Guide,* 21 June 1967.

Kent, Doris. "'Petit Versailles' a Memory: Only Charred Wall Remains." *Times-Picayune,* 25 April 1920.

Kirk, F. M. "Springfield Plantation." http://www.rootsweb.com/scbchs/spring.html (accessed 5 November 2007).

———. "White Hall Plantation, White and Porcher Families." http://www.rootsweb.ancestry.com/~scbchs/whitehall.html (accessed 23 February 2008).

Kleiner, Diana J. "Eagle Island Plantation." *Handbook of Texas Online*, http://www.tsha.utexas.edu/handbook/online/articles/EE/ace1.html (accessed 23 October 2005).

———. "Orozimbo Plantation." *Handbook of Texas Online*, http://www.tsha.utexas.edu/handbook/online/articles/OO/aco1.html (accessed 9 October 2004).

LaFourcade, Emile. "Elmwood as a Park?" *Times-Picayune/States-Item*, 22 May 1982, sec. 1, p. 15.

———. "Elmwood Paints Picture of Past." *Times-Picayune/States-Item*, 14 March 1983, sec. 1, p. 15.

———. "La. Money Sought for Plantation House." *Times-Picayune/States-Item*, 30 January 1982, sec. 1, p. 18.

———. "Preservationists Are Given 6 Months to Buy Elmwood." *Times-Picayune/States-Item*, 21 January 1982, sec. 1, g. 13.

Langley, Mrs. Lee J. "Malmaison, Palace in a Wilderness, Home of General LeFlore." *Chronicles of Oklahoma*, vol. 5, no. 4, 371–380.

Lathrop, Barnes F. "The Lafourche District in 1862: Confederate Revival." *Louisiana History*, vol. 1, no. 4 (Fall 1960): 300–319.

Lawlis, Lea Ellen. "Glen Eden Furniture Returns to Sherman, Prize Antiques Show Sophia's Style." *Sherman Democrat*, 8 July 1979.

———. "Memories of Glen Eden Recalled." *Sherman Democrat*, 24 August 1979, p. 16.

Lawrence, Elisabeth Garr. "Preserve Farm's Brilliant History." *Lexington Herald-Leader*, 18 November 2002.

Lee, Vince. "Orange Grove Will Stand a Little Longer." *Times-Picayune*, 19 May 1979, sec. 1, p. 5.

"Letter Explains Wyalucing Sale." *Marshall News Messenger*, 2 December 1962.

Lewis, Kathleen. "The Woman Called Lucy." *The Houston Chronicle Rotogravure Magazine*, 1 March 1953, p. 14.

———. "The Woman Called Lucy." *The State Magazine*, 2 November 1965, p. 18.

Longley, Lee J. "Italians in the Cotton Fields." *Manufacturer's Record*, vol. 45, 7 April 1904.

"The Loss of Mount Brilliant." Joint Statement of Blue Grass Trust and Greg Goodman, http://www.bluegrasstrust.org/news/stories/BRILLIANt–2.htm (accessed 30 March 2005).

Lucia, Joseph. "Century-Old Mansion Falls Under Order to Move Back Levees." *Times-Picayune*, 10 March 1940.

Magee, Lucie. "Vaiden . . . a Romantic Past and a Promising Spot for Industry." *Jackson Daily News*, 30 April 1950.

"Malmaison." *The Conservative*, 10 April 1942, p. 1.

"Malmaison Destroyed by Fire Last Tuesday Night." *The Conservative*, 3 April 1942, p. 1.

Marshall, M. E. "Marshall Hall on the Potomac." *Marshall Hall Foundation, Inc.*, http://marshallhall.org/history.html (accessed 24 May 2006).

Martin, Bob. "Historic Forks Burns." *Tri-Cities Daily*, 6 June 1966, p. 1.

Martin, Lisa. "Elmwood's Fate Seems Uncertain As Deadline Nears." *Times-Picayune/States-Item*, 4 July 1982, sec. 7, p. 1.

———. "Owners 'Sitting on' Plantation." *Times-Picayune*, 5 August 1984, A-20.

Martin, Wanda, and H. B. Arnold, Jr. "Col. Joseph Allen Whitaker and the 'Rosedale' Plantation." *Clark County Historical Journal* (Winter 1979–80): 250–260.

Matrana, Marc R. "Old Mansion Gone Forever." Letter to the editor, *Times-Picayune*, 9 August 2003, B-6.

———. "On Cane and Coolies: Chinese Laborers on Post-Antebellum Louisiana Sugar Plantations as Exemplified on the Millaudon Plantation of Jefferson Parish." *Jefferson History Notebook*, vol. 7, no. 1 (February 2003).

———. "Seven Oaks Plantation: A Lasting Legacy, The 25th Anniversary of the Demolition." *Jefferson History Notebook*, vol. 6, no. 1 (February 2002).

McMillan, John. "Capote vs. Seven Oaks." *Dixie Roto Magazine, Times-Picayune*, 17 June 1973, p. 10.

Miller, Herschel. "Goodbye Seven Oaks." *New Orleans*, May 1969, 28–31.

Mims, Sam. "Our Dream House: Beautiful Belle Grove." *Louisiana Conservation Review* (Winter 1940/1941).

Mitchell, Sarah E. "Similar Federal Homes in Southside Virginia and Northern North Carolina." http://www.vintagedesigns.com/architectuer/fed/vanchome/.

Montgomery, Susan. "Malmaison Purchase Completed." *The Conservative*, 8 November 2001, p. 1.

Moody, V. A. "Slavery on Louisiana Sugar Plantations." *Louisiana Historical Quarterly*, vol. 7 (April 1924): 191–303.

Moreland, George M. "Vaiden: City of Fine Traditions." *Commercial Appeal*, 1 December 1929, sec. 1, p. 12.

Morgan, David L. "Help Groups Get Ahead of the Wrecking Ball." *Lexington Herald-Leader*, 25 October 2002.

"Much of Mount Brilliant Restored." *Lexington Herald-Leader,* 7 November 2002.

Murphy, Caryle. "Historic Plantation Razed by Arson." *Washington Post,* 17 March 1977, E1+.

Newberry, Farrar. "Manchester Mansion and Its Master." *Southern Standard,* 11 November 1965.

"News of Some of the Plantation Houses in Southern Louisiana." *Préservation,* Louisiana Landmarks Society, March 1958.

Newton, James E. "Slave Artisans and Craftsmen: The Roots of Afro-American Art." *Black Scholar,* vol. 9 (November 1977): 35–42.

O'Byrne, James. "Parish Paid Dearly for Colorful Politics." *Times-Picayune,* 12 July 1993.

"Offer for Wyalucing Withdrawn by Society." *Marshall News Messenger,* 6 September 1962.

"An Old Landmark Gone." *Florence Herald,* 17 June 1897.

Pargas, Damian Alan. "Work and Slave Family Life in Antebellum Northern Virginia." *Journal of Family History,* vol. 31, no. (October 2006): 335–357.

Perry, James A. "Elmwood Dig: Archeologists, Preservationists Study Plantation Site for Historical Data." *Times-Picayune,* 28 November 1982, sec. 2, p. 8.

Pitts, Stella. "Even in Ruins, the St. Louis Was Inspiring." *Times-Picayune,* 22 January 1978, sec. 2, p. 4.

———."Magnificent Windsor Ruins Due Historical Restoration." *Times-Picayune,* 7 April 1977.

———."Orange Grove Only Ghost of Former Self." *Times-Picayune,* 14 January 1979.

———."Plantation Post-Mortem: Grand Home of Another Era Is Dead; Indifference Killed It." *Times-Picayune,* 16 June 1974.

———."Seven Oaks in Westwego Is on Path to Disintegration." *Times-Picayune,* 14 April 1974.

"Plaquemines Acts to Save Home from Demolition." *Times-Picayune,* 8 May 1979, sec. 1, p. 2.

"Plea for Seven Oaks Goes to Panel." *Times-Picayune,* 27 July 1976.

Pope, John. "A Forward Step for Jeff History?" *New Orleans States-Item,* 19 January 1977.

———. "Don Lee Keith, 62, Writer, Instructor." Obituary. *Times-Picayune,* 30 July 2003.

———. "History Is Bulldozed at Seven Oaks." *New Orleans States-Item,* 5 September 1977.

———."Hope Among the Ruins?" *New Orleans States-Item,* 13 March 1976.

———. "Land Acquisition May Save Mansion." *New Orleans States-Item,* 20 March 1976.

———."Politics and the Plantation." *New Orleans States-Item,* 17 April 1976.

———. "River Mansion Traces Doom." *New Orleans States-Item,* 27 February 1976.

———. "Seven Oaks Safe for Now." *New Orleans States-Item,* 27 November 1976.

———. "Seven Oaks Wins Stay of Execution." *New Orleans States-Item,* 9 November 1976.

———. "Stay of Execution May Save 7 Oaks." *New Orleans States-Item,* 6 November 1976.

———. "When It Was Home . . ." *New Orleans States-Item,* 6 June 1977, sec. B.

"Possessions Saved, Pillars Remain, the Past Remembered." *Historically Speaking, A Quarterly Newsletter of Historic Columbia,* vol. 43, issue 3 (Winter 2005).

Price, C. W. "Rich Lands Fading into River Current as New Levees Rise." *The Progress,* 19 August 1938.

"Price Discussed for Wyalucing." *Marshall News Messenger,* 4 November 1962.

Price, H. B. "Terrebonne Parish, Louisiana." *Debow's review, Agricultural, commercial, industrial progress and resource,* vol. 8, issue 2 (February 1850): 146–147.

Prichard, Walter. "The Effects of the Civil War on the Louisiana Sugar Industry." *Journal of Southern History,* vol. 5, issue 3 (August 1939): 315–332.

———."Routine on a Louisiana Sugar Plantation under the Slavery Regime." *Mississippi Valley Historical Review,* vol. 14, issue 2 (September 1927): 168–178.

Pugh, W. W. "Recollections of an Old Citizen of Bayou Lafourche and Its Inhabitants from the Year 1820–1825." *Thibodeaux Sentinel,* 15 August 1903.

Puneky, Claire. "Bayou Landmarks." *Times-Picayune,* 26 February 1978.

Quinn, Mary Alice. "The Homes of La Belle Village." *Commercial Appeal,* 22 January 1967.

Ray, G. B. "Glen Eden: Frontier Story of Romance and Tragedy in Life of Sohpia Coffee." *Sherman Democrat,* 19 September 1948.

"Razing Starts on Wyalucing." *Marshall News Messenger,* 26 November 1962.

"Razing Wyalucing to Start Tuesday." *Marshall News Messenger*, 28 October 1962.

Richard Marshall Scott Obituary. *Alexandria Gazette*, 13 September 1833.

Rivers, Bill. "Pink Mansion Gutted by Fire." *State Times* (Baton Rouge), 17 March 1852.

Roark, Allen. "Choctaws Purchase Carroll County Land of Former Chief Leflore." *Delta Business Journal*, August 2002.

"Seven Oaks." *Préservation*, Louisiana Landmarks Society, March 1957.

"Seven Oaks." *Préservation*, Louisiana Landmarks Society, July 1958.

"Seven Oaks." *Times-Picayune*, 29 February 1976.

"Seven Oaks 1840–1977." *Préservation*, Louisiana Landmarks Society, November 1977.

"Seven Oaks Is Denied Federal Aid." *Times-Picayune*, 2 September 1976.

"Seven Oaks Last Chance." *Dixie*, 14 May 1972.

"Seven Oaks Mansion in Westwego Crumbling." *Times-Picayune*, 22 February 1967.

"Seven Oaks Torn Down." *Times-Picayune*, 31 August 1977.

"Seven Oaks Plantation, Westwego: The Roof's On—What Next?" *Préservation*, Louisiana Landmarks Society, August 1957.

Shea, William L. "Battle of Ditch Bayou." *Arkansas Historical Quarterly*, vol. 39 (August 1980): 195–207.

Shofner, Jerrell H. "Mary Grace Quackenbos, A Visitor Florida Did Not Want." *Florida Historical Quarterly*, vol. 58 (January 1980): 273–290.

Shugg, Roger Wallace. "Survival of the Plantation System in Louisiana." *Journal of Southern History*, vol. 3, issue 3 (August 1937): 311–325.

Sibley, Marilyn M. "Jackson, Abner." *Handbook of Texas Online*, http://www.tsha.utexas.edu/handbook/online/articles/JJ/fja29.html (accessed 1 August 2004).

Smith, Carolyn Vance. "Dana and Dockery Charged with Murder." *Natchez Democrat*, 19 August 1984.

———. "Goat Castle: 52 Years Ago, A Calamity Shocked the World." *Clarion-Ledger*, 26 August 1984.

———. "In 1933, Goat Castle Opened for Tours." *Natchez Democrat*, 26 August 1984.

Soniat, Meloncy C. "The Tchoupitoulas Plantation." *Louisiana Historical Quarterly*, vol. 7, no. 2 (1924): 308–315.

"St. James Plantation Owner Moise J. Hymel Is Dead at 86." *Times-Picayune*, 23 January 1990, B-4.

Stamper, John. "Mount Brilliant to Be Razed." *Lexington Herald-Leader*, 19 October 2002.

Stine, Jeffrey K. "The Tennessee-Tombigbee Waterway and the Evolution of Cultural Resources Management." *The Public Historian*, vol. 14, no. 2 (Spring, 1992): 7–30.

Stokes, Karen. "Generations: Plantation Christmas." *Lowcountry NOW*, http://www.lowcountrynow.com/stories/121602/LOCgenerations.shtml (accessed 1 August 2005).

Stone, Alfred Holt. "The Italian Cotton Grower, the Negro's Problem." *South Atlantic Quarterly*, vol. 4 (January 1905): 42–47.

"Sugar in the Dirt: Excavations at Lake Jackson Plantation." *Texas Beyond History*, http://www.texasbeyondhistory.net/jackson/ (accessed 1 August 2004).

Swanson, Betsy. "Seven Oaks: Lost Forever?" *New Orleans States-Item*, 30 October 1976.

———. "What Will Happen to Seven Oaks?" *Friends of the Cabildo Newsletter*, December 1976.

Swanson, Betsy, and Bethlyn McCloskey. "The Saga of Seven Oaks." *Préservation*, Louisiana Landmarks Society, October 1976: 1+.

———. "Seven Oaks: Hope, Despair, and Hope Again." Abbreviated version. *Préservation*, Louisiana Landmarks Society, July 1976: 4+.

Swindell, Ray. "Bishop Property Acquired by City." *Marshall News Messenger*, 15 March 1961.

Swope, Brad. "Mulberry Grove: Historic and Ecological Treasure." *Savannah Magazine*, May/June 2002.

"The Thorough Bred Stallion" (advertisement). *North Alabamian* (Tuscumbia, Alabama), 6 April 1838.

Tolbert, Frank X. "A Fight to Save Old 'Wyalucing.'" *Dallas Morning News*, 2 October 1962.

———. "About a Girl Called 'Lady Paul Revere.'" *Dallas Morning News*, n.d.

Toledano, Roulhac B. "Louisiana's Golden Age: Valcour Aime in St. James Parish." *Louisiana History*, vol. 10, issue 3 (1969).

Treadway, Joan. "Plantation Must Go—Unless." *Times-Picayune*, 10 May 1977.

"Trespassing Permitted . . . Today Only." *Dixie Roto*, *Times-Picayune*, 11 May 1958, p. 28+.

"Update of Seven Oaks Plantation House." *Préservation*, Louisiana Landmarks Society, February 1977.

"Valuable Real Estate in Alexandria, Virginia . . ." (advertisement). *Alexandria Gazette*, 8 April 1858.

Vaughn, Nell Blair. "Polio Fight Part of Mt. Brilliant's History." *Lexington Herald-Leader*, 21 October 2002.

Vaughn, R. C. "Glen Eden Described in Greene's Book." *Herald Democrat*, 12 December 1999.

Vlach, John Michael. "The Plantation Tradition in an Urban Setting: The Case of the Aiken-Rhett House in Charleston, South Carolina." *Southern Cultures*, vol. 5.4 (Winter 1999).

Walker, Ewing. "Fabulous Belle Grove." *Holland's: The Magazine of the South,* May 1939.

Wall, Maryjean. "History Repeating." *Lexington Herald-Leader*, 11 September 2002.

Wardlaw, Jack. "Terminal Illness Hits Seven Oaks." *New Orleans States-Item*, 29 July 1976.

Washburn, Karen. "The Gunnell Family of Fairfax County." In *Yearbook: The Historical Society of Fairfax County, Virginia*, vol. 20. Edited by Joseph L. Harsh (1984–1985).

Weber, Aaron. "A Farm Called Bush Hill." *Brookland–Bush Hill Civic Association.* http://www.bbhca.org/Farm_called_Bush_Hill.htm (accessed 22 July 2007).

"Wego Board Agrees to Back Restoration." *Times-Picayune*, 13 April 1976.

Weir, Merle. "Phelps, James Aeneas E." *Handbook of Texas Online,* http://www.tsha.utexas.edu/handbook/online/articles/PP/fph2.html (accessed 9 October 2004).

———. "Wharton, William Harris." *Handbook of Texas Online,* http://www.tsha.utexas.edu/handbook/online/articles/WW/fwh8.html (accessed 23 October 2005).

Wiener, Jonathon M. "Class Structure and Economic Development in the American South, 1865–1955." *American Historical Review*, vol. 84 (October 1979).

Wiggins, D. "Good Times on the Old Plantation: Popular Recreations of the Black Slave in Antebellum South, 1810–1860." *Journal of Sport History*, vol. 4, no. 3 (Fall 1977).

Williams, Buzz. "General Wade Hampton III, Noble Summer Resident." *Chattooga Quarterly* (Spring 1999).

Wilson, Samuel, Jr. "Famous La. Plantation Mansion Crumbling to Ruins Across River." *New Orleans States-Item*, 14 November 1953.

Womack, Lillian. "Proud Old Manor of Preston Bend Being Torn Down." *Sherman Democrat*, 29 March 1942, p. 10.

Woodsman, Harold. "Post–Civil War Agriculture and the Law." *Agricultural History*, vol. 53 (January 1979): 319–337.

"Wyalucing, 5-Acre Tract Are Offered for $50,000." *Marshall News Messenger*, 6 November 1962.

"Wyalucing Future in Doubt: Wreckers Start Monday, Society Asks Rezoning." *Marshall News Messenger*, 25 November 1962.

"Wyalucing Is Given Respite." *Marshall News Messenger*, 31 October 1962.

"Wyalucing Work Is Held Up Day: Commission Declines Intervention In Razing of Historic Structure." *Marshall News Messenger*, 30 October 1962.

Zelinsky, Wilbur. "The Greek Revival House in Georgia." *Journal of the Society of Architectural Historians*, vol. 13, no. 2 (May 1954): 9–12.

Zepp, George. "Choctaw Leader Educated in Nashville by Local Family." *Tennessean*, 27 August 2003.

———. "Tribal Chief Revered by Whites, Scorned by Choctaw Nation." *Tennessean,* 3 September 2003.

Zollman, Peter M. "Plantation Object of Preservation Drive." *Alexandria Daily Town Talk*, 11 April 1976.

## Note to the Reader

There are literally thousands of colonial and antebellum southern plantations that have been lost to time. Some of these are only vague memories held by a few, while others are meticulously well documented. Those readers with information (personal accounts, narratives, primary source material, published accounts, references, articles, photographs, drawings, documents, clippings, etc.) on other "lost" plantations or other architectural landmarks are invited to send copies of these materials to the author for possible subsequent studies. Inclusion of any of these materials in a published volume will warrant proper acknowledgment of the donor. The author can be contacted on the Web at www.MarcMatrana.com.

# Index

Page numbers in *italics* indicate illustrations.

A. McAlpin and Brothers, 99

Abendanone, Hannah Margarite, 131

Abraham, A. Lee, Jr., 166

Adams, John, 136

Adams, Lennie, 41

Adams, Penelope Lynch, 184

Addison, Lorenzo, 21

Advisory Council on Historic Preservation, 264ch3n2

Afton Villa Plantation, 273ch7n46

Agricultural Adjustment Act (1933), 252

Aime, Fèlicie, 182, 183

Aime, François, II, 180

Aime, François Gabriel. *See* Aime, Valcour

Aime, Gabriel, 180, 182, 183

Aime, Josephine, 183

Aime, Michel, 180

Aime, Valcour, 180, 182–83, 272ch7n10, 272ch7n17

Airliewood Plantation, 142

Alabama: Historical Commission, 120; history of, 110–11

Alario, Daniel P., 211

Alario, John, Jr., 210

Alario, Zenobia, 211

Alexander, Charles A., 107

Alexander II (Russia), 239

*Alexandria Gazette*, 23

Alexis (Horton House slave), 106

Aliquot, Marie Jeanne, 207, 275ch7n65

Altamount Plantation, 52

American Baptist Home Society, 239, 240, 241

American Liberty Oil Company, 208

American Oil Company, 179, 258

American Revolution: Georgia in, 2; the Hermitage in, 97; Maryland in, 82; Mount Oswald Plantation in, 134, 135; Mulberry Grove Plantation in, 88; New Smyrna Plantation in, 128; Virginia in, 82

American Society for the Suppression of Jews, 42

American Sugar Company, 179, 253

AmSouth Bank, 120, 256

Anderson, Frances, 29

Anderson, James, 136

Andressen, Henry, 210–11

Andressen, Kay, 210–11

Andrews, Emily, 190

Andrews, John, 184–85, 189–90

Annandale Plantation, 142

Annandale Volunteer Fire Department, 14; logo, *14*

Antoine (Hermitage slave), 98

Appleyard, Lula D., "Plantation Life in Middle Florida, 1821–1845," 112

Archer, Branch T., 248

Arkansas, history of, 32–33

Arlington House, 17

Armstrong Cork Company, 86

Ascension Parish Courthouse, 188

Asfeld, Marquis d', 274ch7n60

Assailly, Joseph, 203

Atchison, David Rice, 45

Atchison, Hamilton, Jr., 45

*Atlanta Constitution*, 85

Audubon, John James, 129

Aughinbaugh, Jesse, 243

Aughinbaugh, Sophia Suttenfield, 243–45, 246

Aunt Rose (Sylvan Home slave), 37

Austin, James E. Brown, 246

Austin, Maria, 247

Austin, Moses, 246, 247

Austin, Stephen F., 228, 235, 246–47, 248

*Austin Corbin* (steamboat), 42, 43

Bailey, Temperance, 27

Baird, J. C., 43

Baird, W. H., 43

Baker, George, 107

Balfour, Elizabeth Davis Gartley, 173

Balfour, William Lovett, 173

Balfour, William Suggs, 172–73, 174

Ballin, Arthur, 225

Balzac, Honoré de, 81

Barataria and Lafourche Canal Company, 203

Barnes, Richard, 256

Barnes, Walton, 256

Barrow, William Ruffin, 256

Barrows Plantation, 79

Battle of Ditch Bayou, 41

Battle of Malvern Hill, 30

Battle of New Orleans, 59, 106, 180

Battle of Port Gibson, 154

Bayley, John, 70

Baylor, George, 234

Baynard, Ephraim, 70

Baynard, William Eddings, 70

Bayou Teche, 183

Beasley, Peter R., 74

Beasley, Thomas Bess, 47

Beauregard, P. G. T., 116

Beauvoir Plantation, 143, 149, 256

Beecroft, Samuel, 97

Bell, Marmaduke, 134

Belle Chasse Plantation, 179

Belle Grove Plantation, 184–92; in the Civil War, 190; description of, 188–89, 191; destruction of, 191, 254; exterior column of, *187*; fans of, 256; first-floor plan of, *186*; front façade of, 184–85; ground floor plan of, *186*; preservation efforts at, 191; second-floor plan of, *186*

Belle Isle, Compte de, 274ch7n60

Belle Mont Plantation, 112

Bellus, Cyrus, 167, 172

Bellus, Cyrus (father of Cyrus Bellus), 167

Bellus, Matilda, 167

Belmont Plantation, 75, 78, 179

Belmont Shook Partnership, 166

Belvidere Plantation, 51–52, 62

Ben Youle, Jacob, 131

Benjamin, Judah P., 179

Benthuysen, Eliza Van, 150

Berry Hill Plantation, 8

Binkley, J. M., 245

Birchard, Sardis, 248

Bishop, Albert, 241

Bishop College, 237, 239–40, 241

Bisset, Alexander, 90

Black, Durel, 221, 222

Blackburn, John, 45

Blair, Elizabeth Saunders, 117

Blake, Minnie Jackson, 245

Blakeley Plantation, 21

Blue Grass Trust for Historic Preservation, 246

Blydenburg, Alma Amelia, 236

Boatner, Amenie Gunell, 26

Boisblanc, Genevieve Aimee de, 221

Bolling, Lucy, 26–27

Bolsterli, Margaret Jones, 35

Bonaparte, Josephine, 164, 180

Booth, Thomas B., 5

Bostick, Douglas, *Sunken Plantations: The Santee Cooper Project*, 52

Boucher, Ann, "Wealthy Planter Families in Nineteenth-Century Alabama," 112

Bowling Green Plantation, 142

Boynton, James S., 85, 266ch4n5

Braddocks Point Plantation. *See* Stoney-Baynard Plantation

Brandon, Elizabeth, 176

Brandon, Gerard, 176

Brashers, John, 27

Brashers, Mary, 27

Brierfield Plantation, 146–50; in the Civil War, 149, 252; description of, 148, 150

Briggs, Eleanor, 239

Bristow, Joseph L. 14

Broun, Elizabeth Allen, 62

Brown, James Ewell, 8

Brown, John, 135

Brown, Peter, 167

Brown, Sarah McLean, 249

Brownrigg Estate, 52

Brunswick Canal Company, 107

Bryan, Guy, 248

Bryan, Hamilton, 112

Bryan, Mary Elizabeth, 248

Bryan, Moses Austin, 247

Bryan, William Joel, 249

Bryant, Randolph, 246

Bulloch, James, 87, 88

Bullock, Agnes, 36

Bullock, Anna Booker, 36

Bullock, Charles, 35–36, 37–38

Bullock, Fanny Lyne, 36, 38

Bullock, James, 36

Bullock, Kate, 36

Bullock, Kim, 36

Bullock, Mary Helen, 36

Bullock, Nancy, 36

Bullock, Nannie, 36, 37, 38

Bullock, Robert, 36

Bullock, Sarah Jane Shaperd, 37. *See also* Shaperd, Sarah Jane

Bullock, Sue, 36

Bullock, Tom, 36

Bullskin Plantation, 21–22

Bulow, Charles Wilhelm, 129

Bulow, Emily Ann, 129

Bulow, John Joachim, 129, 131

Bulowville Plantation, 129–31; ruins of, *130*

Burglass, Bruce D., 208

Burleson, Rufus, 245

Burns, Emily, 146

Burns, John, 22

Burnside, 183

Burr, Aaron, 92, 174, 176

Burt, Virginia, 26

Bush, George W., 45

Bush Hill Plantation, 22–26; description of, 23; destruction of, 26; exterior of, *23*

Butler, Fanny, 82

Butler, John, 92, 267ch4n23

Butler, Pierce, 91, 92–93, 102, 267ch4n23

Butler, Sally, 92

Butler's Point Plantation. *See* Hampton Plantation

Butt, George W., 244–45

Bynum, H. D., 117

Byrd, William, II, 4

Byzantine style, 142

Cabahanoce Plantation, 179

Caesar (Pooshee slave), 56

Calgett, Anna, 20

Calhoun, John C., 41–42

Calhoun, Patrick, 41

Calhoun Land Company, 41–42

Calvert, George, 2

Calvert, Leonard, 19

Calvit, Mary Ann, 167

Calvit, Thomas, 167

Calvit, Zepha, 167

Calviton Plantation, 167

Campbell, J. K. P., 231

Camper, Paul, 48

Campest, Ross, 191

Camps, Pedro, 127

Canale, Ann Shook, 166

Canebrake Plantation, 121

Cannon's Point Plantation, 82–83, 90

Capote, Truman, 208

Cappo, Peter, 191

Captain Jack (Forks of Cypress slave), 116

Carew, Dr., 134

Carpenter, Jim, 80

Carradine, Keith, 93

Carrigan, Jane, 120

Carter, Mary, 38

Carter, Robert, 5

Casasnovas, Bartolemeo, 127

Castellani, John, 21

Casulon Plantation, 83–86; description of, 83; destruction of, 83, 86, 254; front façade of, *84–85*; slaves on, 85

Catlett, John T., 5

Ceard (Ste-Reyne director), 220

Center for American History (University of Texas at Austin), 229

Central Coast Wetlands Ecosystem Project, 250

Chaires, Benjamin, Jr., 138

Chaires, Benjamin, Sr., 136, 138

Chaires, Green, 136

Chaires, Martha, 138

Chaires, Thomas (son of Benjamin Chaires, Sr.), 138

Chaires, Thomas Peter (brother of Benjamin Chaires, Sr.), 136

Chambers, S. Allen, *Buildings of West Virginia*, 5

Champion, Aaron, 99

Champlin, George, 68

Champollian, René C., 42

Charles I, 50

Charles II, 50

Charles Town, 22

Charleston Light Dragons, 77

Chastellux, Marquis de, 26

Chatham Manor, 4

Chatsworth Plantation, 26–27, 179

Chauvin, Nicholas, 220

Cherokee, 57, 82, 117

Cherry Hill Plantation, 24

Chickasaw, 46

Chicora Foundation, 24

Chinese laborers, 200, 252

Chocolate Plantation, 83

Choctaw, 159, 161, 164, 166

Christ Episcopal Church, 193

Church of St. Louis, 274ch7n61

Churchill, Winston, 1, 251

Citrus County Federation of Women's Clubs, 134

Civil War: Alabama in, 111; at Belle Grove, 190; at Brierfield, 149, 252; at Bush Hill, 25; at Cottonwood, 133; at Devereux, 80; Eagle Island, 234; Elmwood, 221; at Eutaw, 67; Florida in, 111; Georgia in, 82; at Glen Eden, 245; at Hamilton, 91; at the Hermitage, 99; at Hurricane, 149, 151; at Le Petit Versailles, 183; at Malmaison, 165; at Malvern Hill, 30; at Mannsfield, 4; at Margarita, 133; Maryland in, 2–3; at Millwood, 59; Mississippi in, 142; at Mulberry Grove, 89; North Carolina in, 50; at Ossian Hall, 14; at Peach Point, 249; at Pooshee, 56; at Ravensworth, 17; at Retreat, 102; at Reverie, 47; at Rocky Hill Castle, 113, 116; Rosedale, 40; Seven Oaks, 207; South Carolina in, 50; at Stoney-Baynard, 71; at Sunnyside, 41; at Sylvan Hall, 38; Texas in, 228; at Umbria, 121, 126; at Verdura, 138; Virginia in, 2; at White Hall, 74; Windsor, 154; at Woodlawn, 193, 198; Wyalucing, 239

Clark, Walter MacKenzie, 62

Classical Revival style, 179

Clay, Clement C., 133

Clay, Henry, 231

Clay, Nestor, 231

Clay, Tacitus Matthew, 231–32

Clay, Tacitus T., 233

Clay Castle Plantation, 231–33

Clay-Clopton, Virginia, 132, 133

Claymont Court Plantation, 21

Clifton Plantation, 45

Clubb, John, 100, 102

Cocke, James Powell, 27, 29

Cocke, Richard, 27

Cocke, Thomas (Capt.), 27

Cocke, Thomas (Col.), 27

Coffee, Eugenia, 244

Coffee, Holland, 143–44, 146

Coffee, John, 117

Colonial Dames, 263ch1n53

Colonial National Historical Park, 7

Colonial style, 90

Columbia Gardens, 207

*Columbian Museum and Savannah Advertiser*, 106

Columns Plantation, 136

Conacanarra Plantation, 79

Confederate Conscription Act, 126

Confederate States of America, 2, 146, 149, 239, 277ch8n37; Trans-Mississippi Agency, 239; Treasury Department, 239

Conner, J. Rutledge, 74, 77, 78

Conner, T. L., 77

Conroy, Pat, *The Prince of Tides*, 49

Constancia Plantation. *See* Uncle Sam Plantation

Coody, Elizabeth, 165

Cook, Jane, 147

Cooper, Chip, *Silent in the Land*, 112

Corbin, Austin, 42, 43

Corbin, Francis P., 90

Corbin House, 43. *See also* Sunnyside Plantation

cotton gin, 50, 87, 88–89, 141

Cottonlandia Museum, 167

Cottonwood Plantation, 131, 132, 133, 134

Couper, Ann, 90

Couper, James Hamilton, 90, 91

Couper, John, 82–83, 90

Couper, William Audley, 90

Courturier, Isaac, 68

Cravat, Rebecca, 159

Creek (Native Americans), 82, 93, 111

Creole style, 178, 228

Crevass, Ethyle Venable, 134

Crittenden, Orlando B., 3

Crockett, Davy, 117

Cross, Wayland, 117

Cuffy (Mulberry Grove slave), 88

Cullison, William R., 200

Culpeper, Lady, 23

Cummings, John, 257

Cunningham, Ann Pamela, 257

Curlee, Abigail, "A Study of Texas Slave Plantations, 1822–1865," 229

Curles Neck Farm, 27

Custis, Eleanor Calvert, 9

Custis, John Parke, 9

Custis, Mary Anna Randolph, 17

Cuthbert, Anne, 87–88

Cuthbert, John, 87

Cypress Land Company, 117

Dakin, James, 188

Dale, John, Jr., 150

Dale, Lessley, 150

*Dallas Morning News*, 241

Damer, Juliet, 126

Damon (Sylvan Home slave), 36

Dana, Charles Backus, 145

Dana, Richard Henry Clay, 145–46

Daniel, Harriet Bailey Bullock, 35, 36, 37

Daniell, Catherine, 154. *See* Freeland, Catherine

Daniell, Smith Coffee, II, 151, 154

Dart, J. E., 103

Daspit, Fred: *Louisiana Architecture: 1714–1820*, 179; *Louisiana Architecture, 1820–1840*, 179; *Lousisiana Architecture: 1840–1860*, 179

Dastugue, Quentin, 222–23

Daunoy, Charles Favre, 203

Davidson Mineral Properties, 86

Davis, Isaac, 150

Davis, Jefferson, 133, 145; and Beauvoir, 143; and Brierfield, 146–49; *The Rise and Fall of the Confederacy*, 48

Davis, Joseph E., 147, 149, 150, 151

Davis, Samuel Emory, 147

Davis, Temperance Williams, 59

Davis, Varina, 146, 148

de León, Ponce, 110

de Soto, Hernando, 110, 141

Dean, Zender, 86

*DeBow's Review*, 193

Delille, Henriette, 275ch7n65

Delong, Arthur, 45

Demere, Raymond, 105

*Denison Herald*, 246

Dent, Rebecca, 20

Destrehan Plantation, 179, 258

Deveaux, Stephen G., 52

Devereux, John, 79

Devereux, John, Jr., 79

Devereux Plantation, 79–80

Dewberry Plantation, 229

Dewey, E. D., 231

Diamond Match Company, 99, 100

Dipple Plantation, 24

*Dixie Roto Magazine* (*Times-Picayune*), 208

Dockery, Octavia, 145–46

Dominique (Hermitage slave), 98

Donly, John, 161

Donly, Priscilla, 165

Donly, Rebecca, 165

Donly, Rosa, 161

Dorchester County Historical Society, 4

Doublehead (Cherokee chief), 117

Douglas, John, 136

Dowdy, Jessie Allen, 119

Dowdy, R. B., 119

Downing, Andrew Jackson, 273ch7n49

Drakies Plantation, 89

Drayton Hall Plantation, 52

du Bignon, Christophe Poulaine, 106

du Bignon, Henry Charles, 106–7

du Bignon, Joseph, 107

Dubignon, John Eugene, 107

Duncan, William, 127

Dungeness Plantation, 89

Dunleith Plantation, 143

Durazno Plantation, 249

Eagle Island Plantation, 233–34; sketch of, 232

ECOL, 253

Eden, Charles, 52

Eden House Plantation, 52

Edgewood Plantation, 4, 237

Edwards, Edwin, 210

Edwards, Eunice, 79

Edwards, Jonathan, 79

Eliza Plantation, 133

Elizabeth I, 2

Elk Hill Plantation, 45

Ellersly Plantation, 234–36

Ellington Manor Plantation, 179

Ellison (Pooshee slave), 56

Elmwood Plantation, 220–25; barn at, 224; in the Civil War, 221; description of, 220–21; destruction of, 221; exterior of, 222–23; preservation efforts at, 222–24, 225; restored, 222, 224

Elmwood Plantation, Inc., 222

Emancipation Proclamation, 8

*Enslavement: The True Story of Fanny Kemble*, 93

*Ethan Allen* (gunboat), 104

Eutaw Light Dragoons, 77

Eutaw Plantation, 62–67; Christmas at, 67; in the Civil War, 67; daily life at, 66–67; description of, 62, 66; first-floor plan of, 64; front façade of, 63, 64–65; horse racing at, 67; interior of, 64; Lodge at, 67; slaves at, 67; submersion of, 62

Evans, Clement A., 85

Everitt, Martha Ann, 190

Exon Plantation. *See* Hermitage Plantation

Fagot, Felicie, 211

Fagot, Marie Emilie Eugenie, 211

Fagot, Pierre Auguste Samuel. *See* Fagot, Sam

Fagot, Sam, 211, 212, 215

Fairfax, George William, 21, 22

Hamilton, James, 90, 229

Hamilton, Phillip, 174

Hamilton Hills (resort), 112

Hamilton Plantation, 90–91

Hammond, Ralph, *Ante-Bellum Mansions of Alabama*, 112

Hampton, Anthony, 57

Hampton, Wade, 57

Hampton, Wade, II, 57–58

Hampton, Wade, III, 57, 59

Hampton Plantation, 91–93, 102

Hampton-Preston Mansion, 59

Hampton's Legion, 59

Hancock Hall Plantation, 74

Hanson, Barbara Hatton Johnson, 19

Hanson, Elizabeth, 19

Hanson, Randolph, 19

Hanson Aggregates, 86

Happy Retreat Plantation, 21

Harang, Alexandre, 203

Hardeman, H. M., *The Free Flag of Cuba*, 237

Harden, Edward, 89

Harden, Edward (son of Edward Harden), 89

Harden, John, 89

Hardesty, Eleanor Ann, 20

Hardie, James, 173

Hare, William, 36

Harewood Plantation, 21

Harris, Bannon, 86

Harris, James Clark, 155, 164

Harris, James W., 83, 85, 266ch4n1

Harris, Jesse, 36

Harris, John, 266ch4n1

Harris, Mary, 85

Harris, Susie, 85

Harris, Whitson Alexander, 47, 48

Harrison, Thomas, 23

Harrison, William, 23

Harrison County Historical Society, 240, 241

Hartwell, Alfred Stedman, 67

Hawes, Carrilla, 249

*Hawk* (ship), 90

Hawkins, Hamilton, 43

Hayes, George D., 150

Hayes, Rutherford B., 248–49

Heard, Cleveland, 240

Hebden, Katherine, 19

Hebden, Thomas, 19

Heiland, Sharon, "The Verdura Place: A Historical Overview and Preliminary Archaeological Survey," 138

Helvetia Plantation, 179

Henry, Edward H., 25

Henry, Patrick, 2, 45

Henry Ford Museum, 100

Herbert, John, 29

Herbert, Martha, 29

Hercules (Eutaw plantation horse trainer), 67

Heritage Preservation, Inc., 120

Hermitage Corporation, 99

Hermitage Plantation, 93–100; in the Civil War, 99; description of, 98–99; first-floor plan of, *95*; front view of, *94, 95*; ground-floor plan of, *95*; plot plan of, *96*; preservation efforts at, 99–100; slave cabins at, *96*; slaves on, *97, 98*, 99

Herries Phillip, 135

Herring, Elizabeth Whitfield, 155

Hewie, Samuel, 134

Heyden Hill Plantation, 75

Hicks, Thomas Holliday, 3

Hilton Head Company, 71

Historic American Buildings Survey, 53, 143, 258

Hitler, Adolf, 25, 26

Hoffman, James, 202

Holcombe, Anna Eliza, 277ch8n36

Holcombe, Beverly LaFayette, 237, 239, 277ch8n36

Holcombe, John Theodore, 277ch8n36

Holcombe, Lucy Maria Anderson, 237

Holcombe, Lucy Petway, 237, 239, 277ch8n36; *The Free Flag of Cuba*, 237

Holcombe, Martha Maria, 277ch8n36

Holcombe, Philemon, Jr., 237

Holcombe, Philemon Eugene, 277ch8n36

Holly Hills Preschool, 26

Holmes, Francis S., 53

Home Oil Fields, 174

Homewood Plantation, 167–74; attic floor plan of, *171*; basement floor plan of, *171*; description of, 173–74; destruction of, 174; front façade of, *168–69*; main staircase at, *172*; observatory and widow's walk floor plan of, *171*; principal floor plan of, *171*; rear view of, *170*; second-floor plan of, *171*; side view of, *170*; slaves at, 167, 172; spiral staircase at, 172

Horton, William, 104–5

Horton House Plantation, 104–7; description of, 105; indentured servants at, 104; ruins of, *105*; slaves at, 106, 107; in the War of 1812, 106

Houmas House Plantation, 183

Houston, Sam, 228, 234, 242, 243, 244, 248

Howard, Henry, 188, 192

Howell, Varina. *See* Davis, Varina

Howell, William B., 147

Hubbs, G. Ward, 121

Hughes, Thomas, 45

Hugo, Victor, 139

Humble, John, 100

Hunt, Abijah, 167

Hunt, Catherine, 172–73, 174

Hunt, David, 167, 172

Hunt, Eugenia Dorothea Vaughn, 237, 239, 277ch8n35, 277ch8n36

Hunt, John, 277ch8n35

Hunt, Robert, 79

Hunter, Robert Eldridge, 47–48

Hunter, William W., 247

Huntington, James Marion, 236

Hurricane Betsy, 179, 208

Hurricane Katrina, 143, 256

Hurricane Plantation, 147, 150–51; in the Civil War, 149, 151; description of, 150–51; slaves at, 149, 151

Hymel, Moise J., 219

Iberville, Pierre Le Moyne, Sieur d', 141

Ickes, Harold L., 100

Illinois Central Railroad Company, 221

indentured servants: at Clay Castle, 233; at Horton House, 104; at Mulberry Grove, 87; at New Smyrna, 126, 127; at Peach Point, 247

Ingleside Plantation, 142. *See also* Clay Castle Plantation

International Paper, 100

*Invincible* (ship), 242

Iron Head Plantation, 75

Isabella I, 131

Israel (Pooshee slave), 56

Italian laborers, 200, 252

Italianate style: at Malmaison, 164; in Mississippi, 142; at Nottoway, 185; at Prairie Mont, 155

Jackson, Abner, 229–30

Jackson, Andrew, 106, 110, 117, 242

Jackson, Arsenath, 230

Jackson, Claiborne F., 277ch8n37

Jackson, George, 230

Jackson, James, 117, 118–19, 268ch5n6

Jackson, James (father of James Jackson), 268ch5n6

Jackson, John, 230

Jackson, Mary Steel, 268ch5n6

Jacob, Camile, 215

Jacob, Jules, 215

James, Jesse, 210

James I, 2

Jamestown, 2

Jane (Rosedale slave), 39

*Jardin des Plantes*, 182

Jarrell, John Fitz, 83

Jarrell Plantation, 83

Jarrell Plantation State Historic Site, 83

Jay, John, 136

Jay, William, 98

Jefferson, Thomas, 82, 177

Jefferson College, 182, 272ch7n11

Jefferson Historical Society of Louisiana, *Elmwood: The Historic Archeology of a Southeastern Louisiana Plantation*, 225

Jefferson Parish Historical Commission, 211

Jeffersonian style, 17, 112

Jenkins Plantation, 4

Johnson, Abner, 41

Johnson, Andrew, 41, 149, 151

Johnson, David, 234

Johnson, George, 22

Johnson, Penelope, 234

Johnston, Francis Benjamin, *The Early Architecture of North Carolina*, 52

Johnston, William L., 199, 273ch7n48

Jonchere, Michel de la, 274ch7n60

Jones, C. Allan, *Texas Roots: Agriculture and Rural Life before the Civil War*, 229

Jones, Daniel Chandler, 85

Jones, Franklin, 241

Jones, Harris, 86

Jones, Hugh, 113, 268ch5n3

Jones, Kenneth T., 45

Jones, Kimbrough, 36, *37*

Jones, Mary, 37–38

Jones, Mary Beth, 250

Jones, Noble, 83

Jones, Roger, 159

Jones, Sallie Maud, 85–86

Jopling, May, 8

Josephine (Empress of France). *See* Bonaparte, Josephine

Jourdain, Emilie, 211

Judah P. Benjamin Confederate Memorial and State Historic
    Site, 111–12

Kane, Harnett, 176, 190

Kansas City Life Insurance Company, 43

Kemble, Fanny, 92, 267ch4n24; *Enslavement: The True Story
    of Fanny Kemble*, 93; *Journal of a Residence on a Georgia
    Plantation*, 92–93

Kempe, Margaret, 147

Kentucky, history of, 32–33

Kimball House hotel, 85, 266ch4n8

Kinder-Morgan, 211

King, Anna Matilda Page, 100, 102–3

King, Benjamin, 66

King, Butler, 104

King, Cuyler, 104

King, Florence, 103, 104

King, Floyd, 104

King, Georgia, 104

King, Henry Lord Page, 103, 104

King, Mallery, 104

King, R. Cuyler, 103

King, Roswell, 92, 102

King, Roswell, Jr., 92

King, Thomas Butler, 102

King, Virginia, 104

Kinloch, Francis, 134

Kirkman, Thomas, 117

Kirkwood Plantation, 112

Kolly, Monsieur, 220

Korn, Ed, 241

La Grange Plantation, 4

La Salle, René-Robert Cavelier, Sieur de, 178, 228

Lafayette, Marquis de, 30

Lafreniere, Alexandro Juan Baptiste, 221

Lafreniere, Nicolas, 220, 221

Laissard, Etienne Marafret, 220

Lake Jackson Plantation, 229–31, 255; description of, 229–30;
    Galveston hurricane at, 231; prison labor at, 231, 252; water-
    color of, *230*

Lake Jackson Sugar Company, 231

Lakeport Plantation, 33

Lancaster, Clay, *Antebellum Architecture of Kentucky*, 33, 34

Landrieu, Mitch, 257

Lane, Mills, *Architecture of the Old South*, 35, 52, 112

Langlois, Perrine, 221

Lanier, Augustus H., 111

Lansdowne Plantation, 172

Lash, Anne Elizabeth, 8

Latta Plantation, 52

Laughlin, Clarence, 198

Laura Plantation, 256

Laurance, Paola, 128

Laurel Hill Plantation, 75

Laurens, Henry, 270ch5n41

Le Noble, Henry, 53

Le Petit Desert, 274ch7n60

Le Petit Versailles, 180–83, 272ch7n10; in the Civil War, 183;
    description of, 180, 182; destruction of, 183; front façade
    of, *181*; gardens at, 180, 182; rear elevation of, *182–83*; self-
    sufficiency at, 182–83

Leake, Richard, 90, 106

LeBlanc, Monsieur, 203, 274ch7n60

LeBreton, Jean-Baptiste Cezaire, 220

Lee, Anne Hill Carter, 17

Lee, Charles, 23, 262ch1n35

Lee, George Bolling, 17

Lee, George Washington Custis, 17

Lee, Mary Randolph Custis, 14

Lee, Richard Henry, 2

Lee, Robert E., 14, 17, 30, 145

Lee, Robert E., III, 17

Lee, William Henry Fitzhugh, 17

LeFleur, Louis, 159, 161

LeFleur's Bluff, 161

Leflore, Greenwood, 159, 161, 164–66

Lemann, Jack, 221

Lenoir, Selina Louisa, 121

Lenoir, Thomas, 121

Lentz, J. Fred, 241

Levy, David. *See* Yulee, David Levy

Levy, Jules, 207

Levy, Moses, 131

Levy, Rachel, 131

Levy, Rachel (daughter of Rachel Levy), 131

Lewis, Lawrence, 22

*Lexington Herald-Leader*, 45

Liendo Plantation, 229

Lincoln, Abraham, 3, 149

Linwood Plantation, 179

Lion Oil Plantation, 179

Littlejohn, Price, 241

Little Wilderness Plantation, 203

*Lively* (ship), 242

Locust Grove Plantation, 147

Logan, William, 105

Lonely Planet Travel Network, 256

Longwood Plantation, 140, 142

Looking Glass Plantation, 79

Los Mosquitos Plantation. *See* New Smyrna Plantation

Lossieux, Marguerite Anne, 106

*Lost Virginia: Vanished Architecture of the Old Dominion*, 4

Louis Philippe, 183

Louis XIV (France), 178

Louisa (Rosedale slave), 133

Louisa Plantation, 133

Louisiana: Department of Culture, Recreation and Tourism, 225; history of, 178; Tourist Commission, 222

*Louisiana Conservation Review*, 191

Louisiana Landmarks Society, 179, 208

Louisiana Purchase, 32, 178

Love, Mary, 23

Love, Samuel, 23

Lowrey, W. M., 159

Lucas, Charles, 71

Lucy (Sylvan Home slave), 36

Lyles, Henrietta Eleanor, 20

Lyles, Sallie Magruder, 20


MacKay, Patrick, 97

Macpherson, James, *The Works of Ossian*, 9, 261ch1n16

Macy, Everett, 107

Macy, Monsieur, 220

Madison, Dolly, 24

Madison, James, 24

*Magnolia, The* (steamboat), 90

Magruder, Sam, 155

Malacare, Pierre de St. Julien de, 53

Mallory, Stephen K., 133

Malmaison (France), 180

Malmaison Plantation, 159–67; cemetery at, 165; in the Civil War, 165; description of, 164; destruction of, 165, 254; dining room at, *163*; front façade of, *160–61*; front hall of, *162*; parlor at, *162*; preservation efforts at, 166; side view of, *163*; staircase at, *162*

Malus, Emilie, 215

Malus, Felicie, 215

Malus, Lucien, 211, 215

Malvern Hill Plantation, 27–30; description of, 27, 29–30; destruction of, 30; front façade of, *28*; plot plan of, *28*; preservation efforts at, 30; ruins of, *29*; in the War of 1812, 30

Mannsfield Plantation, 3–4

Manresa House, 272ch7n11

Mansfield Plantation, 52

Marathon Oil Plantation, 202

Marboro Iron Works, 24

Marcello, Joseph, 222, 225

Margarita Plantation, 131; in the Civil War, 133; description of 132; preservation efforts at, 134

Maria Alexandrovna, 239

Marist Fathers, 182

Marshall, Eleanor Douglass, 24

Marshall, George, 172

Marshall, James, 24

Marshall, John, 24

Marshall, Levin, 172

Marshall, Margaret, 20

Marshall, Thomas, I, 19, 20

Marshall, Thomas, III, 20

Marshall, Thomas, V, 20

Marshall, Thomas Hanson, II, 20

Marshall, Thomas Hanson, IV, 20

Marshall, William, I, 17, 19

Marshall, William, II, 19

Marshall Hall Plantation, 17–21, 24, 253; description of, 19–20; destruction of, 21; first-floor plan of, *18*; front elevation of, *18*; map locating, *19*; preservation efforts at, 21; second-floor plan of, *18*

Marshall Historical Society, 241

*Marshall New Messenger*, 240

Martin, Clement, 105–6

Martin, Phillip, 166

Maryland, history of, 2–3

Mason, James W., 41

Mason, Martha W., 41

Mason, William Fredrick, 221

Masse, Monsieur, 220

Masterson, Harris, 234

Mathurin (Hermitage Plantation slave), 98

Matrana, Marc R., *Lost Plantation: The Rise and Fall of Seven Oaks*, 179, 207

Matthews, John, 16, 261ch1n19

Maxey, Samuel B., 38

Mayo, Mark, Jr., 26

McAlpin, Angus, 99, 267ch4n34

McAlpin, Claudia, 99, 100

McAlpin, Donald, 99, 267ch4n34

McAlpin, Ellen, 267ch4n34

McAlpin, Henry, 89, 98, 99, 267ch4n34

McAlpin, Henry (son of Henry McAlpin), 267ch4n34

McAlpin, Henry (grandson of Henry McAlpin), 99

McAlpin, Isabel, 267ch4n34

McAlpin, James Wallace, 99, 267ch4n34

McAlpin, Joseph, 99

McBride, Gordon, 117

McCaskill, Charles Neill, 39

McCaskill, Martha, 39

McCaskill, Mattie Bullock, 38–39

McCaskill, Neill, 39

McCaskill, Neill (son of Charles McCaskill), 39

McCaskill, William Fletcher, 39

McClellan, George B., 30

McCracken, James, 22

McCreery, Harold, 232

McCreery, Vibella, 232

McCrocklin, Jesse L., 232

McCullough, Samuel, 268ch5n7

McCullough, Sarah Moore, 117, 268ch5n7

McDaniel, Henry D., 85

McDowell, Ron, 40

McGehee, Edward, 142

McGillivray, Alexander, 111

McKenzie, John Witherspoon Pettigrew, 245

McKenzie College, 245

McKinley, Andrew, 117

McLean, Donald, 135

McLeRoy, Sherrie, *Red River Women*, 145

McMillan, John, 208

McNeel, George Washington, 235

McNeel, John Greenville, 235, 276ch8n23

McNeel, John Greenville, Jr., 236

McNeilly, Donald P., *The Old South Frontier: Cotton Plantations and the Formation of Arkansas Society, 1819–1861*, 35

Mead, Cowles, 155

Meade, Mary Everard, 120, 121

Mease, John. *See* Butler, John

Mease, John (father of John Mease/John Butler), 267ch4n23

Mease, Pierce. *See* Butler, Pierce

Mease, Sarah, 267ch4n23

Melville, Herman, *Malvern Hill*, 30

*Memphis Commercial Appeal*, 48

Merrill, Ayres P., 145

Merrill, Jennie, 145–46

Mexican American War, 39

Middleton, Polly, 91

Middleton Place Plantation, 52

Miles, William Porcher, 53

Millard, James, 46

Millaudon Plantation, 252

Miller, Mary Carol, *Lost Mansions of Mississippi*, 143

Miller, Phineas, 88, 89

Miller, Samuel, 116

Millionaires Club, 107

Millwood Plantation, 57–59; in the Civil War, 59; description of, 57; preservation efforts at, 59; ruined columns at, 58; slaves at, 57

Minor (Devereux slave), 80

Mississippi: Department of Archives and History Properties Division, 155; history of, 142–43

*Mississippi: The WPA Guide to the Magnolia State*, 142, 143

Mississippi Band of Choctaw Indians, 166. *See also* Choctaw

Mississippi Central Railroad, 155, 159

Missouri, confederate government of, 239, 277ch8n37

Missouri-Pacific Railroad Company, 208

Molhausen, Henry, 188

Molyneaux, Charles, 102

Montague, Daniel, 243

Montalet, Jean de Berard-Mocquet-Montalet, Chevalier Marquise de, 97–98

Montalet, William Polycarp, 98

Montgomery, Benjamin Thornton, 151, 270ch6n11

Montgomery, Isaiah Thornton, 151

Monticello, 4

Montpelier Plantation, 111

Montrose Plantation, 79

Moore, Francis, *A Voyage to Georgia Begun in the Year 1735*, 104

Moore, James, 268ch5n7

Moorish design, 142

Mordecai, Margaret Lane, 79

Morel, Jim, 82

Moreland, George M., 159

Morgan, Benjamin, 199

Morgan, George, 200

Morgan, J. P., 107

Morgan, Thomas Ashton, 199, 273ch7n50

Morgan County Historical Society, 86

Morris, William, 260

Mosca, Nick, 83

Moss, Joseph, 83

Moultrie, John, 111

Mound Bayou, 151

Mount Airy Plantation, 3, 24

Mount Brilliant Plantation, 43–46; demolition of, 43, 45–46, 253, 255; evolution and transformation of, 44; front façade of, 44; site plan of, 44

Mount Locust Plantation, 143

Mount Oswald Plantation, 134–36; description of, 135; overseers at, 134–35; preservation efforts at, 136; slaves at, 134, 135–36

Mount Vernon, 3, 4, 17, 20, 22, 257

Mount Vernon and Marshall Hall Steamboat Company, 20–21

Mount Vernon Ladies Association, 22, 257

Mulberry Grove Plantation, 87–89; in the Civil War, 89; description of, 87, 88; indentured servants on, 87; slaves on, 87, 88

Muldoon, Father, 234

Muller, Joseph, 182

Mumford, Lewis, *The South in Architecture*, 1

Murphy, Francis, 244

Murphy, Thomas, 244

Murray, Charles, 97

Murray, David, 97

Murray, John, 97

Murray, Lucia, 97

Myers, Moses, 131

Narváez, Pánfilo de, 110

Natchez Spring Pilgrimage, 146

Natchez Trace, 143, 161

National Colonial Farm, 21

National Historic Preservation Act, 263ch3n2

National Park College, 4

National Park Seminary, 4

National Park Service: and Chatham Manor, 4; Heritage Preservation Services of, 258; and Malvern Hill Plantation, 30; and Marshall Hall, 21; and Uncle Sam Plantation, 219

National Register of Historic Places, 258; and Bullskin, 22; and Elmwood, 225; and Malvern Hill, 30; and the Rocks, 79; and Rosedale, 40

National Society of the Colonial Dames of America, 4

Native Americans: Cherokee, 57, 82, 117; Chickasaw, 46; Choctaw, 159, 161, 164, 166; Creek, 82, 93, 111; in Kentucky, 32; Seminole, 128, 129, 131; in Texas, 243

Nattiel, Dollie, 132, 134

Nehrbass, Frederick J., 191

Nelson, Emily, 25

Nelson, Robert, 30

Nelson, Thomas, 30

Neo-Palladian style, 2

New Deal, 51

New Orleans, 33; architecture of, 173; Battle of, 59, 106, 180; settlement of, 178, 202; *Social Life of Old New Orleans*, 182

New Smyrna Plantation, 126–28

Newport, Christopher, 2

*News and Courier*, 77

Nicolau, Ann Amelia, 106

*North Alabamian*, 119

North American Trading and Import, 208

North Carolina, history of, 50–51

North Carrollton Baptist Church, 166

North End Plantation, 82

Nottoway Plantation, 185

Nunnally, G. A., 85

Nutt, Haller, 142

Oak Alley Plantation, 180, 182, 210

Oak Grove Plantation, 190

Oak Hill Plantation, 7–8

Oakland Memorial Chapel, 155

Oakland Plantation, 145

Oakley Grove Plantation, 167

Oaks Plantation, 237

Oglethorpe, James, 82, 91, 100, 102, 104, 105

Oisín, 9

Old Santee Plantation, 62

Omron, John P., 113

O'Neill, Maurice B., 146

Ophir Plantation, 52, 71, 74

Orange Grove Plantation, 199–202; Chinese laborers at, 200;

description of, 199–200; destruction of, 202; front façade of, *201*; Italian laborers at, 200; preservation efforts at, 200, 202; rear façade of, *201*

Orange Hall, 102

Orozimbo Plantation, 242–43

Osmun, Benijah, 174, 176

Ossian Hall Plantation, 9–14; attic floor plan of, *13*; basement plan of, *12*; cemetery at, 14; description of, 9; destruction of, 14; first-floor plan of, *12*; front façade of, *10–11*; rear view of, *12–13*; second-floor plan of, *13*

Oswald, Richard, 134, 135–36

Ottolenghe, Joseph, 93, 97

Owenson, Sydney, 227

Packenham, Edward, 106

Page, Francis Burwell, 5

Page, Hannah Timmons, 100

Page, John, 5

Page, Judith, 5

Page, Mann, I, 5

Page, Mann, II, 5

Page, Mann, III, 3

Page, Margaret, 5

Page, William, 100, 102

Palladian style, 2, 3, 16, 62

Palmer, Alice, 74

Palmer, John, 68

Palmer, Joseph, 70

Palmer, Thomas, 68

Pamor, David, 68

Pamor, Elizabeth, 68

Pamor, John, 68

Pamor, Joseph, 68

Pamor, Thomas, 68

Parham, John, 48

Parke, George Washington, 17

Parks, John T., *Florida's Antebellum Homes*, 112

Parks, William E., 150

Patrick, James, *Architecture in Tennessee, 1768–1897*, 35

Patterson, Doug, 121

Pavich-Lindsay, Melanie, 102; "Retreat: Palimpsest of a Georgia Sea Island Plantation," 104; "A Slave Speaks of Silence," 104

Peach Point Plantation, 246–50; in the Civil War, 249; description of, 247–48; Galveston hurricane at, 249; indentured servants at, 247; preservation efforts at, 249, 250; slaves on, 249; in the Texas Revolution, 248

Peach Point Wildlife Management Agency, 250

Pearl River Resort, 166

Pearls, George, 146

Pearson, Simon, 262ch1n31

Pearson, Thomas, 23

Pebble Hill Plantation, 83

Pemberton, James, 105, 147, 148

Percival, John, 82

Percy, LeRoy, 43

Perez, Chalin O., 200, 202

Perry, Emily Margaret Austin, 246, 247, 248, 249

Perry, James, II, 249

Perry, James Franklin, 246, 247, 248

Perry, Josiah, 88

Perry, Lavinia, 247

Perry, Stephen, 249

Perry, Stephen, Jr. (son of Stephen Perry, Sr.), 249

Perry, Stephen, Sr. (son of Stephen Perry), 249

Persac, Marie Adrien, 189

*Perseverance, The* (schooner), 129

Petway, Rhoda, 277

Phelps, James Aeneas E., 242, 243

Phelps, Orlando, 242–43

Phelps, William W., 230–31

Phelps Plantation. *See* Orozimbo Plantation

*Phenix Gazette, Bush Hill*, 26

Phillips, Donald B., 26

Phillips, Mary Gunnell, 26

Phillips Petroleum Company, 236

Pickens, Andrea Dorothea Olga Liva Lucy Holcombe Douschka Francesca, 239

Pickens, Francis Wilkinson, 237, 239

Pickens, Isreal, 121

Pickens, James, 121

Pickens, John, 121

Pickens, Louisa, 121

Pickens, Mary, 121

Pickens, Samuel, 120, 121

Pickens, Samuel (Capt.), 120

Pickens, Samuel (son of Samuel Pickens), 121, 126

Pickens, William, 121

Picot-Boisfeuillet, Angélique Servanne Charlotte de, 98

Pierce, Franklin, 148

Pierrepont, Sarah, 79

Pilgrimage Garden Club, 142

Pinckney, Thomas, 52

Pinckney, Thomas, Jr., 52

Pine Island Plantation, 133

Piney Grove Primitive Baptist Church, 8

Piscataway Park, 19, 21

Pitot House Plantation, 179

Pitt, Mary, 27

plantation system: decline of, 252, 254–55; post–civil war workforce on, 252

Poindexter, George, 167

Point Comfort Plantation, 52

Polenta Plantation, 79

Polk, James K., 45

Pollock, Francis, 79

Pollock, Oliver, 221

Pollock, Thomas, III, 79

Pontchartrain Levee District, 219

Pooshee Plantation, 53–57; Christmas at, 53, 55–56; in the Civil
War, 56; description of, 53; first-floor plan of, 55; front
façade of, 54; practical jokes at, 55–56; slaves at, 56; submersion of, 56–57

Poplar Farm, 45

Porcher, Elizabeth, 74, 75. See also Gaillard, Elizabeth

Porcher, Frederick Augustus, 75

Porcher, Marianne E., 74

Porcher, Thomas, 71

Porter, James, 245

Powell, Margaret, 27

Prairie Mont Plantation, 155–59, 164; demolition of, 159; description of, 155, 159; front façade of, 156–57; interior of, 158;
side view of, 158

Pratt, John Lee, 4

Prefontaine, Monsieur, 220

Prene (Hermitage Plantation slave), 98

preservation efforts: at Bulowville, 129; at Elmwood, 222–24,
225; at Forks of Cypress, 120; at Glen Eden, 246; at the Hermitage, 99–100; at Malmaison, 166; at Malvern Hill, 30; at
Margarita, 134; at Marshall Hall, 21; at Mount Oswald, 136;
at Orange Grove, 200, 202; at Peach Point Plantation, 249,
250; at the Rocks, 78; at Rocky Hill Castle, 117; at Rosedale,
40; at Seven Oaks, 208, 210; at Stoney-Baynard, 71; at Verdura, 138; at Windsor, 155; at Wyalucing, 240–42

Preston, William, 276ch8n22

Price, Madeline, 176

Prospect Hill Plantation, 59–62; description of, 59, 62; destruction of, 62; first-floor plan of, 61; front façade of, 60–61;
slave cabin at, 61

Proverbs, 49

Pugh, Josephine, 198

Pugh, Thomas, 192

Pugh, Welman F., 193, 198

Pugh, William Whitmell, 192, 193, 198

Pulitzer, Joseph, 197

Pushamataha (Choctaw chief), 161

Putnam, Major, 129, 131

Pye, John, 105


Quackenbos, Mary Grace, 43

Quitman, John A., 237


Raintree County, 155

Raleigh, Walter, 2

Rambo, Reuben, 39

Randolph, Anne, 27

Randolph, Beverly, 27

Randolph, John, 184

Randolph, Peter, 26

Randolph, Peter Skipwith, 27

Randolph, Robert, 27

Randolph, William, 27

Randolph, William, I, 26

Randolph, William, III, 4, 26

Randolph, William, IV, 27

Randolph, William Beverly, 27

Ranson, Matthew, 22

Rattle and Snap Plantation, 33–34

Ravenel, Henry, 53, 55

Ravenel, Henry William, 53

Ravenel, René Louis, 53

Ravenel, Samuel Wilson, 53, 56

Ravensworth Plantation, 9, 14–17; in the Civil War, 17; description of, 16–17; destruction of, 17; front view of, 15; interior
of, 15; stables at, 16, 17

Rawlins, John Aaron, 47

Rehder, John B., *Delta Sugar: Louisiana's Vanishing Plantation
Landscape*, 179

Reid, Robert Raymond, 132

Restwood Memorial Park Cemetery, 233

Retreat Plantation, 100–4, 255, 267ch4n40; in the Civil War,
103–4; description of, 102; Grasshopper Hall at, 102; ruins
of, 101; side view of, 101; slaves at, 102; slave hospital at, 101,
102

Retrieve Plantation, 229

Reverie Plantation, 46–48; front view of, *47*

Reynolds, Thomas, 277ch8n37

Rhodes, Mrs. Willie, 119–20

Richmond Plantation, 68, 172

Rillieux, Norbert, 178

Ripley, Eliza, *Social Life in Old New Orleans*, 182

River Road Historical Society, 179, 258

Roane, Laura V., 236

Roanoke Colony, 2, 50

Roberts, Charles, 210

Robertson, Fredrick, 135

Robin Plantation (Mulberry Grove Plantation), 88

Robinson, Pickering, 93

Robinson, Willard B., *Gone from Texas: Our Lost Architectural Heritage*, 229

Rock Hall Plantation, 21–22

Rockefeller, William, 107

Rocks Plantation, 71, 74–79; Christmas at, 75; description of, 75; destruction of, 78; fireplace at, *78*; staircase at, *78*; preservation efforts at, 78; renovations to, 77; slave cabin at, *78*; smokehouse at, *78*; tournaments at, 77

Rocks Pond Campground, 78

Rocky Hill Castle Plantation, 112–17; in the Civil War, 113, 116; description of, 113; front façade of, *114–15*; pocket doors at, 113, *116*; preservation efforts at, 117; slaves at, 113, 116

Rogers, Charles, 83

Rolfe, John, 27

Roman, Andre Beinvenu, 179

Roman, Jacques Etiennè, 272ch7n2

Roman, Jacques Télésphore, 180, 182

Roman, Josephine, 180, 267ch4n34

Roman, Louise Patin, 267ch4n34

Romance Plantation. *See* Rock Hall Plantation

Ronde, Pierre Denis de la, 221

Roosevelt, Franklin D., 25

Rose (Sylvan Home slave), 36

Rose Hill Plantation, 39

Rosedale Plantation, 39–40, 263ch2n19

Rosetta Plantation, 111

Rosewell Plantation, 5–7; cemetery at, 6; side view of, *6*

Ross, John, 265

Rosswood Plantation, 142

Routhland Plantation, 143

Rudd, Robert Mark, "Apocryphal Grandeur: Belle Grove Plantation in Iberville Parish, Louisiana," 179, 188, 189

Runiroi Plantation. *See* Devereux Plantation

Runiroy Plantation. *See* Devereux Plantation

Ruspoli, Emanuele, 42, 43

Russell, Elizabeth Henry, 45

Russell, Henry, 43

Russell, James, 129

Russell, Robert Spotswood, 45

Russell, William, 45

Russell, William (son of William Russell), 45

Rutherford, Robert, 22


Sagan, Carl, 81

Sala Pablo, 207–8, 211

Sampson (Eutaw slave), 66

San Francisco Plantation, 253

Santa Ana de Afafa, 126

Santa Anna, Antonio López de, 242, 243

Santee Cooper Hydroelectric and Navigation Project, 51–52, 254, 264ch3n2; and Eutaw, 62, 67; and Pooshee, 53; and the Rocks, 74, 78; and Springfield, 70; and White Hall, 71

Saunders, Dudley, 117

Saunders, Ellen Virginia, *The Little Rebel*, 117

Saunders, James Edmonds, 112–13, 117; *Early Settlers of Alabama*, 116

Saunders, Lawrence, 116

Saunders, Turner, 112

Saunders, William, 116

*Savannah Daily Morning News*, 268ch4n49

Schiff, Edward, 190

Schiller, Friedrich von, 31

Schley, William, 267ch4n34

Scip (Devereux slave), 80

Scott (Sylvan Home overseer), 38

Scott, Anna Constance, 25

Scott, Eleanor, 25

Scott, Frank, 25

Scott, John Mordecai, 25

Scott, Lucinda Fitzhugh, 25

Scott, Richard M., Jr., 24–25

Scott, Richard M., III, 25

Scott, Richard Marshall, 23, 24–25, 262ch1n35

Scott, William, I, 98

Sea Island Golf Club, 104

Sea Pines Plantation, 71

Seminole, 128, 129, 131

Seven Oaks Plantation, 179, 202–11, 252–53, 256; in the Civil War, 207; demolition of, 210, 253; description of, 203, 207;

first-floor plan of, *206*; front door view of, *209*; and Hurricane Betsy, 208; preservation efforts at, 208, 210; second-floor plan of, *206*; side view of, *204–5*; slaves at, 275ch7n64; in World War II, 208

Seward, Bettie, 233

Seward, George, 233

Seymour, Jane, 93

Shadrack (Sylvan Home slave), 36

Shaperd, Sarah Jane, 36, 37

Shaperd, Thomas, 36

sharecropping, 252; at Hampton, 93; in North Carolina, 51; in South Carolina, 51; at Sunnyside, 42, 43; in Texas, 229; at Woodlawn, 254

Shelby, Joseph, 38, 239

*Sherman Democrat, The*, 245

Sherman Historical Museum, 246

Singleton, Mary Ellen, 86

Sinkler, Charles, 66

Sinkler, James, 62

Sinkler, William, 62

Sisters of the Holy Family, 275ch7n13

Skelly, Isabel, 244

*Skeleton Key, The*, 272ch7n13

Skipwith, Mary, 27

Slavery: advocacy for, 113; in Alabama, 110; in Arkansas, 33; beginning of, 2; cotton gin and, 89; in Florida, 110; in Georgia, 82; in Kentucky, 33; in Maryland, 2; in Mississippi, 141; movement against, 91, 93; slave resistance to, 8, 74, 172; in Tennessee, 32, 33; in Texas, 247; in Virginia, 2

Slaves: at Bulowville, 129; at Bush Hill, 24; at Casulon, 83, 85; as Christmas gifts, 56; at Cottonwood, 132; at Devereux, 80; at Eagle Island, 234; at Ellersby, 236; emancipation of, 3, 8; at Eutaw, 67; family separations among, 36; at Forks of Cypress, 118; freed, 38, 67, 116; at Hampton, 91, 92–93; at the Hermitage, 97, 98, 99; at Homewood, 167, 172; at Horton House, 106, 107; at Hurricane, 151; at Malmaison, 164; at Marshall Hall, 20; memoirs of, 167, 172; at Millwood, 57; at Mount Oswald, 134, 135–36; at Mulberry Grove, 87, 88; at Oak Hill, 7, 8; at Peach Point, 249; at Pooshee, 56; at Retreat, 102; at Reverie, 47; at Rock Hall, 22; at Rocky Hill Castle, 113, 116; at Rosedale, 39; at Rosewell, 5; runaway, 88, 106; at Seven Oaks, 275ch7n64; slave holders relations with, 36, 37, 41, 198; at Sunnyside, 41; at Sylvan Home, 37

Sloan, Samuel, 142

Small, Neptune, 103, 267ch4n40

Smith, George W., 24

Smith, John, 2

Smith, Mary Elizabeth Amy, 40

Smith, Samuel Webb, 40

Smith, T. L., *A History of Brazoria County, Texas*, 229

Smith, William, 47

Smyth, J. F. D., 27

Society of the Sacred Heart, 207

Somerset Place Plantation, 52

Sommer, Janice Burrell, 86

Sommer, Wil, 86

Sotterly Plantation, 4

South Carolina: Department of Archives and History, 53; history of, 50–51; Public Service Authority, 67

Southern Railroad Corporation, 111

Southern Railway System, 200, 202

Southwestern University, 246

Spalding, Randolf, 83

Spate, Ursula, 274ch7n61

Spaulding, Thomas, 100, 102

Speight, Jesse, 147

Spirit of America (theme park), 21

Springfield Plantation, 68–70; description of, 68, 70; front façade of, *69*; interior of, *69*; old brick oven at, *69*; submersion of, 68, 70

*St. Augustine Packet* (ship), 135

St. Foix (Hermitage Plantation slave), 98

St. James Sugar Refinery, 182, 272ch7n10

St. Joseph Plantation, 258

St. Louis Hotel, 200, 274ch7n51

Stampley, Margaret, 167

Stanton, Beatrice, 176

Stanton, Fredrick, 143, 145

Stanton, Maude, 176

Stanton, William, 176

Stanton Hall, 176

Star Enterprises, 21

Stehle, William Howard, 208

Stephanolpoli, Antonio, 127

Stephen A. Douglass Convention, 113

Stephens, Alexander H., 85

Stephens, William, 87

Stepney (Mulberry Grove slave), 88

Ste-Reyne estate, 220

Sternberg, Mary Ann, *Along the River Road: Past and Present on Louisiana's Historic Byway*, 179

Stoddert, Elizabeth Bishop, 19

Stoddert, James, 19

Stone, John Phillip Read, 184, 190

Stone, Mary Read, 190

Stoney, Jack, 70

Stoney, James, 70

Stoney, John, 70

Stoney, Samuel Gaillard, *Plantations of the Carolina Low Country*, 52

Stoney-Baynard Plantation, 70–71

Strickland, Alice, *Ashes on the Wind: The Story of Lost Plantations*, 112

Strobel, Abner J., 229

Strobel, Margaret, 229

Strong, James, 40

Stuart, Columbia, 8

Stuart, David, 9, 14

Stuart, Eleanor, 14. *See also* Custis, Eleanor Calvert

Stuart, Willie, 8

Sunnyside Company, 42

Sunnyside Plantation, 40–43, 252; in the Civil War, 41; Italian immigrant labor at, 42–43; sharecropping at, 42, 43; slaves at, 41; tenant farming at, 41–42

Swanson, Betsy, 200, 208

Swarbeck, Edward, 83

Sylvan Home Plantation, 35–39; in the Civil War, 38; description, 36–37; destruction of, 39, 254; renovation of, 39; slaves at, 37

tabby, 90

Tatum, Elizabeth, 39

Tayloe, Mary, 3

Taylor, Fletch, 245

Taylor, Sarah Knox, 147

Taylor, Zachary, 45, 147, 149

Tchoupitoulas Plantation, 179

Temple, Richard, 127

tenant farming: at Marshall Hall, 20; at Ossian Hall, 9; at Ravensworth, 16; at Rock Hall, 22; at Sunnyside, 41–44

Tennesse, history of, 32–33, 50

*Tennessee Gazeteer*, 48

Tennessee-Tombigbee Waterway, 264ch3n2

Terrett, Margaret Pearson, 262ch1n31

Terrett, William Henry, 262ch1n31

Texas: Declaration of Independence, 242; history of, 228–29; revolution, 242; State Cemetery, 245; State Library and Archives Commission, 229

Texas-Pacific-Missouri-Pacific Railroad, 208, 210

Tezcuco Plantation, 179

Thomas (Sylvan Home owner), 39

Thomas, Mary Gaillard, 121

Thompson, Aunt Sis, 85

Thompson, Sarah Strong, 85

Thorne, Samuel, 59

Thorne, William Williams, 59

Thoroton, Thomas, 135

Three Oaks Plantation, 179, 253

tobacco production, 7

Toledano, Roulhac, 200

Tomoka State Park, 136

Tom Seabrook Plantation, 52

Tonyn, Patrick, 128

Town, A. Hays, 210–11

Treadway, William Marshall, Jr., 8

Treaty of Adams Onis, 110

Treaty of Ildefonso, 178

Treaty of Dancing Rabbit Creek, 161, 164

Treaty of Fort Stanwix, 32

Treaty of Fountainebleau, 178

Treaty of Paris (1763), 141

Treaty of Paris (1783), 110

Treaty of Sycamore Shoals, 32

Trefontaine, Monsieur, 220

Trinity Espiscopal Church, 145

Trudeau, René, 180

Tudor style, 199

Tureaud, Benjamin F., 179

Tureaud, Jacques Auguste Demophon, 211

Turkey Island Plantation, 4, 26

Turnbull, Andrew, 125, 127–28

Turnbull, Andrew (nephew of Andrew Turnbull), 128

Turner, Saunders Mansion, 112

Turney, Frank, 241

Tuttle, Lisa, "Retreat: Palimpsest of a Georgia Sea," 104; "A Slave Speaks of Silence," 104

Tweedy, R. E., 117

Ulmer, Philip, 89

Umbria Plantation, 120–26; back gallery of, *124–25*; basement floor plan of, *123*; in the Civil War, 121, 126; description of, 120–21; destruction of, 126; first-floor plan of, *123*; front façade of, *122–23*; rear view of, *123*

Uncle Billy (Sylvan Home slave), 37

Uncle Sam Plantation, 211–20; bird's eye view of, *216*; demolition of, 219; description of, 212, 214–15; first-floor plan of, *216*; front elevation of, *217*; front façade of, *212–13*; garçonnières elevation, *219*; outbuilding at, *218*; pigeonnier at, *218*; plot plan of, *217*; second-floor plan of, *216*; vacuum pans at, *219*

Union Bag and Paper Company, 100

Uniroy Plantation, 79

United Daughters of the Confederacy, 111

United States Department of State, 43

University of Kentucky Graduate Program in Historic Preservation, 46

University of North Carolina Southern Historical Collection, 52; Peter Gaillard Plantation Records, 74–75

Ursaline convent, 274ch7n61

USS *Constitution*, 90

Vaiden, Cowles Mead, 155, 159

Valcour Aime Guards, 183

Van Court, Catharine, *In Old Natchez*, 173

Vanderbilt, Cornelius, 107

Varner-Hogg Plantation, 229

Vaughn, Nell Blair, 45

Venable, Abraham B., 24

Venable, Monroe, 134

Vens, Guillermo, 128

Verdier, John Mark, 70

Verdura Plantation, 136–38; cemetery at, 138; in the Civil War, 138; description of, 136, 138; destruction of, 136; front elevation of, *137*; preservation efforts at, 138; ruins of, *137*

Victor Farms, 22

Victor Products Company, 22

Virginia, history of, 2

Virginia Historical Society, *Lost Virginia: Vanished Architecture of the Old Dominion*, 4

Wade, Ross, 142

Wall, Samuel, 97

Wallace, Mrs. A. J., 119

Wallace, James, 89

Waller, Hiram, 276ch8n22

Walley, Betty, 48

Walley, Janis, 48

Walley, John, 48

Walley, Page, 48

Walley, Scott, 48

Walnut Grove Plantation, 75

Walter Reed Army Medical Center, 4

Walton, Seth, 241

Walton-Oconee-Morgan Environmental Group, Inc., 86

*Wanderer* (slave ship), 107, 268ch4n49

War of 1812: at Horton House, 106; at Malvern Hill, 30

Ward, A. J., 231

Ward Hall Plantation, 33

Ware, Henry, 190

Ware, James Andrew, 190

Ware, John M., 190

Ware, John Stone, 190–91

Warren, Billy, 120

Washington, Charles, 22

Washington, George: and Bullskin Plantation, 21, 22; and W. Fitzhugh, 17; and C. Greene, 88; and C. Lee, 262ch1n35; and T. Marshall II, 20; and Mount Vernon, 22; and Rock Hall Plantation, 21; and R. Scott, 24, 262ch1n35; slaves and, 22; and D. Stuart, 9

Washington, Jane Charlotte, 22

Washington, John Augustine, III, 22

Washington, Lawrence, 21

Washington, Martha, 9, 17

Washington, Thomas, 97

Waterloo Plantation, 24

Waterman, Thomas T.: *The Early Architecture of North Carolina*, 52; *A Survey of the Early Buildings in the Region of the Proposed Santee and Pinopolis Reservoirs in South Carolina*, 52

Watkins, Mary, 112

Watson, Josiah, 23

Waverly Plantation, 142, 264ch3n2

Webb, Arianna Shaperd, 36, 37

Welham Planatation, 202

Wellington Construction Company, 26

Werner, Valentine von, 203

West, John, 23, 262ch1n31

West, Roger, 23

West Virginia: Department of Culture and Tourism, 4; history of, 2

Westall, Ann Augusta, 236

Westover Plantation, 4, 237

Westwego Historical Society, 211

Wharton, Emily, 66

Wharton, John A. (brother of William H. Wharton), 276ch8n22

Wharton, John Austin, 234, 276ch8n22

Wharton, Kate Ross, 234

Wharton, Waller. *See* Wharton, James Austin

Wharton, William H., 233, 234, 248, 276ch8n21, 276ch8n22

Whitaker, Helen, 40

Whitaker, Joseph Allen, 39, 40

Whitaker, Joseph Allen "Jodie," 40

White, Blake Leay, 71

White, John, 50

White, John Blake, 71

White Hall Plantation, 71–74; in the Civil War, 74; description of, 71, 74; fireplace at, *73*; master house at, *72, 73*; stairway at, *73*; submersion of, 71, 74

White House, 24

Whitney, Eli, 82, 87, 88, 89, 141

Whitney Plantation, 179, 257

Wickes, John, 191

Wickes, William, 191

Wickliffe, Charles Anderson, 132

Wiencek, Henry, *The Hairstons: An American Family in Black and White*, 8, 9

Wight, Limon, 244

Wilber, Isabel E., 99

Williams, A. L., 86

Williams, J. W., 244, 246

Williams, Laurice, 86

Williams, Martha, 59

William Starling Company, 41

Willis, Elizabeth, 22

Willis, Nathaniel Hite, 22

Willoughby, W., 25

Wilson, Agnes John Peter, 261ch1n3, 261ch1n11

Wilton Plantation, 2, 27, 263ch1n53

Windsor Plantation, 151–55; in the Civil War, 154; description of, 154; destruction of, 154–55; preservation efforts, 155; ruins of, *152–53, 155, 156*

Windy Hill Manor Plantation, 174–76; Burr at, 92; curved staircase at, *176*; demolition of, 176; description of, 174; front façade at, *175*; rear view of, *175*

Winkler, Van, 89

Winkler, Zachariah, 89

Winkler, Zachariah M., 89

Winslow, Arthur, 79

Winston, Edmund, 46–47

Winston, Mary Elizabeth, 47

Wollaston, John, 27

Woodlawn Plantation, 192–99; in the Civil War, 193, 198; description of, 52, 192–93; destruction of, 254; first-floor plan of, *197*; front façade of, *51*; interior of, *196*; Ionic capitals at, *196*; second-floor plan of, *197*; side view of, *194–95*; third-floor plan of, *197*

World War II: Bush Hill during, 25; Hampton during, 93; Horton House during, 107; Seven Oaks during, 208

Wormsloe Plantation, 83

Worthington, Elisha, 14

WPA: Federal Writer's Project, 43; slave narratives, 167, 172

Wright, James, 82

Wyalucing Plantation, 237–42, 252; in the Civil War, 239; demolition of, 241; description of, 237; first-floor plan of, *238*; mausoleum at, 239; and Missouri, 239; preservation efforts at, 240–42; second-floor plan of, *238*; side view of, *238*

Wynne, Lewis N., *Florida's Antebellum Homes*, 112

Yarborough, Ralph, 241

Yarborough, Rebecca Parry, 39, 40

Yarbrough, Al, 86

Yeamans, John, 268ch5n7

Yellow Bluff Plantation, 133

Young, Mary, 100

Yulee, Charles Wickliffe, 109, 133

Yulee, David Levy, 131, 133

Yulee Sugar Mill Ruins Historic State Park, 134

Zeigler, W. H., 148

Zerhinger, Johann Michael, 203, 274ch7n61

Zeringue, Camille, 203, 207, 275ch7n64

Zeringue, Michael. *See* Zerhinger, Johann Michael

Zeringue, Michel, 203

Zimpel, Charles Frederick, 221